CONTEMPORARY MANAGEMENT CONCEPTS

GRID SERIES IN MANAGEMENT

Consulting Editor
STEVEN KERR, University of Southern California

Adams & Ponthieu, *Administrative Policy and Strategy: A Casebook*, Second Edition
Anthony & Nicholson, *Management of Human Resources: A Systems Approach to Personnel Management*
Clover & Balsley, *Business Research Methods*, Second Edition
Chung, *Motivational Theories and Practices*
Deitzer, Shilliff & Jucius, *Contemporary Management Concepts*
Deitzer & Shilliff, *Contemporary Management Incidents*
Kerr, ed., *Organizational Behavior*
Knapper, *Cases in Personnel Management*
Lewis, *Organizational Communications: The Essence of Effective Management*
Lundgren, Engel & Cecil, *Supervision*
Murdick, Eckhouse, Moor & Zimmerer, *Business Policy: A Framework for Analysis*, Second Edition
Ritti & Funkhouser, *The Ropes to Skip and The Ropes to Know: Studies in Organizational Behavior*

OTHER BOOKS IN THE GRID SERIES IN MANAGEMENT

Balsley, *Basic Statistics*
Klatt & Urban, *Kubsim: A Simulation in Collective Bargaining*
Morris, *Decision Analysis*
Nykodym & Simonetti, *Business and Organizational Communication: An Experiential Skill Building Approach*
Roman, *Science, Technology and Innovation: A Systems Approach*
Rosen, *Supervision: A Behavioral View*
Steinhoff, Deitzer & Shilliff, *Small Business Management: Cases and Essays*

CONTEMPORARY MANAGEMENT CONCEPTS

Bernard A. Deitzer, Ph.D.

Professor of Management
The University of Akron

and

Karl A. Shilliff, Ph.D.

Professor of Management
The University of Akron

and

Michael J. Jucius, Ph.D.

Emeritus Professor of Management
University of Arizona

Grid Publishing, Inc., Columbus, Ohio

© COPYRIGHT 1979, GRID PUBLISHING, INC.
4666 Indianola Avenue
Columbus, Ohio 43214

ALL RIGHTS RESERVED. No part of this publication may be reproduced, stored in a retrieval system, or transmitted, in any form or by any means, electronic, mechanical, photocopying, recording or otherwise, without prior written permission of the copyright holder.

Printed in the United States

2 3 4 5 6 ☒ 4 3 2 1 0

Library of Congress Cataloging in Publication Data

Deitzer, Bernard A.
  Contemporary management concepts.

  (Grid series in management)
  Bibliography: p.
  Includes index.
  1. Management. I. Shilliff, Karl A., joint author.
II. Jucius, Michael James, 1907- joint author.
III. Titls.
HD31.D4215   658.4   79-11974
ISBN O-88244-187-6

Humbly dedicated to all those teachers, colleagues and friends, present and past, who by their efforts in the vineyard of management have added measurably to the development and progress of this, a most fascinating subject.

CONTENTS

PREFACE, xi

ACKNOWLEDGEMENTS, xiii

1 MANAGEMENT: A PERSPECTIVE AND OVERVIEW   1

Nature of Management; Managerial Specialists; Management Defined; Functions of Management; Organizational Factors of Management; Constraints Governing Management; Key Characteristics of Management; Management: An Art or Science?; Management As a Career

2 DEVELOPMENT OF CONTEMPORARY MANAGEMENT   15

Early Contributions to Management Thought; Various Approaches to Managerial Thought; Scientific Management; Functional or Process Approach; Fayol's Principles of Management; Other Functional Contributions; Human Relations Approach; Behavioral Science Approach; Quantitative Approach to Management; Systems Approach to Management; Contemporary Approach to Management

3 THE DECISION-MAKING PROCESS   29

Introduction; The Decision-Making Process; Subject Matter of Decision Making; Interdisciplinary Nature of Decision Making; Techniques for Decision Making

4 THE CONTEMPORARY ORGANIZATION   43

Nature of Organizations; Kinds of Organizations; Purpose of Organization Structure; Types of Organization Structure; Departmentation; The Concept of Span of Control; Problems Involved in Narrow Span of Control; Narrow Versus Wide Span of Control; Tests of a Sound Structure; Informal Organization; Adaptive Styles of Organization Structure

5 DESIGNING—LINE—AND STAFF RELATIONSHIPS 65

Introduction; Effects of Organizational Growth; Managerial Solutions to Problems of Growth; Kinds of Staff; Characteristics of Staff Personnel; Staff Specialists and Their Functions; Aspects of Staff Authority; Staff Assumption of Line Authority; Staff Influence Without Line Authority; Adequate Use of Staff Services By Line Units; Domination of Line by Staff; Relationship of Central Staff to Regional Staffs; Limitations in Using Staff Departments

6 MANAGERIAL AUTHORITY AND RESPONSIBILITY 79

Introduction; Nature of Authority; Sources of Authority; Delegating Authority; Nature of Responsibility, Bilateral Dimensions of Responsibility; Specifying Authority Limits; Specifying Responsibilities

7 PLANNING FOR RESULTS 95

Introduction; Development of Planning; The Preliminary Phase; The Specialist Phase; The Group-Action Phase; Subject Matter of Planning; Factors Affecting Planning; Guides to Effective Planning; Planning Process

8 PLANNING TECHNIQUES FOR MANAGEMENT 109

Introduction; Quantitative Models; Types of Models; The Gantt Chart; Network Analysis; Break-even Analysis; Inventory Analysis

9 MAKING OBJECTIVES OPERATIONAL 125

Nature of Objectives; Kinds of Objectives; Time Basis of Objectives; Uses of Objectives; Responsibility for Objectives; Size of Firm; Aids to Establishing Objectives; Criteria of Sound Objectives; Maintaining Objectives

10 POLICIES AND STRATEGIES 139

Introduction; Nature of Policies; Purposes of Policies; Coverage of Policies; Characteristics of Policies; Nature of Strategy; Types of Strategies; Strategy Formulation; Interdependence of Objectives, Policies, Policies, and Interdependence of Objectives, Policies, and Strategies; The Role of Central Management

11 UNDERSTANDING INDIVIDUAL BEHAVIOR 151

Introduction; Motivation Process; Motivational Theories; Need Theories of Motivation; Maslow's Need Hierarchy; Herzberg's Two Factor Need Theory; McClelland's Achievement Need Theory; Expectancy Theory of Motivation; Money as a Motivator; From Concepts to Practice

12 UNDERSTANDING GROUP BEHAVIOR 163

Why Understand Group Behavior?; What are Groups?; Reasons People Form Groups; Types of Organizational Groups; Functions of Groups; Characteristics of Groups; Group Cohesion; Decision Making and Goal Attainment; Effect of Larger Organization upon Groups; Group Adjustment to the Larger Organization

13 COMMUNICATION: AN ORGANIZATIONAL VIEWPOINT 181

Nature of Communication; Formal Communication in the Organization; Informal Communication in the Organization; Communication Networks and Interpersonal Relations; Objectives of Organizational Communications; Organizational Barriers to Effective Communications; Structural Barriers; Socio-psychological Barriers; Semantic Barriers; Improving Organizational Communications

14 LEADERSHIP BEHAVIOR: STYLES AND DETERMINANTS 195

Nature of Leadership; Bases of Power; Some Theories of Leadership; Trait Approach; Personal Behavior Approach; Situational Approach; Contingency Approach

15 DEVELOPING THE MANAGERIAL TEAM 209
Introduction; Purposes of Manager Development; Forces behind Development of Managers; Some Concepts of Manager Development; Content of Developmental Programming; On-the-job Developmental Methods; Off-the-job Developmental Methods; Training and Developmental Techniques; Evaluation of Developmental Programs

16 APPRAISING THE PERFORMANCE OF MANAGEMENT 225
Introduction; Purposes of Manager Appraisal; Dimensions of Measurement; Methods of Appraisal; Procedure for Appraisal; Benefits of Appraisals

17 CONTROLLING DESIRED PERFORMANCE 239
Nature of Control; Definition of Control; The Basic Control System; Requirements of Control Systems; General Characteristics of the Control Process; Factors to Be Controlled; Interrelationship of Factors and Functions; Responsibility for Control

18 CONTROLLING TECHNIQUES AND THEIR APPLICATION 251
Introduction; Financial Control; Quality Control; Quality and Product Design; Control Charts; Manufacturing Process Control; Other Quantitative Methods

19 MANAGEMENT AND ETHICAL BEHAVIOR 267
Introduction; Changes in the Environmental Climate; Nature and Significance of Ethics; Definition of Ethics; Sources of a Code of Ethics; Role of Value Systems; Self-perception of Ethical Behavior; A Basis for Professional Conduct; Guidelines for Personal Ethics; Development of Professionalism; An Organizational Program for Business Ethics

20 EMERGING DIMENSIONS IN MANAGEMENT 281
Introduction; The Changing Work Force; Impact of the Computer; Corporate Social Responsibility

INDEX 289

PREFACE

This is a basic, introductory text that attempts to highlight the essential elements in the study of contemporary management.

Our guiding principle in its preparation was to provide a fundamentally basic, yet eclectic and integrated approach to the important functions, factors, and behavior of management.

It is our belief that a correct approach to the subject is one that combines the several and various schools of thought in an interdisciplinary mix to accomplish organizational results.

Consequently, this text enjoys no special orientation (functional, behavioral, quantitative or systems), since we feel management in today's organization includes elements of all these approaches.

Moreover, our intent was to create a classroom text, concise yet challenging, easily read and understood by the student, and also, and importantly, realistic and germane to managerial settings. Upon the strength of field evaluations, we feel that *Contemporary Management Concepts* satisfies our purpose and is adaptable to either junior or senior college levels when the instructor desires an appropriately manageable but yet relevant text.

Further to assist the instructor in course administration, two supplemental materials are available.

- *Instructors Manual for Contemporary Management Concepts,* available from Grid Publishing with text adoption, provides examination materials as well as suggested responses to the exercises at the end of each chapter.
- *Contemporary Management Incidents*, (Bernard A. Deitzer and Karl A. Shilliff) is a paperback, purchasable from Grid Publishing, which presents stimulating short cases, exercises, and projects corresponding with the textual material in *Contemporary Management Concepts.*

ACKNOWLEDGEMENTS

We are especially grateful to Richard J. Gigliotti, Department of Sociology, The University of Akron, for developing and contributing Chapter 12, "Understanding Group Behavior." The inclusion of this critical interpretation of the dynamics of group behavior adds a truly measurable dimension to the integrative and contemporary character of our work.

The authors, moreover, recognize additional help in the development of this text. From the contributions of earlier writers and various associates we have developed and distilled many of our own views. We are indebted to our many colleagues at The University of Arizona, The Ohio State University, Pennsylvania State University, as well as The University of Akron for their ideas, views and reviews of our material.

We appreciate, too, the many constructive comments and suggestions of manuscript reviewers Steven Kerr, University of Southern California, Kenneth Lundahl, Jamestown Community College, and Robert M. Stuart, Sinclair Community College. Their efforts have indeed resulted in an improved manuscript.

Our thanks must be extended to Professors Alan G. Krigline, Donald C. Becker, Richard C. Lutz, Jonathan S. Rakich, Bonita Melcher, William Maltarich, and Milan Savan, and Graduate Assistant David Baker, and Debbie Catanzarite, Department of Management Secretary, all of The University of Akron, who patiently reviewed our materials and offered much constructive help, particularly from a teaching viewpoint.

We want to thank President Dominic J. Guzzetta, Vice-President and Provost Noel Leathers, Business College Dean James W. Dunlap, and Managment Department Chairperson Frank L. Simonetti, all of The University of Akron, for their continuing encouragement and support of this and other faculty efforts in a climate conducive to publishing and research.

Unquestionably, the quality of any prepared manuscript depends on the combined interest, skill, and unending patience of stenographic assistance. In this respect we are eternally grateful to Mrs. Rita Chine who had all of the above while preparing and editing our manuscript.

To James Wilson, President, Nils Anderson, Vice-President, and Marlene Woo-Lun, Management Editor, Helen Mischka and Debbie Parks of Grid Publishing we nod our thanks not only for their collective confidence in our work but also for direct material assistance in bringing this text to fruition.

Finally, while we recognize the contributions of many, we, of course, assume full responsibility for our interpretations of the subject.

Bernard A. Deitzer
Karl A. Shilliff
Michael J. Jucius

CHAPTER 1

MANAGEMENT: A PERSPECTIVE AND OVERVIEW

Purpose of Chapter 1:

1. To define and describe management and to present an overall model of its functions, resources, and characteristics
2. To highlight the universality of the management process in organizational environments
3. To present the fundamental theme and approach of this text

Essential elements you should understand after studying this chapter:

1. Nature and definition of management
2. Basic functions served by management
3. Key characteristics ascribed to management
4. Major organizational factors and their relationships
5. The question resolved—is management an art or science?
6. Management as a career choice

NATURE OF MANAGEMENT

Unquestionably, a unique feature of our contemporary society is the predominance of organized group effort in the pursuit of certain and defined objectives. However, pursuing and attaining any of those various organizational objectives is seldom achieved by any particular individual effort. Rather, groups of people, in organized activities, combine their knowledge, skills, and resources in order to maximize the achievement of individual and group objectives.

Group activities are found in every endeavor of human life. Goods and services that satisfy our economic needs, for example, are principally produced and distributed by business units comprised of more than one individual. The defense of our nation is a mission of a military organization consisting of several million men and women. Similarly, our political parties, our religious affiliations, our labor unions, governmental and welfare institutions, and our recreational and social activities are all characterized by organized group efforts and interpersonal relationships.

However, groups and their activities, in and of themselves, are not enough to support the explanation of organizations. Rather, the effective explanation lies in the coordination of human effort and technical resources. This is the nature and essence of management. Very simply, organizations exist to assemble various knowledges, skills, and resources to produce either a product or a service. Consequently, each organized group, whatever its purposes, combines human effort and technical resources in a manner that accomplishes more than could be achieved by individuals operating independently.

But effective coordination, that is, the combination of human knowledges, skills, attitudes, and nonhuman resources, is accomplished neither arbitrarily nor automatically. For example, computer programmers in a business office do not automatically coordinate their efforts with those for whom they perform such services. Neither do production workers automatically synchronize their output with the efforts of salespersons. Nor do such specialists as engineers, accountants or personnel managers automatically serve the needs of production units. Similarly, in nonbusiness areas, such specialized personnel as athletes, ministers, social workers, nurses, or civil service employees, do not automatically work together in their respective spheres.

MANAGERIAL SPECIALISTS

Coordinating the activities of the specialists we mention must be accomplished through the efforts of another type of specialist—the manager specialist. The manager is responsible for getting other specialists to cooperate effectively and must unite the technicians of production, distribution, politics, welfare, recreation, or whatever the particular field may be. The manager is as indispensable to effective organized human effort as are the technical specialists themselves.

The coordinating specialist is known by many names. In the governmental field the person may be called president, governor, or mayor to mention a few. In the religious field he may carry such titles as pope, cardinal, or bishop. In recreational areas he or she may be called coach, manager, or director. In the business arena we find such titles as chief executive officer, executive, vice-president, superintendent, supervisor, and foreman.

Common to all these titles certainly is the implication of group leadership. Fundamentally, therefore, the task of each title is to increase group effectiveness. Each is concerned with the work of developing and maintaining environments in which people can accomplish goals efficiently and effectively. Each should elicit from a group more than the group itself could accomplish without such leadership or more than the individuals of the group could accomplish independently.

Performing in this leadership role, then, is known as *managing*. While each leader-manager must be technically equipped in a specialized area such as business, government, religion, or recreation, the person must also add managerial capabilities to his or her mix of conceptual, technical, and human skills in order to operate successfully.

As a student of management, you should recognize from the onset, however, that management practices are universally applicable and would be reasonably similar in other areas of human activity. But while management is indispensable to any organized effort with a purpose, this text emphasizes the business organization as the setting for both discussion and treatment of the subject of management.

Business is, obviously, not the only organized activity in our society. It is, though, a priority activity because all other institutions—government, education, or defense—depend on profits and savings that only economic performance can generate.[1]

Furthermore, the term *management* is applied to all levels of leadership in a business enterprise. The president manages the vice-presidents, who manage the directors, who manage the division managers, who manage the supervisors, who, in turn, manage the workers. Each is a manager of a particular group of subordinates. So, while there may be differences in degrees of emphasis or coverage, the essential features of management are much the same at all levels of the organization.

But just how is this mix of managerial attributes and capacities acquired? For a long time organizations felt, as some still do, that managers were born with certain desired attributes or possibly developed them over long years of practical experience. More recently, though, it is solidly recognized that managers, like engineers or accountants, can be developed or helped by formal training. This is true, since there is now a crystallized body of information that professes the knowledge, functions and skills required of management.

MANAGEMENT DEFINED

Over the years the term *management* has developed multiple connotative meanings. The word is loosely used as a synonym for the field of business administration itself. Management is sometimes used as the opposite of labor, as in labor/management relations. And regularly, the term is employed to identify that group of people at the top echelon of an organization.

But while there is no universally accepted, scientific definition of the word *management*, there is, nonetheless, a conceptual definition of management as an organizational process.

You may define management, then, as that field of human endeavor in which managers plan, organize, staff, direct, and control human, physical,

and financial resources in an organized group effort in order to achieve desired individual and group objectives with optimum efficiency and effectiveness.

Important to recognize in this definition is the interaction of its many elements. Each element affects and is affected by the other elements. Each element is part of a greater entity—no one element stands alone in explaining the success of a manager. Each must be manipulated carefully in relation to the others if a manager is to increase any chances of success as a leader of a group.

Moreover, the relationships between the elements of this definition are simultaneously and, oddly enough, static as well as dynamic. When perceived statically, the relationships within an organization are constant and fixed as of a given moment.

A static model of management is illustrated in figure 1-1. Here the manager's success is measured by the degree in which various group and invidividual objectives are obtained. Any success in reaching these objectives is determined largely by the manager's ability to coordinate the efforts of group members. Furthermore, the ability to coordinate is dependent largely upon acquired skills in performing the managerial functions of planning, organizing, staffing, directing, and controlling.

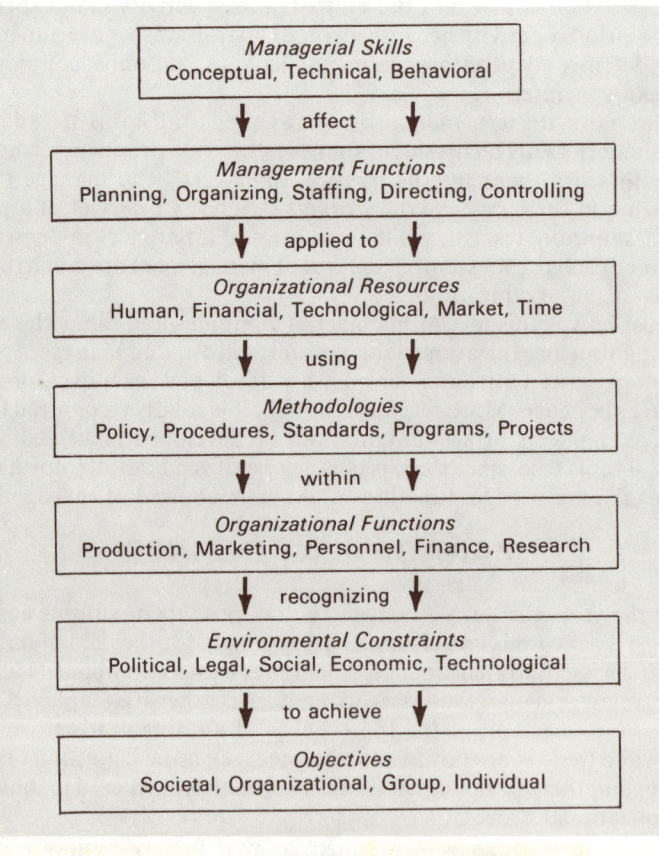

```
           Managerial Skills
      Conceptual, Technical, Behavioral
                 ↓ affect ↓
           Management Functions
  Planning, Organizing, Staffing, Directing, Controlling
                ↓ applied to ↓
          Organizational Resources
    Human, Financial, Technological, Market, Time
                 ↓ using ↓
              Methodologies
     Policy, Procedures, Standards, Programs, Projects
                 ↓ within ↓
          Organizational Functions
    Production, Marketing, Personnel, Finance, Research
              ↓ recognizing ↓
         Environmental Constraints
    Political, Legal, Social, Economic, Technological
               ↓ to achieve ↓
                Objectives
     Societal, Organizational, Group, Individual
```

Fig. 1-1. Static management model

These functions are then applied to human and physical resources using certain organizational methods within the framework of the total organization itself (as in the case of top management) or within the setting of an organizational function (as with middle or lower management) in order to achieve stated individual and group objectives.

A dynamic management process model, on the other hand, is illustrated very simply in figure 1-2. Here, as in the case of the static model, essential inputs are converted through the management functions into desired objectives. But there are, however, additional features in the dynamic process model. Management as a process implies continuing activity over varying spans of time. It implies that management can plan, organize, staff, direct, and control, to some extent, the nature and degree of change itself occurring within the organization.

Process, as a concept, also implies the organization has a built-in mechanism for creating ongoing decisions and activities and for regularly setting and achieving objectives. The management process keeps repeating itself. As one objective is attained, or being attained, there is constant feedback to both the group effort and management functions in reaching succeeding objectives. Activities, based on a plan and predetermined objectives, generate consequences and these consequences when monitored and evaluated are compared to the basic intent of the plan.

Consequently, this facilitates both planning and control and the process begins again. As a result, there is a continuing, interacting, iterating system of relationships between the various functions, factors and elements of the organization.

FUNCTIONS OF MANAGEMENT

What do managers do that separates them from nonmanagers? Our definition of management isolates five distinct and definite functions common to managers in organizations. Termed *managerial functions* they are *planning, organizing, staffing, directing,* and *controlling.* Future chapters will describe their use and purpose more fully, but here we will only examine each briefly.

Planning is the managerial function of determining in advance what a group or an individual should accomplish. It is the initial decision-making step that precedes organized activity. Planning is the conceptual function dealing with needed resources, future actions, events and activities. It concerns itself with the direct questions of the who, the what, the when, and where, and the how, prior to managerial action.

Organizing is the managerial function that provides various factors and resources necessary to carry out plans once they have been programmed. It means establishing an organization structure to define properly the position and relationships of management and subordinates. Policies, procedures, and systems must be established to effect the projects specified in plans. Personnel, materials, methods, equipment, finances, and other resources required to carry out plans must be procured. Organizing is essentially the function of setting up the structure and machinery needed to operate the plans.

Staffing concerns itself with management's responsibility for procuring manpower required by the organization structure. It involves not only de-

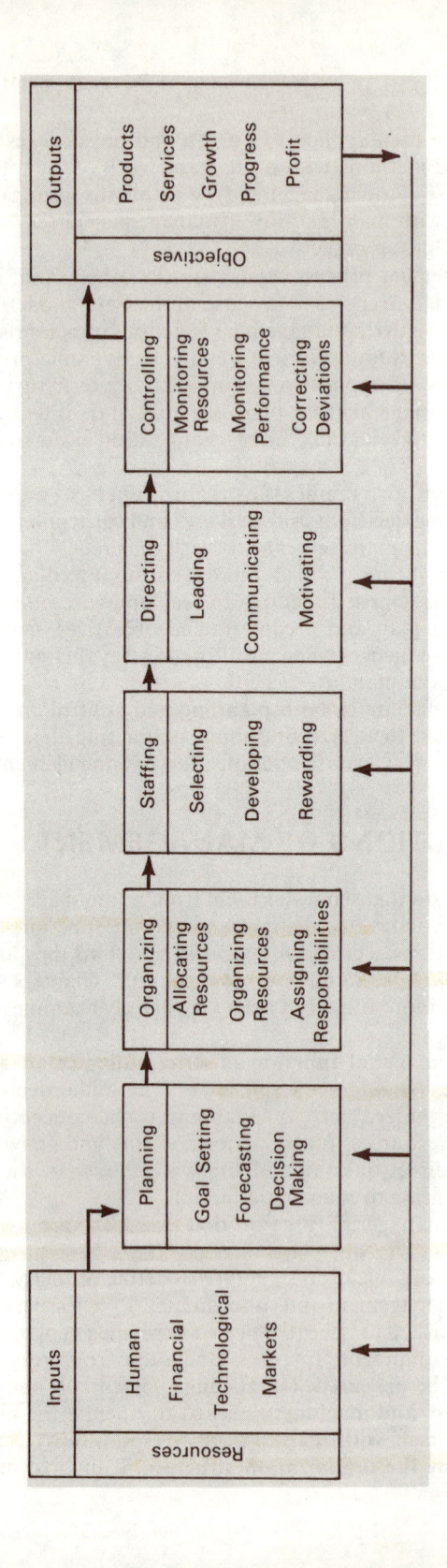

Feedback: Identification of significant deviations from desired performance.

Fig. 1-2. A dynamic process model

fining manpower requirements, but also recruiting, selecting, appraising, compensating, and developing organizational personnel.

Directing is the managerial function of leading, motivating, and communicating to subordinates as the organization carries out desired plans. Once the organization structure is established, positions determined, and objectives and responsibilities identified, the manager has yet additional duties. The person must continue guiding the organizational group; motivating it toward improved performance while communicating assignments and results as the organization converts its plans into results.

Controlling is the managerial function of monitoring, evaluating, and correcting subordinate activities and performance to insure that actual events conform to predetermined plans. Controlling includes evaluating organizational operations and results so that deviations from the plan may be minimized or corrected. Through controlling, management assures itself that the right quantity and quality of output is being produced by various organization units at the right time.

Controlling involves the use of objective criteria or control devices, such as budgets and standards, to insure conformity to plans. But in the final analysis, compelling events to conform to plans really means identifying people responsible for causing any deviations from plans and then taking necessary action to realign current activities or operations to improve performance.

It should be remembered, too, that these five broad managerial functions are neither mutually exclusive nor independent. Nor are they performed in an uninterrupted, undeviating sequence. The function of planning must be executed with respect for ultimate controlling. How one plans, moreover, depends in part on how one can control. Directing is often conducted concurrently with controlling. And very often available and important resources, such as people, will determine the limits to planning and organizing.

So, while it is convenient to discuss the functions of management under separate headings, in actual practice there is much overlapping and interfacing of the exercise of these functions.

Furthermore, it should be recognized there is not an equal and proportionate distribution of time and energy spent by managers on these functions. While they are central to all management, certainly there are wide variations in both the intensity and extent of their application even among various managers at different levels of the same organization and also in different types of organizations.

ORGANIZATIONAL FACTORS OF MANAGEMENT

But what especially do the managers plan, organize, staff, direct, and control? What factors do they work with? In all instances careful consideration must be given to the involvement and interaction of the following organizational factors we illustrated in figure 1-1:

1. Philosophy
2. Resources
3. Functions
4. Objectives
5. Policies
6. Procedures
7. Structure

Management Philosophy

This refers to the basic principles and guidelines that underlie all actions of management. A management philosophy answers certain fundamental questions about the firm. Does the manager's beliefs correlate with both the need and justification for the very existence of the particular business? What is the manager's basic attitude toward subordinates? What system of ethics and ideals guides the manager in decisions regarding employees, customers, clients, stockholders, and the community?

Every executive has a basic philosophy of life—one that definitely helps shape or influence any managerial action inside, as well as outside the institution. A conscious understanding of the person's own self and personal philosophy is genuinely essential to effective management, since it constitutes much of the underlying cause that precedes managerial action and activities.

Organizational Resources

Resources are what the manager works with. The basic organizational resources are human, material, financial, technology, markets, and time.

Human resources—people—are, of course, the most essential of all resources. The performance of functions is entrusted to individuals. It is imperative, then, for management to procure and develop human skills to perform the required technical and managerial functions. Simultaneously, management must attend to matters of morale and motivation as they affect the employees.

Material resources have to do with the range of basic materials and ingredients that are procured and utilized in the development, manufacturing, or processing of goods or services. Financial resources, simply, are those that relate to the acquisition and disposition of the organization's money and funds. Technology is a resource in the sense that it is the mix of equipment, processes, and facilities employed to convert material resources into desired products and services.

Markets, the ultimate distribution the user of the product or service, also constitute a resource. Markets include all those sources for product or service use. They include also any distribution channels that facilitate movement from producer to ultimate user. And finally time, while not generally recognized as a given resource, nevertheless, remains an inelastic commodity. An indispensable resource, time is limited in volume and quantity. Irrevocable in character, it can neither be accumulated nor inventoried but must be used judiciously by management as it becomes available.

Organizational Functions

By functions is meant whose prime activities in an organization that are absolutely basic to producing and distributing the product. They vary, of course, from institution to institution depending on the nature of the business and type of final product. In a manufacturing-directed organization the basic functions may be production, finance, marketing, and personnel. For a service-directed industry, like insurance, they may be underwriting, claims, finance, marketing, and personnel.

Objectives

Goals, purposes, or end results to be achieved are considered objectives. As a business institution, an enterprise must produce and distribute some worthwhile good or service. To its owners, a profit over the life of the concern should certainly be realizable. To its employees, satisfactory monetary and nonfinancial rewards should be anticipated. Moreover, for the community in which it operates, various social values must be protected and responsibilities satisfied. Each subdivision of an enterprise has an impact upon these services, personal goals and social purposes. Just how well these various goals are established and balanced in relationship to each other is dependent in part upon the philosophy and ethics that regulate the thinking of the managers.

Policies

Policies are those guidelines within those boundaries both the managerial and organizational functions must be performed if objectives are to be attained effectively. In a sense, they are directives established in advance for the guidance of subordinates. Thus subordinates need not seek a decision from their superiors about any contemplated action if a policy governing that the specific situation has been already established. Policy, in effect, recites those decisions the superiors themselves would make if they were personally involved.

Procedures

This term refers to the fact that activities and the people who perform them must be arranged in orderly sequences. For example, in the process of selling a car to a buyer there are many related actions. Unless these activities are arranged in sequences, each advancing the work from beginning to end, then the efficient completion of the sales contract will not be accomplished either economically or effectively. In any organizational function—engineering, marketing, or accounting—management must see that procedures for detailed activities are properly related in orderly sequences.

Organization Structure

By structure is meant that invisible framework that ties together various technical and managerial experts and specialists. Thus, a line on an organization chart extending downward from a national sales manager to a district sales manager informs all concerned as to who has authority over whom, and for what, in this important function.

To sum up, the organization structure indicates relationships and lines of authority, responsibility, and accountability, all of which help unify the group members into a more cohesive unit while concurrently pursuing defined objectives.

CONSTRAINTS GOVERNING MANAGEMENT

While performing required tasks, the manager operates under two major constraints; situational and resource. Situational constraints are the various laws, regulations, customs, and socially accepted institutions which impose limits on the manager's freedom of action. Legally, there are rules, decisions, and directives of various political bodies that govern managerial action. Then there are those social customs, traditions, and ethics that can be violated only at greater or lesser peril to management. Finally, and somewhat conclusively, such institutional groups as governmental agencies, business associations, industry groups, and unions very much circumscribe the limits within which management must act.

Resource constraints, on the other hand, identify the limitations of time, finances, knowledges, and skills. What managers seem to have enough time in which to make decisions? What managers have ever had enough funds to support the various projects which could increase their effectiveness? And perhaps above all, who has ever possessed enough skill not only in a professional discipline, but also in such complex areas as economics, the behavioral sciences or organizational systems?

These constraints, however, are certainly not cause for alarm. Ideally, the manager would prefer they do not exist. But by being fully aware and alert to changes in situational factors, the person can function wisely within them. Managers can reduce the possibility of conflict with various groups, laws, and customs. And by increasing their skills in pertinent areas of required knowledge, they certainly can be reasonably effective and competitive in making decisions for their organization. Managers do not have to be perfect—only as good or better than their competitors.

KEY CHARACTERISTICS OF MANAGEMENT

Management is an attitude. Management is an essential function in modern society. As such it is an attitude, a way of thinking, distinctly different, that focuses on processes, people, and functions to achieve desired results. Attitudinally, the good managers differentiate between *doing* and *managing.* They recognize that when they do things themselves, they are operators, not managers. While it is true that in every managerial position there does exist certain operational work itself, it is important to recognize those times when the manager is operating and those times when the person is managing.

Management is change oriented. Contemporary managers are confronted with regular and, at times, wholesale change. Change is expected of the firm's leadership by society, government, labor, the consumer, and the employee. In this respect the manager occupies a unique position when modifications and adjustments are required. Managers must recognize and identify causal forces and their meaning to the organization. They must assess and evaluate the impact of change upon the objectives of the firm. Consequently, management is pivotal in the firm's strategy for progress and growth through innovation.

Management achieves results through people. While management is results or goal oriented, those same results are accomplished through people. Technology, structure, equipment, and resources are important ingredients in accomplishing goals. But in the final analysis, it is people using resources who work to achieve objectives.

Management is results oriented. The business enterprise must always put economic performance first. It can justify its existence and its authority only by the economic results it produces. Management must supply goods and services desired by the consumer at a price the consumer is willing to pay. It must improve or at least maintain the wealth producing capacity of the resources entrusted to it.[2]

Management is activity oriented. Management is an activity that makes things happen. Effective managers are catalysts. They do not *wait* for things to happen; they cause things to happen. They do not let the flow of events determine what they work on. This means that the manager acts rather than reacts to situations. Moreover, it means that effective managers do not *depend* on the future. They really *make* the future. Successful management deals with economic resources aimed at economic performance and at the same time is measured by the economic results it produces.

Managers perform a great quantity of work at an unrelenting pace.

Managerial activity is characterized by variety, fragmentation, and brevity.

Managers prefer issues that are current, specific and ad hoc.

Managers sit between their organization and a network of contacts.

Managers demonstrate a strong preference for the verbal media.

Despite the preponderance of obligations, managers appear to be able to control their own affairs.

Adapted from Henry Mintzberg, "Managerial Work: Analysis from Observation," *Management Science,* October 1971, B97 - B110.

Fig. 1-3. Some characteristics of managerial work

MANAGEMENT: AN ART OR SCIENCE?

An inevitable question in discussions of management is whether it is an art or science. Actually management cannot be defined as a true science such as the physical or natural sciences. The physical or social scientist is concerned with *analysis* of things or events while the artist is primarily involved with the *synthesis* of materials, human efforts, and ideas.[3]

One contributor to management thought has pointed out: "It is the function of the arts to accomplish concrete ends, effect results, produce situations that would not come about without the deliberate effort to secure them. These arts must be mastered and applied by those who deal in the concrete and for the future. The function of the sciences, on the other hand, is to explain the phenomena, the events, the situations of the past. Their aim is not to produce specific events, effects or situations, but explanations which we call knowledge."[4]

The art of management is nothing more than the practice of management. Unlike a science as such there are many aspects of organizational life where it is impossible to control all factors, where rigorous experimentation is impossible, as in the exact sciences.

Management is an activity that applies creativity, knowledge, and skill to achieve objectives. Consequently, it can be classified as both an art as well as a science.

As to management being a discipline for study, there is no doubt. While management's boundaries are inexact, a condition true of all disciplines including the natural and physical sciences, it is nevertheless a formal discipline with an organized body of knowledge and is taught in universities and colleges. Moreover, the status of management as a discipline increases when it is challenging enough to engage efforts of scholars and practitioners and becomes the basis of professional careers in society. Finally, management as a discipline increases in favor as it continually develops and tests its own theories, codifies principles, and disseminates this knowledge.[5]

MANAGEMENT AS A CAREER

The expanding field of management offers multiple opportunities for exciting careers. Just about every enterprise requires management personnel in its major functions. Moreover, increasing numbers of women and minority members are discovering satisfying opportunities in business, government, education, and health-care institutions. Furthermore, the nation's need for personnel with managerial knowledges and skills will increase through the 1980s.

Requirements for salaried managers will continue to grow as rapidly as firms broaden their needs for trained managerial specialists. Newer technologies, applications of research and development, and computerbased operations all demand trained management.

Employment of managers and administrators is projected to reach 10.9 million in 1985, up from 8.9 million in 1974. This represents a slightly faster rate of growth (22 percent increase) than the 20 percent increase for the nation's total employment during this period. The share of total employment held by managers and administrators is expected to rise slightly to about 10.5 percent in 1985. In other words, more than one of every 10 workers will be management.

Management employment, coincidentally, is expected to increase at different rates in various industries. In the manufacturing sector, for example, employment of managers is projected to increase about 10 percent between 1974 and 1985. While, in contrast, managers in the fast growing service industries are expected to expand by more than 40 percent.[6] It all boils down to continuing demand and continuing opportunities for careerminded management personnel in the decade ahead.

QUESTIONS FOR DISCUSSION

1. Explain the nature of group activity. What must occur in group operations if their results are to be optimized?
2. Develop a working definition of management as an organizational process.
3. Identify the managerial functions and describe the relationship of each of the functions to each other.
4. Managerial functions must be applied to certain organizational factors for successful completion of the management process. Please explain.
5. Discuss both the differences and the relationships among objectives, policies, and procedures.
6. Identify certain and key characteristics of management.
7. Discuss whether management is an art or a science.

REFERENCES

1. Peter F. Drucker, *Management Tasks, Responsibilities, Practices,* (New York: Harper & Row Publishers, 1974), p. 23.
2. Ibid., p. 40.
3. Henry M. Boettinger, "Is Management Really An Art," *Harvard Business Review*, January-February, 1975, p. 58.
4. Chester I. Barnard, *The Functions of the Executive,* (Cambridge: Harvard University Press, 1938), p. 290.
5. Dalton E. McFarland, *Management Principles and Practices*, 4th ed. (New York: Macmillan Publishing Co., Inc., 1974), p. 7.
6. *Monthly Labor Review*, vol. 99, no. 11, November, 1976, pp. 12-15. Bureau of Labor Statistics, U.S. Department of Labor.

SELECTED BIBLIOGRAPHY

1. Drucker, Peter F. *Management: Tasks, Responsibilities, Practices.* New York: Harper & Row, Publishers, 1974.
2. Jucius Michael J.; Deitzer, Bernard A.; and Schlender, William E. *Elements of Managerial Action.* 3d ed., Homewood, IL: Richard D. Irwin, Inc., 1973.
3. Lorsch, Jay W.; Baughman, James P.; Reece, James; and Mintzberg, Henry. *Understanding Management.* New York: Harper & Row, Publishers, 1978.
4. McGregor, Douglas. *The Professional Manager.* New York: McGraw-Hill Book Company, 1967.
5. Mintzberg, Henry. *The Nature of Managerial Work.* New York: Harper & Row, Publishers, 1973.
6. Sayles, Leonard R. *Managerial Behavior.* New York: McGraw-Hill Book Company, 1964.

CHAPTER 2

DEVELOPMENT OF CONTEMPORARY MANAGEMENT

Purpose of Chapter 2:

1. To trace the origin and evolution of management thought
2. To discuss and evaluate those people who have been instrumental in the initiation and advancement of the subject

Essential elements you should understand after studying this chapter:

1. Contributions of early writers
2. Different approaches to management
3. Scientific management and Frederick Taylor
4. Process approach and Henri Fayol
5. Human relations school
6. Behavioral science contributions
7. Quantitative approach and its applications
8. Systems theory and management
9. The contemporary school of thought

EARLY CONTRIBUTIONS TO MANAGEMENT THOUGHT

First of all, the question of the origins of management as we know the subject today should be examined. Actually, aspects or elements of management thought can be traced far back into antiquity. The roots of management go deep just as do those of other, older professions such as law, medicine, and education.

Management has been of great concern to organized groups and institutions throughout the world's civilized history. Most of the earlier contributions, however, were derived from practice rather than theory. Formalized management theory, as such, is a recent phenomenon and begins with the ideas of such men as Henri Fayol and Frederick Taylor. Their conceptual contributions date back just a few short years to the early 20th century and will be discussed later in this chapter.

Various early cultures offered significant managerial contributions along the way, however. The Egyptians, in different centuries before Christ, recognized the need for planning, organizing, and controlling, for decentralization, and for the use of staff advice. They appreciated the need for managerial authority and responsibility.

Similarly, the Chinese saw the need for planning, directing, and organizing and for recognizing the basic principle of specialization. It was Mencius, the Chinese philosopher, who indicated the concern for system and methodology—"whoever pursues a business in this world must have a system."[1] But it remained for the Greeks to be the first to understand the principle that maximum productivity is achieved through the application of uniform methods at measured rates of speed. It was Plato who first espoused the theory of specialization of the division of labor: "which would be better—that each should ply several trades, or that he should confine himself to his own? He should confine himself to his own."[2]

It was Xenophon, in a discourse on Socrates in the fifth century B.C., who enunciated one of the first beliefs of the universality of management. He wrote, "for those who conduct public business make use of men not at all different in nature from those whom the managers of private affairs employ, and those who know how to employ them, conduct either private or public affairs judiciously while those who do not know, will err in the management of both."[3]

Among the first to recognize the need for effective organization were the Hebrews under Moses. Chapter 18 of the Book of Exodus illustrated the concept of delegation of authority and with it the fact that the span of control can be too large. The Bible further recites how "Moses sat to judge the people and the people stood by Moses from the morning unto the evening . . ." Jethro, father-in-law to Moses, observed this and told Moses, "The thing thou doest is not good. Thou wilt surely wear away—for the thing is too heavy for thee; thou art not able to perform it thyself alone." Whereupon Jethro devised a scalar organization for Moses who decentralized decision-making authority to lower levels of his organization. Up to this point the Israelites had spent thirty-nine years on a journey that accomplished only half the distance to the Promised Land. After reorganization took place, as visualized in figures 2-1 and 2-2, the final half of the exodus was completed in less than a year.[4]

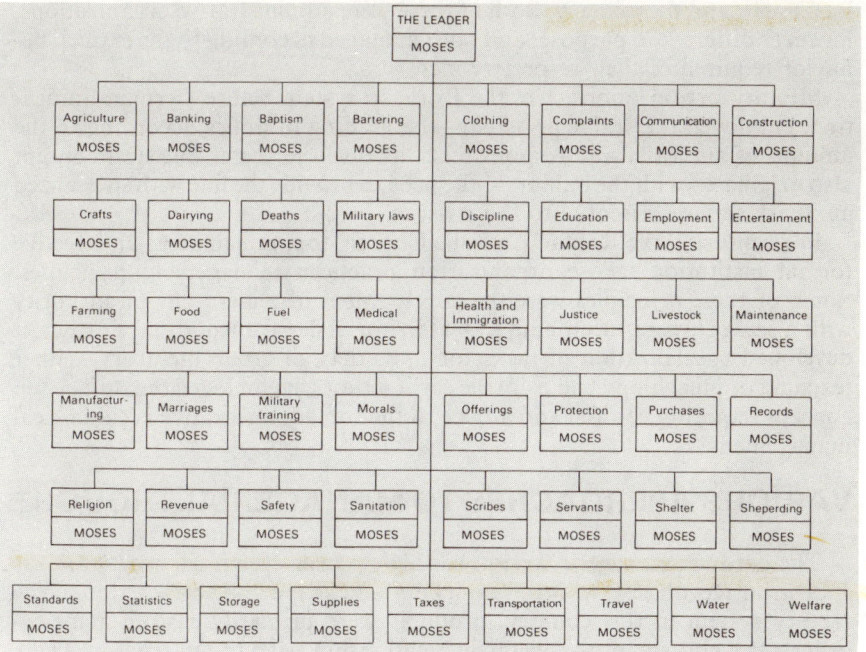

FIGURE 2-1. Moses Span of Control Before Reorganization

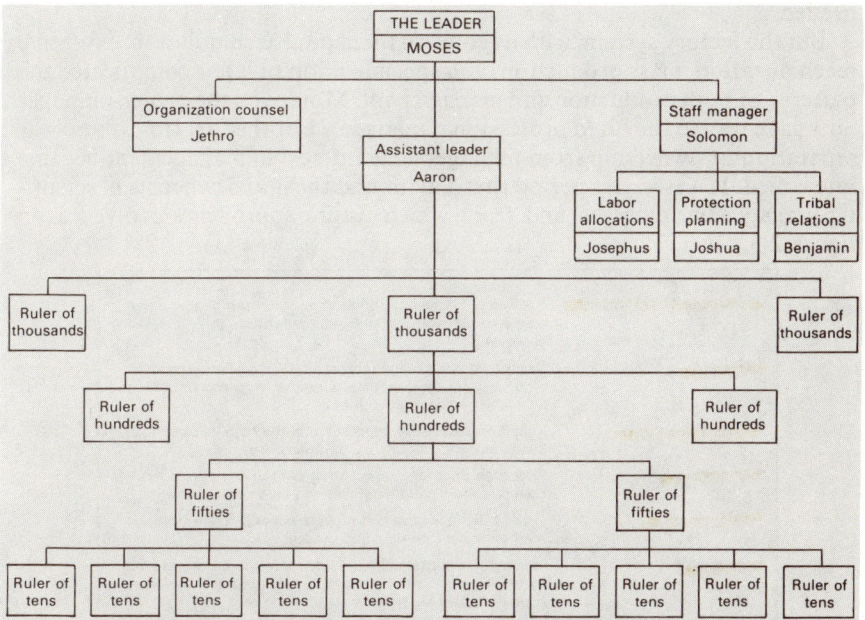

Source: Dale, Ernest, *Management: Theory and Practice,* (New York: McGraw-Hill Book Company, 1973), 3d ed., pp. 193-194. (Used with permission.)

FIGURE 2-2. Moses Span of Control After Reorganization

Two major institutions preceding industrial times were the Roman Catholic Church and the military. Both of these were administrative organizations, however different in purpose, and both managed according to the explicit behavior required of their respective members.

Military organizations, like the Prussian system before German unification, employed the scalar principle—the grading of duties according to the amount of authority and responsibility involved in them. The staff concept also originated with the military—the need to provide the line with specialized auxiliary services essential to the mission.

For centuries, the Roman Catholic Church, too, remained as an effective formal institution whose organization practiced management principles. Some of these principles were the development of a hierarchy of authority with a scalar organization built upon territorial departmentation. Further, it developed specialization of tasks for its variety of group members—either teaching or preaching. And from the earliest times, it employed the staff group concept requiring counsel and advice to the top administrative ecclesiastical management.

VARIOUS APPROACHES TO MANAGERIAL THOUGHT

The need for managerial action has always been identified, but it took the Industrial Revolution to facilitate its definite shape and form. Prior to the factory system in this country, products were primarily custom made-to-order—the craftsman was in direct relationship with the purchaser. There were few problems with this type of production. Little management was needed.

But the factory system, with its concern for capital accumulation, extensive mechanization, mass production, and specialization of labor complicated the patterns of both production and management. Moreover, the owner-manager now gave way to the hired professional manager. For the first time, there was separation of ownership from management. Interest in management became intensified. It was in this period that Taylor and the initial concepts of scientific management emerged and from which future approaches evolved as in figure 2-3.

Scientific Management	Applying the scientific method; increasing productive efficiency of workers and machines through systematic observation
Process	Describing what management should do; exercising planning, organizing, directing, coordinating, and controlling as key activities in goal pursuit
Human Relations	Initially isolating the importance of the human aspects, of needs and motivations in the enterprise
Behavioral	Increased understanding of interpersonal relations, leadership, cultural relationships, and group dynamics
Quantitative	Solving management and organizational problems through mathematical formulas and models
Systems	Interrelating parts and subsystems to the overall system by identifying inputs, processes, and outputs to produce objectives of management
Contemporary	Integrating the process approach with the behavioral, quantitative and systems to maximize organizational efficiency

Fig. 2-3. Approaches to management thought

SCIENTIFIC MANAGEMENT

Frederick W. Taylor (1856-1915), is considered "the father of the scientific management" movement. While he enunciated principles for management, his main efforts dealt with improving the productive efficiency of workers and machines through the techniques of time and motion study. Taylor's orientation was engineering. His interest in management was at the shop level in the steel industry, where there was direct association between operating management and the workforce.

A two-fold contribution to the development of management thought belongs to Taylor. He applied the scientific method to the solution of factory problems and from these analyses developed basic principles which he substituted for the trial and error methods then in use.

Beyond this was his declaration of the universality of the scientific method and its approach to all kinds of human effort. The four principles of scientific management as Taylor outlined them for management were:[5]

1. The development of a science to replace the old rule-of-thumb method
2. The scientific selection and progressive teaching and development of the workman
3. The bringing together of the scientifically selected workmen and the science to accomplish work
4. The almost equal division of the work and the responsibility between management and the workers, with management taking over work for which they are better fitted than the workmen

A second contribution was Taylor's crystallization of a philosophy of management—a "mental revolution" as he termed it. He believed that management was not solely an art, but a field with its own principles and logical relationships. Through study and experimentation, these basic principles and relationships could be ascertained and codified. Moreover, he believed the knowledge so acquired could be transmitted from generation to generation just as were the findings of chemistry or physics. He believed, too, that management was intended to serve the interests of employees, customers, and the community as well as those of the owner.

Working either with Taylor or independently about the same time were several sympathetic associates of the movement in the United States. Henry L. Gantt (1861-1919) for a time worked closely with Taylor. In many respects, their viewpoints were similar. Both stressed management's broad obligation to society, but whereas Taylor emphasized organization and efficiency, Gantt perceived the importance of the human element in productivity and approached the concept of motivation as we presently understand it. His most memorable contribution, the Gantt chart, a device used by management to compare actual to planned performance, and his task-and-bonus renumeration plan remain in use today.

While there were several other contributions in this scientific management era, two remaining notables should be identified. Harrington Emerson (1853-1931), the apostle of efficiency, and also a contemporary of Taylor, stressed the importance of ideas more than resources. His major work, *Twelve Princi-*

ples of Efficiency, was a distinct appeal for clearly defined organizational ideals (objectives); common sense; use of competent counsel; discipline; fair dealing; reliable and adequate records; dispatching; use of standards and schedules; standardized conditions; standardized operations; written standard practice instructions; and reward for efficiency. Incidentally, the first five of these focus on interpersonal relations while the remaining seven relate mainly to methodology or systems in management.[6]

Frank B. Gilbreth (1863-1924), and his wife, Lillian, were also original contributors to the scientific management approach. Their collaborative activities formed the basis for the advancement of motion study and the application of basic hand motions (therbligs).[7] The Gilbreths' efforts in time and motion established this practice as a fundamental concept in productive efficiency.

FUNCTIONAL OR PROCESS APPROACH

One of the first, and moreover lasting, efforts to synthesize a general theory of management appears in Henri Fayol's *General and Industrial Management*, first published in France in 1916. Fayol (1841-1924), also an engineer, and using analytical techniques similar to Taylor's, originated his concepts independently, but applied them not to operative but to top administrative management.

Both Taylor and Fayol worked on developing a formalized concept of management. Taylor arrived at his conclusions from the bottom up—the shop level and highlighted worker efficiency. Fayol, on the other hand, derived his from the top—the administrative level where he sensed the universality of the management process in the theories of planning, organizing, commanding, coordinating, and controlling. He saw these essential activities as something distinct from, but contributive to, the typical business organizational functions of production, finance, marketing, or personnel.

FAYOL'S PRINCIPLES OF MANAGEMENT

Fayol believed management was a teachable process common to all organized human effort. (It should be noted that at this time there was no formalized, acceptable management agenda for learning.)

He perceived six independent activities in the organization:[8]

1. Technical (production, manufacturing)
2. Commercial (buying, selling, exchange)
3. Financial (search for and optimum use of capital)
4. Security (protection of property and persons)
5. Accounting (stocktaking, balance sheets, costs, estimates)
6. Managerial (planning, organizing, commanding, coordinating, and controlling)

A further elaboration of the above managerial activity shows Fayol's understanding of these concepts:[9]

planning—examining the future and drawing up a plan or action

organizing—building a structure of human and mental elements to achieve objectives
commanding—maintaining activity among the personnel of the organization
coordinating—bringing together, unifying, and harmonizing all activity and effort
controlling—seeing that everything was accomplished in conformity with the established plan and command

Certainly, with no attempt to expand needlessly on Fayol's contribution, but to stress his foresight in conceptualizing a doctrine in management, you should be aware of the fourteen and still germane **principles** he felt should be the basis for effective management:[10]

1. Division of Work. (The object of specialization is to produce more and better work.)
2. Authority and Responsibility. (Authority is the right to give orders—responsibility is a corollary of authority.)
3. Discipline. (Discipline is respect for agreements that are directed at achieving obedience, application, energy, and the outward marks of respect.)
4. Unity of Command. (An employee should receive orders from one supervisor only.)
5. Unity of Direction. (One head and one plan for a group of activities having the same objectives.)
6. Subordination of individual interest in general interest.
7. Remuneration of Personnel. (Should be fair and should encourage keenness by rewarding well-directed effort.)
8. Centralization. (In every organism, sensations converge toward the brain or directive part, and from this orders are sent out which set all parts of the organism in movement.)
9. Scalar Chain. (The line of authority of the chain of supervisors ranging from the ultimate authority to the lowest ranks.)
    In large organizations it is too lengthy to follow this path. Therefore, an alternate "gang plank" is suggested. Suppose person F needs to work with P to accomplish a project. Following the scalar chain depicted in figure 2-4, F ordinarily goes through E, D, C, B, A, then $L, M, N,$ and O in turn to reach P. Fayol suggested that F, being on the same level, could contact P directly on a "gang plank," as long as the procedure concurs with top management.
10. Order. (A place for everything and everything in its place. A place for everyone and everyone in his place.)
11. Equity. (Equity is a combination of knowledge and justice.)
12. Stability of Tenure of Personnel. (Managerial personnel of prosperous concerns is stable; that of unsuccessful ones is unstable.)
13. Initiative. (A manager able to permit the exercise of subordinate's initiative is infinitely superior to one who cannot.)
14. *Esprit de Corps.* (Union in strength, for dividing one's own team is a grave sin.)

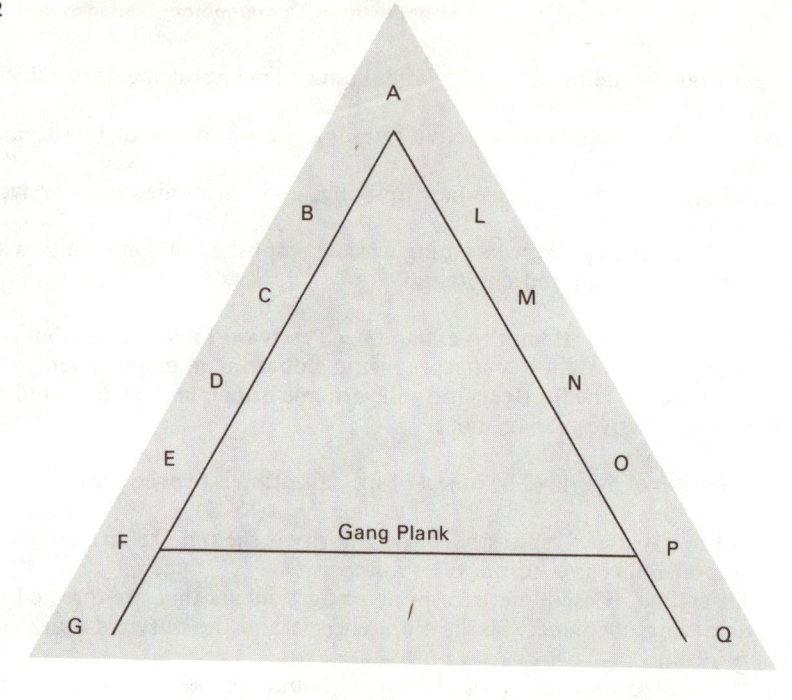

Fig. 2-4. Fayol's scalar chain of organization

In summary, Fayol's legacy to management as founder of the process school was singularly manifested in three aspects. He postulated the universality of management as a body of knowledge applicable to all forms of group activity. Secondly, he left us a complete and comprehensive theory of management—one that has resolutely defied the challenge of other and different approaches. Finally, he synthesized the knowledge and art into a curricular form for students of management.

OTHER FUNCTIONAL CONTRIBUTIONS

An often unheralded contributor to the process or functional stream of thought is Ralph Currier Davis—also an engineer by orientation and for many years a professor at The Ohio State University in Columbus, Ohio. His first significant work, *The Principles of Factory Organization and Management*, appeared in 1928.[11] Here he isolated the organic functions of planning, organizing, and controlling and identified their relationship to the firm's objectives, policies, and leadership and to its business functions of production, personnel, and distribution as a general method of approach to the solution of business problems. *The Fundamentals of Top Management* in 1951 further refined his process of management philosophy into a complete work of principles that prescribes normative managerial behavior in decision making.[12]

Another earlier contributor of the process school was James D. Mooney (1884-1957), who collaborated with Alan C. Reiley in producing *Onward Industry*. This work is a classic treatment of the universality of management principles, along with a concept of organization based on scalar processes and the functional definition of jobs.[13]

Other contemporary authors who belong more to the process stream of thought are Peter F. Drucker, Harold Koontz, and Cyril O'Donnell. Their writings and analyses provide continuing insights into the ever-growing body of management knowledge.[14]

HUMAN RELATIONS APPROACH

Probably no other event than the Hawthorne experiments of 1927-32 stimulated interest in and concern for human relations. Studies by Harvard professors Elton Mayo and Fritz J. Roethlisberger of environmental factors in industry disclosed the importance of human attitudes upon efficiency and productivity and introduced the human relations movement.[15] Earlier contributors like Taylor, Lillian Gilbreth, and Gantt did not ignore the human element, but for the first time, significant and continuing conclusions began to evolve from sociologists, anthropologists, social psychologists, and psychologists.

In addition to the contributive research of academicians, much was added by informed business practitioners. Central to their efforts was an increased understanding of the individual worker. Terms such as motivation, needs, group dynamics, interpersonal relationships, and leadership, now became commonplace in the vernacular of writers.

Hugo Munsterberg (1863-1916), a German-born, experimental psychologist, pioneered the role of industrial psychology in satisfying three chief purposes of business life—"how we can find the men whose mental qualifications make them best fitted for the work . . . secondly, under what psychological conditions we can serve the greatest and most satisfactory output of work . . . and how can we produce most completely the influences on human minds which are desired in the interest of business."[16]

Mary Parker Follett (1868-1933) was a Boston social worker whose writings stressed the application of the scientific method to human relations problems. She advanced the concept of management as a profession and defined leadership as being the ability to organize all available forces in the organization to serve a common purpose. She was one of the first to see leadership as being based not on power but on the influence the leader exerts on the follower, and the follower on the leader, depending on the context of the situation.[17]

Chester I. Barnard (1886-1961) deserves mention here for his application of sociological concepts to management. He focused on the firm as a social system of interactions whose continuance rested on the balance of the member's contributions and the satisfactions they derived. Barnard saw the organization as an opportunity for joint cooperation and collaboration; where effectiveness could be achieved through group effort.[18]

Ordway Tead (1891-1973), was primarily concerned with a study of the working-class psychology. In his *Instincts in Industry*, he attempted to show for the first time the influence of instincts upon organizational behavior. He worked toward a better understanding of people in their capacity as manual workers. Tead identified nine different instincts whose functioning throw light upon human behavior in industry. These were: parental, sex, workmanship, acquisitiveness, self-assertion, self-abasement, the herd instinct, pugnacity, the play impulse, and the instinct of curiosity.[19]

BEHAVIORIAL SCIENCE APPROACH

The behavioral science movement, a consequence of the human relations school focused its emphasis on a better understanding of the individual's motivations and interpersonal relations within the organization. Leadership, its nature and elements, increasingly became a prime area of study by both psychologists and sociologists who contributed extensively to the behavioral science school of thought.

Some of the more important contributors during the onset of this movement were Abraham Maslow who presented a theory of individual needs, Frederick Herzberg who advanced a motivational model of human behavior, and Ralph M. Stogdill who initiated his lifetime studies of organizational leadership. Others who made significant contributions during this period are such people as Chris Argyris, Rensis Likert, and David C. McClelland.[20]

QUANTITATIVE APPROACH TO MANAGEMENT

While quantitative or mathematical methods may be employed by other schools of management thought, there is one group of theorists who view management more specifically in these terms. Formally known as either operations research or management science, this view supports the use of scientific analysis employing mathematical models in the solution of mangement problems, and particularly, in those areas of programmed decision making. Elemental to the advancement of this approach has been the simultaneous progress of the computer which has facilitated the use of complex mathematical calculations in managerial decisions.

Among the quantitative tools used in this area are descriptive and inductive statistics, probabilities and decision theory, and regression and correlation analysis. But whatever the specific mathematical tool, its use in decision making generally revolves around four distinct steps.[21]

1. The construction of a mathematical model to reflect the important factors in the situation to be analyzed.
2. The definition of decision rules or measures for comparing the relative merits of possible courses of action.
3. The gathering of empirical estimates of the numerical parameters in the model that specify the particular situation to which it is to be applied.
4. The execution of mathematical calculations to find the course of action which for the specified parameter values, maximizes the criterin function.

Just to name a few of the more active management science contributors are Herbert A. Simon, C. West Churchman, Russell L. Ackoff, E. Leonard Arnoff, and Jay W. Forrester.[22]

SYSTEMS APPROACH TO MANAGEMENT

An offshoot of operations research is the development of the systems approach. It is a concept that treats management as a dynamic whole, as a system with its part being subsystems. As such, it is a set of attitudes and a frame of mind rather than a definite and explicit theory. Contributors to this field, among others, are the noted Nobert Wiener and Ludwig von Bertalanffy, and again, C. West Churchman.[23]

Systems theory people see management as the manipulation of levels and flow rates, through the use of decisions based upon information and related to standards. Systems theory is integrative. It corporates the use of quantitative methods and applications from the behavioral as well as other disciplines.

In sum, its authors say it provides a "conceptual framework to better understand any organization; an architecture on which organizations can be more effectively built and maintained; a system within which all systems may be interrelated to produce whatever harmony or conflict is seen to be appropriate within the ensemble."[24]

CONTEMPORARY APPROACH TO MANAGEMENT

So far we have seen that the field of management has been variously approached from the differing viewpoints of which the scientific management, process, human relations, behavioral, quantitative, and systems theories are predominent. Each approach, distinct and definite, builds upon and adds incrementally to the work and developments of preexisting contributors as visualized in figure 2-5.

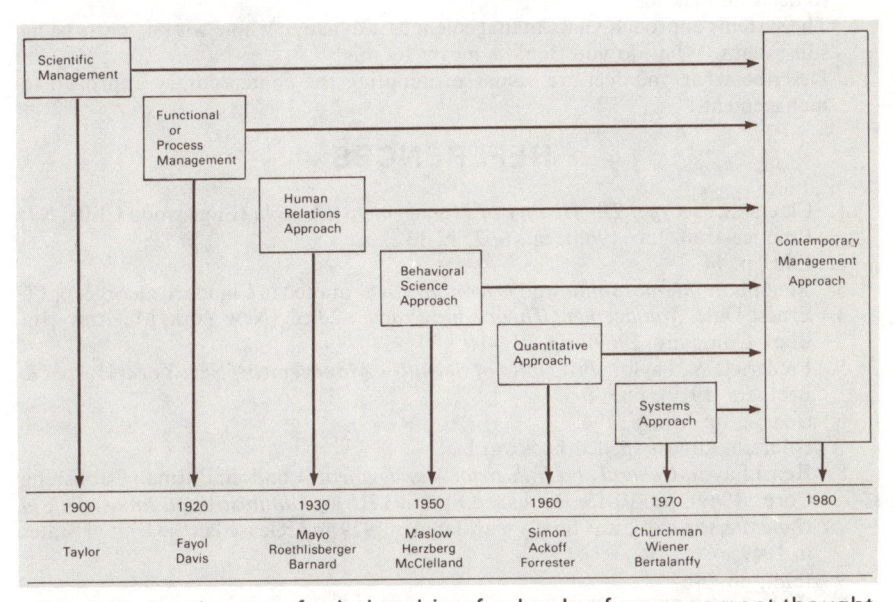

Fig. 2-5. Continuum of relationship of schools of management thought to the contemporary approach to management

So it is that we view management as being dynamic, embodying the concepts, techniques, and models from various approaches. Today's manager must be essentially integrative and eclectic, deriving behavior and decision-making performance from the spectrum of previously successful contributions. The complexity of today's contemporary organization requires that managers have considerable knowledge and skill of a fundamental business discipline along with a solid understanding of the behavioral, quantitative, and management sciences. Sole dependence upon a particular approach such as the behavioral or the management science will result only in failure to utilize effectively human and physical resources in the process of achieving the organizational mission.

This then, the contemporary or integrative approach, that is, combining the contributions of the various approaches, is the model offered in this text. It is an approach that is both flexible and contingent, and yet, consistent with the ever-changing forces which impact upon the organization and its people.

QUESTIONS FOR DISCUSSION

1. What is your opinion of the impact and influence of the Industrial Revolution upon the emergence of management as an activity?
2. What were the specific contributions of the scientific management school of thought?
3. In what manner was Fayol's functional or process approach both similar to and dissimilar to the scientific management school of thought?
4. Do you feel the behavioral approach truly introduced a significant contribution? What was the major effort of Abraham Maslow?
5. Evaluate the usefulness of the quantitative four-step method as used in its approach to decision making.
6. The systems approach views management as a dynamic whole with its parts being subsystems. What do you think is meant by this?
7. Describe what you feel are values of adopting the contemporary approach to management.

REFERENCES

1. Claude S. George, *The History of Management Thought* (Englewood Cliffs, NJ: Prentice-Hall, Inc. 1968), pp. 6, 7, 12-13.
2. Ibid., p. 14.
3. Xenophon, *Memorabilia,* and *Oeconomicus* as quoted in Claude S. George, p. 17.
4. Ernest Dale, *Management Theory and Practice* 2d ed. (New York: McGraw-Hill Book Company, 1969), pp. 215-16.
5. Frederick W. Taylor, *Principles of Scientific Management* (New York: Harper & Brothers, 1919), pp. 36-37.
6. George, op. cit., p. 194.
7. Gilbreth, almost spelled backward.
8. Henri Fayol, *General and Industrial Management* (London: Pittman Publishing Corp., 1949), pp. 10-15. Published first in 1916 as *Administration Industrielle et Generale,* the work was finally translated in 1929 and released in the United States in 1949.
9. Ibid., pp. 3-6
10. Ibid., pp. 19-20.
11. See Ralph Currier Davis, *The Principles of Factory Organization and Management* (New York: Harper & Brothers, 1928. Revised in 1940 as *Industrial Organization and Management.*)
12. See Ralph Currier Davis, *Fundamentals of Top Management* (New York: Harper & Brothers, 1951).
13. George, op. cit., pp. 130, 147.

14. See Peter F. Drucker, *The Practice of Management* (New York: Harper and Row, 1954). Idem, *Management: Tasks, Responsibilities, Practices* (New York: Harper & Row, 1974).
15. Fritz J. Roethlisberger, and W.J. Dickson *Management and the Worker* (Cambridge: Harvard Univesity Press, 1939).
16. Hugo Munsterberg, *Psychology and Industrial Efficiency* (New York: Houghton Mifflin Co., 1903), pp. 23-24.
17. Daniel A. Wren, *The Evolution of Management Thought* (Englewood Cliffs, NJ: Prentice-Hall, Inc., 1968), pp. 307-308.
18. See Chester I. Barnard's *Functions of an Executive* (Cambridge: Harvard University Press, 1938), for an insight into leadership decision-making responsibilities of the executive.
19. Ordway Tead, *Instincts in Industry* (New York: Houghton Mifflin Co., 1918), p. 14.
20. See Chris Argyris, *Interpersonal Competence and Organization Effectiveness* (Homewood, IL: Richard D. Irwin, Inc. and the Dorsey Press, 1969). Rensis Likert, *New Patterns of Management* (New York: McGraw-Hill Book Co., 1967). Ralph M. Stogdill, *Individual Behavior and Group Achievement* (New York: Oxford Press, 1959). David C. McCelland, *The Achieving Society* (Princeton: Van Nostrand Co., 1961).
21. Herbert A. Simon, *The New Science of Management Decision*, rev. ed., (Englewood Cliffs, NJ: Prentice-Hall, Inc., 1977), pp. 55-58.
22. See C. West Churchman, Russell L. Ackoff, and E. Leonard Arnoff, *Introduction to Operations Research* (New York: John Wiley and Sons, 1957).
23. See Ludwig von Bertalanffy, *General Systems Theory: Foundations, Development, Applications* (New York: George Braziller, 1968). Norbert Wiener, *Cybernetics* (Cambridge: Massachusetts Institute of Technology Press, 1961) and *Human Use of Human Beings* (Garden City: Doubleday and Company, Anchor Books, 1954). C. West Churchman, *The Systems Approach* (New York: Delacorte Press, 1968).
24. John A. Hackett, *Management Dynamics: The New Synthesis* (New York: McGraw-Hill Book Co., 1971), p. 158.

SELECTED BIBLIOGRAPHY

1. George, Claude S., Jr. *History of Management Thought* Englewood Cliffs, NJ: Prentice-Hall, Inc., 1968.
2. Herzberg, Frederick; Mausner, Bernard; and Snyderman, Barbara Block. *The Motivation to Work*. New York: John Wiley & Sons, Inc., 1959.
3. Maslow, Abraham H. *Motivation and Personality*. New York: Harper & Row, Inc., 1970.
4. Mee, John F. *Management Thought in a Dynamic Society*. New York: New York University Press, 1963.
5. Merrill, Harwood F., ed., *Classics in Management*. New York: American Management Association, 1960.
6. Miner, John B. *Management Theory*. New York: The Macmillan Publishing Co., 1971.
7. Wren, Daniel A. *The Evolution of Management Thought*. New York: The Ronald Press, 1972.

CHAPTER 3

THE DECISION-MAKING PROCESS

Purpose of Chapter 3:

1. To define the decision making process and its importance to the manager
2. To present the interdisciplinary subject matter of decision making
3. To introduce the scientific method of decision making

Essential elements you should understand after studying this chapter:

1. The dynamic character of the decision-making process
2. Important elements involved
3. Decision making and its interdisciplinary nature
4. Specific techniques employed by management
5. Application of the steps involved in the scientific method

INTRODUCTION

Decision making is an increasingly important area of study to teachers, students, and practitioners of management. Decisions are an inescapable aspect of everything a manager does or is concerned with. The process of making decisions is complex, but yet definable. Indeed, the term decision maker could well be a synonym for manager.

A simple definition of a decision is a choice between alternatives. But how are choices made? Which alternatives should be decided upon? What means should be chosen to attain what objectives? What assumptions, data, theories, personal aspirations and constraints govern choices? These questions and more are full of perplexities which characterize decision making as a complex subject. One that is worthy of separate and special study.

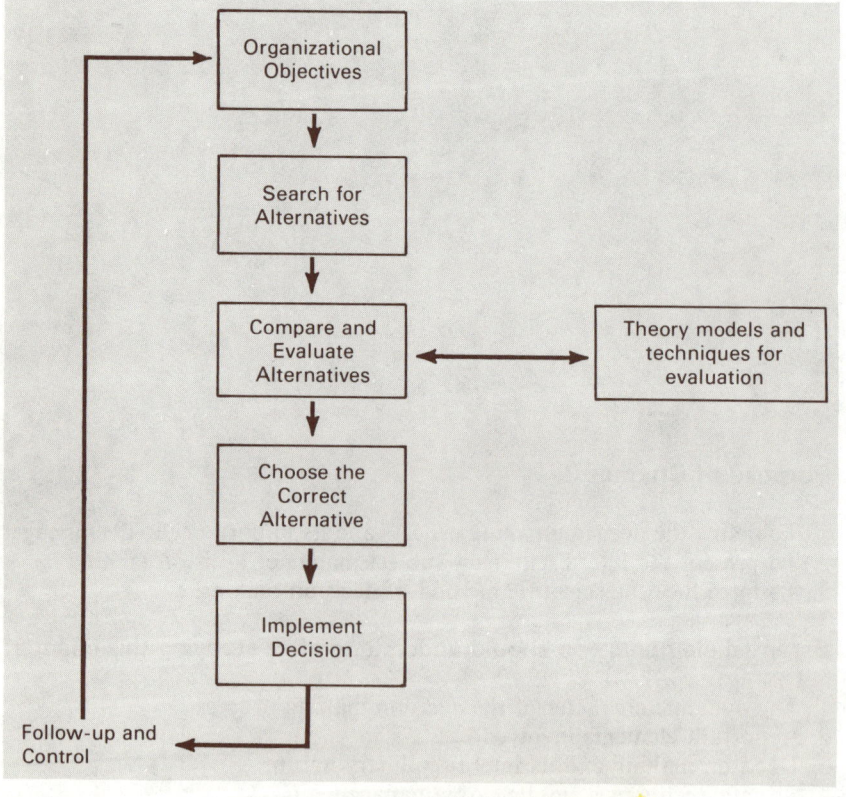

THE DECISION-MAKING PROCESS

The decision-making process is a dynamic one. It begins with setting objectives, continues through the search, evaluation, and choosing of an alternative, and then culminates with the implementation and follow-up stages of the process. Figure 3-1 illustrates the scope, implications, and the components of the process.

Fig. 3-1. The decision-making process

Defining decision making as the choice among alternatives is useful as a springboard for further analysis. Important to note here is that choices must first be made among the goals or objectives and the means of attaining them. For example, a business executive may place profits as his basic objective. But if he attempts to maximize profits at the expense of everything else, he will soon find that others, such as customers and workers with their own personal goals and needs, may soon become dissatisfied. The manager must instead seek a reasonable profit, not a maximum, so that the customer may receive reasonable service and the workers reasonable wages.

The continuous nature of decision making also deserves emphasis. A manager is not finished with just one decision. Every decision is a part of a continuum of decisions, affected by past decisions, related to current decisions, and serving as a basis for future decisions. For instance, the manager who is deciding how to introduce a new manufacturing process should give consideration not only to past decisions in similar cases, but also to the immediate consequences of his past action, as well as to the future implications of his decision.

Implications of Decision Making

What choices of methodology do managers have to assist them in making a decision? Such methods as intuitive guesswork, past experience, logical reasoning, in addition to sophisticated statistical analysis are just a few of the choices available to management.

Who is involved when making a decision? Certainly every manager is a decision maker. But is it an exclusive jurisdiction? Far from it! Each executive must be cognizant of three directions from which other participants may enter into the decision. First, there are superiors whose decisions must be considered. Second, there are subordinates, whose views should not be slighted. And third, there are those management peers whose reactions must be regarded. To illustrate, the specific manner in which funds are to be expended must be decided in light of the superior's directives, subordinates' expectations, and peer's possible reactions.

How does a manager know when to make a decision? This is a difficult question. It is not valid to assume that every manager either at the top or bottom level is an effective decision maker. One of the most important qualities of management is the ability to recognize that a situation has arisen which requires a decision. Moreover, it should be noted that in certain situations the decision to make no decision is in fact a decision.

Components of Decision Making

The nature of decision making can be better appreciated by examining the model depicted in figure 3-2. Here it is seen that managers make choices among alternative means, evaluated in various ways, to attain objectives. The process, as you will observe, is a dynamic one which continues in various concurrent and sequential stages.

In making a choice the available alternatives must be evaluated or compared to some pre-established standards or value system, established either by superiors or by prior study of knowledge. Information on decisions is derived

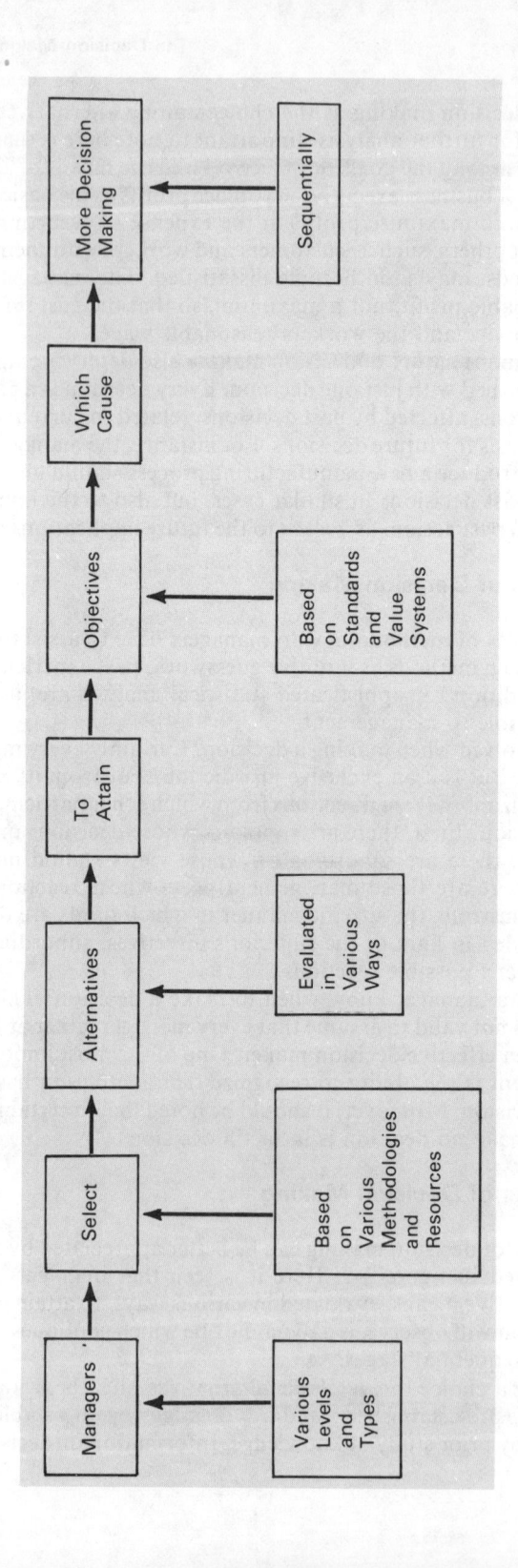

Fig. 3-2. A managerial decision-making model

by the manager's own experience or supplied from other channels. For example, in choosing between various wage incentive plans, a manager would want to compare each of these plans to the environmental and personnel conditions in the business. In this way, a choice could be made to determine which is better for the company and personnel.

The continuous feature of decision making calls for flows of information to evaluate the effectiveness of decisions. This insures that adjustments, if needed, may be made. This process is known as "feedback." It requires a sensor to gather information about the results of the decision, a discriminator to compare the results to plans, and a channel to transmit messages from point to point.

Feedback systems are of two major types: open-end and closed-end. the most common type, open-end, is illustrated in figure 3-3. figure 3-4 illustrates the closed-end type of feedback system. Both types of systems essentially place reliance upon information that is already in the hands of the manager.

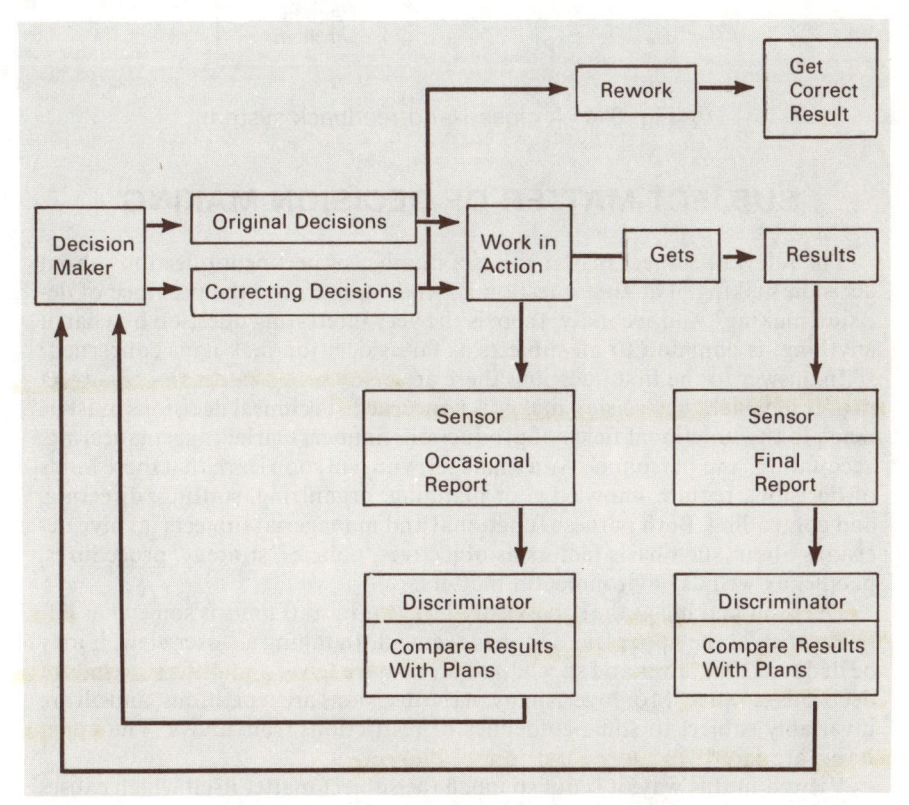

Fig. 3-3. An open-end feedback system

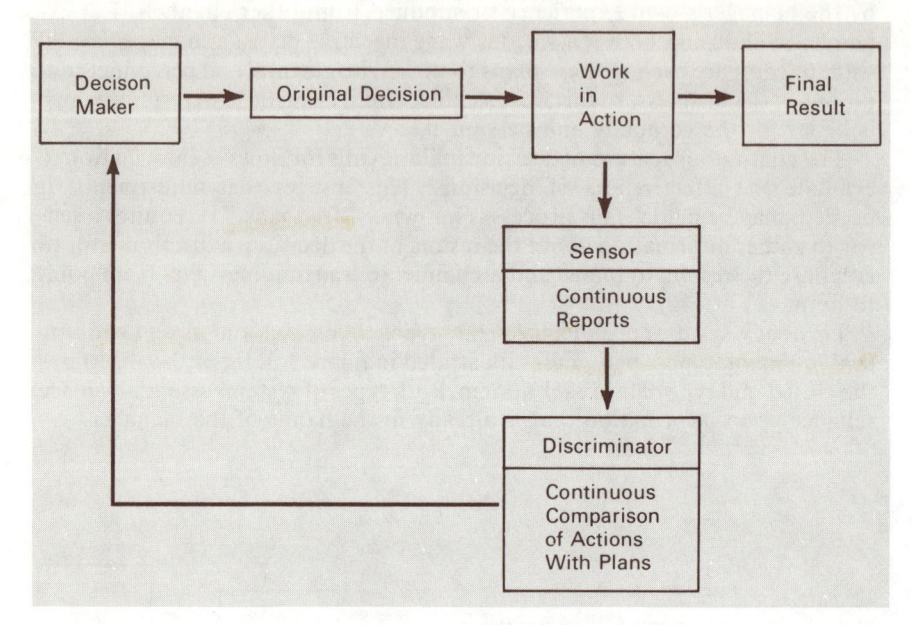

Fig. 3-4. A closed-end feedback system

SUBJECT MATTER OF DECISION MAKING

The relevant subject matter raises a number of pertinent questions about decision making. The first question is, what subjects are the province of decision making? And secondly, there is the very interesting question of what, if anything, is common to all subjects as far as decision making is concerned?

In answer to the first question, there are many broad categories of subject matter in which the decision maker is concerned. Technical decisions must be made in the functional fields of production, finance, marketing, engineering, accounting, and personnel. As a manager, you will soon learn that these kinds of decisions require knowledge of planning, organizing, staffing, directing, and controlling. Both of these functional and managerial subjects involve decisions about such basic factors as objectives, policies, strategy, procedures, people, as well as environmental matters.

Decision making at the supervisory levels or in staff units is somewhat different than at the upper levels of management. In taking a closer view, it may be deduced that lower and specialized levels have fewer and different kinds of decisions to make. Moreover, many of the decisions are repetitious, and all are invariably subject to some guidelines or restrictions from above. The upper levels are faced with more freedom of choice.

Viewed in this way, it is not so much the subject matter itself which causes differences in decision making, but rather the differences in the conditions surrounding that area of subject matter which fall within the manager's jurisdiction. The unknowns and variables with which one must contend when deciding whether or not to automate a process are different from and more numerous than those which an engineer, detailed to design electrical switches, must consider after an affirmative answer has been given by the higher executives in regard to the automation of a manufacturing process.

This brings us to the second question: What, if anything, is common to all decision making? Besides differences in decision making at various levels, there must also be similarities—or the executive ladder would indeed be a series of unrelated steps and advancement would follow no logical pattern. Something must be learned at lower levels that is useful at higher levels. Knowledge of subject matter at lower levels helps one to make decisions as one progresses to higher levels. Granted, though, there are innumerable instances of people moving successfully from one functional area to another (and often unrelated) field. Personal experiences of many people give credence to the thesis that those whose managerial skills make them successful managers at lower levels will be successful at higher levels also.

INTERDISCIPLINARY NATURE OF DECISION MAKING

Is such success in decision making due to the executive's *knowledge* of subject matter or is it in fact due to skill in *handling* the subject matter? It is impossible to say. Certainly the methods one uses have much to do with successful decision making. There are many disciplines, such as are shown in figure 3-5, which influence both the subject matter and methods of decision making.

BEHAVIORAL SCIENCES
Psychology
Sociology
Social Psychology
Anthropology

THE TECHNICAL SCIENCES
Engineering
Mathematics
Statistics
Economics

THE DECISION—MAKING PROCESS

FUNCTIONAL BUSINESS AREAS
Production
Personnel
Finance
Marketing
Accounting

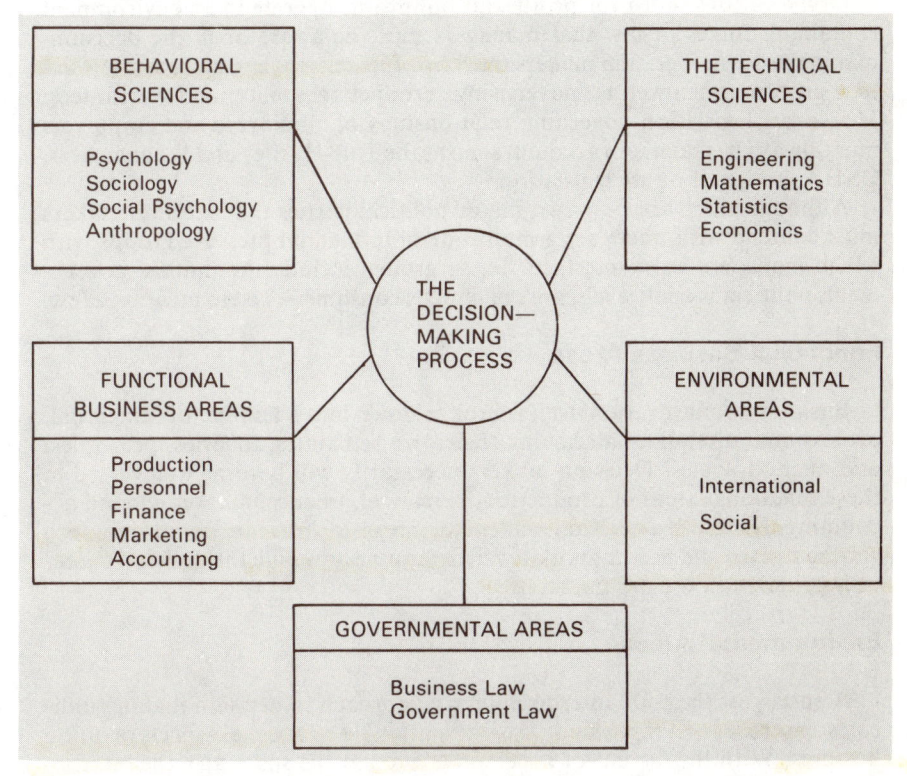

ENVIRONMENTAL AREAS
International
Social

GOVERNMENTAL AREAS
Business Law
Government Law

Fig. 3-5. The interdisciplinary structure of decision making

Behavioral Sciences

As a starting point let us consider the manager's value system. The person's religion, morality, and code of ethics all play an important role in the decision making process. Attitudes, beliefs, and personal philosophy with respect to individuals, profits, competitors all help guide the decision making powers. Incidentally, certain theories of psychology and sociology strive to explain the influence of individual and group behavior in decision making. Aspects of these topics are covered elsewhere throughout this text.

Technical Sciences

The quantitative aspects of decision making have their basis extensively in the disciplines of mathematics and statistics. The focus of these disciplines, as related to decision making, is to gather, organize, and clarify data descriptively. Then, the task of analyzing follows, using classical statistics, probabilities and tests of hypotheses, and possibly expected value. Often the entire gamut of mathematics from adding and subtracting to differential and integral calculus is used in management decision making.

Politics and the Law

Organizations, both for profit and nonprofit, operate in an environment containing forces of law that managers must be aware of in the decision-making process. Decision makers must consider current and emerging legislation governing marketing, advertising, product reliability, and warrantees. Moreover, legislation governing relationships of employees and employers must always be taken into account, such as the Taft-Hartley and Wagner Acts, OSHA, and civil rights legislation.

Although there are only two major political parties that decision makers must contend with, there are a multitude of influential pressure groups with which managers must interface. These groups include the unions, government, politicians at all levels, and, of course, consumers, just to mention a few.

Functional Business Areas

Business administration itself is broken down into a number of functional, professional disciplines all having their own semantics, theories, principles, and methodologies. Decision makers necessarily will become well versed in these functional areas of production, personnel, finance, marketing, and accounting. How well a decision maker can integrate these functional areas into strategic plans and programs may well determine how high the decision maker may progress in the organization.

Environmental Areas

A survey of the total interdisciplinary approach to decision making indicates a more recent emphasis on the international and societal aspects of doing business. With the advent of supersonic jets and the space age, the international aspects of doing business have also come of age. With energy crises, and emphasis on trade balances, most large corporations are faced with continual international decisions.

Within the last decade or so, societal goals such as pollution, minority employment, health, education, and welfare have intruded into the scope of management decision making. Concepts like "enlightened self-interest" and "quality of life", wherein managers forego short-run profits for the long-run well-being of society and industry as a whole, now surface into the corporate philosophy and replace profits only as an enlightened objective.

Literally, decision making draws from every discipline. The integration of these disciplines depends upon the backgrounds, education, and experience of each decision maker. Effective decision making requires a multidimensional as well as an integrative approach. The final decision lies with management. But it is difficult to deny the benefits from the concepts and principles set forth throughout this section.

TECHNIQUES FOR DECISION MAKING

Decision making implies the use of various methods. But before placing these various methods in their proper perspective we offer here some general comments regarding certain differing viewpoints on decision making.

General Survey Methods

In the past, most scholars believed that a person either did or did not have the ability to make sound business decisions. They believed only practical experience could demonstrate this ability. Such a view is based on the thesis that there is no formal way to teach judgment. So reliance has to be placed upon the "school of hard knocks"; and only those who have "it" in them succeed. How "it" got in them and how "it" developed were beyond analysis. There simply wasn't anything to be taught, and investments in teaching judgment would be futile. One generation of successful executives could neither teach nor transmit anything of its methods to the next. Each generation of executives had to build its methods from scratch.

Many now question this thesis. But our accumulated store of knowledge is still insufficient to discard this view entirely. Even now, many managers cannot tell how they arrived at a particularly successful decision. Often one hears of managers to whom a solution to a difficult problem came "out of the blue" after a good night's sleep. So respect for informalized judgment must be retained to some extent.

Indeed, there seems to be a logic to decision making. There is a method of reasoning from premises, for example, which can be taught. In this sense, the logic which is applicable in other forms of human activity—philosophy, law, and science—is pertinent to business organizations. If this is not granted, then economics, which is universally accepted as a basis of business, can contribute nothing to business decisions. So the conclusion seems inevitable that one generation of business executives can learn from another and thereby build a progressively better system of decision making from the principles and processes of logical reasoning.

Increasingly, too, quantitative areas of human knowledge are making gratifying contributions to decision making,[3] because managers must not only decide qualitatively but also quantitatively. It is now enough to conclude—for example—that unit production must be increased. The decision must establish a quantitative level to the increase. Nor is it enough to arbitrarily increase the price of a company's product. The increase must be stated quantitatively, while keeping in mind both the customer and competitor reactions. To these and similar decisions, various statistical, mathematical, graphical, and computational techniques and methods are making contributions of real value.[4] (Some of these techniques and methods will be described later in this text.) These types of quantitative aids, which are being continually improved upon, can be explained and passed on to succeeding generations of management.

Findings of various experts seem to justify the assertion that decision making is certainly not incapable of being explained. Merely to mention the emergence of linear programming is sufficient to indicate a new attitude toward decision making. Here, as well as in other examples of techniques and research, a fundamental fact is that knowledge and skills developed and utilized in many other scientific areas can be combined effectively in the solution of business problems. Thus, what is learned in one area can be applied and extended in other areas. Indeed, many improvements in decision making have been accomplished by experts from other fields, such as operations research, who have applied their skills to the field of business.

To summarize, it is admitted that many situations arising in business are novel, unique, and highly abstract. Often, the decision maker must rely upon judgement, intuition and hunch. Conversely, there are many situations within the realm of systematic analysis. Here, the decision maker would be wise to take advantage of the growing body of applicable, quantitative knowledges and techniques.

The Scientific Method

The scientific method is an imposing contrast to judgment or experience as a means of decision making. This method is based upon facts, classified and organized through a series of logical steps. It gains its name, therefore, from the attempt to adopt the attitudes and processes of the physical scientist who seeks solutions to problems from data supplied by careful experiments. Similarly, scientific organizational managers, faced with problems, seek data that will serve to provide answers to their questions.

Although enthusiasm for scientific decision making is easy to generate, it has two serious weaknesses that should be noted. First, facts are difficult to obtain in the managerial field—particularly facts about people and about the future. Second, facts are difficult to obtain in time. Often, decisions must be reached within a time interval that permits little or no fact gathering.

Despite these shortcomings, the scientific method has the best hope for successful planning. Hence, it deserves a fuller description. To do this we need to view the following steps of the scientific method as depicted in figure 3-6.

Statement of Purpose

The first step of the scientific method is to establish as precisely as possible one's purpose. The purpose may be either to accomplish particular objectives

The Decision-Making Process 39

```
        Statement of Purpose
                 ↓
        Preliminary Analysis
                 ↓
        Suggested Solutions
                 ↓
    Testing and Selection of Alternatives
                 ↓
        Testing Selected Solutions
                 ↓
            Application
                 ↓
             Follow up
```

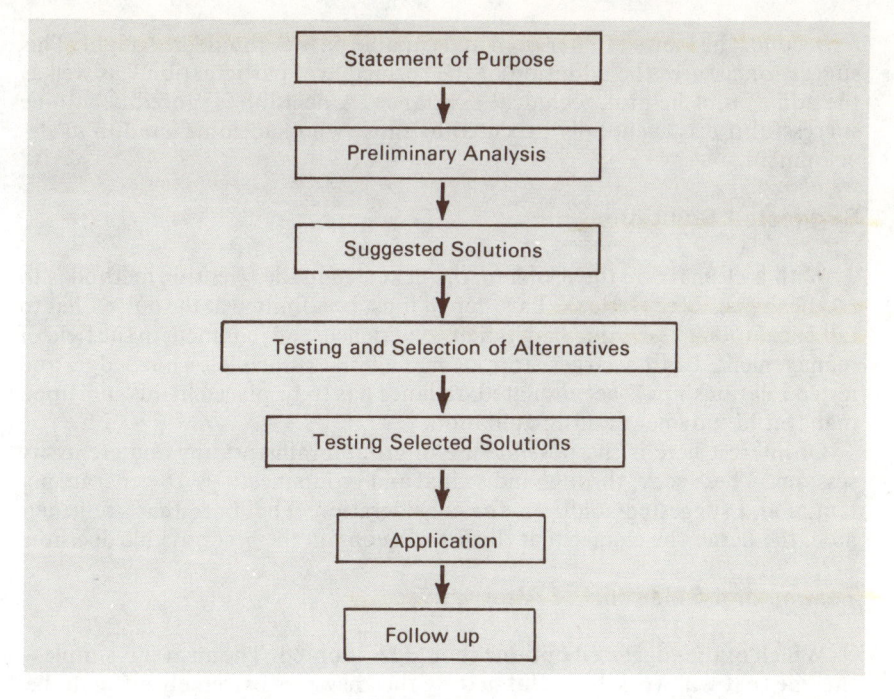

Fig. 3-6. Scientific method of decision making

or to solve problems. The former is exemplified by such statements as "Sales are to be increased in the next period by 10 percent" or "Accounting for customer accounts is to be converted to computers within two years." The latter is exemplified by such statements as, "How can collective bargaining be placed upon a factual basis?" or "How should our decentralized warehouses be integrated into a more efficient distribution system?"

The statement of a problem is particularly difficult. To say, for example, that sales are low does not state a problem. Low sales are an undesirable result. The desired result—high sales—was not attained because some problem was not solved.

Preliminary Analysis

An accurate statement of purpose, objectives, problems, or questions is so important that whatever is determined in the initial step should be considered tentative until the case is examined more carefully. This is in line with the dictum that a correct statement of a problem is half its solution.

Two suggestions are in order while making a preliminary analysis of a problem to be solved. First, it is well to know something about the people involved and the general circumstances in the problem area. As an organizational example, if a manager wanted to convert an office operation from a manual to an automated process, the approach to the problem should not be strictly from an engineering point of view. There are personal considerations and organizational relationships to be considered.

Second, the views of interested and capable parties should be sought. This suggestion assures the adoption of the "principle of participation," as well as the addition of helpful, technical assistance. A decision is more likely to be successful if it is eventually executed by those who had some hand in its development.

Suggested Solutions

With a clear fix on the problem, the next step in the scientific method is to establish possible solutions. This step, it must be admitted at the outset, has to fall back upon guess, educated hunch, experience, and judgment in the field of management. Until a larger store of managerial principles, knowledge, and tested relationships is accumulated, reliance has to be placed in this step upon managerial judgment and imagination.

Of interest here is the possible use of group brainstorming and creativity sessions. These seek, through individual and group meetings, to generate potential and suggested solutions for consideration. The more that are generated, the better the chance that the list will contain the best possible decision.

Testing and Selection of Alternatives

Which of the suggested options should be adopted? The answer is simple—the one that will work best. But getting the answer is extremely difficult, because it means getting the facts on each plan. How does one go about determining, for example, whether a ranking or forced choice plan of evaluating employees is better? Or whether, in collective bargaining, employees will be offered a 5, 10, or 20 percent increase? Suggestions on approaches to getting answers have been made in the preceding paragraphs of this chapter, so further discussion is unnecessary here.

Whatever method is used, however, they all tend to follow somewhat the same formula. The advantages and disadvantages of the several alternatives (suggested solutions) are weighed on the scales of available information. The option with the best net score is judged the one to be employed. In a sense, data decide the course to be followed. This might sound as though executive judgment were being discarded. On the contrary, much judgment is still necessary throughout all stages to insure that logical rules are being followed.

Testing Selected Solutions

Having determined what is the best alternative, applying it would logically seem to be the next step. Often this is so; and indeed time limitations may require this. But where possible an intermediate stage of testing is desirable. This may be done on a trial basis in a limited area or on a "pilot plant" basis. The former provides a check to see whether or not the plan works out in practice as expected. An advertising plan may be checked in a local area before it is put into effect on a national scale, or a training program may be tried out in a branch plant before it is installed companywide.

A "pilot operation" has similar advantages. An accounting system may be operated under the jurisdiction of a consulting concern until all the bugs are worked out. Thus, a trial run permits corrections to be made, unforeseen situations to be handled, and refinements to be included before final application under normal, full-operating conditions.

Application and Follow-up

The adopted decision should be first applied and then continuously checked. Initially, adequate instruction and guidance should be provided to insure that the plan is operated as intended. It is unfortunate when managers conclude that their work is mostly finished when a good decision is made and subordinates can now take over completely. This seems to be a strange point of view. If an executive has struggled for some period of time to arrive at a decision, how can subordinates be expected to grasp the technicalities of its ramifications without careful supervision?

Secondly, it is desirable to check the degree of success attending the operation of an adopted plan. Checking will permit adjustments so the plan will better serve the purposes which it was intended. Certainly, the so-called flexible budget, for example, is a plan whose usefulness depends upon changing the basis of the plan as fundamental conditions change during the period for which it was intended to be used.

Checking will also permit lessons to be learned which can be applied to the improvement of future decision making. So, year by year, better decisions will be developed because of close scrutiny of past successes and failures. For the real test of success is not perfection, but gradual improvement. And this can be assured by good follow-up.

QUESTIONS FOR DISCUSSION

1. Define the term *decision making* and then note some of the reasons why decision making is difficult for any manager.
2. Differentiate between statistical and economic tools and then discuss the relation of these terms to the goal aspect of decision making.
3. Of what significance are standards and value systems to the process of decision making?
4. How does follow-up or feedback contribute to managerial decision making?
5. How does the breadth of narrowness of subject matter with which a manager must deal affect his decision making?
6. List and describe the steps of the scientific method of decision making.
7. What resources may be brought to bear upon decision-making problems?

REFERENCES

1. Herbert Simon, *The New Science of Management Decisions* (New York: Harper and Row. 1977), pp. 5-6.
2. James H. Donnelly, James L. Gibson, and John M, Ivancevich, *Fundamentals of Management* (Dallas: Business Publications, Inc., 1978), pp. 131-133.
   Harold Bierman, Charles P. Bonini, and Warren H. Hausman, *Quantitative Analysis for Business Decisions* (Homewood, IL: Richard D. Irwin, Inc. 1973).
4. L.J. Savage, "The Theory of Statistical Decision," *Journal of American Statistical Association,* March 1951, pp. 55-67.

SELECTED BIBLIOGRAPHY

1. Aigner, Dennis J. *Principles of Statistical Decision Making.* New York: Macmillan Co., 1968.
2. Bross, Irwin, D.I. *Design for Decision.* New York: Macmillan Co., 1953.
3. Churchman, C. West *Prediction and Optimal Decision.* Englewood Cliffs, NJ: Prentice-Hall, Inc., 1961.
4. Fishburn, Peter Co. *Decision and Value Theory.* New York: John Wiley and Sons, Inc., 1964.
5. Schlaifer, Robert. *Analysis of Decisions under Uncertainty.* New York: McGraw-Hill Book Co., Inc., 1967.
6. Simon, Herbert A. *The New Science of Management Decision.* New York: Harper & Brothers, 1977.

CHAPTER 4

THE CONTEMPORARY ORGANIZATION

Purpose of Chapter 4:

1. To illustrate the nature of organizations and the purposes they serve
2. To identify the different types of organization; the line, functional and line and staff
3. To discuss the concept of departmentation as a framework for organizational work
4. To point out how the design of the structure must meet certain tests

Essential elements you should understand after studying this chapter:

1. A clear distinction of the different kinds of organizations and their functions
2. A definition and distinction among the line, functional and line and staff types of structure
3. Departmentation and the rationale for assigning and dividing work into logical units
4. Tests of a sound organizational structure
5. The informal organization: its role and purpose
6. Adaptive styles of organizations, such as systems, project and matrix management

NATURE OF ORGANIZATIONS

Just about all of us—parents, professors, or students—find ourselves in an environment surrounded by and comprised of organizations. Daily we are exposed to organizations of some type or kind. Most of us spend much of our lives working for and being influenced by one.

Earlier we defined organizing as one of the major functions of management. As such, organizing has to do with the need for providing appropriate organization structures, processes, procedures and systems, as well as personnel, material, and technical resources. From this function, then, logically flows the necessary rationale for creation of an organization and its implementation.

Essentially the basic reason for an organization's existence is that certain objectives or goals can be reached only through the combined action of groups of people working together. Whether the goal is profit, providing education, religion, or health care, getting a candidate elected, or having a new football stadium erected, organizations are characterized by their goal-directed behavior.[1]

FORMS OF ORGANIZATIONS

Although organizations have definite common attributes, such as goals, people, structure, processes, and resources, they can nevertheless be classified into certain forms.[2] A primary form of organization is the *production or economic* organization which is largely concerned with the production of goods and the provision of services needed by a consuming society. This category would include manufacturing, marketing, transportation, utilities, mining, wholesale and retail firms, to name a few. It is this form—the business organization—that we largely use for illustrative purposes in this chapter.

The second form is what is known as the *maintenance organization*. Its purpose is intended to support, through socialization, the mental, physical, and spiritual welfare of people in other organizations and in the larger society. This form is comprised of those organizations directly involved in the maintenance of people such as churches, hospitals, universities, colleges, religious organizations, rehabilitation and reform, in addition to health and welfare institutions.

The third form is referred to as the *adaptive organization*. Its purpose is to create and disseminate knowledge, develop and test theories, and to apply information to existing problems. Examples here, of course, would be universities through their research functions, research type organizations, and foundations. Some artistic and altruistic organizations would qualify here because of their interest in, and extension of, human understanding and experience.

A final form is the *managerial or political* organization that deals with the control of resources, people and subsystems. Obviously, the state is the most central and visible example of such organizations. Through its power to use and control force, the state becomes the central power source. Other organizations in this class would be government subsystems, pressure groups, labor unions, and special-interest organizations.

PURPOSE OF ORGANIZATION STRUCTURE

An organization—any organization—essentially is a coordinated group of people involved in achieving desired objectives. Coordination, however, does not automatically occur. Instead, it is necessary to provide certain mechanisms to insure both coordination and control.

One of these mechanisms is the organization structure. The term structure as used here refers to the fixed relationships that exist among jobs and people in the organization. It identifies authority, responsibility, status, and the expected roles of people. It also defines the interpersonal relationships that will exist in various jurisdictional levels and diversions. Moreover, organization structure provides an invisible framework which serves to unify people working together toward common goals. It provides for management control of the various units in the organization. It identifies the various centers of decision making and is ultimately a vehicle for the exercise of leadership throughout the institution.

Organization structure, therefore, provides an indispensable tool of coordination in the human organization. As such, it defines and subdefines jobs. It also combines the groups together through departmentation those jobs having a common basis, and clarifies through the span of control the appropriate size of a group reporting to one manager.

The framework of an organization structure is not an inert, static arrangement. Rather it is dynamic in nature. It delineates the working relationship between the various team members and organizational units. Moreover, the lines of authority and responsibility from higher and lower levels, and between units at the same level, constitute lines of communication. These communication lines are, in a sense, channels of information flows which, both horizontally and vertically, insure a dynamic interaction among all the members.

TYPES OF ORGANIZATION STRUCTURE

Organization structures may be classified in the business field, for example, as being (1) formal (line, functional, and line and staff), (2) informal, and (3) adaptive in design. When studying structures, you should understand, however, that there really is neither an ideal nor optimal design for a given business institution. Organization structures are designed by the firm's management to satisfy specific organization needs. As such, then, they are means to an end—not the end itself.

Line Organization

The traditional and formal line organization is characterized by direct vertical relationships which connect positions and tasks of each level with those above and below it. Each manager in a line organization has comprehensive authority and responsibility concerning all activities directly or indirectly related to the person's primary area. This is depicted in figure 4-1. Authority extends in a direct line from supervisor to subordinate down to the operating level.

This form of structure, incidentally, has important advantages. Since each person reports to one and only one superior, the line of command is clear,

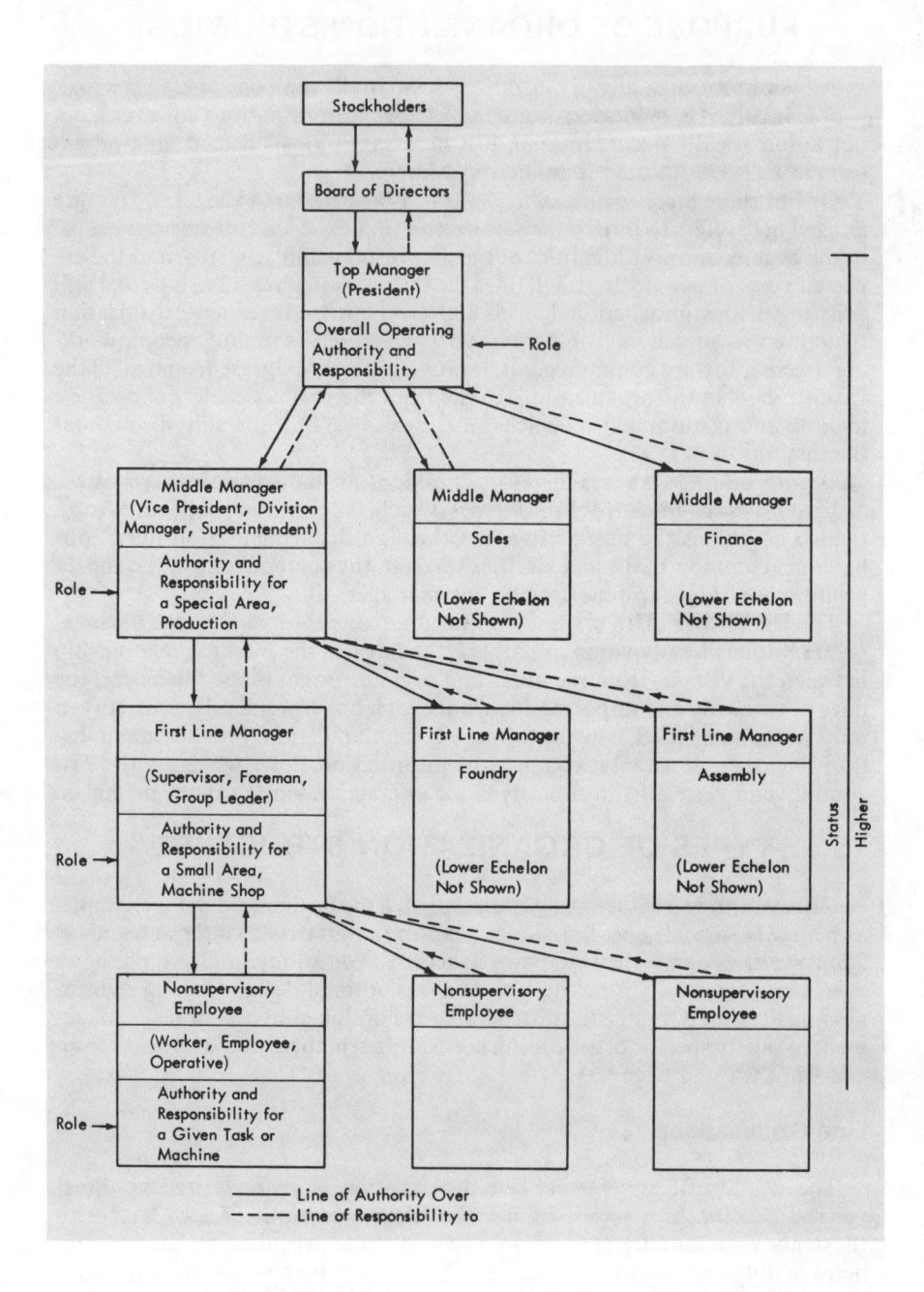

Fig. 4-1. Line of authority and responsibility in organization structure

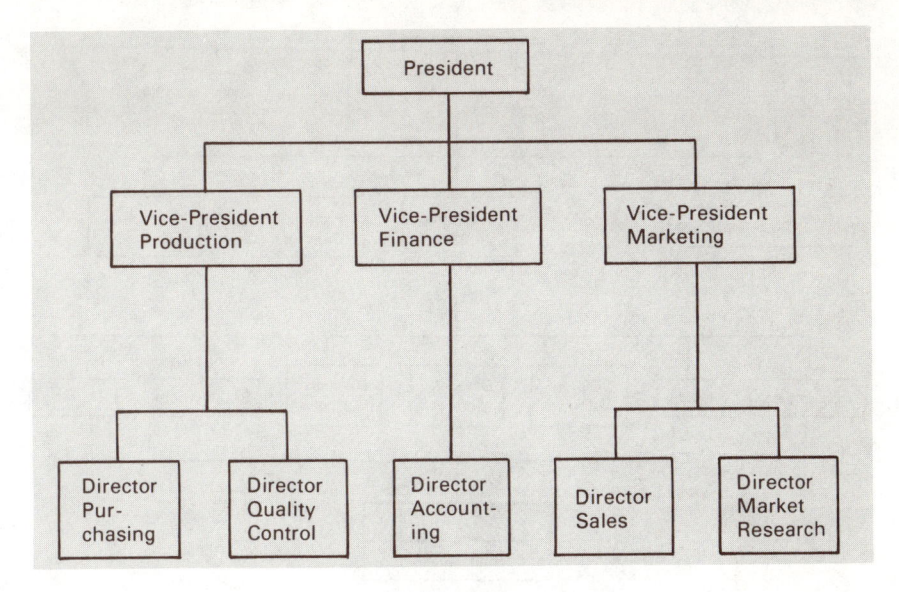

```
                        President
          ┌────────────────┼────────────────┐
   Vice-President    Vice-President    Vice-President
     Production         Finance          Marketing
      ┌──┴──┐              │              ┌──┴──┐
  Director Director    Director      Director Director
   Pur-    Quality    Account-        Sales   Market
  chasing  Control      ing                  Research
```

Fig. 4-2. Line organization

misunderstandings in communication are minimized, and "buck passing" is almost impossible. However, such direct and undiluted authority insures management flexibility and quick decision making. Figure 4-2 illustrates a simple line structure.

But the line structure also has major disadvantages. Line executives must take care of all the varied details and complexities that arise in their jurisdiction. Few executives, though, can be experts in all fields of needed knowledge. Consequently, the line type lacks leadership in specialized fields.

In sum, the effectiveness of the pure line structure is limited to the following conditions: first, a firm must be fairly small and its problems relatively simple and unchanging; secondly, well-rounded executives are generally available and finally, undivided authority is absolutely essential in the management of the business.

Functional Organization

The functional structure is intended to supply the specialization lacking in the line model. In this form, each specialist has authority only over his specialty. In turn, each subordinate reports to several specialists but only for the person's respective area or specialization as illustrated in figure 4-3.

An advantage of the functional form lies in its focus on specialization. Each executive is a specialist, concerned only with functional expertise when dealing with subordinates and, in turn, reports to a specialist. As a consequence, there is specialized managerial direction of various technical subjects.

But what happens when a subordinate has dual accountability and reports to several specialists, even though to each for some different responsibility? Generally, in practice the answer is unsatisfactory. Lines of authority, though abundantly clear on paper are seldom as clear in practice. Subordinates are

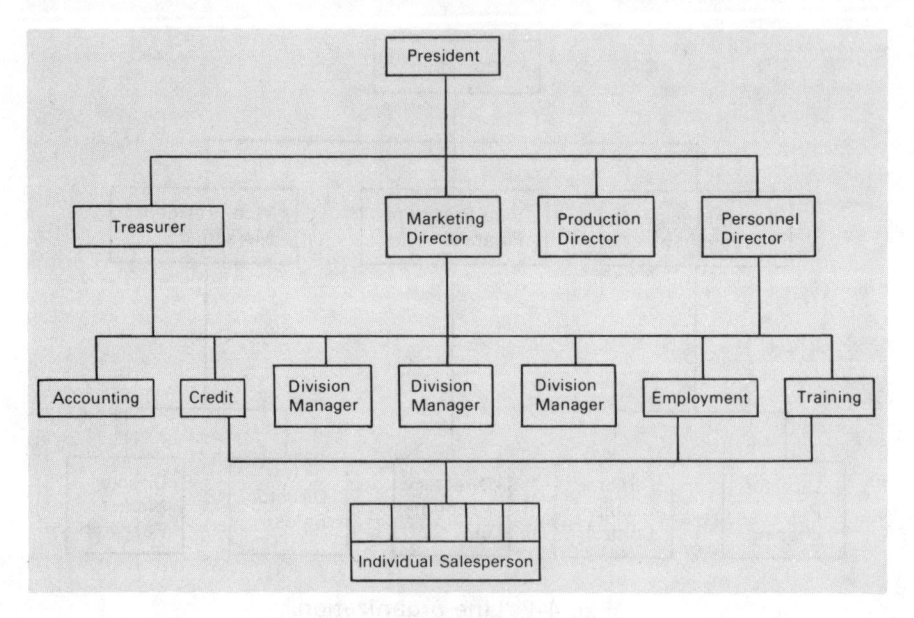

Fig. 4-3. Functional organization

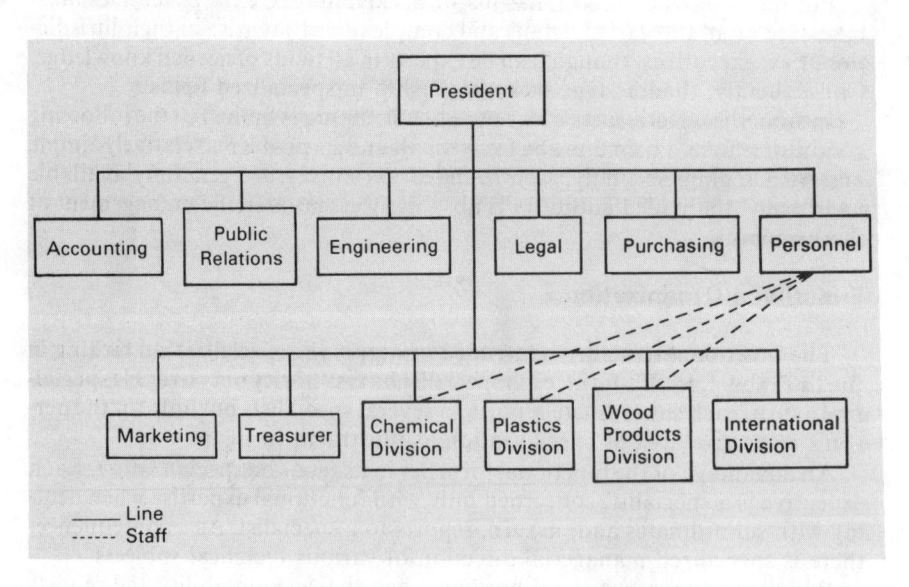

Fig. 4-4. Organization with line and staff relationships

never quite sure to whom they should report. Uncertainty and delay are seemingly the results.

So consequently, this form has not gained popular use. It is adopted occasionally in emergencies or in complex situations (such as automated processes) when direct authority must be given to a specialized executive. But as a general practice such specialized leadership must not be bought at the price of divided leadership. On the other hand, functional structures can be built into an organization structure so that both single accountability and specialized leadership are attained. This is the case in the line and staff form, which we present next.

Line and Staff Organization

The line and staff type of structure represents a favorable combination of the pure line and functional types of organizations. Single accountability, so basic to sound vertical relationships, is preserved, since there is only one superior to whom any individual is directly responsible. Concurrently, specialized staff advice and assistance are, nonetheless, available to any unit of the organization. Figure 4-4 is a typical example.

In this type of organization the service of the functional specialist can truly be developed to a fine degree. Yet, assuredly the advantage of single accountability is still maintained. Maximum effectiveness of effort is made possible since every subordinate takes orders from and reports to only one superior. Moreover, "passing the buck" is somewhat difficult since the scope of one's responsibilities can be more clearly defined. Another definite advantage is this: line executives are allowed to devote more of their time to their own specialty, which, of course, is executing the satisfactory performance of their basic and primary work.

Possible disadvantages of the line and staff design are twofold. Staff units may attempt to take over line authority and line units may, conversely, fail to take advantage of staff services. But these are human failings and not necessarily an inherent weakness of the line and staff form as such.

DEPARTMENTATION

As soon as two or more individuals are engaged in an enterprise, some division of the work becomes necessary. Since the organization is the mechanism established to carry out the work, then any work to be performed must be executed logically and effectively. *This division of the work in an organization into the most logical units is called departmentation.* It means establishing groupings of functions and activities in order to assign them to particular positions or people. It means subdividing the organization structure so that managers specialize with restricted ranges of activity.

Departmentation is a basic element in the organizing process and is genuinely essential to establishing effective relationships between superior and subordinate. Departmentation is arrived at through what is known as functional *analysis* and functional *differentiation*.

Functional analysis is the examination of objectives of the organization as a whole and for each unit, and of the work to be done in order to achieve such objectives. It consists of breaking down the duties of each job and examining each duty to determine its relationship to other duties, its relevance to the organizational unit and the requirements for its performance.

Functional differentiation, which goes one step farther, consists of grouping in an orderly pattern the activities that have been analyzed. These activities are, furthermore, grouped together to facilitate their execution. In arranging these duties, management must give real consideration to the position in which these duties can best be performed and to the proper sequence of their performance as well.[3]

Departmentation, then, classifies and groups the work to be done into manageable units. There are essentially five bases for grouping, with a sixth basis serving as a combination of the first five:

1. Functions
2. Product
3. Processes or equipment
4. Geography
5. Customer
6. Combinations of above

Departmentation by Functions

Similarity of functions is the most frequently used basis for departmentizing. Functions that are alike are grouped into individual organizational units. Thus, it would be logical to group all sales activities together, even though selling might be concerned with different products, customers, and territories. Such classification and arrangement take advantage of specialization. It is true that sales activities may later be grouped further on additional basis as the entire sales function expands and the need for specialization of sales according to customer or product develops. Primarily, however, many activities are departmentized by function.

Departmentation by Product

Another common base of departmentation is to group together those functions pertaining to specific products in a company. An example is the division of operations of a meatpacking company into such major units as beef, pork, and lamb products. Some automobile firms departmentize major divisions on the basis of make of automobiles, such as Chevrolet, Pontiac, Oldsmobile, and Buick. A rubber company may classify its major units into rubber products (such as footwear and rubberized fabrics) and plastics. Concentration of all efforts peculiar to a particular product or service is thus made possible. (Figure 4-5).

Departmentation by product not only permits the maximum use of managerial expertise and specialized knowledge, but also permits the exaction of profit responsibility from the product department managers. This is a natural consequence since under departmentation by product, all activities necessary to both the production and distribution of goods and services are combined within the same organizational subdivision of the firm.

Departmentation by Process or Equipment

This type of departmentation is often employed to permit certain economic advantages materializing from bringing manpower and materials together to

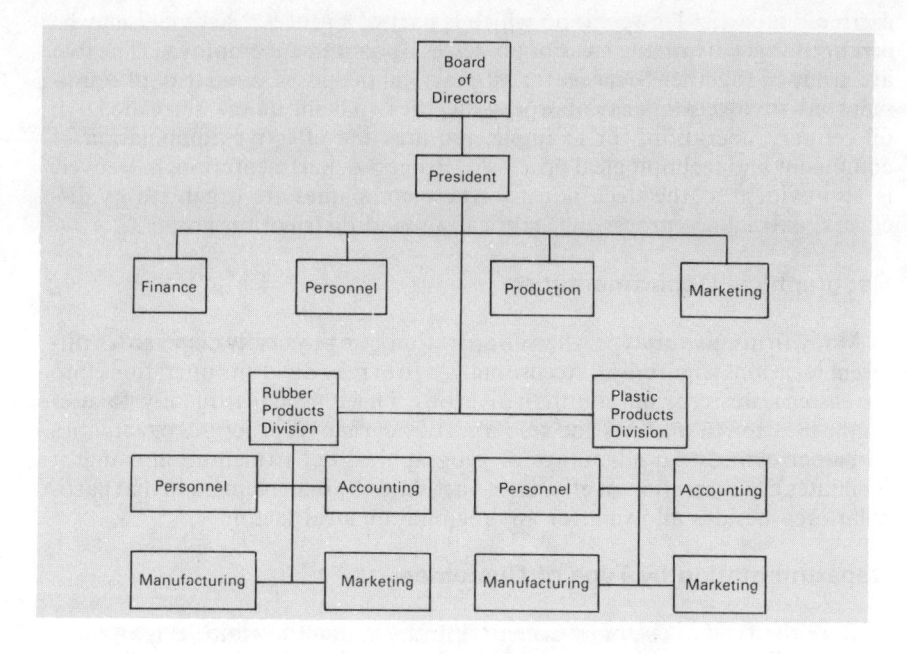

Fig. 4-5. Departmentation by product

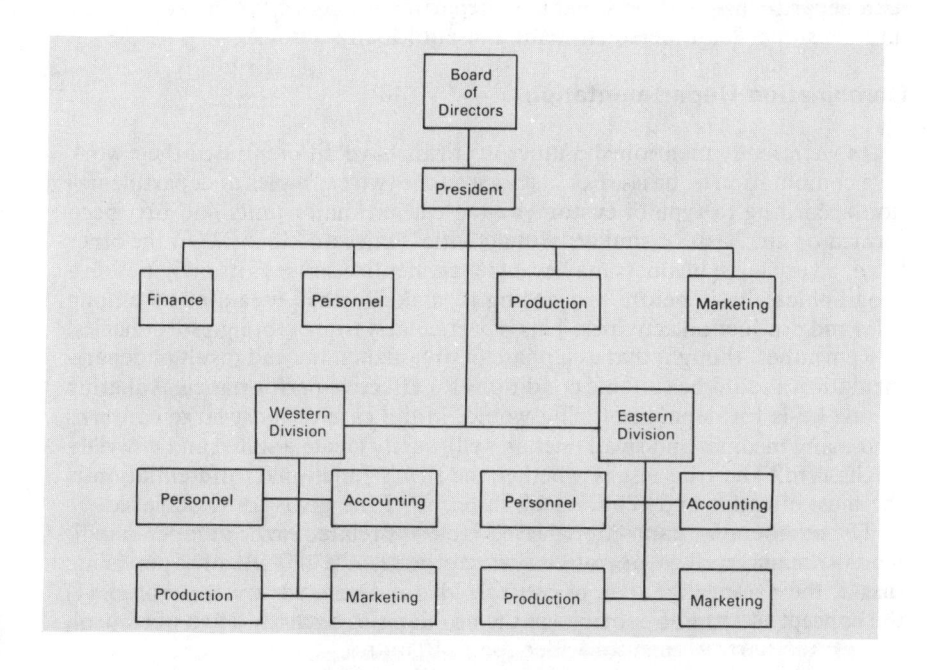

Fig. 4-6. Geographical Departmentation

carry out a particular operation which is part of a process. Activities may be arranged logically on the basis of processes or equipment employed. The two are grouped together because, for all practical purposes, similarity of equipment will involve similarity of processes—the two being quite interrelated. An oil refinery operation, for example, requires the effective combination of equipment and technological processes. Process departmentation, moreover, is also evident in the steel industry where companies are organized by discovery, extraction, processing, fabricating, and distribution groups.

Geographical Departmentation

Many firms use this type when its operations are physically dispersed in different locations (figure 4-6). Accordingly, a firm may divide its operations into the eastern, western, and southern divisions. This type, consequently, focuses on the location of markets and resources rather than on processes or activities to be performed. An advantage of geographical departmentation is that it facilitates concentration of efforts and activities by management in that particular area besides allowing for any regional or local factors.

Departmentation by Type of Customer

Here the type of customer is central to the manner in which activities are grouped. For example, a firm may departmentize its sales activities into retail, wholesale, and institutional selling units. A bank may divide its loan function into such categories as commercial loan, mortgage loan, and personal loan departments. The personal loan department may be further subdivided into consumer loan, personal loan, and auto loan sections.

Combination Departmentation

As we already mentioned, numerous firms have differentiated their work on a combination of bases. For instance, in the two examples of departmentation according to type of customer cited earlier, major units had first been formed on the basis of similarity of activities (sales and loans). On the other hand, a very large business may even departmentize some of its activities on a geographical basis before proceeding to make further breakdowns among sales and production activities. This is particularly true of foreign subsidiaries.

Remember, though, that as a phase of organizing, the end result of departmentation should be suitable conditions for effective performance. Adhering to one basis for departmentizing would, in the case of most large concerns (and many medium and small ones as well), surely create a stilted and unwieldy mechanism. The true test is whether the firm's functional differentiation is the most effective and economical, in terms of the goals to be achieved.

The number of organizational levels is closely related to the number of individuals, managerial or operative that executives are capable of supervising; that is, their respective span of control. This is discussed now in terms of (1) the concept of span of control, (2) the problems of a narrow span of control, and (3) the narrow versus a wider span of control.

THE CONCEPT OF SPAN OF CONTROL

The term span of control refers to the number of individuals an executive can personally and directly supervise with effectiveness. The number varies between operative employees and managerial employees. As a rule of thumb, a span of 10 to 30 is generally indicated for operative and from 3 to 8 for managerial employees. This is true because of the nature of the work involved.

In operative jobs the employees are usually trained to perform their activities in a set way. Once they attain proficiency, their work requires control of a somewhat routine nature. Contacts necessary in performance of their jobs are usually simple in nature and made briefly and directly with their supervisor. When interpersonal contacts are made at the operative level, they do not normally require frequent coordination by the supervisor but are usually routinized by some formalized procedure.

Since the administrative activities of managers above the first level of supervision are more complex, the effective span tends to be limited to fewer subordinates. Normally the complexity of executive duties tends to increase with each advancing level of the organization.

At upper managerial levels, span tends to be much less extensive. Managerial work is less standardized and involves much decision making. The managerial functions must be supervised and integrated with activities of other subordinate executives. Supervision and coordination of all executives on the same level in a division require frequent personal contacts, both between superior and subordinate and, often, among subordinates. Thus, superiors must devote proportionately more of their time to each of their subordinate executives than must first-line supervisors to each of their operative subordinates.

PROBLEMS INVOLVED IN NARROW SPAN OF CONTROL

But keeping a narrow span of control means that more levels must be added to an organization as it grows. This increases the possibility of such managerial problems as: (1) layering, (2) inaccurate communication, (3) additional supervisory expense, and (4) unsatisfactory morale.

Layering

Layering refers to inflexibility in performing managerial duties brought on by the addition of numerous organizational levels. Interpersonal contacts between individuals in different units must be routed through the formal chain of command, as indicated in figure 4-7. A bridge of communication as shown by the dotted line cannot be established, and all contacts must be made by working up through all levels in the pyramid. Certain decisions, as a result, will take longer to make and communicate since needed information and coordination can be less easily secured.

Layering is sometimes insisted upon, though, as a control measure in order to assure that the superior executive is kept informed of activities conducted below. However, when action at lower levels does not actually require the superior's advice or other participation, the person can be kept informed of action taken by the subordinate, without actually becoming a link in the chain

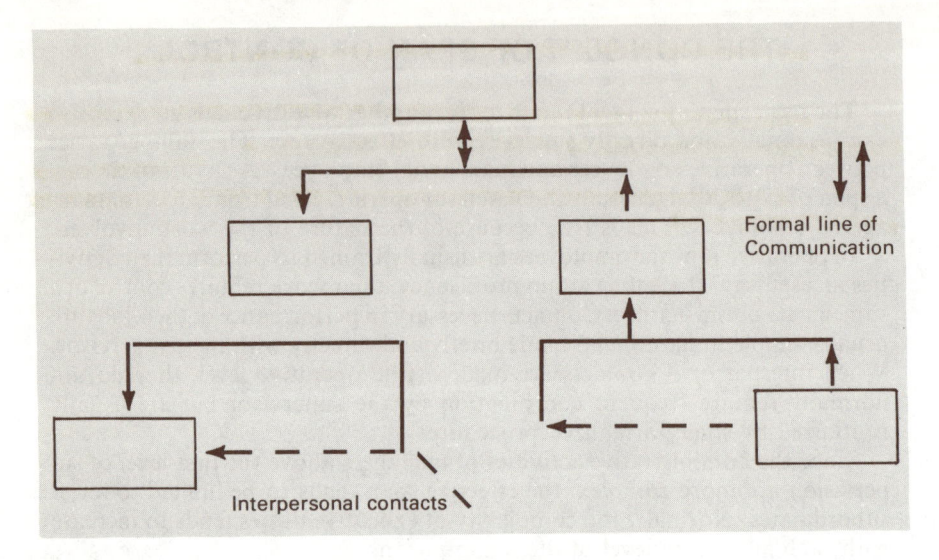

Fig. 4-7. Effect of layering in communications

of communication.

Inaccurate Communication

Obviously, an increase in the number of echelons in the firm lengthens the channel of communication. The more positions a communication must pass through, the greater the possibility that information may become distorted. Consequently, the danger that communications do not remain clear and understandable and are not transmitted with a minimum of delay is increased.

Additional Supervisory Expense

Supervisory expense may be increased because more levels of supervision are added with a narrow span of control. For example, if a span of 5 was maintained consistently throughout an organization comprising 6 organizational levels, the number of managers would be significantly greater than if the span were increased to 10 and the levels reduced accordingly.

Unsatisfactory Morale

It is said that when a manager administers through a narrow span of control, morale can possibly be affected unfavorably. Layering and an extended chain of command may be conducive to subordinate isolation. In the next section we shall examine the hypothesis that morale is improved in a wide span.

NARROW VERSUS WIDE SPAN OF CONTROL

In recent years, questions have been raised by both the management theorist and the practitioner about the traditional views of span of control. These views generally hold that a span of three to eight or nine[4] subordinates is unrealistic. In practice, executives frequently exercise a larger span of control without difficulty. Some executives can supervise more than others, and the conditions under which they manage are different. Furthermore, a wide span of control permits decreasing the levels in the organization thus minimizing the problems resulting from numerous levels as we discussed above.

While the desirability of minimizing levels cannot be denied, the span of control cannot, however, be widened indiscriminately. When a large number of subordinates is supervised by an executive, there is the distinct possibility that communication and coordination problems may develop. Although delays due to layering may not be present, problems within a unit may be increased.

Under what conditions, then, can widening the span of control be considered? There are several. First, when the subordinate managers are engaged in specialized and independent functions, a wider span is possible. An illustration of these two sets of conditions is shown in figures 4-8 and 4-9.

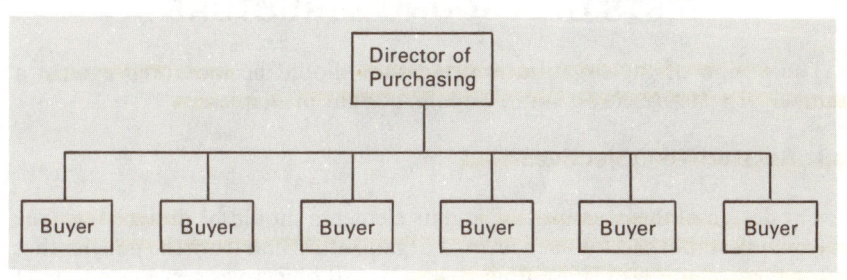

Fig. 4-9. Span of control with relatively independent subordinates

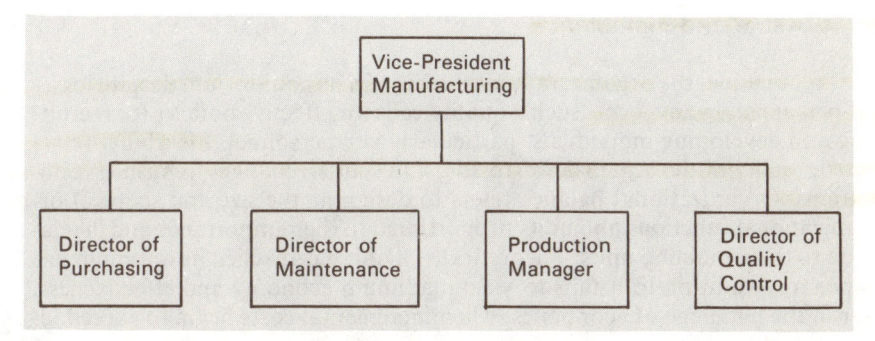

Fig. 4-8. Span of control with interdependent subordinates

In figure 4-8, the four directors must frequently contact one another as well as the common superior. In figure 4-9, however, each buyer is a specialist in a particular field. Not only may contacts among buyers be infrequent, but also the contacts between individual buyers and the director of purchases may be limited.

A number of other factors also determine the practical span of control. A manager who must perform certain duties such as public relations will have little time left for supervising immediate subordinates. The manager's personal skill, knowledge, adaptability, and even physical fitness will figure in the number to be successfully managed. The rate of growth of an organization will also be a determinant, since rapidly changing business situations will influence the executive span. Then too, the extent to which an organization remains stable will decidedly influence the width of span.

Where subordinates are capable of exercising individual discretion and decision-making authority, and where the policy is one of considerable delegation of authority, a wider span of control is feasible. In certain instances, some of the duties of an executive can be assumed by an assistant or an "assistant to." With the assistant acting as a personal staff or aide, the executive then has more time freed up to devote to subordinate unit managers, thus increasing the span of control.

TESTS OF A SOUND STRUCTURE

The design of the organization structure should be measured against a number of tests based on sound organizational principles.

Is It Related To Objectives?

The design of the organization and its elements should be derived from the objectives established for each level of organization and from the policies that guide the execution of those objectives. Overall objectives serve as points of departure for planning subobjectives. In order to achieve subobjectives, objectives can be stated for each lower level unit and its jobs. Moreover, the objectives of jobs must be consistent with the objectives of the next higher level. Similarly, the structures of each unit and level should be integrated and consistent with the next higher level.

Is It Stable and Flexible?

To be stable, the organization must maintain its equilibrium despite losses of personnel on any level. Such a quality calls for effective policies for recruiting and developing individuals, particularly key personnel. Flexibility refers to the ability of the organization to adjust to sudden changes in business conditions. Organizational balance refers to designing the size and scope of organizational functions and units proportional to their importance and in relation to the remaining units. Theoretically, a unit has reached its optimum size when any addition to it fails to yield maximum economy and effectiveness. Or in the language of economics, when incremental costs begin to exceed incremental benefits.

Is It Simply Constructed?

Furthermore, an organization should remain as simple in structure as is consistent with work needs. This point is so fundamental that it may appear superfluous. Yet, too often, firms, especially in periods of rapid growth, evolve such complex frameworks that control is made difficult. Labor costs go up; stability, flexibility, and balance are all jeopardized by the resulting unwieldy mechanism.

Does It Provide For Change?

A sound organization furthermore allows for growth or contraction over a long-run period. Many firms have expanded rapidly in an extended sellers' market, only to be confronted with insurmountable obstacles when an economic slowdown dictated retrenchment. The challenge is to provide for dynamic equilibrium—that is, to allow the organization to expand or contract, and still maintain a stable, flexible, balanced, and simple organization structure. Flexibility, of course, refers to its ability to adjust to both short- and long-run growth and change.

Are Functions Logically Grouped?

A sound organization will be marked by a logical grouping of functions within units. In other words, departmentation has been performed effectively, and jobs within units have been organized on the basis of suitable grouping of activities. Lastly, the objectives, policies, functions, authority, responsibility, and relationships that have been planned and organized into existence should be known and understood by all those concerned.

INFORMAL ORGANIZATION

When contrasted with the formal type organization, which we have been discussing, the informal takes on special significance. *The informal organization can be identified as a group of two or more people who communicate more or less regularly for purposes of exchanging information, rendering group support, developing group consensus, or providing needed leadership.* It is a system of relationships and associations which supplement the formal organization.[5]

Role and Purpose of Informal Organization

Just about every organization has some type of informal organization. As its recognized purposes, the informal organization:

1. Provides for the satisfaction of certain socio-psychological needs not provided by the formal structure.[6]
2. Provides communications through the medium of the well-known grapevine. The grapevine is the system of networks that circulate within organizational groups. Its purpose is to supplement information released through formal channels as depicted in figure 4-10.

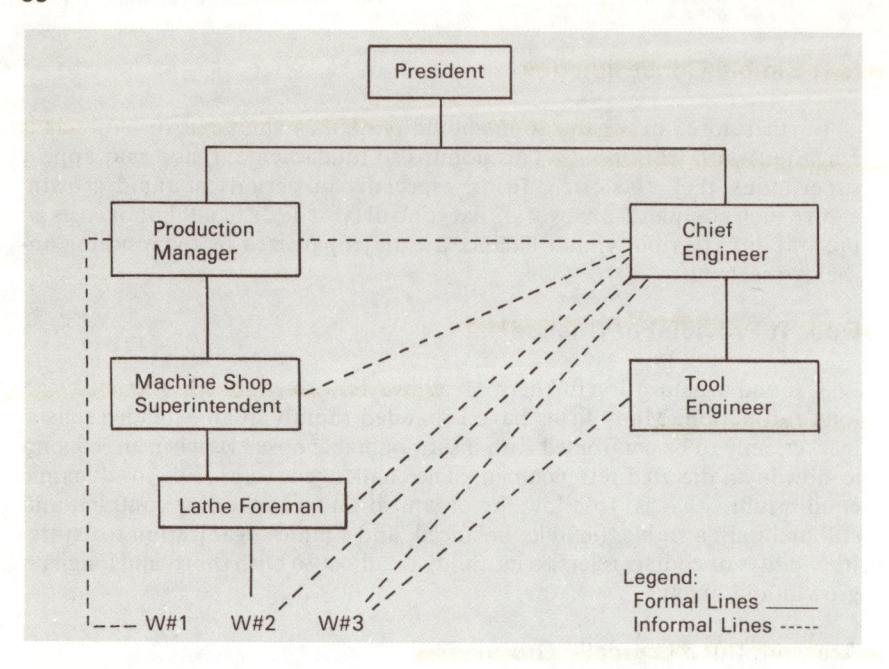

Fig. 4-10. Informal contact chart

3. Establishes and maintains group norms and standards of behavior and performance. Violations may result in disapproval and censure by the group.
4. Offers leadership through the informal leader in contrast to the formally designated leader. Informal leaders may not have official authority as such but are recognized and accepted by a particular group on the bases of such characteristics as age, skill, knowledge, social, physical, or certain personal attributes.

Certain personal attributes of informal leadership which seem to have a strong bearing on member acceptance are the facility to communicate information to the group; the ability to embody the values of the group, to verbalize these as its spokesman; and to provide linkage or liason with other managers or work groups.

Essential for management is the need to recognize the informal organization, its structure, and its leadership as positive rather than negative realities in accomplishing certain organizational objectives. Whenever the informal structure is compatible with the formal organization, institutional objectives can be more readily realized. By using the grapevine within the informal structure, management can communicate certain information quickly. By identifying sources of informal power and leadership, management can build additional and sound structural relationships while cooperatively pursuing its objectives.

ADAPTIVE STYLES OF ORGANIZATION STRUCTURE

The increasing complexity of today's organization along with an advancing technology have created a need for more adaptable and flexible models of organization. Among these are (1) systems management, (2) project management, (3) matrix management, and (4) the office of the president.

Systems Management

Systems management is achieved by identifying all components necessary for organizational effectiveness and by designing a plan that will assure their optimum interaction.

In this context, then, the organization is regarded as a system containing a number of subsystems—for example, production or marketing or accounting—and surrounded by larger systems such as the industry or even society as a whole. The business organization system includes: (1) inputs of information, facilities, materials, and effort; (2) a systematic process whereby the inputs are combined into an orderly arrangement of interacting components; (3) outputs such as products, customer service, wages, and profits; and (4) a feedback process which reports the results of operations and corrects the input mix if necessary so that the output meets predetermined objectives and standards, as simply illustrated in figure 4-11.

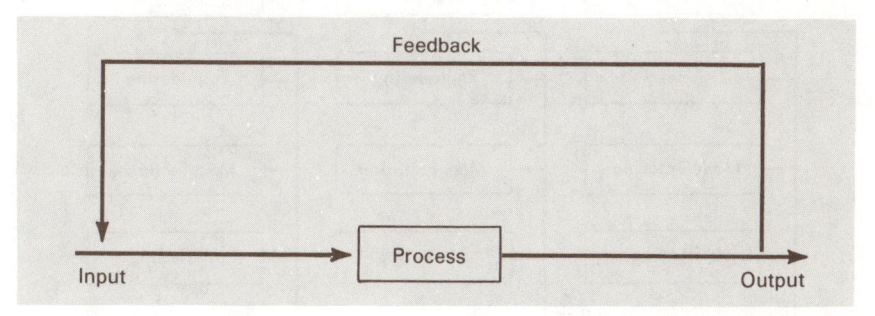

Fig. 4-11. Simplified concept of a system

Advocates of the systems management concept point out that the conventional functional design of the organization with its line-staff format does not always permit optimum efficiency in the various departmental activities involved in specific project undertakings. The functional division of tasks, they argue, imposes barriers to smooth cooperation among the many different skills needed for completing any particular project. Systems management purports to achieve a smooth flow of activities under conditions which allow human effort to be fitted to the work process with high efficiency.

Project Management

Under project management a group of individuals possessing the required skills is organized into an autonomous unit for a particular task or project.

Project management is an offshoot of the weapons systems concept applied by the aerospace industry in the development of ballistic missiles. The need for reduced lead time to develop an operational weapon system necessitated a different kind of organizational model. More recently it has been adapted to such large-scale projects as the building of a skyscraper and to the construction of a nuclear reactor boiler vessel where a huge input of resources, manpower, materials, and equipment must be precisely integrated.

Project management is carried out by a project director appointed to coordinate the activities of engineering, marketing, production, accounting, and to motivate personnel drawn from these respective departments or a separate pool who make up the project team for a particular project. Figure 4-12 illustrates the concept of project organization. Each project then has a complete line organization managed by the project manager who has full authority over all personnel, facilities, and operations required to complete the product.

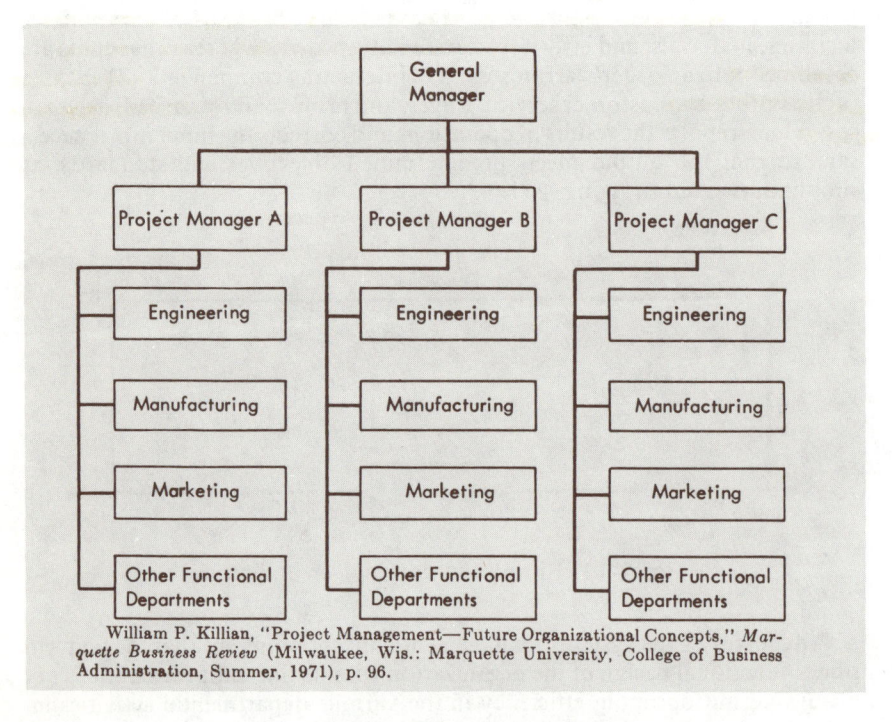

William P. Killian, "Project Management—Future Organizational Concepts," *Marquette Business Review* (Milwaukee, Wis.: Marquette University, College of Business Administration, Summer, 1971), p. 96.

Fig. 4-12. Project organization

The advocates of project management point to its clear visibility of project goals and to the team members understanding of their role and task. Responsibility for the project is definitely pinpointed; coordination is facilitated; and motivation and innovation increased. On the other hand, one of the strongest disadvantages of the pure project organization is that the cost in a multiproject company would be prohibitive because of the required duplication of effort and facilities among the projects.

Matrix Management

Matrix Management is a form of organization that combines or mixes both the project structure and the traditional functional structure. It is desirable for producing large projects within desired cost, schedule, and performance standards. Figure 4-13 shows a simplified matrix organization chart.

```
                        General Manager
         ┌──────────────┬────────┴────────┬──────────────┐
     Engineering    Manufacturing     Marketing         Other
                                                     Departments
    ┌────────────────┐          │      Project
    │Project Manager A├─────────┼──────Responsibility─────────→
    └────────────────┘          │
    ┌────────────────┐    Functional
    │Project Manager B├────Responsibility────────────────────→
    └────────────────┘          │
    ┌────────────────┐          │
    │Project Manager C├─────────┼─────────────────────────────→
    └────────────────┘          ↓
```

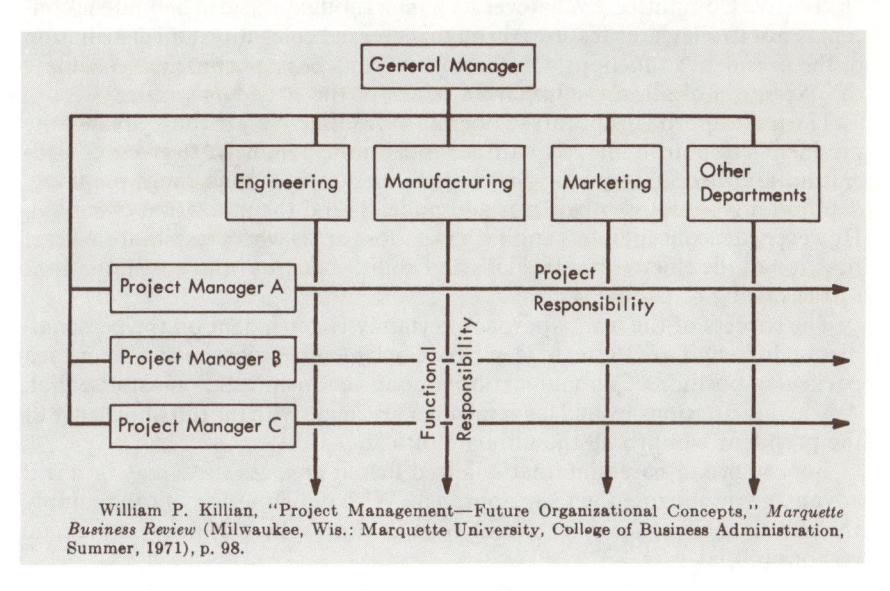

William P. Killian, "Project Management—Future Organizational Concepts," *Marquette Business Review* (Milwaukee, Wis.: Marquette University, College of Business Administration, Summer, 1971), p. 98.

Fig. 4-13. Matrix organization

In a matrix organization each of the functional groups such as marketing or engineering is headed by a department manager who is responsible for a particular function, and has assigned responsibilities according to the needs of the project. Concurrently, the project manager, on the other hand, is fully responsible for the project's total success.

Advocates of the matrix form argue that it combines strengths of both the functional and project organizations. It also provides for specialized knowledge for carrying on a number of specific projects. And furthermore, it allows for quicker responsiveness of specialists by virtue of its established communication lines and its functional levels of decision making.

Conversely, there are certain disadvantages of this type of organization. Possible problems may arise out of the dual accountability of personnel involved in the project. Then too, possible conflicts of objectives and purposes may exist between project and functional managers and finally there is the potential difficulty of pinpointing profit and loss accountability for individual managers and groups in the project.

Office of the President

In the majority of corporations, the traditional chief executive is at the helm. However, within the last decade the pressures on the president have been so intensified that some firms have offered assistance by establishing an "office of the president." Diversification, decentralization, increasing technology, and product complexity are forcing some firms to set up a multiple chief executive function to ease the burdens of the chief executive.

This concept is widely used in Europe, and it may function under such various designations as "Office of the President," "Management Forum," or "Executive Committee." Whatever its name, though, the idea behind the concept is not to alleviate pressures through increased delegation and distribution of the president's functions. On the contrary, its basic purpose is to facilitate the execution of all of the important tasks of the president's office.

The team approach appears to operate more effectively in those areas of the president's responsibilities that are generally more conducive to group consideration and decision making—responsibilities such as long-range planning, determining corporate objectives and policies, and the utilization of capital. However, the concept is less applicable in those areas where results are a direct function of the chief's singular skills and abilities such as in labor negotiations or the raising of capital.

The success of the team approach certainly is dependent on the personalities and strengths of the team members. Each member must be competent at a particular position. Communication among the members is most essential. Any major decisions by any team member are made with the full knowledge of the president who is still the ultimate officer.

For the broad-based internationalized firm it appears there may be a real advantage in utilizing the team approach. With judicious use, it can multiply the effectiveness of the chief executive in an atmosphere of heavy duties and responsibilities.

QUESTIONS FOR DISCUSSION

1. What elements are included in the definition of organization structure?
2. Identify and give actual illustrations of the four main types of organizations.
3. What factors explain the origin of the concept of the functional organization at this particular time in history?
4. What are the chief advantages of the line-and-staff type of organization?
5. What is included in functional analysis?
6. What are the tests of a sound organization structure?
7. What type of needs does the systems concept of management appear to fill?
8. To what extent does the wide span of control eliminate the problems generally associated with the narrow span?
9. Identify the major differences among the project and matrix organizational forms and the traditional functional structure.
10. Discuss the advantages of the "office of the president" concept. Can you foresee any possible disadvantage to its use?

REFERENCES

1. James L. Gibson, John M. Ivancevich, and James H. Donnelly, Jr., *Organizations: Behavior, Structure, Processes* (Dallas: Business Publications, Inc.,) p. 4.
2. Adapted largely from Daniel Katz and Robert Lester Kahn, *The Social Psychology of Organizations* (New York: John Wiley and Sons, Inc., 1966), pp. 111-128. Functional arrangement as described here is sometimes critized by students of organization on the ground that the definition of jobs and departments creates a

structure which discourages coordination among functions. Those within a functional unit, it is contended, become so preoccupied with effective performance in their unit that they fail to see their role in and relationship to other units and to the whole organization. Sound procedures, however, should effectively integrate the various functions into a total balanced and coordinated system, with each function making its specialized contribution to the objectives of the firm.
4. The range of three to eight or nine subordinates has often been cited as representing generally the most effective span. Usually such citations recognize the possibility of exceptions. See, for example, Ralph C. Davis, *The Fundamentals of Top Management* (New York: Harper & Bros., 1951), p. 276.
5. Michael J. Jucius, Bernard A. Deitzer, and William E. Schlender, *Elements of Managerial Action* (Homewood, IL: Richard D. Irwin, Inc., 1973), p. 279.
6. Jucius et al., op. cit. p., 143.

SELECTED BIBLIOGRAPHY

1. Blau, Peter M. *On the Nature of Organizations.* New York: John Wiley and Sons, Inc., 1974.
2. Burack, Elmer. *Organization Analyses: Theory and Applications.* Hinsdale, IL: The Dryden Press, 1975.
3. Galbraith, Jay R. *Organization Design.* Reading, MA: Addison-Wesley Publishing Company, 1977.
4. Hall, Richard H. *Organizations: Structure and Process.* Englewood Cliffs, NJ: Prentice-Hall Inc., 1972.
5. Litterer, Joseph A. *The Analysis of Organizations.* 2d ed. New York: John Wiley and Sons, 1973.

CHAPTER 5

DESIGNING LINE-AND-STAFF RELATIONSHIPS

Purpose of Chapter 5:

1. To discuss the different functions and purposes that exist between line and staff components in the firm
2. To illustrate specific types, kinds and responsibilities of staff specialization
3. To show how staff authority works in the typical organization

Essential elements you should understand after studying this chapter:

1. Inherent differences between line and staff responsibilities
2. Specific characteristics of staff personnel
3. A description of personal and also specialized staffs
4. Staff specialization and its relationships to the managerial functions
5. Those situations when staff assumes line authority
6. Handling conflict in line and staff situations

INTRODUCTION

In the previous chapter we discussed the distinctive characteristics, advantages, and limitations of the organizational structure. In this chapter we will explore more fully the place of staff in its relationship to the line organization. This relationship to the basic line structure is so vital in the achievement of the company's objectives that it justifies special consideration. For as the organization grows, it necessarily relies more and more on services of specialized staff experts to maintain managerial efficiency.

An organization may grow in terms of (1) technical factors such as machines, processes, materials, and buildings; (2) specialization within those technical factors such as particular people working exclusively on particular tasks as purchasing, production control, or traffic; (3) absolute numbers of personnel; and (4) spatial coverage, that is, the firm's geographical expansion either in one location or through branches. Consequently, to handle such growth, both specialized management and an accomodating structural system must often be established.

EFFECTS OF ORGANIZATIONAL GROWTH

As the small organization sees opportunity for increasing the volume of business, the means for doing so must be organized. Generally such increased activity will require more equipment or materials, more personnel, more space for operations, or a combination of these. And if such additional factors are to be integrated with the present organization then, obviously, additional managerial functions are also required.

Indeed, the management difficulty is increased by more than the equivalent of the mere addition of factors. The entire new organization is a more complex system of units, levels, and relationships. Thus, while technical, personnel, and space factors, for example, are added, the managerial functions are multiplied. That this is uniformly true has led to the recognition of the *law of functional growth. This law states that as necessary functions are added to handle the increased volume of an organization, the number of relationships tends to increase in geometric ratio, although the actual functions may increase arithmetically.*

So, as work expands, the organization also expands both horizontally and vertically. To basic line production functions are added differentiated staff technical functions, such as purchasing, engineering, and warehousing. Levels, as well as more units on the same level, are developed. Relationships become more complex at an accelerated rate, and assistance to those original managers of basic functions must be provided. To the management of operative work is now added another highly significant problem, namely, the management of more managers.

MANAGERIAL SOLUTIONS TO PROBLEMS OF GROWTH

The solution to the problems of providing sufficient management for the growing organization are several. An obvious alternative is simple to multiply the number of line executives. As technical factors, personnel, and spatial coverage increase beyond the scope of present line executives, additional line officers, each with the same scope of responsibilities, are appointed as in figure 5-1. In actual circumstances this solution would be applied in relatively few and limited instances. As soon as the firm expanded beyond the point of being very small, such a move would become a most uneconomical one.

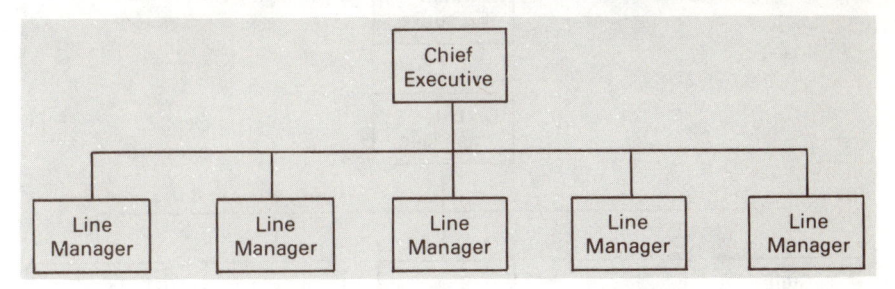

```
                    ┌──────────┐
                    │  Chief   │
                    │Executive │
                    └────┬─────┘
       ┌──────────┬─────┼──────┬──────────┐
   ┌───┴───┐  ┌───┴───┐ │  ┌───┴───┐  ┌───┴───┐
   │ Line  │  │ Line  │...│ Line  │  │ Line  │
   │Manager│  │Manager│   │Manager│  │Manager│
   └───────┘  └───────┘   └───────┘  └───────┘
```

Fig. 5-1. Initial development of line management

More probably, another course of action would be followed to supply adequate management capacity. A manager, sensing the drag on time caused by attending to many details, would probably employ an assistant to take over such detail and routine work as keeping time records of employees, distributing routine work instructions for the day, or making up a report on work progress.

Let us assume that the individual has been employed to assist the manager in the purchasing function. At first the individual will probably do the routine work of making out purchase orders, checking supply levels, and ascertaining that deliveries are made on time. As the individual learns about specifications, rate of use, sources of supply, and negotiations, additional purchasing duties will be assumed. When the activities in this function rise to the point where the assistant can no longer do all of them, authorization may be given to employ additional clerical help in order to free up time for the more important part of the job as in figure 5-2.

The assistant now has taken over, at this point, all or nearly all procurement duties, but still reports to the line manager who still has the responsibility for this function. The purchasing assistant, however, has assumed the role of staff specialist to the line manager.

As the organization increases in volume a further development may take place. The potential advantages of having a common procurement function for all organizational units becomes apparent. The purchasing officer now is given authority and responsibility for organization-wide procurement. Commensurate with this new authority and responsibility, the purchasing agent now moves up to a higher echelon in the organization.

At this point, the agent may not be placed on the same level with former superiors, and both the purchasing manager and line manager may be responsible for a common line manager as depicted in figure 5-3. Thus, a staff unit may be elevated to a level where the executive in charge is responsible directly to the president. When a firm becomes multiplant in size, we find frequently that a staff unit is set up at the home office level, while similar units operate at the plant level and below. This is generally called staff parallelism.

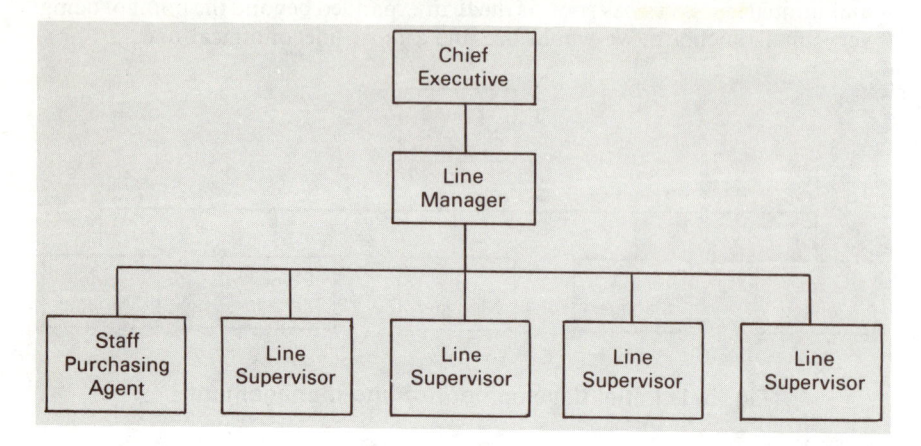

Fig. 5-2. Addition of staff specialization

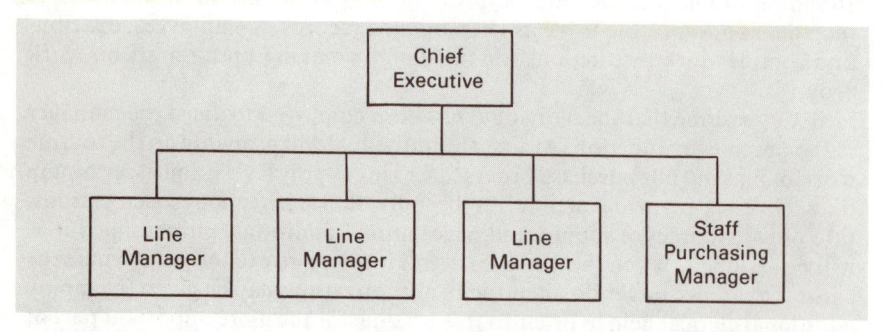

Fig. 5-3. Progression of staff specialization to staff management

KINDS OF STAFF

Generally, there are two basic kinds of staff. These are *personal* staff and *specialized* staff.

Personal Staff

These are positions with the distinct purpose of assisting the managers in executing those aspects of their job which they cannot and do not wish to delegate to others. Personal staff mainly consists of three kinds of assistants: the line assistant, the staff assistant, and what is known as the general staff assistant.

Designing Line-and-Staff Relationships

The line assistant, while in the direct chain of command, is nevertheless staff to his or her superior because the job is to advise, counsel, and take over, when required, for the manager only. The line assistant has no responsibility separate from that of any immediate superior; consequently there are no powers of redelegation. Typical of the line assistants are the various "assistant managers" of production, marketing, and so on.

The staff assistant is also known as an "assistant to," or "administrative assistant." More confined than the line assistant, staff assistants exercise no authority over other personnel, nor ever assume the responsibility of the line executive. Responsibilities of staff assistants differ widely. An assistant to the president may range in use from a personal valet in one firm, to a presidential alter ego in another who may sit in on board and other important meetings and also handcraft important reports and speeches for the president.

The general staff assistant serves as an advisor to top management in specific areas, and often is a member of another particular staff group and is employed in addition to the regular corporate specialized staff.

Specialized Staff

This type of staff provides both advice and service to the line organization and other staff departments. Specialized staff departments restrict their activities to one specialized function or area. They may be called upon by all other line and staff units of the firm. In contrast, personal staff, on the other hand, works primarily for one executive in helping carry out responsibilities. Some typical staff positions are illustrated in figure 5-4.

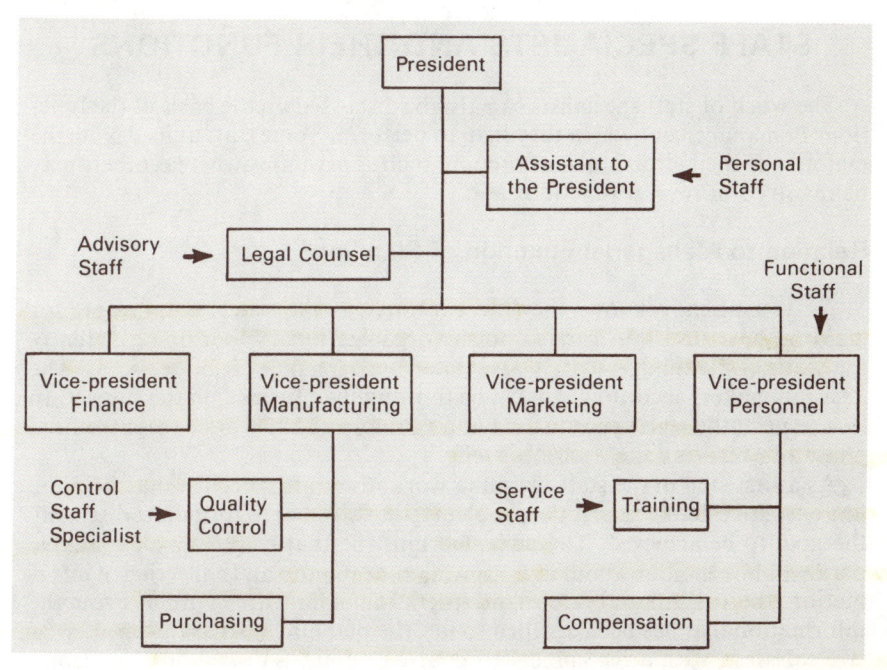

Fig. 5-4. Some examples of staff positions

CHARACTERISTICS OF STAFF PERSONNEL

Due to the very nature of the work, its inherent responsibilities and functions, the staff person assumes distinctly different characteristics than those of the line counterpart in the organization. What are some distinctive differences worth identifying?

1. Staff personnel evidence certain comparative social differences. Generally, staff people have more education and are younger than their line counterparts.
2. Staff personnel, moreover, are professionals who have a sense of pride, obligation, and commitment to the profession itself. This may, at times, override any loyalty to the organization.
3. Staff personnel must rely heavily upon winning the voluntary cooperation of the line. Lacking formal authority, staff must use effective influence and persuasion to win support of the line organization.
4. Irrespective of their personal ambitions, staff people must at times subordinate their own personality to the situation. Occasionally others, including the superior, may receive credit and recognition for recommendations and suggestions which may have been generated previously by the staff specialist during the course of staff work.

While these differences are recognized, they nevertheless should not impede the necessary and required integration of talents, and coordination of activities which are so necessary to achieve organizational efficiency.

STAFF SPECIALISTS AND THEIR FUNCTIONS

The work of staff specialists can also be discussed on the basis of the functions of management which they help to perform. Some staff units devote the majority of their efforts to one function, such as planning, whereas others may be involved in several functions.

Relation to Managerial Function of Planning

As you already know, the line executive is ultimately responsible for making those decisions carried out by organizational subordinates. Hence, the work of planning is closely associated with the making of decisions. The decision maker, accordingly, must be thoroughly informed on the subject. In this respect, the staff specialist may do virtually all the work except the final phase of executing the decision itself.

As a first step in the staff planning work, the staff specialist may help the line executive define clearly the problem to be solved or to formulate distinctly the goal to be achieved. The next step must be that of getting all available pertinent information about it. Following such inquiry and collecting of information, the analysis and careful interpretation of data are in order. From the information that has been distilled so far, the planning staff draws up alternative solutions with a recommended course or courses of action. The recommendations are submitted to the superior for subsequent consideration and final approval.

Completed Staff Work

The principle of *completed staff work* is often invoked here. This principle states that whenever possible the staff should prepare the complete report of plan to the point where only the superior's approval or disapproval is required.

An example of staff assistance in planning is the marketing research and planning department which is within the marketing function. The research unit of a coffee manufacturer, for example, may be directed to determine the cause of a drop in product profitability. From its research, the marketing research department may suggest several alternative courses of action. It may recommend that the company process its own instant coffee, or even purchase it from a current producer. In either event it will propose a recommended decision and a plan for carrying it out.

Relation to Managerial Function of Organizing

In the area of organizing, staff units have developed their contribution substantially. For if line managers in modern business would concern themselves with providing all the necessary factors for operation then this would leave little time for seeing that operational activities were performed adequately. Staff assists thereby in procurement of the various technical factors and resources. The work done by the purchasing department or the material storage department is a case in point. These staff units not only do much of the planning for procuring equipment, materials, supplies, and services in cooperation with other departments; but they also see to it that these resources are brought together at the right place and right time, subject to the approval of line personnel.

Procuring personnel is another organizing factor performed mostly by staff. Recruitment, selection, and assignment to jobs (subject to the line manager's approval) are organizing functions that are the responsibility of personnel departments or their equivalent.

A third instance is this: the work of providing the various technical factors often requires that the staff department provide its services on a continuing and regular basis. Maintenance departments are typical of this. Such departments are now referred to as service departments and are at times distinguished from other staff units. The basis of their distinction is the assigned right to perform their services anywhere in the organization.

Relation to Managerial Function of Staffing

By its work in such areas as the recruitment, selection, training, development, compensation, and evaluation of operative and managerial employees, staff very much assists in the staffing function. These programs are, of course, essential in the utilization of human resources within the organization.

Relation to Managerial Function of Directing

Staff may assist in the direction function in several ways. The staff specialist may prepare written instructions, standard operating procedures, or specifications which are released as authorizations to perform in a certain way or by a certain time. Staff specialists may also further assist line management in the active supervision of the work. The dispatcher who distributes work orders and schedules to individual operatives at machines, or the inspector who points out to employees ways of avoiding defective workmanship, are specific examples.

Relation to Managerial Function of Controlling

Finally, staffs may assist in the function of control. They are particularly helpful in comparing results with plans and in determining and recommending corrective action.

Measurement of results implies the existence of standards against which to measure. Standards of material, quality, time, method, personnel, and service must first have been established. Moreover, ways and means of comparing performance against standards must be set.

A typical example is the work done by the production control staff unit. Within the framework of overall production goals, it determines production quotas and time goals for various units. It constantly keeps in touch with operating units and, perhaps, such units as purchasing and stores, helping to coordinate needs and production of all interrelated units. It makes minor adjustments as necessary in order to keep all operations on time and in proper order of performance. At the end of a specified time period, a comparison is made with the quota originally planned. When there is a deviation, it is investigated and explained, and suggestions are made for improvement or adjustment.

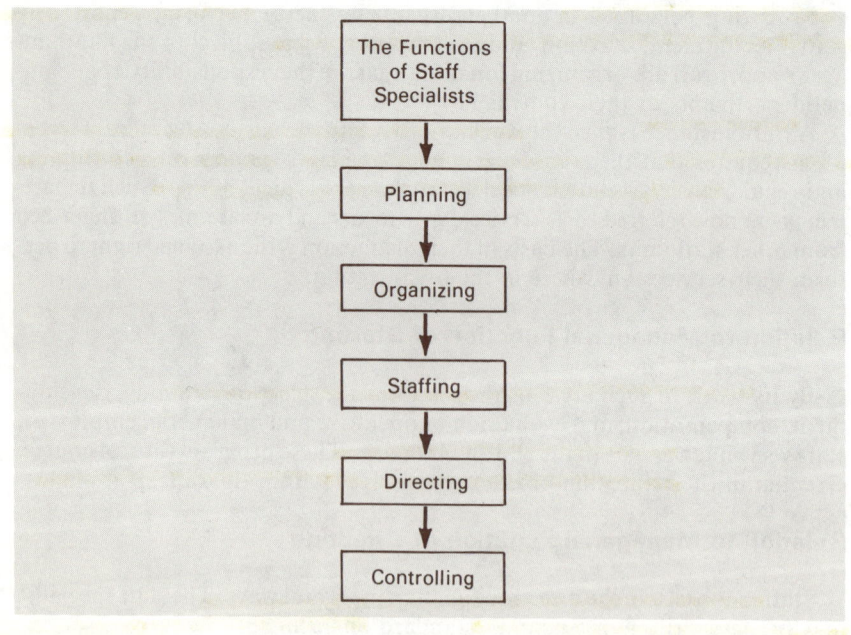

Fig. 5-5. Staff specialization

ASPECTS OF STAFF AUTHORITY

A great variety of tasks performed by staff specialists gives rise to a significant question. How does staff get and exercise the authority to discharge its obligations? Actually, whatever rights it has are delegated by a superior line officer. Staff is outside the basic line structure and is auxiliary to it. So it must ordinarily carry out its responsibilities of assisting and facilitating through other than the formal line structure. The ramifications of the exercise of authority by staff are a subject of particular discussion that follows.

Authorization of Staff to Act for Line

All formal authority that staff may exercise is received from a higher line executive. Consequently, the line may authorize staff to act in its behalf. The staff specialist is asked to assume certain responsibilities of the line unit and commensurate authority is concurrently delegated along with it. But the ultimate authority over this action remains nonetheless with the delegating line executive. This is so because the line retains its responsibility for performance of that action. Since it cannot delegate its responsibility or obligation to a higher level, it must also continue to have the right to change its authorization to the staff.

Line Authority Within Staff Unit

While staff does not ordinarily exercise direct line authority toward other units, the executive in the staff unit exercises direct authority over staff subordinates. Direct supervision is needed in order to effectually produce the service for which the staff unit exists. For instance, the corps of inspectors in a plant may all be assigned to a quality control department and may act in a staff capacity to various production departments. They will have direct line accountability to the chief inspector, who will in turn have line accountability to the quality control manager. As a result, the principle of single accountability is maintained in a line and staff organization.

STAFF ASSUMPTION OF LINE AUTHORITY

There are circumstances in which it may be desirable, even urgent, for staff to assume line authority. Such occasions, which should be kept to a minimum, are dictated at times by certain factors of conditions.

Emergencies

Emergencies may arise when the combination of line authority and the staff's special talents should rest with a staff executive. For example, the medical department may refuse to permit a worker to continue at the present job because of an allergy, even though the supervisor may wish to retain the worker.

Technical Knowledge

Other special situations may warrant delegating to a specialized staff unit. The knowledge and skills demanded in the management of a technical function may be of such caliber that the staff specialist alone is capable of planning and organizing as well as directing and controlling it.

Procedural Authority

The work involved in machine maintenance may be so complex that only the department head and subordinate managers can supervise maintenance and repair of machines. The authority of maintenance thus extends into the organization wherever its services are needed, and it exercises line authority over its function. The staff performs its work through procedures, drawn up and approved as the accepted ways, in which staff operations will be done. Actually it exerts its authority by virtue of a procedure, which means it exercises procedural authority.

Professional Skill

Even where no formal procedural authority exists, staff sometimes exercises influence that is almost indistinguishable from line authority. To illustrate, after exploring alternatives the operations research staff may submit a recommendation, arrived at through involved and quantative means, as to the most desirable product mix that a company should offer. The recommendation is then adopted with little question as to its validity simply because the line manager is not capable of evaluating the procedure from which it resulted.

Since the placement of line authority in a staff position is not without organizational hazards, such a decision should be justified. Every additional assumption of authority by staff is really an inroad into the authority of the line organization and therefore confuses the placement of responsibility. For this same reason the assumption of line authority by staff is often only a temporary condition.

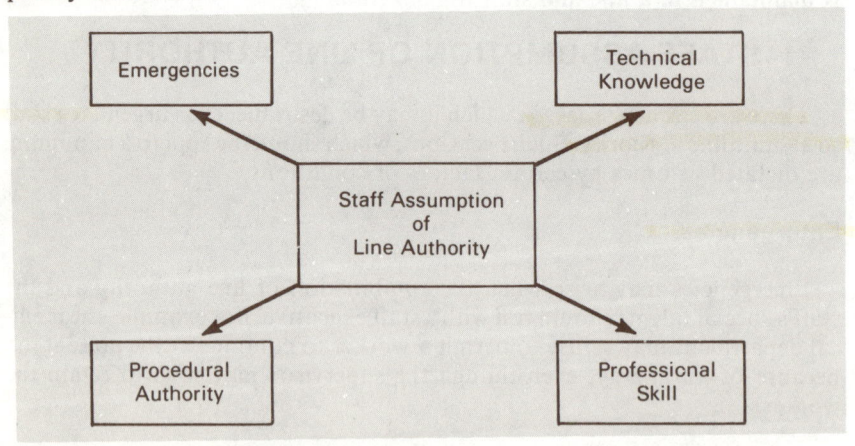

Fig. 5-6. Line and staff

STAFF INFLUENCE WITHOUT LINE AUTHORITY

For the staff unit to depend heavily on assumed line authority in order to exercise its duties would be to invite confusion and conflict among management. Effective staff specialists can use other alternatives beyond that of assuming line authority. They can engage in activities such as the following to further their staff influence.

Advisory Council

This staff job exists to advise and assist other units. By loyal and superior service in the interest of the organization, staff can go far in earning respect for and acceptance of its work. Usually staff's special skills and knowledge inherently command the respect of those not directly involved in their execution. When these are applied in facilitating the discharge of the line manager's responsibilities, the staff people are not only sought after, but their suggestions and directions are readily followed.

Consultative Skill

Ability to persuade other executives of staff's value is another helpful tool for influencing others. Staff personnel often have the background and attitude that make them conscious of maintaining good personal relationships. Recognizing their lack of formal authority over other units, they may well realize the value of good salesmanship.

Indeed, the personal popularity that the persuasive staff person generates is often a more potent force than the formal right to manage which is conferred through line channels. Such an individual often combines the influence of personal relationship with the weight of the position. When such personal magnetism is combined with a tactful and logical presentation of the staff offerings, staff influence is well assured and accepted.

Recourse to Higher Authority

A third way available to staff in influencing other units is that of recourse to higher line authority. There may be occasions when the staff specialist feels it imperative that a recommendation be followed. Or, staff personnel may feel that their limited right is being unnecessarily challenged by other executives. A case in point is the sales supervisor who refuses to heed the admonition to restrict granting of credit to certain customers who are questionable credit risks. If the credit manager cannot directly take action to discourage such behavior, the credit manager may report the matter to the sales manager. It is then up to the latter to take remedial action. If the credit manager's position is justified, this influence will be felt through the sales manager.

ADEQUATE USE OF STAFF SERVICES BY LINE UNITS

The line organization is often reluctant to use the services of the staff. There are several possible reasons for this. Line executives may not understand the services available and applicable to their own problems, or they may be reluctant to use staff because of intrafunctional hostility or fear of encroachment on their own authority. If line managers are inclined to be independent, they may regard the need to consult staff purely as a sign of weakness. Additionally, they may feel that there is always insufficient time to consult and involve staff services.

Some organizational philosophies stress the avoidance of the required use of staff advice by units. This constraint puts the staff person in the position of either "selling" the special services, or being out of a job. On the other hand, there are firms in which the rule of compulsory staff advice is mandatory for management. This, in effect, requires the line manager to consult appropriate staff units prior to making a significant decision. Line is not under obligation to use the advice, but must, nevertheless, listen to it before taking action. There are exceptions to this rule, but in general the level of significance of the decision can be specified.

Generally, good service should sell itself. Once quality service is rendered without adversely affecting the status or goodwill of the unit manager who has benefited, further requests for service can be expected. Line units less willing to avail themselves of staff help may be persuaded by the example of more enthusiastic ones who have been recipients of staff services.

If staff advice and support are to be effective in content and really pertinent to the situation, they must be given with the assurance that the staff specialist will not suffer retribution because of ideas or recommendations which may conflict with those of the immediate superior. Staff advice is less than useless when it deteriorates to the level of merely echoing what the superior already has voiced, or if it attempts to give the answer which the superior expects to hear. It may help compound mistakes rather than avoid them, a situation that is certainly to be deplored.

DOMINATION OF LINE BY STAFF

At times line authority is assumed by staff under unfavorable organizational conditions. The line manager for certain reasons may not be able or may not even care, for that matter, to exercise all the management prerogatives. Line may prefer to let the staff unit exercise line jurisdiction over certain of the responsibilities. While this abandonment of authority is a symptom of organizational weakness, it nevertheless exists.

Staff people may, by virtue of developing strong informal authority, succeed in dominating line executives. Oftentimes their proximity and frequent access to the president's office may give staff personnel undue weight of influence. Staff personnel may gradually broaden their procedural authority beyond its intended scope. Or, staff personnel may seize upon gaps in assignment of organizational responsibility and gradually build for themselves additional responsibilities and authority in the process of creating an empire and with it greater deference. By periodically reviewing the organizational responsibilities and authority of all units, both line and staff, and by providing training and development for management people of all units, management can help to minimize greatly the dangers of excessive staff influence on the line structure.

RELATIONSHIP OF CENTRAL STAFF TO REGIONAL STAFFS

A related question of line-staff relationships is that of the relationship of the central office staff of multiunit companies to the regional staffs. Frequently, a parallel pattern of staff arrangement can be found; that is, the staff unit at the home office is duplicated at the plant level. This may not apply to all staff services. Certain highly specialized activities as central legal and public relations staff units, for example, may satisfy needs for the entire organization.

Such duplication of staff is usually founded on good reason and is done to a greater extent where the organizational philosophy is that of decentralization. Here, the lower staff units are set up to help the regional plant manager exercise greater initiative in making decisions. The headquarters office, consequently, is in a position to exercise staff help for the entire company. Its more comprehensive resources can help the regional staffs do their job better. Proper relationships can minimize time involved in, and maximize amount of, assistance given by headquarters to units.

LIMITATIONS IN USING STAFF DEPARTMENTS

Even though we have shown that staff groups are a vital and necessary part of the total organization structure, the very nature of the staff-line relationship creates certain practical limitations. Staff departments have little formal responsibility, as such. A marketing research department, for example, gathers the data, analyzes it, and prepares and presents a report on what should or could be done. However, the sales group must first accept, then adopt, and finally implement the plan. The responsibility of the marketing research group ends with the presentation of the final report.

Sometimes staff personnel may undermine line authority. If the president of the organization has hired the Marketing Research Director to investigate and make recommendations on certain markets and then commands all of the sales personnel to cooperate and follow these recommendations to the letter then the authority of the line people is being undermined.

In some cases both line and staff groups may have certain responsibilities for dealing with the same problem. A clear definition of who is really responsible for the problem may not exist within the organization. To illustrate, in one corporation both the Director of Advance Planning (a staff function) and the Divisional President (a line function) felt they were responsible for corporate acquisitions and mergers. When an opportunity to acquire a small business arose, both executives fought for the right to make the decision. The responsibility had not been included in either job description. The dispute was eventually brought before the corporate president, who listened to each proposal, then accepted the Divisional President's plan, much to the frustration of the Director of Advance Planning.

Students should not infer that all line-staff conflict is inherently bad. In some cases, such as in consumer demand forecasting, each group—production, sales, marketing research, and advance planning—may all have their own perceptions of an acceptable forecast. For example, the sales groups are eternally optimistic and desire large amounts of inventories to sell, and therefore, forecast higher than most groups. The production group, which is internal, and might not be up-to-date on new trends, will often forecast conservatively on past performance. The theory-oriented marketing research group using quantitative models and the computer, and moreover, having no responsibility to implement the forecast, may sometimes issue forecasts of extreme variance. In sum, each group presents a different forecast.

To resolve the apparent impasse, top management often brings together representatives of each of the group to work out a consensus forecast that everyone in the organization can live with. The important thing for top management to do is minimize the potentially disruptive effects of line-staff conflict in this instance with a consensus forecast.

QUESTIONS FOR DISCUSSION

1. What are some of the reasons why managerial specialization is not as prevalent in a small company as in a large company?
2. It has been said that the influence of the individual executive decreases as the size of the organization increases. Do you agree?
3. In what way does staff assist in the managerial function of planning? Of controlling?
4. Should staff units ever assume line authority? Under what circumstances?
5. Many firms follow the practice of cutting back or eliminating staff units at a considerably greater rate than the line personnel as the organization encounters economic difficulties. Does this seem to be a logical action on the part of the company?
6. Why are staff services resented or ignored by many line managers?
7. How does procedural authority effectuate the work of the staff department?
8. What are some important limitations when using staff groups?
9. Is all line and staff conflict inherently harmful? Why or why not?

REFERENCES

1. D.R. Hampton, C.E. Summer, and R.A. Webber, *Organizational Behavior and the Practice of Management*, rev. ed. (Glenview, IL: Scott Foresman and Co., 1973), chapter 7.
2. R.C. Sampson, *The Staff Role in Management* (New York: Harper & Row, 1965), pp. 42-44.
3. Louis A. Allen, "The Line-Staff Relationship," *Management Record*, vol. 17, no. 9, September, 1955, pp. 346-49.
4. Max D. Richards and Paul S. Greenlaw, *Management: Decisions and Behavior* (Homewood, IL: Richard D. Irwin, Inc., 1972), pp. 282-85.

SELECTED BIBLIOGRAPHY

1. Dennis, Warren G. *Changing Organizations*. New York: McGraw-Hill, Inc., 1966.
2. Blau, Peter M. and Scott, W. Richard. *Formal Organizations: A Comparative Approach*. San Francisco: Chandler Publishing Co., 1962.
3. Mitchell, Terence R. *People in Organizations*. New York: McGraw-Hill, Inc., 1978.
4. Sampson, Robert C. *The Staff Role in Management*. New York: Harper & Brothers, Publishers, 1955.
5. Sisk, Henry L. *Management and Organizations*. 3d ed. Cincinnati: South-Western Publishing Co., 1977.

CHAPTER 6

MANAGERIAL AUTHORITY AND RESPONSIBILITY

Purpose of Chapter 6:

1. To analyze both the concept and sources of authority
2. To discuss the delegation of authority to subordinate management
3. To investigate the relationship between managerial authority and responsibility
4. To point out the range and limits of executive authority

Essential elements you should understand after studying this chapter:

1. A clear definition of managerial authority
2. The three different sources of authority: formal, acceptance, and competence
3. Delegation and reasons why some managers hesitate before its execution and subordinates resist its acceptance
4. Relationship between authority and responsibility
5. Specific situations in which authority is formally delegated in the firm

INTRODUCTION

The many technical, managerial, and operative groups must cooperate to advance both the organizational and personal objectives of an organization. It is in this context then, the achievement of objectives, that the concepts of authority and responsibility should be examined. Because it is through the interrelationship of both these elements, particularly the relationship of prescribed and delegated authority with resultant responsibility, that objectives are reached.

NATURE OF AUTHORITY

Authority is the right to do something. It may be the right to make decisions, to give orders and to require compliance, or simply the right to perform a work assignment. Authority may also be defined as a relationship between two individuals, one "superior" and the other "subordinate." The superior frames and transmits decisions with the expectation that they will be accepted by the subordinate. The subordinate expects such decisions, and his conduct is determined by them. Authority may also be defined as the right to command. Implicit in the word *power* is the ability to impose sanctions, grant rewards, and to exact compliance or obedience to the authoritative source. This logically brings us to a discussion of the sources of authority.

SOURCES OF AUTHORITY

In academic circles there is considerable discussion about the source of managerial authority in the organization. Several main theories, however, seem to evolve from any investigation. These are the formal authority theory, the acceptance theory, and the competence theory.

The Formal Authority Theory

The formal source of authority derives from the institution of private property in our democratic society. It is the authority of ownership. Formal authority when delegated by the immediate line superior can be traced back up the line structure to the board of directors, the stockholders, and eventually to society itself. The extent of this authority is determined by the specific duties for which the job incumbent is responsible.

The Acceptance Theory

The acceptance theory of authority dilutes the power implication of management and emphasizes that the real authority rests with the subordinate who will "accept" the authority of management. This view, the acceptance theory, holds that any commands, from an authoritative source, become somewhat ineffectual, unless those people affected by the commands understand them and find them consistent with their purpose.

The Competence Theory

The competence theory is an aspect of informal authority in which there is authority generated by the personal competence of the individual. It is developed by way of informal relationships among personnel and represents the authority ascribed to an individual by others. People voluntarily accept command out of deference for the person's status. The person's status, in turn, is built up as a result of personality characteristics, job importance and location, skill and knowledge, and similar recognition-gaining factors. Others thus subordinate themselves to the person's leadership and direction.

Competence theory is, in a real sense, most similar to the acceptance theory—since it is "earned authority." It may serve to modify formal authority and help to effectuate it by determining how much formal authority will actually be accepted and acknowledged by subordinates.

In practice, however, all these theories—the formal, acceptance, and competency—have a basis for application. Formal authority envelops the entire structure of the organization within a societal framework, while the acceptance and competency theories more narrowly relate to superior-subordinate relationships. These concepts are further discussed in this chapter under the bilateral dimensions of responsibility and are also illustrated in figure 6-1.

Type	Description
Formal	This is formal power; derives from institution of private property; it is authority of ownership; it is top-down authority imposed upon others.
Acceptance	People subject to commands voluntarily accept them; real authority rests with subordinates who accept the authority of management; it is bottom-to-top authority; it is self-imposed.
Competence	Authority is generated by the personal competence of the individual; authority is a derivitive of leader's personality characteristics, job position and location, knowledge and technical skills.

Fig. 6-1. Sources of authority

DELEGATING AUTHORITY

Delegation in the business institution, occurs when certain of the executive's functions, responsibility, and authority are released and committed to designated subordinate positions[1]. By delegating authority an executive turns over various aspects of jurisdiction to subordinates. The manager lets them do the work for which they were hired. But the manager is, nonetheless, responsible to superiors for the success or failure of the subordinates. As a consequence, the manager may be reluctant to delegate authority as fully as one should. On the other hand, subordinates may be equally reluctant to accept authority to proceed on their own. So this subject of delegating authority must be seen from the viewpoints of both the delegator and the recipient.

The Delegator of Authority

The first task of an executive in delegating authority is to overcome any built-in reluctance to delegate caused by an overdeveloped sense of obligation to the organization. Indeed, this is worth observing in any candidate for a managerial position, since an overriding sense of obligation is characteristic of successful management.

But carrying this characteristic to an extreme, however, is undesirable. Refusing to delegate, for example, will eventually weaken the executive as well as his subordinates. An executive will be physically unable to keep up the pace of doing all that is attempted. And subordinates will never develop to the point where they can carry on their legitimate tasks as competent people should.

The executive may also fail to delegate due to lack of trust in subordinates. This is an indirect criticism of the executive. Perhaps if the manager had spent more time on the managerial function of organizing, there would be a trained and dependable team with the technical ability to carry out assigned tasks.

Other executives refuse to delegate because it gives them a feeling of superiority to do technical jobs themselves. It bolsters their egos in front of subordinates. It does not, however, give people a chance to grow, their self-respect is reduced, teamwork is weakened, and even the executive's own chances of success are ultimately minimized.

Finally, some executives refuse to delegate out of fear that the subordinates will replace them in their jobs. Worry won't help an executive protect the job, nor will such tactics prevent good subordinates from climbing over the superior. If good subordinates leave, an executive is in even poorer shape, because only inferior subordinates remain.

Recipients of Authority

Subordinates themselves may be reluctant to accept authority. Unless this reluctance is reduced, management will end up doing the work of others whether planned this way or not. The initial step in removing reluctance of subordinates is to make sure that one is not surrounded by people who avoid authority because they are incapable of handling it.

Assuming that subordinates have the actual or potential ability to accept authority, why may they be reluctant, and how may the reluctance be overcome? Perhaps the major explanations are lack of confidence and fear of failure. The two go together. A subordinate thinks he or she cannot do the job expected and will have to pay the penalty of failure. So one finds some way of evading or ignoring the authority that is being bestowed. The manager must now do what should have been done earlier. The subordinate must be encouraged and coached with patience in actual situations.

Subordinates, particularly at lower levels, may refuse authority obligations because they do not wish to lose seniority privileges or the associations of present friends. Overcoming the argument against losing out with current associates is not easy. When a person moves from the rank of worker to that of supervisor, one often acquires a new set of characteristics as well as opportunities for further growth—professional, financial, and social.

Finally, subordinates may be unwilling to accept authority because they lack confidence in their superiors who may possibly issue ambiguous orders, play one subordinate manager against another, and look for scapegoats for their own mistakes. Under such circumstances, one would be hard pressed to take on authority delegations.

NATURE OF RESPONSIBILITY

Responsibility refers to the obligation of a subordinate to perform a duty or specific service for someone else. When an individual assumes an obligation, the result is a direct accountability to the person who has assigned the responsibility. Each person in an organization has an obligation for something to someone. Generally, and here too, the term *responsibility* is used to denote both dimensions of obligations. Some authorities prefer to designate the obligation *for something* by the term *responsibility* and that of *to someone* by *accountability*. Part of the organizing function discussed in the previous chapter is to help insure that all necessary functions will be performed. This is done by seeing that each phase of work in each functional unit is made the responsibility of some organization member.

This requirement of organizational development has important implications for the relationship of responsibility to formal authority. To discharge effectively the responsibilities of a job, the incumbent must have sufficient authority or right to carry out the obligation connected with it. Although authority is delegated from a higher line executive, the amount of responsibility for which the subordinate will be held accountable determines the amount of delegated authority.

BILATERAL DIMENSIONS OF RESPONSIBILITY

When management does delegate authority downward, then subordinates are held responsible for the assigned delegations. And the subordinates themselves must not avoid the responsibilities for which they have accepted authority. So, an analysis of responsibility may be considered from the viewpoints of the executive who is holding subordinates responsible, the subordinate who accounts for his responsibilities, and the distinct relationships of authority to responsibility.

The Executive and Responsibility

The large number of functions, factors, and forces can be applied in the task of holding subordinates responsible for their acts. To begin with, getting results from subordinates—holding them responsible—is basically founded on the right that management must exercise authority. This right is obtained in the first place by delegation from above. Every executive is acquainted with this source of authority, and great reliance is invariably placed upon it.

Therefore, people are held responsible through the right to command obedience and the right to penalize the nonperformer. Up to the present time, authority by delegation still gets results, but not as effectively as it once did—and not with as much personal satisfaction to the user of such authority alone.

Were this the only source of authority, the right to command would be full of harsh and undesirable implications. Management would be not much more than a dictatorial process. But the right to require compliance has a more pleasing facet, because there is yet another source of delegation. Authority may be earned from below. Subordinates may willingly follow orders. They may willingly obey commands. Indeed, they may anticipate orders and cooperate in the performance of desired acts even without being ordered.

The wise executive, then, is the one who seeks to supplement the authority received by delegation with that earned from below. Assuredly one should seek the willing cooperation of subordinates. But how is authority earned from below? Several courses suggest themselves. First, an executive should possess competence in a technical field. Secondly, the executive should exhibit managerial skills; and finally, he or she should be fair and alert to the problems and needs of subordinates.

The first of these, technical competence, has an impressive value. Subordinates are impressed by the superior who knows the technical aspects of the job: of production, of accounting, of sales, of engineering, and so on. The need for technical competence is particularly useful to an executive when taking over a new department. Then the past reputation will be a favorable force in the eye of new subordinates, who will be reserving judgment. Moreover, technical competence is something people can readily interpret for themselves. As time goes on, however, this factor of technical judgment will weigh less and less with subordinates. They will be concerned with an executive's managerial and human relations skills.

Subordinates sooner or later, and consciously or unconsciously, evaluate an executive on the ability to manage. They will be aware of the results of good management, if not of managerial performances which help cause the results. They will be aware of the absence of continuous emergencies, of controversy and conflict, of jurisdictional bickering, of shortages of materials and machine time, and of poor designs and procedures.

Respect and authority are earned also by the skill the executive has in dealing with the personal needs and problems of subordinates. Does the executive convince them by deeds as well as words, that their best interests are being considered? Does the executive procrastinate about employee wants and problems, or anticipate them and deal with them fairly and voluntarily?

Dealing with personal problems and needs is considerably more than a question of being fair. An executive must also display an active, voluntary, interested, and sincere attitude in this connection. The loyalty of subordinates flows out to executives who are voluntarily interested in employees' concerns.

To summarize, earning authority from below depends upon a proper combination of technical, managerial, and human relations skills. There is no single right combination for all executives. Each must work out the emphasis that will work best for each situation. All too often, however, executives rely almost entirely upon technical competence to the exclusion of managerial and human relations skills in order to add earned authority to delegated authority.

The Subordinate and Responsibility

A number of reasons may be advanced as to why subordinates do not carry out obligations as desired. They may, initially, not possess requisite capacities. Poor selection or no training would be causes of the problem. Some subordinates shirk responsibilities because they are indifferent and want to avoid work. Here is a problem in motivation. Is the indifference due to boredom, to lack of interest, or to the absence of a challenge in the job itself. If the difficulty is in the job, the executive must figure out what, if anything, will remove the cause of the indifference. It may be that a job change or new assignments are called for. It may be that the employee has not been shown the interesting facets or challenges in a job. It may be that the subordinate has never been asked to participate in aspects or activities relating to the work.

Furthermore, the source of trouble may be in a negative reaction to managerial behavior. Employees may be indisposed to a particular supervisor and, consequently, take their grudge out on all management. Or they may not like the attitude of all management toward employees. They may have the feeling of being inferior to one or all of the management group.

There is yet another group of reasons. Subordinates may shirk responsibilities, because they fear criticism for poor results. This fear may arise because of lack of self-confidence or because of negative leadership. A subordinate who is uncertain about performing a job well may avoid performing the work altogether. So, if this is the case, the subordinate must be trained how to do the work correctly.

It should be apparent by this time that a discussion of why employees do not always execute responsibilities as required invariably regresses to poor management techniques.

Management itself is the cause of many shortcomings ascribed to labor or to subordinate executives. Perhaps even more importantly, the intent has been to provide enough evidence to make the following statement more convincing: that the best way to effect change in others is first to change oneself. As managers improve their managerial behavior, they will soon find that great changes have "automatically" taken place in their subordinates.

Relation of Authority to Responsibility

Is there a relationship between authority and responsibility? Generally, the proposition is accepted that the two should be coequal. Under this proposition, the right to command should be equal to the obligations assigned to a given individual. Indeed, some interpret this proposition to mean that unless authority and responsibility are coequal in every position, a nonsensical relationship exists. Figure 6-2 represents the flow of coequal authority, responsibility, and accountability in a typical firm.

Without attempting an exhaustive analysis, some study of the proposition is in order. First the question, is it equally easy to delegate authority as to assign responsibility? Anyone with practical experience in management knows that authority is relinquished with greater reluctance. The president may, for example, give the chief accountant the responsibility of keeping an accurate set of books. But the president may reserve unto himself the right to decide what system of accounts to keep, who should be hired, and what kinds of accounting machines may be purchased. Under these circumstances, some might argue that the chief accountant would be responsible for accuracy only within the limits of the personnel, equipment, and system supplied by the president. The accountant will have the right to command the available re-

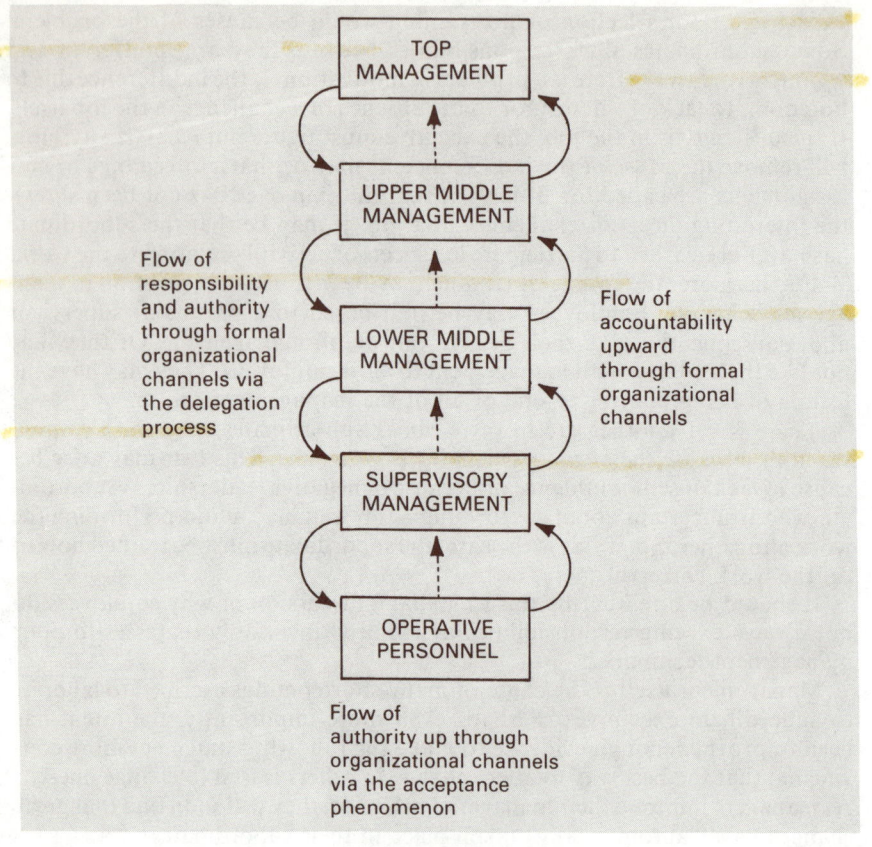

Fig. 6-2. The flow of authority, responsibility, and accountability in a Formal Organization

sources and will be responsible for results obtained from them.

However, if inaccuracies resulted from unqualified personnel, one might assume the chief accountant is not responsible because he had no authority over their selection. Such an argument may possess theoretical soundness, but it is doubtful whether the chief accountant could use it in explaining inaccuracies to the president.

So, for practical purposes, it is not uncommon for responsibilities to be assigned in greater amounts than authority. As the chief gains in experience, the president should gradually release increments of power until his total responsibilities are equaled by the total grants of authority.

It might be argued in this case that the president has more authority than responsibility and that these should be equated for him too. In one sense, it is as indefensible to have too much authority relative to responsibility as the reverse. But, in this case, is not the president responsible for the acts of the chief accountant? Or, to generalize the case, isn't every executive responsible for the acts of his subordinates, no matter how many levels removed?

The answer lies in the generalization that while executives may delegate responsibility, they never are divested entirely of it. In the present case, then, the president is still responsible for the accuracy of the books and, of course, has the authority to take action to get it. The authority is not greater than the responsibilities.

What are the "authority" and "responsibility" of subordinates then, if in the end, both reside in the chief executive? Essentially, authority is nothing more than the right to act in behalf of the president. Responsibility is nothing more than a sharing of the obligations of another. For instance, when the chief accountant recognizes that the orders issued are really those of the superior, and the responsibilities shouldered are really those of the superior, then this fact removes one of the greatest dangers to teamwork—the feeling of independence. In its place comes the quintessence of cooperation—the recognition of being a sharer in the results, one who must work with and for each associate and not as an independent agent.

Authority and responsibility are equated, therefore, not only in a given position for particular duties but also to and through executive channels, as we illustrate in Figure 6-2. In the accounting case cited above, for one to look solely at the job of the chief accountant in equating authority and responsibility is not enough. The authority and responsibility must be related to what degree the president may also desire involvement in order to best handle his ultimate authority and responsibility.

SPECIFYING AUTHORITY LIMITS

As in most fields of human knowledge, it is one thing to grasp the theory of a subject and another to apply it. This is very true of the concept of authority. The following presents statements on how such authority rights may be defined, first, in relation to organizational and procedural jurisdictions and, second, in terms of specific delegations.

Organizational and Procedural Authority

Although provision is generally made for the organizational authority of executives, their procedural authority is often overlooked. Yet, due consideration for each is very important. **Organizational authority refers to the rights an executive has in connection with the organization unit being managed.**

As an illustration of organizational authority, take the case of the executive in charge of a traffic department. The executive is given the right to manage the department. The right would spell out the relation to each superior, to each subordinate, and to other departments with which contact is made. This means the traffic manager would have line authority within the boundaries of the traffic unit, and staff relationships with all other departments which serve or are served by traffic[2].

Procedural authority, on the other hand, refers to the rights executives are granted in connection with the portions of a procedure that pass through their organizational units. Referring to the traffic manager, again, what right does the person have to initiate less carload as requested by the sales department or to hold up these less-than-carload (l.c.l.) deliveries until a carload quantity can be accumulated? If the manager has no such rights, then each order must be shipped by seller and each l.c.l. order must be handled separately.

In the latter event, the organizational authority indicates what rights the manager has and what duties to perform in connection with the projects that pass through the department. Procedural authority is limited to the areas or directions prescribed by those in the procedure who preceded the manager.

The relation between organization and procedure is depicted in Figure 6-3. Here, the structure of the traffic department is shown in relation to a project that originates elsewhere, passes through this department, and is completed elsewhere. In this case, the traffic department is concerned with only one function in the project. This diagram, in and of itself, does not disclose what rights the traffic department has in connection with this function. but in some fashion or other such rights should be delineated.

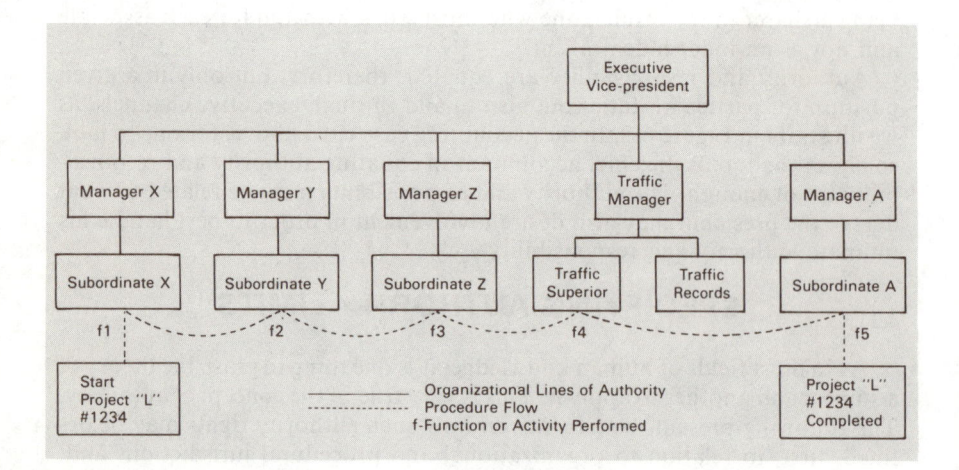

Fig. 6-3. Organizational and procedural relations

Since organization charts and procedural layouts, as described in Figure 6-3, do not give a good picture of authority limits, other means must be provided for this purpose. Simple devices of oral communication or past practice may be employed, but these have obvious weaknesses. More preferred are written statements in organizational manuals, procedural manuals, job specifications, and standard practice instructions[3]. Important too is that such written methods must be coordinated with the other written media and are kept current. If these precautions are not taken, the manuals will be more than ineffectual.

Specific Delegations

In the modern firm, specific delegations of authority are regularly granted to managers. Moreover, the phrasing of these delegations is truly important in guaranteeing not only the individual's performance but also the achievement of standards established for the job.

Delegated authority expresses the degree of freedom that a superior grants to a subordinate while taking action in the organization unit or in a phase of a procedure[4]. Such expressions may range from relatively complete freedom of action to almost complete restriction. Each firm needs to work out a classification which will meet its particular needs. In the following, authority delegation has been classified into five general categories which have been found helpful in working out specific delegations incorporated in managerial job descriptions and similar purposes. These are:

1. Authority of full administrative discretion
2. Authority within established objectives and policies
3. Authority within general direction and procedure
4. Authority limited to standard practice instructions
5. Authority limited to acting when and as directed

Authority of Full Administrative Discretion

Wide administrative discretion involves the right to exercise a very high degree of initiative and freedom in the performance of managerial functions. This includes decision making within certain broad limits. It permits setting objectives and making policies in areas of major importance. A typical example is the independent firm that becomes a subsidiary but is permitted to remain for most purposes an independent unit, carrying on nearly all the functions in the same way as it had prior to the merger.

Authority within Established Objectives and Policies

This type of delegation of authority is more commonly found than full administrative discretion. While discretionary privileges are broad in scope, full conformity with general overall policies is expected. Even where broad administrative authority is delegated in some areas, the unit must still operate within established policies in such matters as finance or personnel.

Today's multiplant organization is characterized by such decentralization so that broad policy-making machinery may be operating at the top executive level, while the remainder of administrative processes are delegated to the next lower level. The plant manager may have the assistance of expert administrative management from the top level, but is free to exercise individual initiative in matters below the broad policy level.

Authority within General Directions and Procedure

Delegation of authority that is limited by general direction and procedure is the third level of decentralized authority. The right to make policy here is almost nonexistent. Actual operating decisions are left to the manager within fairly wide limits. Broad general standards of time, expense, quality, and quantity are often given, while control is exercised by measuring performance against such standards, and by requiring reports periodically.

Such level of authority is particularly effective at middle management levels and lower levels of some firms. It still permits the exercise of initiative so basic to the motivation of managers. It trains managers to assume responsibility and permits a high degree of flexibility. Furthermore, top executives, particularly at the plant level, are still free to spend more time on administrative matters.

Authority Limited to Standard Practice Instructions

At this level where conformity with standard practices is required, considerable initiative has already been removed from subordinates. Objectives or quotas are determined quite precisely. Little or no discretion as to approach and method remains with the unit manager. Rather, procedures are planned in detail, and specific, step-by-step instructions are developed for carrying them out.

This type of limitation of delegated authority by standardization is often operational at lower levels where repetitive work occurs. Normal examples may be found in an order-filling department, in some garage service departments, or in certain chain restaurants where simple and fixed menus are offered.

Here, the manager must secure approval before taking action on any matter that is uncertain and must keep superiors regularly informed of results, and immediately informed of any exceptions to standard practice that may have occurred.

Authority Limited to Acting When and As Directed

The most restricted level of authority is where action can be taken only when and as instructions are specifically received. Theoretically, a complete absence of administrative discretion exists. Policies, procedures, and instructions are supplied for each instance. Obviously, this degree of delegation is not to be found frequently.

There are organizational instances, however, where such limitation may be necessary because of the complicated and unrepetitive nature of work to be done, or because of the state of development of the individuals involved in the excercise of authority. The manager in this situation makes decisions only when told, or the subordinate acts only when ordered.

With the above descriptions of authority levels as a basis, statements of authority can be drawn up for job descriptions, program assignments, and similar purposes. Each manager, consequently, has a clear understanding of rights and responsibilities.

SPECIFYING RESPONSIBILITIES

Assuredly, the obligations placed upon subordinates should be spelled out as precisely as are rights and privileges, and the coverage should be the same as in the case of authority. Thus, the organizational and procedural aspects of responsibility should be specified to balance the authority specifications. Since the relation between organization and procedure has been covered in the preceding sections, it will be unnecessary to repeat this material in connection with the matter of responsibility.

There is a definite phraseology that should be employed to describe the kind and degree of obligations placed upon subordinates. The phraseology suggested below does not imply there is common agreement as to the mean-

Managerial Authority and Responsibility 91

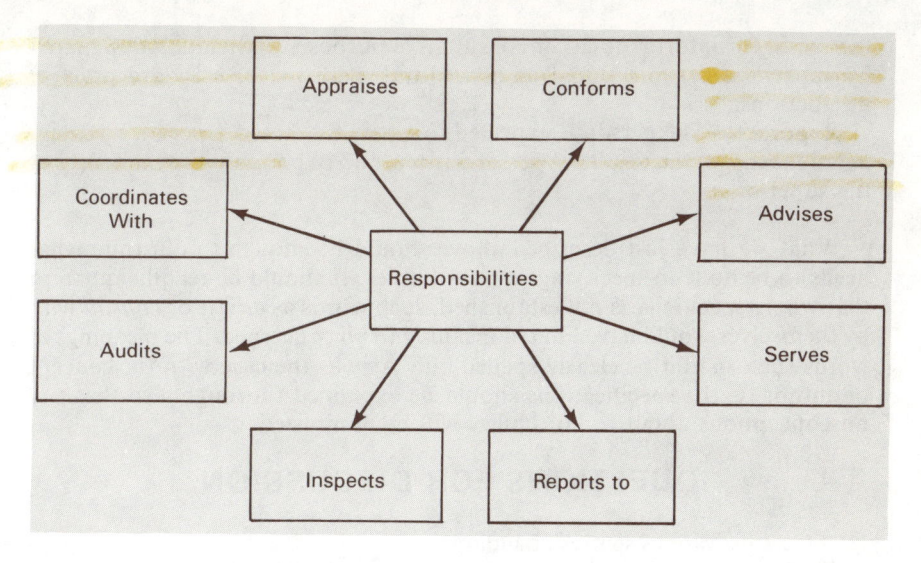

Fig. 6-4. Specifying responsibilities

ing of these actions in various firms. It is argued, however, that within a given company the action statements should be uniformly understood by all those involved.

Words alone are often used to define responsibilities. This is not enough. It is necessary to define the words. Some action terms commonly used to specify responsibilities, and suggested definitions and explanations of them, are listed in the following[5]:

Conforms: The person is expected to carry out duties exactly as specified in procedures, manuals, blueprints, specifications, or oral instructions.

Advises: The person is expected at regular intervals, or as requested, to submit recommendations, or to advise, and counsel on specified matters or problems.

Serves: The person is expected to provide resources, facilities, personnel, or services to various parties either (a) as specified by the various parties and within their budgeted allotments, or (b) through budgets, personnel, and resources assigned to the individual.

Inspects: The person is expected to check products, services, processes, or equipment in conformance with preestablished standards, and to report any deviations from those standards.

Audits: The person is expected to examine processes, services, or resources in conformance with such tests and standards as is necessary, and to report deviations to interested parties.

Appraises: The person is expected to make current or periodical evaluations of personnel, organizational, or procedural performances not otherwise subject to quantitative measurements, and to report those findings to interested parties.

Coordinates with: The person is expected to work with and/or make contact with, for informational or consultative purposes, individuals designated by superiors, organizational or procedural manuals, or standard practice instructions.

Reports to: The person is expected to notify the stated superior, by designated means, of the results of performances, and to be subject to the orders of the superior.

What we have just described above should be enough to illustrate what needs to be done in specifying responsibilities. It should be readily apparent that where specificity is not established, such words as *advise* or *consult with* by themselves would have limited meaning to all concerned. The meanings of words then should be clearly spelled out. As was the case with the concept of authority, the specifications should be explained thoroughly so that any misconceptions about responsibility will be minimized.

QUESTIONS FOR DISCUSSION

1. Discuss the various sources of authority.
2. How do you explain the failure of managers to delegate the proper amount of work to subordinates?
3. Why do subordinates avoid acceptance of responsibility? What are some remedies for such a situation?
4. How does procedural authority differ from organizational authority?
5. Discuss the different specific delegation levels of authority as it may be delegated to lower levels.
6. How can management determine the degree of authority to delegate to a lower unit?
7. What is an example of authority delegated to act only when and as directed?

REFERENCES

1. Chester I. Barnard, *The Functions of the Executive* (Cambridge: Harvard University Press, 1938), pp. 92-94.
2. Richard E. Bogatzis, "The Effective Use of Power," *Supervisory Management*, March 1972, pp. 40-44.
3. James D. Mooney, *The Principles of Organization* (New York: Harper & Brothers, 1947).
4. John R.P. French and Bertram Raven, "The Bases of Social Power," in Dorwin Cartwright (ed.), *Studies in Social Power* (Ann Arbor, MI: Institute for Social Research, 1959), pp. 150-67.
5. Michael J. Jucius, Bernard A. Deitzer, and William E. Schlender *Elements of Managerial Action,* (Homewood, IL: Richard D. Irwin, Inc. 3rd ed., 1973), pp. 240-60.

SELECTED BIBLIOGRAPHY

1. Dalton, Gene W.; Barnes, Louis B.; and Zalesnik, Abraham. *The Distribution of Authority in Formal Organization.* Boston: Division of Research, Graduate School of Business Administration, Harvard University, 1968.
2. French, John R.P., and Raven, Bertram. "The Bases of Social Power." Cartwright, S. Desmond, ed. *Studies in Social Power.* Ann Arbor: Research Center for Group Dynamics, University of Michigan, 1959.
3. Katz, Daniel, and Kahn, Robert L. *The Social Psychology of Organizations.* New York: John Wiley and Sons, 1966.

4. McConkey, Dale D. *No-Nonsense Delegation.* New York: Amacom, American Management Association, 1974.
5. Newman, William H. *Administrative Action.* 2nd ed. (Englewood Cliffs, NJ: Prentice-Hall, Inc., 1963.
6. Steinmetz, Lawrence L. *The Art and Skill of Delegation,* Reading, MA: Addison-Wesley Publishing Company, Inc., 1976.

CHAPTER 7

PLANNING FOR RESULTS

Purpose of Chapter 7:

1. To define the nature, role and importance of the planning function
2. To identify the subject matter of planning
3. To explore those factors that affect planning's effectiveness

Essential elements you should understand after studying this chapter:

1. Planning defined
2. The preliminary phases of planning
3. Manager's role as a planning specialist
4. Subject matter involved in planning
5. Important factors management must recognize
6. Guidelines to follow in planning

INTRODUCTION

The purpose of this chapter is to focus on the most basic of managerial functions—the planning function. Fundamentally, planning is an activity which consists of a number of consciously deliberate and integrated decisions. *By this we mean that planning is a continuous and systematic process of setting organizational and departmental objectives and goals; of determining methods and resources of accomplishing them, of preparing programs to achieve those goals, and of identifying and evaluating alternative choices of action.*

Planning is determining in advance what a group or an individual should accomplish and how it should be accomplished. Planning is deciding in advance the who, what, when, where, and how of activities.

Nearly everyone in the organization has a responsibility for planning.[1] Implicit as a manager's responsibility, planning varies only in the degree and intensity of its application at the various levels of the firm. In today's modern organization guesswork and intuition are used less and less. The accelerated forces of economic, technological, social, and political change demand more emphasis on objective forecasts and analyses.

DEVELOPMENT OF PLANNING

As we defined earlier, planning is the managerial function of determining in advance what a firm should accomplish and how its goals are to be attained.[2] Too often in the past, firms were more likely attuned to current, short-run conditions than to long-run strategies. However, modern firms are placing increasing importance on long-run planning, strategy formulation, and goal setting. In fact, in many modern organizations a new corporate executive, the advance planner, who often reports to top management itself, has emerged with greater organizational responsibilities. So while all management has the responsibility for planning, corporations, more and more, appear to be shifting towards establishing top-level corporate staffs with planning expertise to assist management in implementing this important function.

Thus, planning has three main elements. First, it is done in advance of the operational activities; secondly, it is done by all management; and thirdly, it has a critical contribution to make to the entire corporate effort.

THE PRELIMINARY PHASE

Planning essentially is something which must be done in advance of operational activities. Its justification lies in the simple fact that programs will be more efficiently performed if they are first planned. This aspect of planning can be seen by examining, first, the contributions of planning, and second, the time aspects of planning.

Planning Contributions

The justification of planning must be found in its possible contributions. To begin with, it has the advantage of specialization in its favor. And, generally speaking, anyone who specializes in a subject, function, or methodology will have a competitive advantage.

So, the manager who practices in planning techniques is more apt to be better at planning than a worker who does both the planning and the work. Assuredly, this does not mean that only managers should plan. Employees often provide useful planning ideas.

Moreover, planning contributes to corporate effectiveness because all details of corporate programs of work and their relationships are worked out in advance. Not only are the best of details selected and designed, but they are arranged in proper sequence. This is truly important.

Essentially, planning enhances ultimate coordination. Each member of an organization performing the right task implies that specific actions are properly related to each other. For an advertising and sales promotion campaign to be successful, for example, not only must the message be appropriate, but also it must be coordinated in time with the production of goods and their distribution to wholesale and retail outlets. This kind of coordination is best achieved through advance planning.

Finally, planning contributes to overall effectiveness by handling possible obstructions to contemplated strategic projects. Planning seeks to anticipate and thereby remove obstacles and problems that stand in the way of attaining goals. Advance steps can be taken to eliminate, circumvent, or minimize undesirable conditions that would otherwise adversely affect project efficiency. By being alert, for example, to the possibility of a strike by a supplier's employees, of changes in styles or consumer preferences, or of governmental regulations affecting one's products, adjustments can be made more readily before rather than after the firm is actually in production.

Time Aspects

The effectiveness of planning is also directly related to the factor of time. Since planning implies a time predetermination, it would seem that the more time allowed for planning, the better the planning should be. In part, this is true. If a company proposes, let us assume, to revamp its marketing channels and policies, the appropriate plans cannot be devised overnight. Several months at least would be required for such changes to be planned successfully. But in part, the longer the interval of time between planning and performance, the less confidence can one place in a plan. The trouble lies in the fact that a plan by its very nature is a forecast or is based on a forecast of the future.

The probability of success in forecasting obviously grows less the farther one looks into the future. And by the time a plan is converted into action, the conditions for which one planned are likely to have changed considerably. This might cause pessimism in planning were it not for two facts. First, if one does not forecast, he will invariably be worse off than if he does. No forecasts are actually forecasts that conditions will not change. And second, techniques of forecasting are continuously being improved so that however the uncertainty of long-range forecasting, it is gradually becoming more accurate.

So, advance planning is the modern theme, even though every planner knows he cannot forecast accurately. But most are learning more about how to handle the probability aspects of forecasting. Some of the plans are based on periods of just a few days; certain shop and sales quotas are cases in point.

Some plans are based weeks and months ahead; budgets, production programs, sales estimates, and financial requirements are examples. And some plans are worked into time spans of five, ten, and twenty years. Growth plans, personnel needs, research projections, and financial flows are of this nature.

THE SPECIALIST PHASE

Planning, in the second place, is done for others by a specialist.[3] Except in financial matters, most planning was for a long time left to chance, to subordinates, or to spur-of-the-moment decisions. Gradually the conclusion was accepted that someone else should coordinate all planning.

That "someone else" is the manager. In exercising the planning role, the manager is supposed to specialize in thinking through, in advance, the action that is to take place in the future. In a small organization this is not much of a problem, since then there usually is only one manager, or several at best, to perform planning.

But what if there are many managers at different levels and covering various specialities and functional areas? Where this occurs, planning must be carefully organized or there will be either costly duplications or vacuums of effort. In general, the design of planning calls for both horizontal and vertical allocations of duties. Horizontally, planning responsibilities are company-wide and cover longer periods of time at the top of an organization and gradually are reduced in subject matter and time spans as one moves to the lower organizational levels.

A few illustrations are worth observing in this connection. The range of planning responsibilities is illustrated in figure 7-1. Here you will see that the president is responsible for company-wide planning,[4] but the lower executives have narrower ranges of responsibility.

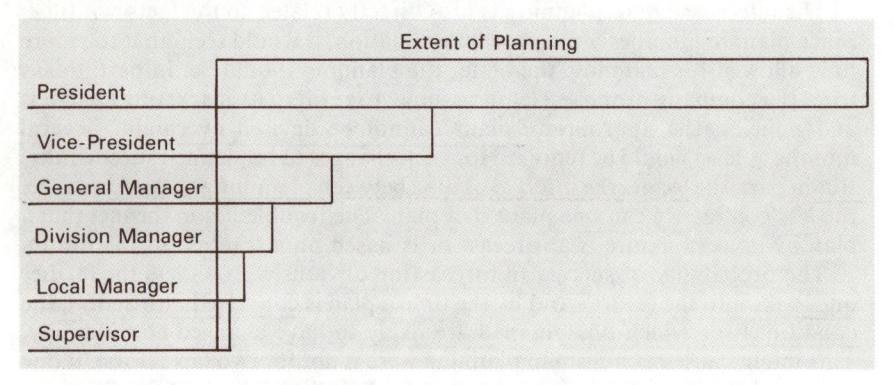

Fig. 7-1. Extent of planning responsibilities (executive level)

The time span of planning responsibilities is illustrated in figure 7-2. Here you will note that the president of a company is responsible for plans that extend from several months to several years, whereas the time span of lower executives tends to be of much shorter duration.

Planning for Results 99

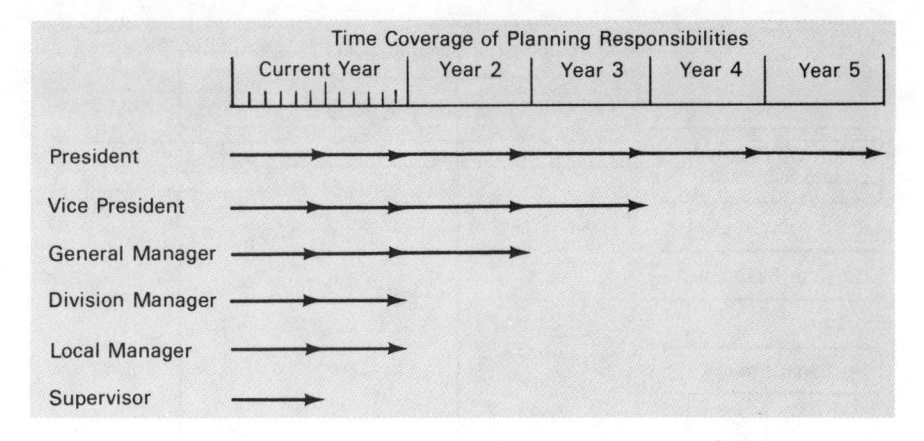

Fig. 7-2. Time planning responsibilities (executive level)

Fig. 7-3. Specifics of planning responsibility

The nature of planning responsibilities is graphically illustrated in figure 7-3. Observe that the president is responsible for broad, qualitative predeterminations of objectives, policies, functions, procedures, organization structures, people, and environmental matters. Lower executives, conversely, tend to establish more detailed, quantitative plans for these factors.

Finally, it should be realized that the work of the various planning specialists must be integrated into strategic plans in order to reach specific goals.[5] In figure 7-4 it is evident that a strategic planning concept results in setting a measurable goal, identifying activities and schedules, allocating resources, controlling progress and eventually reaching the goal.

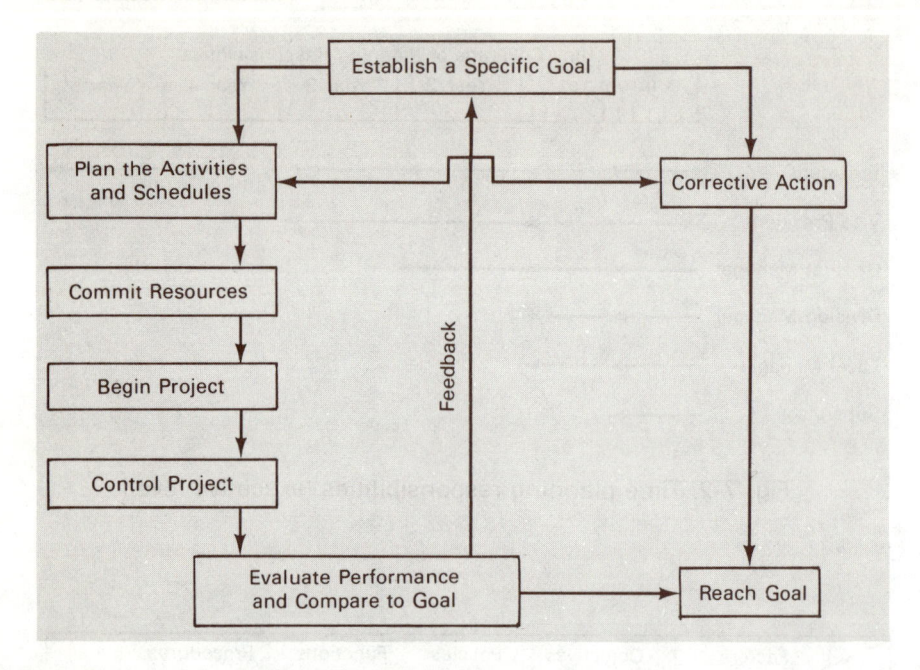

Fig. 7-4. Strategic project concept

THE GROUP-ACTION PHASE

Planning, thirdly, has a contribution to make to group effort. In this respect it should provide the basis for group action. This is done initially by a clear statement of the common and personal objectives of the group. Armed with this knowledge, all will know in what directions efforts are to be expended. Group coordination, consequently, is on a firm foundation when the planning also specifies what is to be done, how, and by whom.

Really, planning is a positive factor in increasing the efficiency of the firm. But planning also contributes to a firm's effort by increasing the effectiveness of the managerial functions of organizing, staffing, directing, and controlling. For example, organizing simply becomes a hit-or-miss proposition unless strategic plans are carefully established. Or controlling will take the major part of a manger's time if the person does not do a good job of preplanning. Indeed, the amount of time that is spent on planning can well reduce the time that is spent on the other functions of management.

SUBJECT MATTER OF PLANNING

It is now pertinent to determine the subjects which apply to planning. There are there major areas, which will be discussed in this section:

1. Managerial functions
2. Basic business factors
3. Strategic projects

Managerial Functions

Planning has already been enumerated as one of the major managerial functions. Planning has been stated to precede organizing, staffing, directing, and controlling. In this sense, organizing provides the resources to carry out the plans of planning, staffing provides the planning personnel, directing then carries out the plans, and controlling aids in comparing the degree to which plans have been successful. Planning can also determine the necessary corrective action that needs to be taken in regard to future plans.

But if organizing, staffing, directing, and controlling are to be well performed by a manager, then the person must plan these functions as well. Before an organization structure can be installed, for example, it must be designed, that is, planned. Before a manager can direct the activities of subordinates, a plan of behavior toward them must be determined. And before a manager can evaluate and measure performance, a system of controlling performance must be planned. As we will discuss more fully later in this chapter, a manager must also plan his planning.

Planning for planning and planning for organizing, staffing, directing, and controlling should be given the time and resources they deserve, particularly as companies grow and business becomes more complex. Such organization units as advance planning departments using operations research and the computer are definite proof that this trend is taking place in larger companies. But smaller companies must also find time for such planning—however, on a more informal basis or through intercompany cooperation—if their operations are to be conducted with greater success.

Basic Business Factors

The basic factors found in every business situation constitute another significant area of planning. Certainly, only by means of planning can the following factors be properly established:

1. Objectives to be sought
2. Policies to be followed
3. Environmental factors to be evaluated and forecasted
4. Organizational and procedural structures to be used
5. Supporting plans to be established
   a. Marketing-sales plan
   b. Financial plan
   c. Production plan
   d. Manpower plan
   e. Research and development plan

As an example, figure 7-5 provides a simple outline of factor planning. This shows selected items for each factor, the responsible executive, and the dates by which preliminary and final plans must be completed. Of course, detailed statements of each factor would have to be derived. For example, output would be expressed in quantitative terms, by style and type, for each product manufactured and sold.

	Responsibility of—	Preliminary Plans by—	Final Plans by—
Plan of Objectives:			
Sales	Vice-president—sales	June 1	July 1
Production programs	VP—production	June 15	July 15
Cost limits:			
Production	Production manager	June 20	July 10
Sales	Sales manager	June 15	July 10
Overhead	Controller	June 25	July 10
Plans of Policies:			
Profit expectations	Executive Vice-president		
Pricing	Sales manager	June 10	June 25
Marketing channels	Marketing manager	June 10	June 25
Advertising themes	Advertising manager	June 10	June 20
Financial	Financial manager	June 20	June 25
Plans of Organizing:			
Executive lines	Executive Vice-president	May 1	May 15
Staff units	Organiz. plan. manager	May 1	May 15
Systems design	Systems plan. manager	May 1	May 15
Purchasing goals	Purchasing manager	June 25	July 20
Environmental:			
Social relations	Public relations	May 1	May 15
Political relations	Executive committee	May 10	May 15
Competitive strategies	Executive committee	May 10	May 20

Fig. 7-5. Responsibility for factor planning

Many of these activities will be considered in more detail in subsequent chapters, so we need only mention them here. Equally required is necessary planning to attack problems of policies, functions, organization structure, and procedures. It is through planning in these areas of basic business factors that the foundation and structure of an effective corporate management is established.

Strategic Projects

Planning is also intended to serve in the area of strategic projects.[6] Certainly, it may be the primary plan of a company to earn a certain profit in the coming year by manufacturing and distributing a given product through a certain marketing channel. But many strategic subordinate plans will be needed to carry out the basic major plans. A factory foreman will need a plan to carry out production; a sales supervisor will need a plan to persuade customers to buy in quantities equal to established quotas; and the service manager will need a plan to repair products returned by customers.

FACTORS AFFECTING PLANNING

You should, of course, recognize that the nature of planning in any company will be affected by a number of factors. Among these are the following:

1. Skill and attitude of management
2. Time and resources available

3. Types of problems encountered
4. Environmental, social, and human conditions
5. Application of plans

Management Skill and Attitude

Management skill and attitude are the most significant factors affecting planning in a company. What can one expect in a company in which the chief executive goes to fortune-tellers in order to make decisions regarding the future? Or how much scientific planning can be expected in a company in which top executives are opposed to quantitative techniques in marshaling data and information? Fantastic as this may sound, such cases are not figments of the imagination. Perhaps as silly, though at the other extreme, are those who want every decision buttressed by vast arrays of schedules and charts and formulas of data. Obviously, then, the key to good planning lies in the skill and attitude of top management toward planning.

Time and Resources

Time and resources available, moreover, to perform the planning function are also crucially important. The time aspect has a number of phases, such as the following:

1. Time available to establish a plan before putting it into effect
2. Time for the plan to be executed
3. Time interval to be covered by the plan
4. Time the plan should either be revised or nullified

The resources aspect also has a number of conditioning phases, such as the following:

1. Funds available to invest in planning
2. Availability of trained or trainable planning personnel
3. Availability of technical facilities for planning
4. Degree of cooperation and understanding of personnel who are expected to use the plans

Space is too limited to explore all these phases. It is perhaps enough to note that the precision of planning cannot be any greater than the time or resources available for planning. Nor should it be any greater than the capacities of those who are to use the plans. Obviously, if only a few days are available to plan a system of warehousing distribution, it would be futile to employ the involved techniques of operations research in developing the plan.

Types of Problems

The types of problems to be encountered present another factor affecting managerial planning. Some problems have only a few variables to be solved, whereas others have numerous interdependent and interaffecting variables. As an example of the former, establishing an employee-suggestion system, though it presents some important questions, is not an overly difficult task to accomplish.

But establishing a plan of distribution from a warehouse complex of several units to a number of retail outlets is another matter. It would have to be determined whether or not each warehouse would carry a full complement of products; make shipments to each retail outlet; bill each retail outlet separately, or take orders from each outlet but ship from another warehouse. To optimize the relationships among warehouses, products carried, distances covered, and retail outlets serviced involves a set of factors that will challenge unaided human skills but certainly provides an excellent problem for electronic computerization.

Environmental, Social, and Human Conditions

Planning is also affected by environmental, social, and human conditions. To illustrate, planning in the field of labor-management relations was not particularly difficult in the days when labor legislation was almost nonexistent and labor unions were usually powerless. But under present-day conditions of involved labor laws and strong unions, management must expend much time and effort and apply itself skillfully and diligently to problems in this area.

Moreover, a company with branch plants and offices scattered throughout the world must plan its operations in the light of social, political, and all environmental conditions in the various areas. Thus, policies that might be very effective in the United States, may well be disastrous in the Near East, or Orient.

Application of Plans

Another factor affecting planning is that it can be applied in a negative or positive way. Too often plans are used as control devices solely to determine the effectiveness of managerial work. As an effect, a negative atmosphere of apprehension may revolve around such plans as budgets, for example. On the other hand, emphasis upon providing correct solutions for future or current operations may be the purpose of plans, so that budgets, correspondingly, are viewed in a constructive and positive light.

GUIDES TO EFFECTIVE PLANNING

If the managerial function of planning is to be performed effectively, certain tests or guides should be kept in mind.

Focus on Objectives to Be Accomplished

Perhaps the most significant test relates to the matter of objectives. At all stages of planning, it is imperative to focus on the purposes that are to be accomplished. This is so because the ultimate success of a plan depends upon the degree to which it achieves desired objectives. If results fall below objectives, the plan has to some degree failed.

Thus, a plan is the means to an end and should be viewed accordingly. Indeed, this emphasis upon objectives is supposed by those who assign to management by objectives—to be discussed in a latter chapter—a major role in all phases of management, particularly planning.

Provide Definite Yet Flexible Approach

A plan must provide a definite route to desired goals, yet it must have some degree of flexibility. A financial budget expresses in monetary terms how much is to be expended in some future period for various items in order to accomplish particular purposes. But during that period, variations may occur from conditions that had been expected. As a result, the budget will then be unrealistic.

Ideally, the answer here is to initially make the budget flexible. That is, the plan should be constructed to provide for deviations from expected conditions. As a result, the budget is stable in that it establishes a financial route to desired objectives. But it is also flexible in that the route can be varied by fixed amounts if conditions vary during the budgeted period.

Consider Basic Strategy

It should, among other things, consider the following factors:

1. Conditions expected to prevail during the time it is effective
2. Attitudes of personnel by whom it is to be used
3. Priority and importance of problems to be solved
4. Nature of obstacles—personal, legal, or political—to be faced
5. Avenues of escape or change, if unforeseen emergencies develop

A plan can almost guarantee certain failure, unless it is designed with the foregoing strategic safeguards in mind.

Be Clear and Understandable

Finally, a good plan should be clear and understandable. A plan may be clear to the planner, but is it equally clear to the intended user? The planner should make certain that the plan is expressed either in clear terms or is communicated to the user so that the latter knows what is expected. And if it is clear to the user, does the user understand and have confidence in the plan? Again, the planner has the responsibility to transmit a plan so that users believe in its efficacy and fairness.

PLANNING PROCESS

Plans are not self-executing. They must be managed. And this, like any other project, requires planning, organizing, staffing, directing, and controlling. Good planners carefully check out their methodologies. They know what areas and factors will require planning. They allow enough time and resources for planning. They give thought to the conditions, obstacles, and guides affecting planning. In short, they plan in the light of the elements of the planning process, as shown in figure 7-6.

```
                    ┌─────────────────────┐
                    │ Statement of Purpose │
                    └──────────┬──────────┘
                               ▼
                    ┌─────────────────────┐
                    │ Preliminary Analysis │
                    └──────────┬──────────┘
              ┌────────────────┴────────────────┐
              ▼                                 ▼
          Forecasting                    Advance Planning
         Uncontrollable                     Controllable
```

External Environment	Internal Dimensions of Strategies
● Demand	● Product
● Economic Conditions	● Price
● Technology	● Personal Selling
● Business Law	● Advertising-Promotion
● Competition	● Channels of Distribution
● Society	● Plant Location
● Energy	

Decision Systems

Opportunities and Problems

Analyzing and Selecting

Alternatives

Objectives and Goals

Strategic Planning

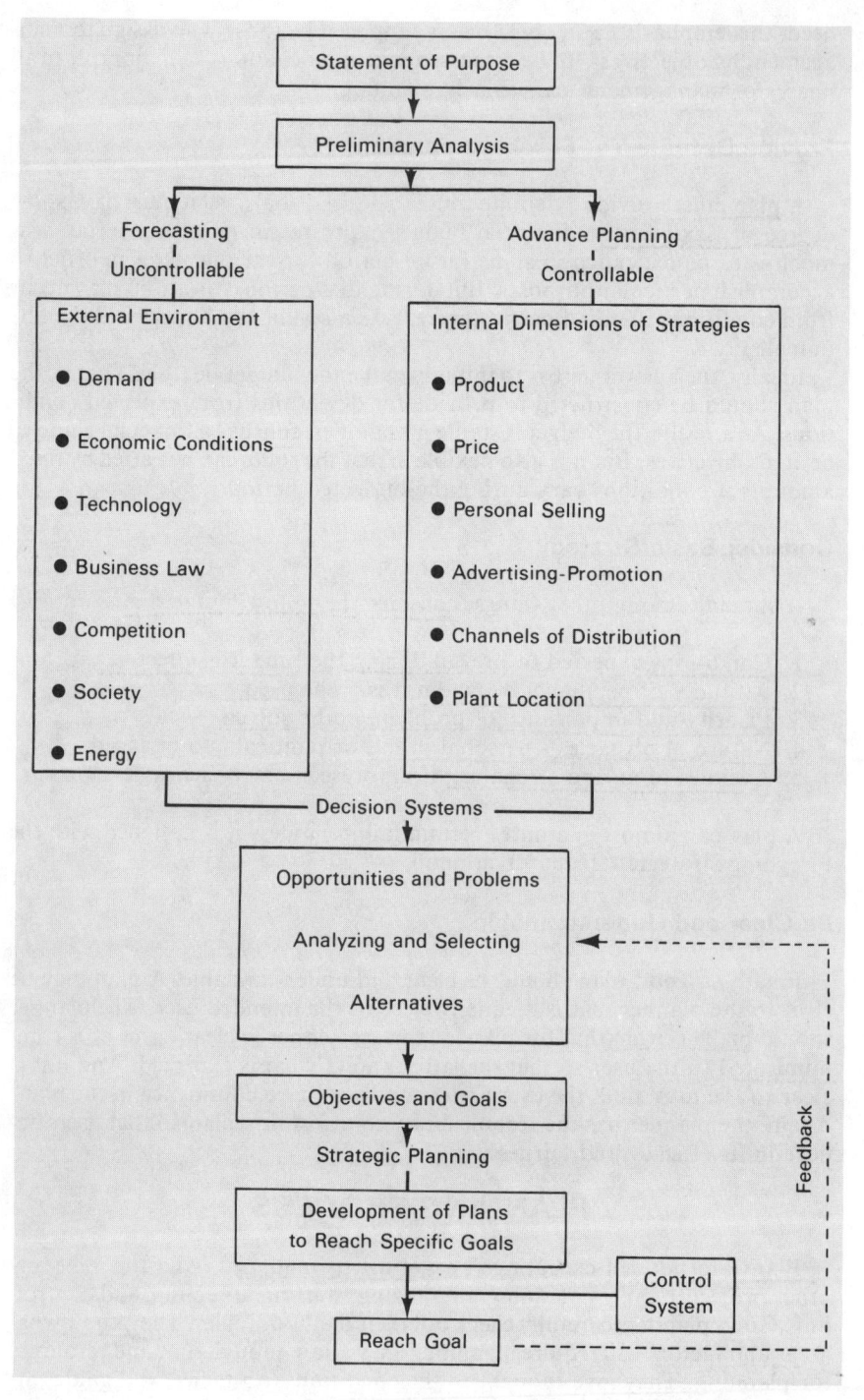

Development of Plans
to Reach Specific Goals

Control System

Reach Goal

Feedback

Fig. 7-6. The planning process

Next, planning involves an organizing phase. It should incorporate a precise determination of personnel responsible for the completion of each part of the plan. Responsible personnel should know to whom they are accountable for results, the times at which they are expected to report on progress, and the manner in which reports are to be submitted. And lastly, determinations should be made as to how the responsibilties of each person are to be finally discharged.

Plans also require directional management. Executives, managers, and supervisors must interpret and communicate planning information to their respective subordinates. This may call for training in the meaning and purposes of the planning. Various motivational efforts may be required to get subordinates to effectively support the plans. Provision should be made for constant and timely information on progress in executing planning. In this manner, interruptions to planning can be identified before they become serious and thereby appropriate corrective action can be taken. The planning in this context is an indispensable part of effective direction.

Finally, by adequate controls the full value of planning may be attained. Results of plans should be carefully measured against desired objectives. For instance, did actual sales equal planned sales, actual cost of sales equal budgeted costs, and actual profits equal anticipated profits? After deviations of actual from planned results are computed, an analysis should be made of causes for deviation.

The analysis of cause and effect is the real value of postoperational control. It provides, first of all, a basis for rewarding the successful planners and penalizing the failures. And it provides, secondly, a basis for improving planning in the future. This latter purpose is more important. Unless control of planning can lead to improvement, it really contributes little to successful management and, in turn, to the successful operation of an enterprise.

QUESTIONS FOR DISCUSSION

1. Describe the three key ideas involved in managerial planning?
2. How does the element of time enter into the planning function?
3. How does top management planning differ from planning at lower organizational levels in terms of extent, time coverage, and time spans?
4. What contributions does planning make to group action?
5. The nature of planning in any company tends to be affected by what factors or conditions?
6. By what tests may the effectiveness of the managerial functions of planning be evaluated?
7. Discuss the controllable and uncontrollable factors that must be analyzed before planning decisions can be made.

REFERENCES

1. Fred Luthans, *Introduction to Management* (New York: McGraw-Hill Book Company, 1976), pp. 83-104.
2. Peter F. Drucker, *The Practice of Management* (New York: Harper & Brothers, 1954).
3. Stanley S. Thune and Robert J. House, "Where Long-Range Planning Pays Off," *Business Horizons*, vol. 13, no. 4, August 1970, pp. 81-87.

4. E. Kirby Warren, *Long-Range Planning: The Executive Viewpoint* (Englewood Cliffs, NJ: Prentice-Hall, 1966).
5. Bernard Taylor and Kevin Hawkins, *A Handbook of Strategic Planning* (London: Longman, 1972, pp. 34-47.
6. Karl A. Shilliff and Robert Smith, "A Forecasting Method for Setting Short-range Research Objectives," *Research Management*, March 1972, pp. 24-33.

SELECTED BIBLIOGRAPHY

1. Ackoff, Russell L. *A Concept of Corporate Planning.* New York: John Wiley and Sons, Inc., 1970.
2. Ansoff, H. Igor. *Corporate Strategy.* New York: McGraw-Hill Book Co., 1965.
3. Ewing, David W., ed. *Long-Range Planning for Management.* 3d ed. New York: Harper and Row, Publishers, 1972.
4. Steiner, George A. *Managerial Long-Range Planning.* New York: McGraw-Hill Book Co., 1963.
5. Warren, E. Kirby. *Long-Range Planning: The Executive Viewpoint.* Englewood Cliffs, NJ: Prentice-Hall, Inc., 1966.

CHAPTER 8

PLANNING TECHNIQUES FOR MANAGEMENT

Purpose of Chapter 8:

1. To present and describe the role of quantitative techniques in planning
2. To identify various types of quantitative models and their features
3. To explore the application of models to specific management problems

Essential elements you should understand after studying this chapter:

1. Definition of the quantitative method used in planning
2. Characteristics of quantitative models
3. The various types of management models
4. Using network analysis techniques
5. Applying PERT in planning and control situations
6. Constructing a break-even analysis
7. Employing the quantitative method in inventory analysis

INTRODUCTION

In the preceding chapter we examined the basic concepts of the planning process and their usefulness in developing a logical and systematic approach to management situations. Here we will elaborate on that process by introducing you to the terminology of management models and selected quantitative techniques employed in specific business planning situations.

The applications of quantitative analysis, including the development of models, reflect the contributions of the management science or quantitative school of thought. More specifically we see here the introduction of techniques that help management structure solutions to those problems of the organizational planning and control functions.

Quantitative techniques or methods are broadly defined as the application of statistics and mathematics coupled with the scientific method. These methods are applied to the solution of management problems that confront business on a daily basis. One of the primary reasons that quantitative analysis is so popular with management is the necessity to examine logically and systemmatically problems using numerical data. In this respect quantitative analysis requires that business data be, therefore, treated descriptively as well as inductively.

Managers must engage in rigorous as well as precise manipulation of business data in order to make certain decisions. While not all decisions lend themselves to mathematical analysis, many lend themselves to applicable quantitative models which are invaluable aids to management.

Once problems are reduced to mathematical formulation, solutions, oftentimes, may easily be effected utilizing the computer. Computers increasingly have available programmed packages to help incorporate the various quantitative techniques that will be developed in this chapter. It remains for you to be aware of and understand these techniques and their potential, when combined with the computer in solving many kinds of problems occurring in the firm.

QUANTITATIVE MODELS

The fundamental basis for quantitative decision making is the use of the mathematical model. The term *math model* is simply an abstraction of the real world. A model is abstract in that it cannot really depict the entire complex reality with its myriad factors. In using models, the manager is attempting to analyze the relationships of a few significant factors in a practical and logical form. In much the same way that scientists use theory to indicate the various relationships of scientific phenomena, managers use models to show the relationships of various numerical business factors. Through the use of models, the manager attempts to:

1. Show logical and meaningful relationships of business factors
2. Gain insight into the various kinds of management problems
3. Develop a structure for management dialogue with better means of communication
4. Prescribe what actions should be taken for problem solving

5. Predict future relationships, changes or other developments regarding the business variables

TYPES OF MODELS

Descriptive, Graphic, and Symbolic Models

There are basically three types of management models. The most simple model is the descriptive type. This can be a simple verbal description, a succinctly written paragraph, a picture, or even a mock-up of a product. Standard operating procedures used in manufacturing a product are often typical examples of descriptive models.

The second type of model is the graphic model. Lines, blocks, and circles which are utilized in systems drawings, in break-even analysis, and economic analysis are some examples. This type of model is often referred to in management literature as the analogue model.

The third model type is the symbolic model. It makes ample use of equations such as those for a straight line, $y = a + bx$, or symbols depicting gross national product, $GNP = C + I + G$. Irrespective of the type of management model, you should be aware of the characteristics of these models as given in figure 8-1.

Normative, Stochastic, and Deterministic Models

Another classification of models should be discussed here. Often models are classified on the basis of what the model attempts to do. To explain further, whenever a model prescribes what management *should* do, it is defined as *normative*. If a model uses probabilities to deal with risk and uncertainties relating to business phenomena, it is referred to as *stochastic* or *probabilistic*. If a model does not use probabilities, it is classified as *deterministic*. And frequently a model may be referred to as *normative-deterministic*, if it prescribes some management action but doesn't utilize any probabilities. It would, furthermore, be possible to create a normative-deterministic-analogue-management-decision-making model, if a few straight lines were used in helping to make a management decision.

While there are a variety of planning techniques, the following sections will illustrate four of the most popular types — the Gantt Chart, network analysis, break-even analysis, and inventory analysis.

THE GANTT CHART

The Gantt chart which follows (figure 8-2) was devised by Henry L. Gantt, the management scholar, as a planning and control technique in production situations. The projects are listed on the left and time is listed across the top. The bars indicate the length of time necessary for the completion of each project.

Since much short-range planning and controlling concerns scheduling of various projects, a Gantt chart which gives a visual production schedule and record is very helpful to the production manager.

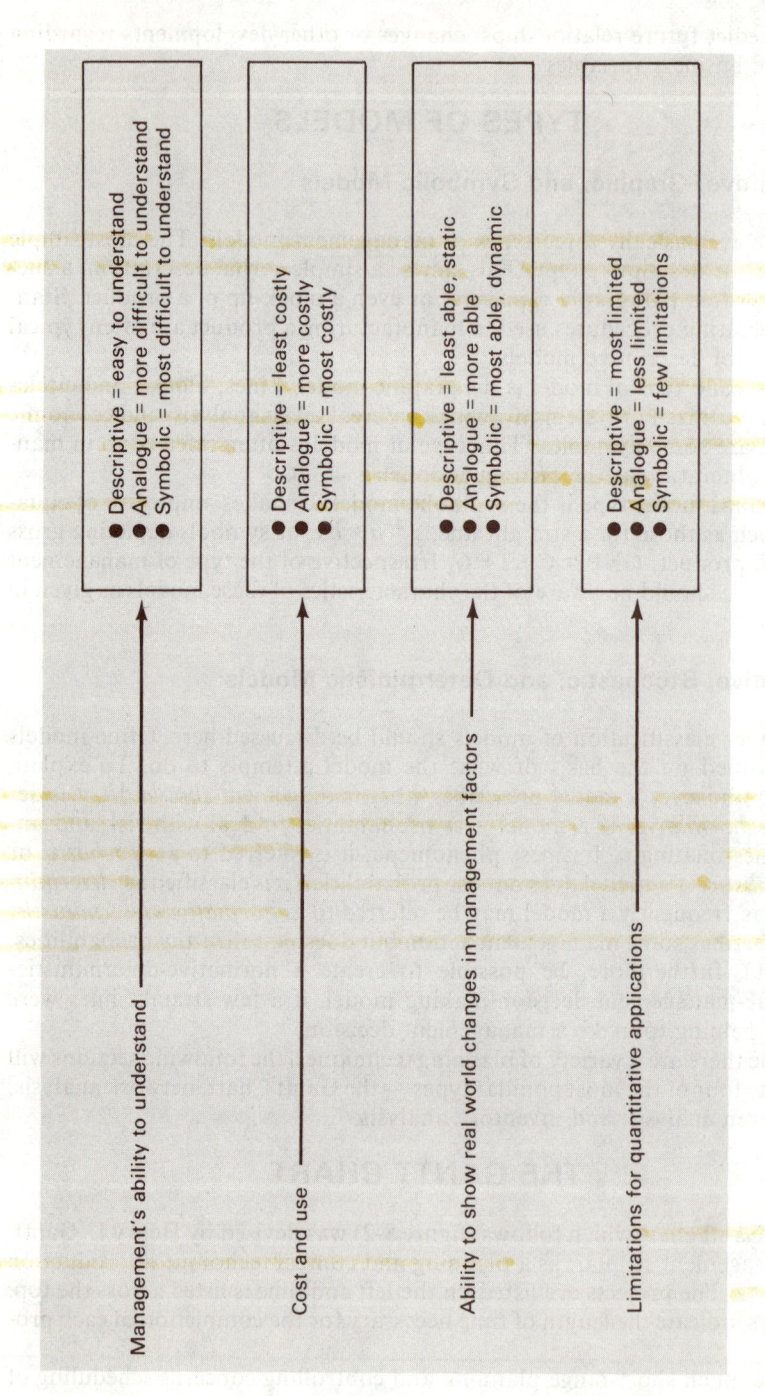

Management's ability to understand	Cost and use	Ability to show real world changes in management factors	Limitations for quantitative applications
• Descriptive = easy to understand • Analogue = more difficult to understand • Symbolic = most difficult to understand	• Descriptive = least costly • Analogue = more costly • Symbolic = most costly	• Descriptive = least able, static • Analogue = more able • Symbolic = most able, dynamic	• Descriptive = most limited • Analogue = less limited • Symbolic = few limitations

Fig. 8-1. Model characteristics

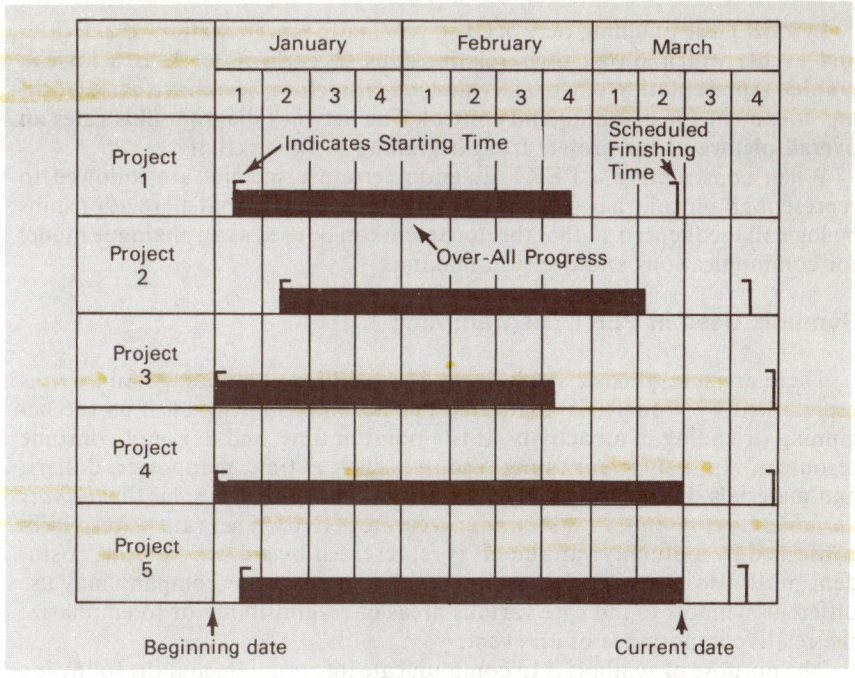

Fig. 8-2. A progress chart for control (Gantt chart)

NETWORK ANALYSIS

One of the most popular and applicable management planning and control techniques developed in recent years is known as network analysis. The term is generally applied to two similar techniques, one military, the other industrial. PERT (Program Evaluation and Review Technique) was developed around 1958 by the Special Projects office of the U.S. Navy.[1] The technique was developed in order to schedule and control the Polaris Missile System efficiently. The network was built up and events that needed to be completed by certain dates, called *milestones*. While this technique did not account for costs, it handled the risks and uncertainty of time estimates required to complete particular activities.

Almost simultaneously, in 1956 an Engineering Control group at the du Pont Company was searching for new techniques to assist in scheduling large complex projects. Out of this search the Critical Path Method (CPM) was devised for that purpose.

The general distinction between PERT and CPM is that with PERT, the results of the analyses are expressed in terms of activities to be performed. In fact, with PERT three different time estimates are used. CPM, however, provides for only one time estimate to be used. Even though there exist some technical differences between the two techniques, they have become increasingly similar. Therefore, throughout this text, for simplification, only PERT will be used for network analysis problems.

PERT Defined

In PERT the planning network is a schematic representation of activities and events which shows their relationships to each other. It is a logical, graphic representation of a project plan, and therefore, becomes a basic working document for planning and control. The network diagram illustrates an overall picture of the project from beginning to final activity.

When constructing a PERT diagram certain principles are followed to represent graphically a project. It is, moreover, essential that all relationships be logically sequenced so that the document can be used as an analogue model for communications and decision making.

Symbols Used in PERT Diagramming

There are several basic symbols used in PERT diagramming. An *event* is represented by a circle. It is a particular accomplishment, such as the beginning or ending of an activity. It is a point in time, and does not consume resources. An *activity* consumes resources such as time, manpower, dollars, and materials. It is represented by an arrow. The third symbol is the *dummy variable*. It represents a constraint on a future activity. There are no resources consumed by a dummy variable. It is represented by a dashed arrow. A student must also be aware that each individual manager or company may use different symbols to indicate various areas of responsibility or to emphasize the relative importance of an event.

The purpose of symbols is to communicate information, and the following in figure 8-3 are some of the generally recognized and used terminologies.

Symbol	Name	Description
Activity ⟶	Activity	The performance of a specific construction job requiring resources (plumbing, digging, sawing, etc.)
Event ◯	Event	Represents the start of finish of a particular job
Duration	Duration	The time required to complete an activity
Network Diagram	Network Diagram	The network representing all of the activities and events for completing the house
Dummy Variable ----▸	Dummy Variable	A restraint on an activity, signified by a dashed arrow
Critical Path	Critical Path	The longest time path in the network of activities

Fig. 8-3. Network terminology

Planning Techniques for Management 115

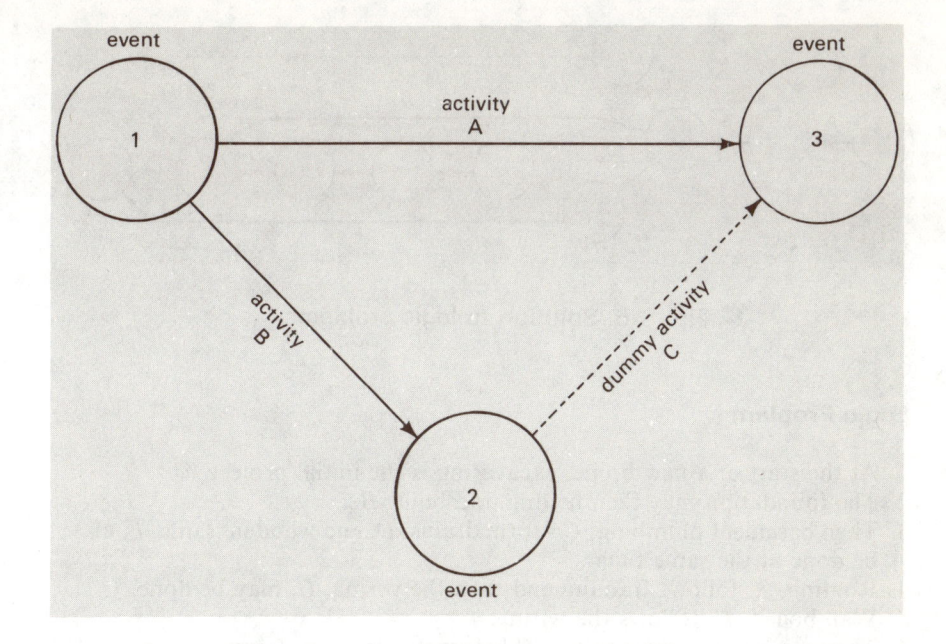

Fig. 8-4. Network diagram

An illustrated network diagram that illustrates how the events and activities appear is shown in figure 8-4.

Activity		Depends on Completion of:
A	Excavation	None
B	Foundation	A
C	Plumbing	B
D	Storm drains	B
E	Frame	B
F	Roof	E
G	Wiring	E
H	Wallboard	G
I	Paint	H
J	Floors	I
K	Finishing	All above

Fig. 8-5. Dependency table

The next most important step in PERT diagramming is the logic problem accompanied by a dependency table such as shown in figure 8-5.

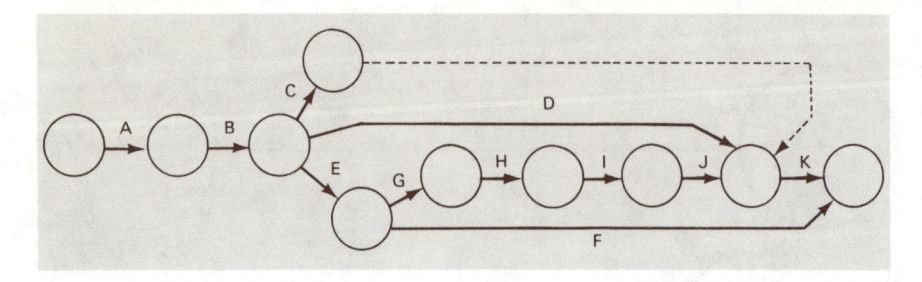

Fig. 8-6. Solution to logic problem

Logic Problem

1. At the start of a new home, excavating is the initial project A
2. The foundation may then be dug and built. B
3. Then basement plumbing, C; storm drains, D; and wooden frame, E, may be done at the same time.
4. Roofing, F, follows framing and then the wiring, G, may be done.
5. Wall board, H, follows the wiring.
6. Then, painting, I, must follow H before the flooring, J, can be completed.
7. The finishing, K, must wait the completion of all above. Figure 8-6 diagrams the solution to this logic problem.

Rules For PERT Analysis

There are some general rules that should guide PERT analysis.

1. An event can be drawn only when the previous activity is finished.
2. No activity or event can be shown twice, unless it occurs twice.
3. No two activities can generate out of the same event and into the same event.
4. A dummy variable should be used to indicate a restraint on an activity, where no resources are used.

Time estimates are an important basis of the analytical operation carried out on the network. The work schedule is no better than the input data from which it is calculated. It is also advantageous to use three time estimates for each activity; the most likely time, the optimistic time, and the pessimistic time. The optimistic time is the shortest possible time than an activity may be completed. The pessimistic time is the longest time that an activity might take, provided some things went wrong. The most likely time is the best estimate, given the present situation.

From these estimated times a single weighted average is calculated using the following formula:

$$\text{Expected time} = \frac{\text{Optimistic time} + (4 \times \text{most likely time}) + \text{Pessimistic Time}}{6}$$

A manager can use this technique simultaneously to plan, organize, and control as many projects as necessary throughout the same time period.

PERT would help keep schedules in order and sequences logical. Later, when time analyses have been perfected, estimates of cost for each activity could be developed in a similar fashion. Other resources such as manpower and materials may also be used in this model.

BREAK-EVEN ANALYSIS

The preparation of a break-even chart can be a valuable quantitative model for use in pricing policies, in planning the firm's capacity, in the making of budgets, and in developing sales strategy. A manager must know what sales volume is necessary in order to break even—that point where total revenue is equal to total cost. *A break-even chart, therefore, indicates what profits or losses should be expected at various potential sales positions.* Moreover, the chart will also indicate what effects, such as changes in costs, or prices will have on profitability.

Break-even analysis or profit-cost-volume analysis, as it is also known, is a quantitative technique for analyzing the relationships among costs and revenue at various sales volumes of operation.[2] In other words, as a planning and also a control technique, it indicates the various sales volumes the firm must achieve in order to generate specified levels of profit, when given the costs of operation.

Therefore, a manager must first make a distinction between variable and fixed costs. Costs that vary directly with output are termed variable costs. For example, each unit of output might require materials, labor, and other resources such as electricity that vary proportionately with output. On the other hand, those costs that remain constant over a period of time, regardless of output, such as rent, insurance, plant and equipment costs, are referred to as fixed costs. It should be recognized, however, that fixed costs remain so only for a short period of time. In the long run all costs may be considered variable. Thus, when the term fixed cost is used it refers to the short run situation.

Graphic Approach to Break-Even Analysis

Break-even analysis relies on the use of a graphic approach, although the break-even point (BE), may be calculated algebraically. Figure 8-7, a straight line break-even chart, illustrates how fixed and variable costs and revenue might look for a manufacturing firm.

It can be seen on figure 8-7 that total revenue is the product of output times the price per unit. Total costs (TC) equals fixed cost plus variable costs (VC). The break-even point is where the total revenue (TR) and total cost (TC) curves intersect. Above the BE point, total revenue is greater than total cost and, therefore, a profit is made. To the left of the BE point, total costs are greater than total revenue, and a loss occurs.

The application of break-even analysis can probably best be demonstrated by presenting a specific problem and showing the relationships of profit-cost-volume both graphically and algebraically. Just to illustrate, assume that a company wants to determine the necessary sales volume required to break even on a new product given the following data:

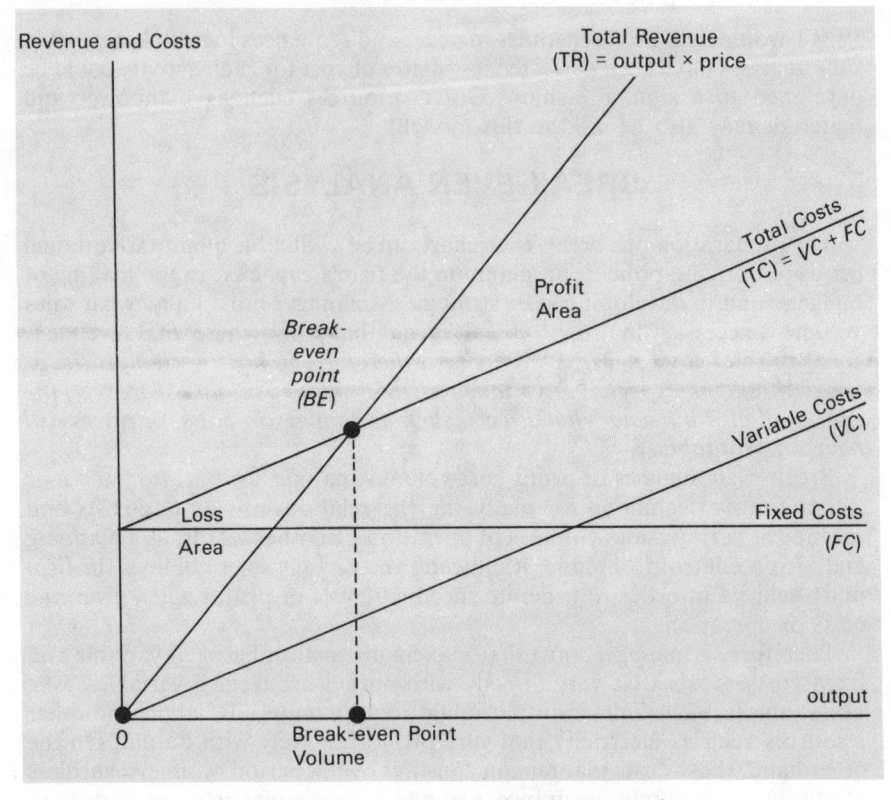

Fig. 8-7. A straight line break-even chart

Price per unit, $4
Fixed cost, $100,000
Variable cost per unit, $2

The break-even position may be calculated by setting up the following equation and substituting the above values.

$$TR = TC, (TC = FC + VC)$$
$$TR = FC + VC$$

Output × $4/unit = $100,000 + $2 × Output
substituting X for Output
$$4X = 100,000 \times 2X$$

where

$$2X = 100,000$$
$$X = 50,000 \text{ units}$$

The 50,000 units is the break-even point for the new product. This analysis is usually accompanied by a break-even chart illustrating the relationships involved in the problem, as we show in figure 8-8.

Planning Techniques for Management 119

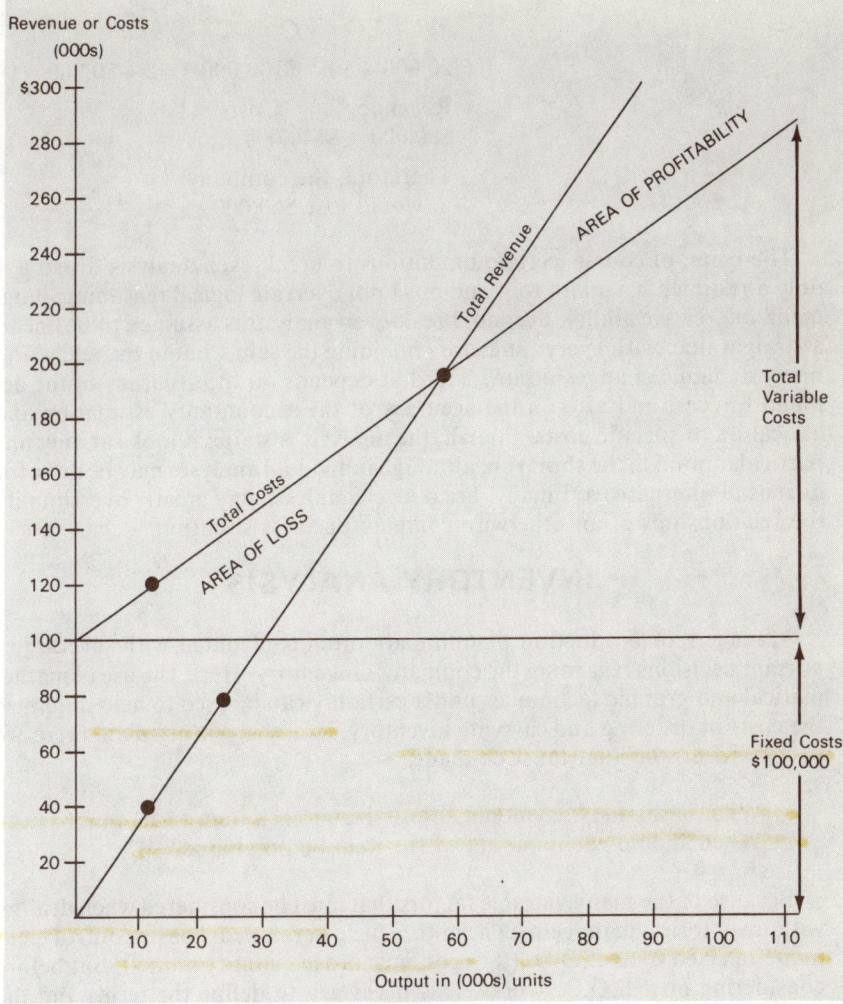

Fig. 8-8. Break-even chart

There are other important questions that could be answered from this chart. Using either the equations or the chart, a manager could determine how much volume must be sold in order to make $80,000 profit.

It is, moreover, simple to modify the equations to include profit (*PR*). For example:

$$TR = FC + VC + PR$$
$$4X = \$100,000 + 2X + = 80,000$$
$$2X = \$180,000$$
$$X = 90,000 \text{ units}$$

Therefore, 90,000 units must be made and sold to insure profits of $80,000. Conversely, if only 20,000 units were sold, the company would lose money.

$$TR = FC + VC$$
$$20{,}000 \cdot \$4 = \$100{,}000 + \$2 \cdot 20{,}000$$

Revenue   Costs
$80,000 = $140,000

Therefore, the company would lose $60,000.

There are, of course, certain limitations to break-even analysis. First, it is only a rudimentary math tool and must not override logical reasoning, judgment, or creative ability. Second, break-even analysis is assumed to be linear, a straight line, with everything else remaining the same, but in the real world many dynamic changes occur.[3] Third, it depends on the accuracy of the demand forecast and also on the accuracy of the accountants' estimation and allocation of specific costs. Fourth, the analysis is static; it looks at only one particular point in the short run, although individual analyses may be done for dozens of alternatives. Finally, break-even analysis may greatly oversimplify the relationships of an otherwise complex business situation.

INVENTORY ANALYSIS

Managers of production planning are often confronted with several important decisions regarding the company's inventory. Here, the use of mathematical and graphic techniques under certainty can be used to help minimize the costs of ordering and carrying inventory. In any inventory plan, there are two key decisions that must be made:

1. What is the most economical lost size of each item to be purchased?
2. When should each amount of the item be purchased?

Because of the many variable factors that must be considered when dealing with inventories, management scientists have developed a basic control technique referred to as E.O.Q. (the economic order quantity model). But before considering how E.O.Q. works, it is necessary to define the terms and the assumptions underlying the model.

Cost Factors

The costs associated with inventory analysis are of two kinds—carrying costs and ordering costs.[4] Carrying costs are those expenses incurred in processing, storing and handling the inventory. This includes such costs as spoilage, breakage and obsolescence. These costs are usually expressed as a percentage of the cost of the inventory. Inventory carrying costs may range from 10 to 25 percent of the total cost of inventories depending upon the kind of space and facilities used.

Second, are the ordering costs. These reflect the costs of ordering and securing the items into inventory. These costs are incurred each time the firm orders more inventory. They are mainly considered clerical and administrative. Together these costs constitute the total costs of carrying and ordering inventory.

Planning Techniques for Management   121

The objective of E.O.Q. is simply to find the lowest point of the total cost curve. For example, if a manager orders too often (places many small orders), the total cost curve will be too high due to high order costs and low carrying costs. If a manager orders too much (but only once or twice a year), the order costs will be low, but carrying costs will be too high, since more than the amount needed is ordered. The objective, obviously, is to order just the right amount so that ordering costs versus carrying costs are a minimum.

Assumptions Underlying E.O.Q.

When applying the E.O.Q. technique, it is necessary to make assumptions regarding demand; that is the amount of inventory needed for a specific time in advance, usually a year. This generally is the sales forecast. The second assumption concerns the lead time necessary. For E.O.Q. analysis the time between placing and receiving an order is assumed to be known. The third assumption is that inventory is depleted at a constant and continuous rate as depicted in figure 8-9.

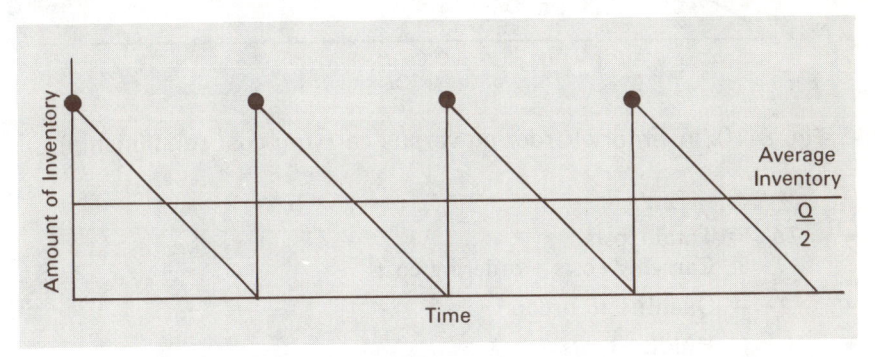

Fig. 8-9. Average inventory

Although these assumptions would rarely hold true for the real-world situation, they allow a student to work through a simple model to show the various possible relations between costs.

It can be seen from figure 8-9 that if there are continuous disbursements and instantaneous receipts of inventory, then the average inventory at any one time is $\frac{Q}{2}$.

Therefore, to minimize inventory costs, managers attempt to minimize carrying costs versus ordering costs. The manager when developing an E.O.Q. is doing an opposing cost analysis as shown in figure 8-10.

If costs for each order size are plotted carefully, the E.O.Q. can be found by graphical analysis as in figure 8-10. While this trial-and-error method involves graphing and manipulation of costs, a formula may be derived based on the assumptions previously made.

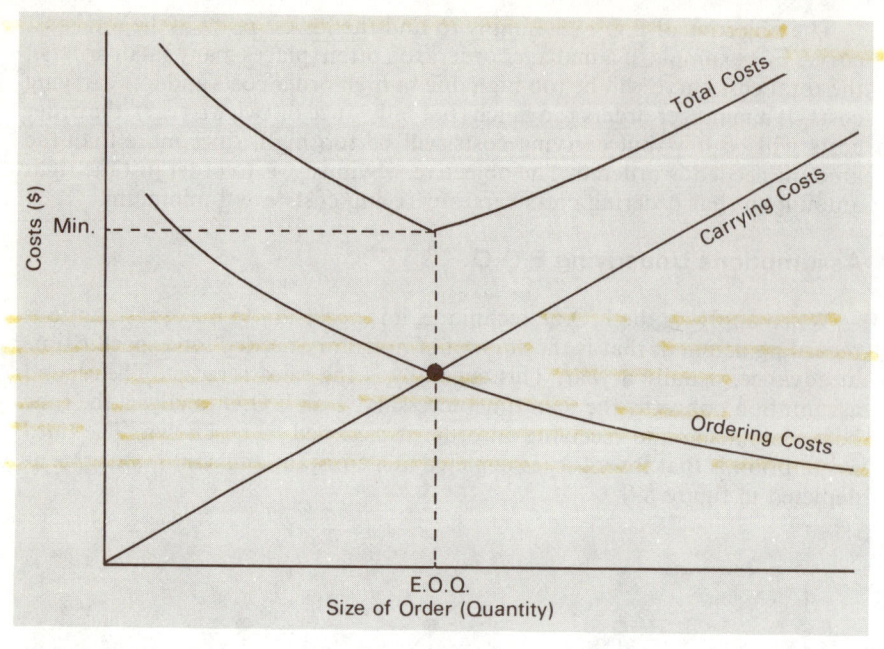

Fig. 8-10. Inventory (Ordering versus carrying cost relationship)

- TC = Total Costs
  = Carrying costs + ordering costs
- Q = Quantity to order
- HC = Holding costs
  V = Value per unit of item under consideration
  C = A percentage figure indicating carrying cost as per cent of unit value of item
- $\dfrac{Q}{2}$ = Average amount of stock in inventory at any one time
- D = The total quantity to be used for a period of time (year)
- O = The cost of placing an order

$\therefore TC = \dfrac{Q}{2} HC \dfrac{D}{Q} O$

From the graph in figure 8-10 it can be seen that to minimize total costs, the amount Q should be ordered at a point where order cost intersects carrying cost.

The first step in the algebraic derivation is to set carrying costs equal to order costs and then solve for Q. This will give an equation for an E.O.Q., which will minimize total costs.

$$\begin{array}{cc} \text{Carrying Costs} & \text{Order Costs} \\ \dfrac{Q}{2}HC & = \dfrac{D}{Q}O \end{array}$$

$$Q^2 HC = 2DO$$

$$Q^2 = \dfrac{2DO}{HC}$$

$$Q = \sqrt{\dfrac{2DO}{HC}}$$

This final equation then determines the economic order quantity (E.O.Q.). Let us assume that a rubber company is working on an inventory problem with the following data:

Estimated demand for year	2,000
Cost of item per unit	$40
Cost per order	$80
Inventory carrying cost (as a % of cost per item)	5%

$$\text{E.O.Q.} = \sqrt{\dfrac{2 \cdot 2{,}000 \cdot 80}{40 \,(.05)}}$$

$$\text{E.O.Q.} = \sqrt{\dfrac{320{,}000}{2}}$$

$$\text{E.O.Q.} = \sqrt{160{,}000}$$

$$\text{E.O.Q.} = 400$$

There are some serious limitations to this type of model since the assumptions previously made are rarely met in the real world. Demand for any item is at best only a rough forecast or estimate. Few if any inventories deplete with continuous flow and instantaneous receipts. It is extemely difficult, moreover, to obtain accurate cost data when a company works with literally thousands of products.

Despite these limitations, though, the primary concern for management is to understand not only the relationships of the various factors but also how a manager may reach more effective decisions. Furthermore, the models do give the student insight to the problems faced by management. They also become the basis for more meaningful dialogue and communications between interfacing management.

QUESTIONS FOR DISCUSSION

1. Discuss the various kinds of management models and their characteristics.
2. How can PERT be used for effective planning and control of new products?
3. Diagram the following activities in the form of a PERT network.
    a. At the start of the project, *A, B, C* are done concurrently.
    b. *E,F,G* follow *B*.

d. *K* is one of the last jobs and follows *D*.
   e. *L* is also a terminal activity and follows completion of *R* and *G*.
   f. *R* must follow the completion of *C*.
   g. *Z* follows *E* and ends with *K* and *L*.
   h. *U* follows *F* and ends with *K* and *L*.
4. What are some of the limitations of break-even analysis?
5. If the selling price of product A is $10 and the fixed cost is $50,000, given a variable cost of $8 per unit, calculate the break-even point.
   Draw an analogue model to illustrate and show relationships of revenue-costs-profit-loss.
6. A plant manager wishes to order some inventory items. The yearly demand is 500 items; each item costs $20. The ordering cost is $30 per order and the carrying cost is 10% of the cost of each item. What is the E.O.Q.?
7. What are the limitations to E.O.Q. analysis?

REFERENCES

1. Herbert G. Hicks and C. Ray Gullett, *The Management of Organizations* (New York: McGraw Hill, Inc., 1976), pp. 275-78.
2. E.V. McIntyre, "Cost-Volume-Profit Analysis Adjusted for Learning," *Management Science,* vol. 24 no. 2 (October 1977), p. 149 B-E.
3. Y.K. Bhada, "Dynamic Cost Analysis," *Management Accounting* (July 1970), pp. 11-14.
4. R. Raplan, "A Dynamic Inventory Model with Stochastic Leadtimes," *Management Science,* vol. 16, 1979, pp. 491-507.

SELECTED BIBLIOGRAPHY

1. Adam, Everett E., Jr., and Ebert, Ronald J. *Production and Operations Management* Englewood Cliffs, NJ: Prentice-Hall, 1978.
2. Buffa, Elwood S. *Production-Inventory Systems: Planning and Control.* Homewood, IL: Richard D. Irwin, Inc., 1968.
3. Kwak, N.K. *Mathematical Programming with Business Applications.* New York: McGraw-Hill Book Co., 1973.
4. Olsen, Robert A. *Manufacturing Management: A Quantitative Approach.* Scranton, PA: International Textbook Co., 1968.
5. Starr, Martin K., and Miller, David W. *Inventory Control: Theory and Practice.* Englewood Cliffs, NJ: Prentice-Hall, Inc., 1963.

CHAPTER 9

MAKING OBJECTIVES OPERATIONAL

Purpose of Chapter 9:

1. To explore objectives, their nature and function in the organization
2. To describe and discuss the program of management by objectives as a means of satisfying organizational goals
3. To illustrate the need for an integrated network of objectives at the various levels of the firm

Essential elements you should understand after studying this chapter:

1. The distinction between economic objectives and objectives based upon time
2. Uses of objectives in the performance of the managerial functions
3. Source of responsibility for setting objectives
4. Criteria for establishing sound objectives

NATURE OF OBJECTIVES

Any organization exists to attain certain objectives. With business organizations, for example, earning a profit is a generally recognized objective. This simplistic statement, though, does not do justice to the numerous other types, uses, and implications of objectives in the business environment. Nor does it disclose the managerial responsibilities imposed by this important factor in the operations of organizations.

Attainment of objectives, therefore, justifies the existence of a business organization. If a business does not satisfactorily attain objectives, it will sooner or later cease to exist. Basically, then, what are these objectives? Objectives are those results which are considered valuable or useful. Specific examples of objectives are profits, goods and services, salaries and wages, job security, control of markets, industry leadership, and so on.

Regularly, during the operations of a firm, objectives are sometimes equated with the terms principles and policies. There is nothing wrong with this as long as everybody has a clear understanding of the meaning intended. Semantically speaking, though, the major differences among these seemingly equivalent terms are that a *principle identifies the reason why a firm is in business, an objective indicates what it desires to achieve, while a policy tells how it conducts its activities in order to accomplish its purpose and attain its objectives.*

KINDS OF OBJECTIVES

Most organizations have more than one objective. Some objectives are usually more significant than others. Accordingly, it is possible to classify objectives in several ways. Since the reason for the determination of objectives is chiefly to do a better job of managing, it is helpful to establish those classifications along two different tracks: (1) the kinds of organization values or service provided, and (2) the length of time required for their achievement. Figure 9-1 illustrates an overview of the various organizational objectives.

Economic Objectives

The primary or basic mission of the business firm is to produce and distribute certain economic products or services which the consumer will buy. Since this economic service is the reason why the company exists, these objectives may be considered primary. Accomplishing them in an efficient and economical manner assures the survival of the firm, provided the objectives themselves are selected on the basis of customer needs and wants. The organization must, first of all, create and then distribute the desired values to its customers. Trade will inevitably flow to that firm which demonstrates it is giving more for the price of its product or service than its competitors.

The growing social conscious of business leadership has created a climate in which certain social objectives such as creating job opportunities appear worthy enough to be considered of primary importance. The temptation to state these as primary objectives of the firm must be resisted, however, since they will probably come about as a result of management's concentration on

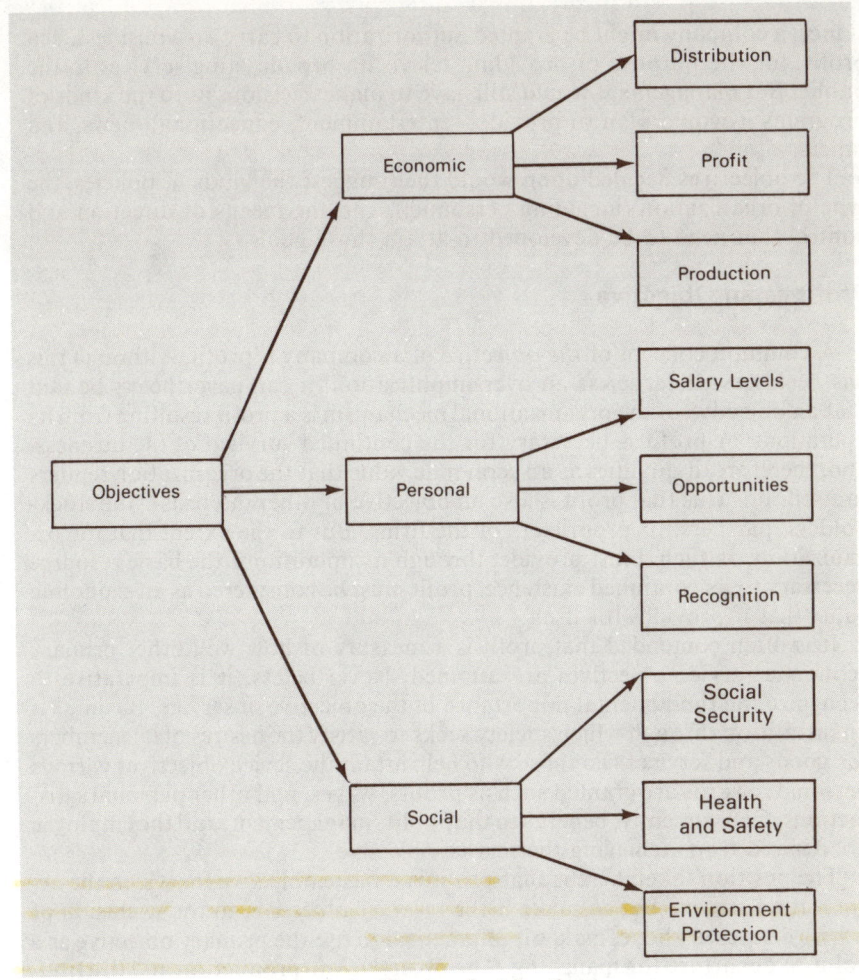

Fig. 9-1. Kinds of objectives

primary economic objectives. If the assumption is made that the company's first obligation is to create jobs, then the values to the customer could be relegated to secondary consideration, and the competitive position of the organization could be affected adversely.

The development of sound basic economic objectives is not always simple. It is easy to state that economic service to the customer is the primary objective, while actually another goal instead, such as maximizing the return on sales. However, if performance is appraised in terms of an annual accounting period, for example, there may arise a real question as to whether the two objectives are always in agreement. An executive may find tht his performance is rated as being deficient in terms of bottom-line results even though he has genuinely provided service.

The economic service expected of a business firm is often stated in a broad way in its legal authorization by the state to engage in the business. For instance, a company might be granted authorization to carry on a business, at a profit, for the purpose of providing television broadcasting services to the public. But management would still have to make decisions as to the kinds of programs it would plan to provide—entertainment, educational, news, and others.

The objectives decided upon would then suggest the kinds of policies, the type of organization (including personnel), and the means of direction and control that need to be developed to attain those goals.[1]

Profit as an Objective

A common concept of *the objective* of a company is profit. Although this has been viewed earlier as an oversimplification, it can nevertheless be said that an objective of the organizational mechanism is a profit resulting from its operations. A profit is necessary for the continued survival of the business, and, therefore, it qualifies as an economic value that the organization renders to itself. It is true that profit is also an objective of other interests—the stockholders, partners, or proprietors of the firms. But to the extent that the organization, as such, must provide, through its operations, the basic resource necessary to its continued existence, profit must be considered as an economic value that it provides for itself.

It is often contended that profit is a measure of how well other primary economic service objectives are attained. Nevertheless, it is imperative to recognize the fundamental importance of the objective of service. Business is an institution through which society seeks to satisfy the desires of its members for goods and services. To those who help attain the sevice objectives various personal rewards are granted such as profits, wages, and other personal satisfactions. Consequently, benefits to the public, management, and the employee are derived from achieving the service objective.

The position taken here is that profit is a basic objective for which the organization strives. But to make it the *primary* objective, to the exclusion of others discussed above, makes it impractical to use the primary objective as a point of departure for managing. The objective of "production and distribution of a complete product line" is a more meaningful objective for planning than is the simply stated goal of "profit." A firm may be able to operate for several years without making a profit (although it certainly will continue to expect to achieve a profit before many years have passed). But it is far less likely that a firm can operate for even a fraction of a year without producing and selling an economic good or service.

Personal Objectives

Management well realizes that other interests must be served as a consequence of its operation. Individuals make up the organization, and they expect to acquire certain values from their association with the organization. Since the organization cannot function effectively without the cooperation of these individuals, it must take as its obligation the satisfaction, in reasonable degree, of the personal objectives of all individuals connected with the organization.[2] Thus, the stockholders or owners have as a personal objective the receipt of a healthy dividend that should result from the company's obtaining a profit. Both manager and nonmanager alike have certain objectives that they seek to attain through their association with the firm. Some of these objectives are: desired salary levels, opportunity for promotion, achievement of status, recognition, and other values.

The fact that the executives do have personal objectives presents a problem in their determination of the organizational objectives. The latter can easily be affected by the personal aims of the executives. It is not difficult to imagine the rationalization possible to define a personal objective as an organizational one. The ambitious chief executive, aspiring to greatness, can easily accept as an enterprise goal "becoming the leader in the industry." Personal objectives are very real and must be taken into consideration in the management of the company.

Social Objectives

What the firm expects, or feels obligated, to supply to social generally constitutes its social objectives. Some of these social objectives, and the manner in which they are achieved, are prescribed by the government through legislative action. For example, social security, unemployment and workers compensation are required by law. Such government influence may take place on the local, state, or national level.

A firm frequently assumes voluntarily obligations to the community in which it is located. Top management may follow a policy of participation in such civic undertakings as a community fund drive, anti-pollution programs, or the backing of a hospital construction program. It may establish a foundation devoted to raising educational and cultural standards of schools, a community, or the entire country. In this manner a business firm behaves as a conscientious citizen of the community, and with its resources contributes very important values to society in general.

Secondary Operational Objectives

Secondary operational objectives are the company's goals with respect to economy and effectiveness of operation. Economy refers to the cost at which the service or product is produced and distributed. Effectiveness, on the other hand, refers to the production and distribution functions being rendered when required, and in the right quantity and quality.

TIME BASIS OF OBJECTIVES

Objectives may be classified not only as to coverage but also as to the time span within which their achievement is expected. Accordingly, we may distinguish among ultimate (or long-term) intermediate, short-term, and immediate objectives.

Long-Term Objectives

Long-term objectives are broad goals which are continuously sought, permanently in view, and never really satisfied. They are basic to all other goals, are broad gauge in nature, and represent the aims of the firm over its business life. The long-term objectives primarily are guides or goals for the highest echelons of management, while more immediate challenges are required at lower levels.[3] Here, for instance, is an example of long-term objectives as defined by a typical firm:

1. To provide for customers a high-quality product at a fair price.
2. To provide for employees working conditions, fair wages, and other forms of compensation that are equal to, or better than, those of other firms in the community.
3. To provide for stockholders an equitable return on their ownership investment.
4. To accept a fair share of responsibilities as a good citizen of the community and to strive to promote the economic well-being of the community.

Intermediate Objectives

These are objectives of a specific nature, indicating definite programs or projects having dimensions and an ending point. They are those objectives which are sought in the near future, usually in the one or two year range. The standard for instance may be in the form of market penetration. In the case of an appliance company the intermediate objective may be to have 30 percent of the market for its products in the next several years. The current penetration may be 22 percent of that market. Intermediate goals are usually expressed as sales, production, or financial criteria.

Short-Term Objectives

These objectives relate to those values that the company hopes to attain in the near future such as the next accounting period, or possibly attain during the next calendar year, the next quarter, or the next month. They are objectives that must be quite precise and are usually subject to careful measurement. To illustrate, an automobile company announced that it had scheduled 40,000 units for production in a given month. This is a short-term objective. At the end of the month the company could check actual production and determine whether its goal had been achieved.

Immediate Objectives

These refer to those goals or aims that are established for a work shift, a day, or some part of a day. Thus, we may set up a daily sales quota for a field representative. This had been established as the sales volume required that day while achieving that month's and that year's marketing goals, so as to move in a planned way toward the intermediate and long-term objectives. This finite objective, however, must be set at the basic operational level for each employee since the long-term objectives furnish too little guidance for the people in their daily work.

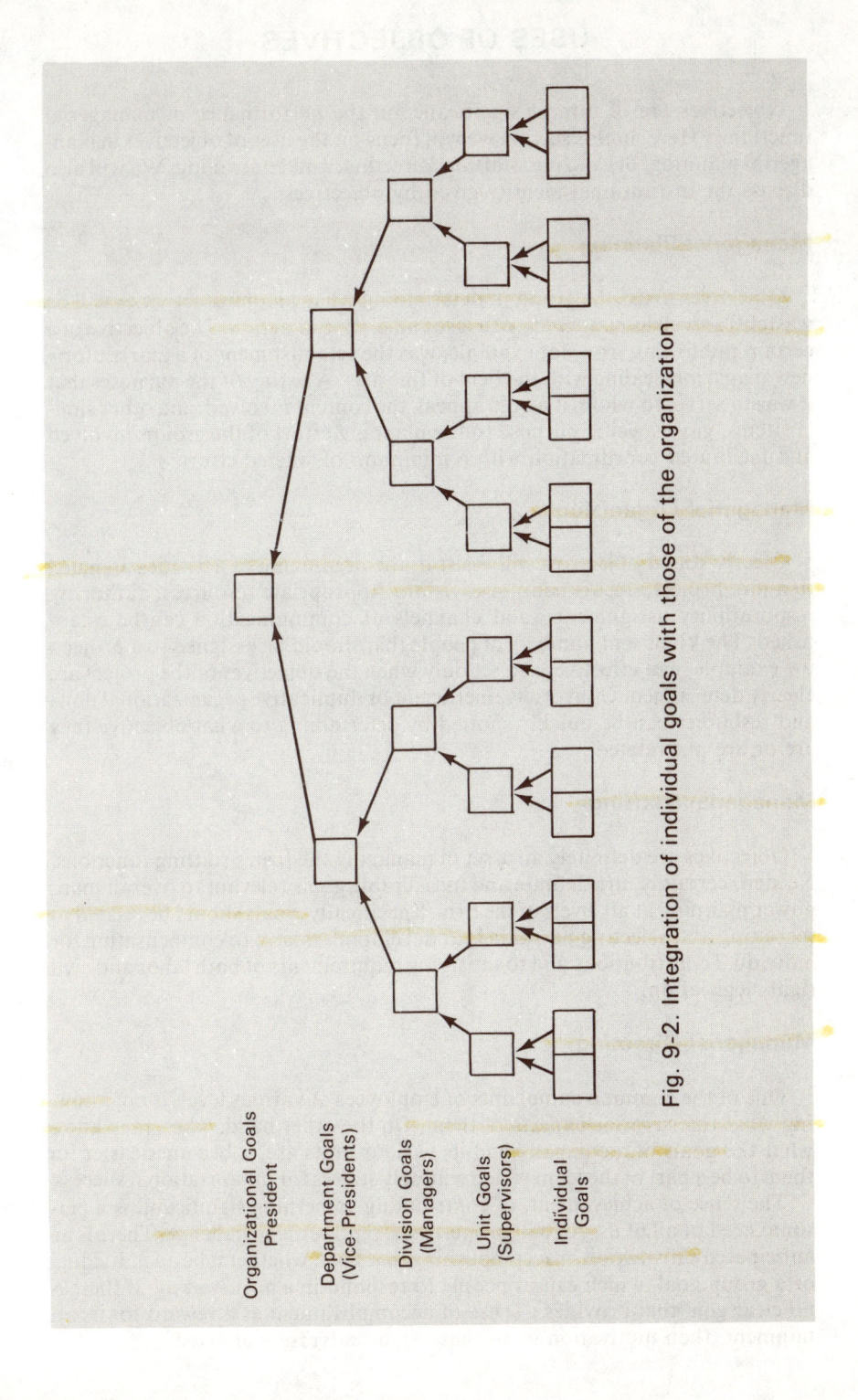

Fig. 9-2. Integration of individual goals with those of the organization

USES OF OBJECTIVES

Objectives are of utmost significance in the performance of managerial functions.[4] Here, in this section we will focus on the uses of objectives in managerial planning, organizing, staffing, directing, and controlling. We will also discuss the institutional identity given by objectives.

Managerial Planning

Objectives assist the group in determining what planning activities will be wasteful as well as contributive to a sound course of action. The objective of a certain publishing firm, for example, was the establishment of a market for a new magazine dealing with the field of fine arts. A listing of the purposes that it was to serve, to whom it would appeal, the content involved, and other similar items, gave specific purpose to the planning effort of the groups involved and facilitated coordination with a minimum of wasted effort.

Managerial Organizing

Clearly stated objectives will assist in the organizing of activities assigned to a job, project, department, or division. Appropriate resources, authority-responsibility assignments, and channels of communication can be established. The kinds and numbers of people that should be assigned to a project, for example, can effectively be set only when the objectives of the project are clearly determined. Conversely, inefficient or duplicative organizational units and resources can be quickly spotted by determining to what objective they are or are not related.

Managerial Staffing

Objectives are definitely an asset in managing the firm's staffing functions. Needed, certainly, are definite and measurable goals relevant to overall manpower planning at all levels of the firm. Specifically, goals should be related to recruiting and selecting personnel; to developing talent; to compensating for individual contributions and to satisfying requirements of both labor and civil rights legislation.

Managerial Directing

One of the common complaints of employees at various levels is not knowing what the superior expects of them. On the other hand, when they know what the goals of a company and its various units are, it becomes easier for them to be a part of the team which willingly strives for organizational success.

The sense of achievement, of contributing something significant, is a personal need of all of us. A goal, properly set, represents a challenge. There is an anticipated satisfaction in accomplishing that goal, whether it be an individual or a group goal, which causes people to respond in a positive way. If there is no clear goal that provides a sense of accomplishment as a reward for its attainment, then motivation is, to that extent, adversely affected.

Many organizations are utilizing what is known as management by objectives as a motivational basis for encouraging a sense of achievement. Briefly a management by objectives (MBO) program consists of the following sequential steps:*[5]

1. Management initially identifies the corporate objectives or goals.
2. These objectives are formulated for the firm, then scaled downward into subobjectives and sub-subobjectives for departments, divisions, and work units as depicted in figure 9-2.
3. The supervisors and their subordinates mutually set personal goals for accomplishment. These are first developed, then written and communicated to the involved and responsible parties.
4. Periodic appraisals are used to analyze progress.
5. There is a discussion of variances in goal achievement, and concurrently there is a mutually developed plan of action for successful goal accomplishment for the future.

As an additional benefit, it appears that MBO programs help in the development of managers since there is evidence that it:

1. Fosters both communication and cooperation between managers who, first of all set and then work regularly toward achieving company and unit goals.
2. Identifies and then integrates the goals of the individual with those of the organization.
3. Facilitates personal development by localizing specific areas for development that are congruous to the defined objectives.
4. Stimulates individual efforts of employees who are working toward common objectives that are consistent, realizable, and accepted.

Managerial Controlling

Objectives aid measurably in exercising control. Some executives have stated that the only thing that counts is results. They mean that whether or not the company's or person's efforts have been properly applied can be seen in the end results of those efforts. While this may be oversimplification, it does show that the ultimate standard or criterion, by which effort is measured, is the objective that was to be achieved. When standards are set for accomplishment of projects or phases of an overall program, they become interim objectives which act as building blocks toward final objectives. Comparison of performance to these objectives thus becomes a means of measurement of progress toward overall program completion.

Institutional Identity

Objectives give identity to the organization and assist in relating it to those groups upon which its survival depends. For example, General Electric's well-known advertised objective of "Progress Is Our Most Important Product" serves as a unique objective of the business, inviting challenge and comparison by both the consumer and the public.

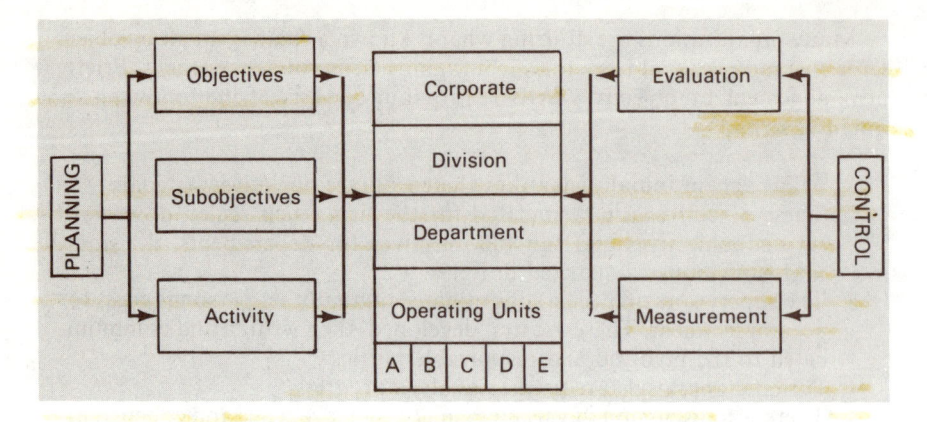

Fig. 9-3. Model of relationship of objectives to planning and control (The function of planning is to determine objectives for the corporation as well as the subsequent determination and integration of necessary subobjectives and finally the activities themselves that initiate the chainlike process.)

RESPONSIBILITY FOR OBJECTIVES

Objectives, obviously, are not self-generating. They arise out of the conscious deliberations of the owners of the firm, and over time are influenced by both management and employees as the objectives themselves are being implemented. Furthermore, the economic, social, and political climates concurrently exercise a profound influence on the development of those objectives.

Actions of Owners

In any system of government embracing the concept of private property, the primary source of the objectives of a firm is the ownership group. These are the stockholders in a corporation, partners in a partnership, members in a cooperative, and the entrepreneur in a proprietorship.

In all firms it is imperative that the owners or board of directors remain active in seeing that their concept of the objectives is sharpened, crystallized, and completely communicated to all employees, both managerial and operative alike. this means a continuing appraisal of the firm in terms of these objectives.

Actions of Management

Where the managers are the owners, the above components apply. Where the managers are hired employees of the owners, these people act as individuals and are able to influence strongly not only the execution of the objectives but also their formulation. In such a case, care must be taken to insure that management focuses on the organizational rather than its personal objectives.[6]

Actions of Employees

Employees, directly and indirectly, affect the objectives of a firm, both in their formulation and, more obviously, in their execution. Certainly it is clear that an organization could not set up objectives with little or no motivational value to the employees of the firm. If, for example, a firm were to announce that its sole objective is to maximize the return on absentee stockholder's capital, it could hardly expect to win the support of all employees. The actions of management, which have an important bearing on successful attainment of such an objective, would no doubt adversely affect employee morale. An illustration of such action would be the decision to pay below-area wages in order to reduce costs so as to maximize profits.

Influence of Environmental Factors

Many environmental factors affect the establishment or modification of organizational objectives. Some of the more significant ones are considered here, such as economic and political environmental forces.

General Business Environment

The general business climate will affect the objectives of a company. Objectives of a firm born in a depression period will often reflect those deteriorated economic conditions. The firm will probably accent survival and the creation of value, rather than maximization or return on capital or sales. The promoters may well be looking for a way to make a living—not a speculative profit, or even, particularly, an investment. They may well have set their goal a break-even operation with attainment of a minimual market position.

Conditions such as monopoly or acute competition can also affect the objectives set by a firm. Management operating in a competitive market will have good reason for deciding, as realistic objectives, the provision of high-quality product, outstanding customer service, lower price, or some combination of all three. Its objectives will need to be concerned with survival and growth among strong competitors.

On the other hand, a company under monopolistic, or near-monopolistic conditions, is not under the same pressure from the marketplace to stress values. It can afford to put greater emphasis on obtaining a better rate of return on invested capital. An effective limit to the maximization of return is the fear that regulatory action may be taken against a monopolistic concern.

Political Environment

The political environment in the nation, state, and locality must be considered, too, in shaping company objectives. In a free economy the individual firm has a wide latitude in determining the goals it will strive to achieve. In a regimented economy the goals will be more limited, or possibly even set, for the enterprise. In the Soviet Union for example, the objectives of an enterprise are usually well defined by the specific trust that controls that segment of the economy.

Size of Firm

While the age and size of a firm may be less influential than are economic and political conditions, they are, nonetheless, general factors that affect the objectives of a company. A large firm tends to be perpetually in the eye of the public. Its conduct has to be more discreet than does that of its smaller business counterpart.

AIDS TO ESTABLISHING OBJECTIVES

Certain scientific management techniques or tools are of some assistance in molding objectives. The technique of market research is of considerable aid in spelling out a practical objective of product quality. It also assists in devising objectives for the distribution of the product. In determining intermediate and short-term goals, market analysis and economic analysis can provide realistic data to help shape market goals for the near future.

Improved production control techniques, too, provide knowledge that can be materially helpful in setting production goals or targets. Time and motion study can give insight into practical output standards (immediate objectives) for individual employees. Job evaluation produces accurate job descriptions, which can be very fruitful in developing objectives that run the gamut of employee activities.

The attainment of all objectives is dependent upon the modern use of progressive, scientific management tools. What does it gain a firm to set up high-sounding objectives that are soon shown to be obviously unattainable? It is better practice to use the devices of scientific management to develop objectives that can be realistically achieveable.

CRITERIA OF SOUND OBJECTIVES

If fullest benefits are to be derived from objectives, they should possess certain desirable characteristics. Some of these are suggested here:

Acceptable

An objective must be acceptable to the people whose actions are involved in its achievement. This means that an organizational objective must be meaningful to the members of the organization. Announced objectives which are inconsistent with the everyday behavior of the firm are readily discounted.

Attainable

An objective must be attainable within a reasonable time. An objective will lose its effectiveness if the people who work for its attainment cannot tell whether or not they have achieved it. This means essentially that the overall, long-term objectives of the firm must be translated into intermediate and more specific objectives; objectives which will provide yardsticks against which progress of the firm and its individual employees may be measured.

Motivational

An objective must have inspirational qualities which motivate all personnel to strive for its achievement. The objective of a medical center has been expressed as "Medical Service To People." This is the sort of objective that can inspire employees to create and distribute values for the patients.

Understandable

An objective must be as clearly and simply stated as possible. there should be a minimum of objectives as far as the individual employee is concerned. Each should be briefly and clearly stated and yet give complete meaning to the expression of purpose.

Communicated

An objective must be communicated to all who are concerned with its achievement. Such communication must not only be initially well executed but must also be continuously maintained with the employee. In effect, management must take every opportunity to stress the goals toward which the firm and its people are striving.

MAINTAINING OBJECTIVES

As the firm continues in existence, it will be necessary to periodically re-examine the objectives to determine if changes are dictated as a result of evolution in the business environment. The basic, original objectives must be constantly reappraised to assure that they are still pertinent.

While the board of directors of a corporation or the owners of an enterprise must be the ones to reappraise the objectives, management must take the lead in identifying the need for such reappraisal. Oftentimes, management itself will be the group that detects the changing environment that requires a reexamination of the original objectives.

Similarly, a new management may come into the firm, and it will be very desirable for that new person or group to meet with the owners to either reaffirm the original objectives or evolve new ones. One need only scan current business news items to see how changes in ownership or top management are accompanied by alterations in both the general and specific objectives of an institution.

Through continuing appraisal of the firm's progress, through annual audits and other means of examination, management will give continual emphasis to objectives. The progress of the institution, and of each individual who is a part of that institution, must be judged against the criterion of the firm's objectives and the degree to which they are achieved.

QUESTIONS FOR DISCUSSION

1. How does the firm determine its objectives? To what extent are influences external to the firm involved?
2. Identify the advantages that accrue from a clear formulation and statement of objectives.

3. Define what is meant by Management by Objectives (MBO).
4. Explain some of the advantages and disadvantages of MBO.
5. What are the influence of environmental factors on objectives? Give examples.
6. How may objectives be utilized in the management's control process?
7. Discuss the criteria of sound objectives.

REFERENCES

1. William Newman, James Logan, *Strategy Policy and Central Management* (Cincinnati: Southwestern Publishing Co., 1976), 7th ed., pp. 66-67.
2. W.S. Wikstrom, "Setting Targets for Staff," *The Conference Board Record*, vol. 1, no. 10, pp. 32-34, (October, 1964).
3. William D. Guth, "Formulating Organizational Objectives and Strategy: A Systematic Approach," *Journal of Business Policy*, vol 2, no. 1, (Autumn 1971), pp. 24-31.
4. Charles H. Granger, "The Hierarchy of Objectives," *Harvard Business Review*, May-June, 1964, p. 70.
5. *See Chapter 16, "Appraising The Performance of Management," for a discussion of management by objectives as a managerial appraisal technique.
6. Harold Koontz and Cyril O'Donnell, *Management* (New York: McGraw-Hill Book Company, 1976,) pp. 168-171.

SELECTED BIBLIOGRAPHY

1. Ansoff, Igor H. *Corporate Strategy*. New York: McGraw-Hill Book Company, 1965.
2. Carroll, Stephen J.; and Tosi, Henry L., Jr. *Management by Objectives*. New York: The Macmillan Company, 1973.
3. Glueck, William F. *Business Policy: Strategy Formation and Executive Actions*. New York: McGraw-Hill Book Company, 1972.
4. Murdick, Robert G.; Eckhouse, Richard H.; Moor, Carl R.; and Zimmer, Thomas W. *Business Policy: A Framework for Analysis*. 2d ed. Columbus, OH: Grid, Inc., 1976.
5. Rogers, David C. D. *Corporate Strategy and Long Range Planning*. Ann Arbor: The Landis Press, 1973.

CHAPTER 10

POLICIES AND STRATEGIES

Purpose of Chapter 10:

1. To define the nature of policies and their purpose in the firm
2. To explain the difference between external and internal policies as they serve the organization
3. To show how policies are related to organizational principles, objectives and strategies

Essential elements you should understand after studying this chapter:

1. A working definition of policies
2. Various coverage of both internal and external policies throughout the firm
3. How policies are also classified into those relating to both managerial and operative functions
4. The concept of strategy formulation and its relationship to objectives and policies

INTRODUCTION

Organizational objectives, policies, and strategies are closely interrelated concepts. Policies provide a broad guide for decision making as to how the objectives of a firm should be achieved. The firm's policies implement the firm's objectives, as departmental policies implement departmental objectives. Strategies, however, signify a general or specific deployment or commitment of resources toward the accomplishment of the firm's objectives, within the firm's policy guidelines.

For effective management, first, each firm must have comprehensive objectives, as we discussed in the previous chapter. Second, the firm must deploy resources to accomplish the objectives, and third, policies must be formulated and utilized as guides for the commitment of the resources and achievement of objectives.

When one analyzes the situations about which management makes decisions, it is found that they can be divided into two distinct classes. First, some situations encountered are unique. Each is different from others, so that each has to be handled on its own merits. As a consequence, a separate and individual decision-making effort must be made by the manager. Second, some situations encountered are very similar to cases met in the past and are likely to be met again in the future. Each of these cases could be decided separately and individually. But it would seem much wiser to establish a standard decision and apply it to the same type of situation.

Such standard decisions for recurring, similar situations are provided by policies. Policies are among the most useful tools of management. Through policies, the manager affects the work of many people, and is in turn affected by them every day of executive life. Such a significant tool should be thoroughly understood, if it is to be used properly.

NATURE OF POLICIES

Policies are guides to action in that they provide standard decisions for recurring problems of a similar nature. They serve to keep action in line with desired objectives. This concept can be better understood if, first, policies are compared with other guides to action; second, attention is directed to what they are and are not; and third, some thought is devoted to what they can and cannot do.

A number of guides to action are generally used by management. For example as in figure 10-1, a firm's philosophy of management may provide a basic guide to action. Or at times the stated principles of an organization are commonly followed as guides to action. The same is true for the firm's objectives, policies and rules. How do these concepts differ?

Certainly, there is no universal agreement as to the exclusive use of these guides. It is possible, however, to grade these terms as to a general, if overlapping degree of universality and specificity of application.

A philosophy is the broadest guide, covering in general terms every situation an executive may encounter. The statement "We believe that a business enterprise is a living, functioning institution, existing to perform a needed and satisfactory purpose" is an example.

Policies and Strategies 141

Philosophy	... A system of thought that explains basic business problems and supplies the basis for an intelligent approach to their solution.
Principle	... A fundamental truth, an accepted guide or rule of conduct, action, or thought.
Objective	... An end to be achieved; a result to be accomplished.
Policy	... A guide to be followed in performing activities to achieve desired objectives.
Rule	... A mandatory, prescribed course of action or conduct to be followed in a specific situation or localized environment.
Strategy	... A term defining how an organization's objectives are to be achieved. It connotes the plan of action within policy guidelines coupled with the commitment of resources.

Fig. 10-1. A ranking of managerial terms

A principle, conversely, is less abstract, more specific that a philosophy and devolves from it in terms of provising a basis for organizational conduct. The following is a statement of principles of a leading insurance organization.

- We believe that people have within their own hands the tools to fashion their own destinies.
- We believe that by working together people can develop an economy of abundance which will provide a maximum of opportunity, freedom, and security for all.

In contrast to principles, objectives, as we discussed in the previous chapter and as depicted in figure 10-2 are future results to be accomplished in carrying out a particular activity. Objectives are usually specific and realistic. To cite a case, the General Electric Company asks its managers to set objectives in eight key result areas: profitability, market position, productivity, technological leadership, personnel development, employee attitudes, public responsibility, and balance between short- and long-range goals.

Correspondingly, a policy is usually predicated on an objective and reflects a managerial decision based on it. To illustrate, a production objective might be "to produce a balance line of profitable high-quality products, for diversified markets, which lend themselves to modern techniques of engineering and manufacturing." A distinct production policy to implement this objective would be "to maintain rigid quality control tests at all stages of the production process." Figure 10-2 depicts the sequential and incremental relationship among these various guides.

	Rule #1	Rule #2	Rule #3	Rule #4	Rule #5	Rule #6	Rule X
Rules Are Built on →	Policy #1		Policy #2		Policy #3	Policy #4	Policy X
Policies Are Built on →	Objective 1		Objective 2			Objective 3	
Objectives Are Built on →	Principle #1			Principle #2			
Principles Are Built on →	Philosophy						

Fig. 10-2. Sequential relationship of management guides

In summary, then, policies are guides (based upon objectives) for making decisions and taking action in recurring situations, in ways that will lead more successfully to desired objectives. In another diagram form in figure 10-3 the role of policies can be shown as follows:

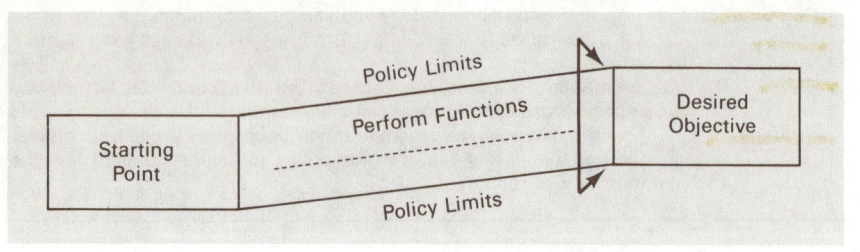

Fig. 10-3. How functions operate within policy limits

By performing functions within the prescribed policy limits, desired objectives will be attained economically and effectively. Policies, it should be noted, are contributors to more effective management, and not a substitute for management.

PURPOSES OF POLICIES

Without policies, managers may reduce their personal effectiveness in a number of ways. They must rethink a decision every time a problem recurs. Beyond that, inconsistency may result since managers may offer different decisions from day to day on given situations. Moreover, they have to be physically present while handing down decisions to subordinates—a great demand on management's limited time.

Without policies, those being managed are subject to a number of disadvantages. To begin with, subordinates must decide for themselves what to do in a given situation or refer the case to their superior. If they decide for themselves, they may be handling something beyond their personal capacities, something beyond their authority limits, or something that involves other organizational units.[1] If they refer the case upwards, they may be repetitiously wasting the time of both their superior and themselves, shrinking from acting in a situation within their capabilities, and simultaneously failing to develop their own skills.

But with policies, all have much to gain. Managers can increase their managerial powers geographically. Through policies they can be in several geographical places at the same time. Management can simultaneously provide decisions in a number of situations involving subordinates literally hundreds of miles apart. Or managers can, through policies, "speak out" from time to time without being physically present.

COVERAGE OF POLICIES

Where and for what subjects may policies be used? In general terms, policies should cover any situations that tend to repeat themselves. Actually, there are few subjects, if any, that could not benefit from the establishment of policies. And while a study of all possible areas is beyond the scope of this text, we will focus on the organizational and functional aspects of policies.

Organizational Coverage

This category classifies policies according to organizational relationships. It may be subdivided into three parts:

1. External policies, or those that guide the organization in relation to various outside groups and agencies
2. Internal vertical policies, or those that, starting from the top, guide successively the various subordinate subdivisions of an organization
3. Internal horizontal policies, or those that serve to coordinate various organizational units at the same level

As the term implies, external policies guide an organization in relation to various outside groups and agencies. They are necessary because an enterprise does not operate in a vacuum. Various dealings and contacts are initiated with governmental, community, business, and union agencies. Merely by way of illustration, such typical policy questions as the following will have to be answered:

1. To what extent should company officials and technical experts be "loaned" to agencies of the federal government?
2. To what extent should financial contributions be made to charitable and educational institutions?
3. To what extent should the company participate in such business groups as trade associations and chambers of commerce?
4. What position should be taken in relation to unions and collective bargaining?

Internal policies of the "vertical" type pertain to those that are intended to guide lower levels of the organization. Initially, broad company policies must be established that serve to guide the entire organization. Just as objectives should be identified for each echelon in the organization, so should accompanying policies be formulated that will facilitate the achievement of those objectives. Then divisions and subdivisions to the lowest level will have policies appropriate for themselves and consistent with higher level policies. (See figure 10-4 for the relationship of policies to organizational principles and objectives.)

Internal policies of the "horizontal" type serve to guide the horizontal relations among various departments. for instance, it may be the stated policy of the company that no department should install a policy until it has determined that the policy is consistent with policies in other departments. To illustrate, if the policy of manufacturing is to stress simplification of product, it would be unwise for salesmen to follow a policy of stressing diversification of lines.

Another area of horizontal policies is that which guides staff departments in their relations with those they serve. As an example of such a policy questions, if the personnel department is assigned the task of hiring, should line departments be forced to accept candidates submitted by the personnel department? Obviously, if there is to be coordination between departments at the same level, policies can serve to achieve this form of integrated effort.

Functional Coverage

This category classifies policies according to the functions to which they pertain. It may be divided into two large classes: policies of managerial functions and those of operative functions.

Policies of managerial functions are established to guide in the performance of planning, organizing, staffing, directing, and controlling.[2] Recurring problems are invariably encountered in connection with each of these functions.

Policies of operative functions are established to guide in the performance of specialized activities. For example, in the field of marketing there is need for policies on such constantly recurring questions as what price systems will be used, what kinds of advertising media will be employed, what allowance there shall be for returned merchandise, and whether private or national brands will be pushed.

Or, in the case of accounting activities, it will be necessary to establish guidelines in such matters as depreciation methods, inventory valuation methods, allowances for reserves and contingencies, and write-offs of bond discounts. Similarly, in other specialized function areas such as public relations, engineering, personnel, and production, policies should be established to guide their performance. (Figure 10-5 is descriptive of some of the areas in which policies are established.)

CHARACTERISTICS OF POLICIES

What constitutes good policy? Policies can be considered effective, if they have the following features:

Purpose

Policies must have adequate purpose and are supposed to guide activities in achieving objectives. They must guide business action to particular goals. A firm that expects its salespeople not only to sell but also to provide technical assistance should be certain its compensation policies, for example, are related to these twin responsibilities. The salespeople, accordingly, should be compensated for their dual functions.

Related to Objectives

Practically all policies serve to attain or affect several objectives simultaneously. So another significant test of any policy is the degree to which it concurrently serves these objectives. Take the case of a firm that has the policy of hiring only college graduates. Assume, moreover, that this policy serves to advance the objectives of producing or distributing the firm's products. But what if there are not enough challenging positions to which the graduates can eventually be promoted? Then the policy fails to serve personal objectives even though it serves the company objectives.

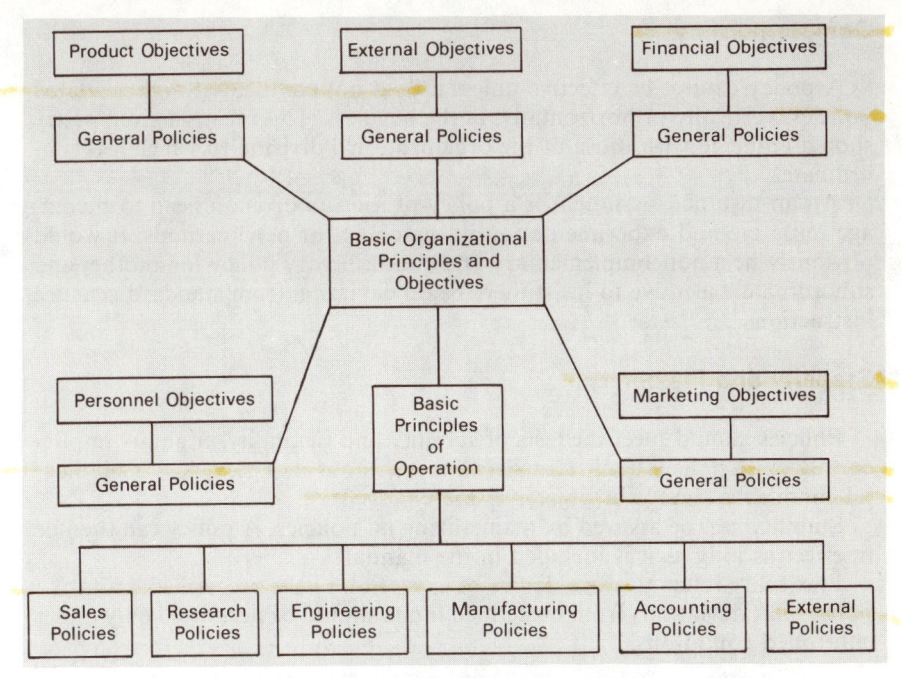

Fig. 10-4. Relationship of policies to organizational principles and objectives

---

Personnel Policies
1. Compensate employees at higher than prevailing rates in the industry.
2. Provide training and developmental opportunities for all employees.
3. Promote, wherever possible, from within the firm.
4. Bear all the financial costs of employee health and welfare programs.

Marketing Policies
1. Distribute products on a national and international level.
2. Advertise only in media directed to the medical profession.
3. Sell a product line of various types and sizes.
4. Keep total expenditures for sales and advertising expenses within 15 percent of gross dollar sales.

Financial Policies
1. Secure capital whenever required by borrowing from long-term creditors.
2. Use profits rather than borrowed funds as a source of additional capital to finance the firm's expansion.
3. Pay regular and stable dividends on both common and preferred stock.
4. Issue preferred stock in preference to common stock as a source of capital.

Production Policies
1. Manufacture products at safety tolerances exceeding industry and governmental standards.
2. Maintain rigid quality control tests at all stages of production.
3. Manufacture products only in the domestic United States.
4. Locate branch production facilities in cities of less than 200,000 population but in densely populated geographical regions.

Fig. 10-5. Functional policies

Complementary

A policy cannot be effective unless it does not conflict with other related policies, vertically or horizontally, in the business. This means a given policy should coincide with those of the organizational division to which it is subordinate.

An an instance, assume it is a policy of a given division head to encourage initiative and experimentation in searching for new methods. It would obviously be a noncomplementary and contradictory policy for another and subordinate executive to insist there be no deviation from standard practice instructions.

Stability and Flexibility

Policies should meet the tests of stability and flexibility. Stability implies constancy. A policy should remain in effect without change, unless fundamental conditions change or objectives are changed.

Stability can be assured by manualizing all policies. A policy can then be in effect as long as it is included in the manual.

Flexibility refers to some degree of exception to the prescribed limits of a policy. But deviations from prescribed limits should be permitted only under controlled conditions.

Fairness and Honesty

Essentially this test is a question of determining that the attainment of a given objective does not unfairly affect other objectives. It might seem fair to produce a high-quality product. Yet, the degree of quality placed into the product should not be at the expense of the employees or stockholders. Or policies that serve to overcharge customers or underpay employees or undercompensate investors are examples of unfairness.

Communication and Acceptance

Finally, a policy must pass the test of being known, understood, and accepted.

Certainly, policies cannot guide, if people are unaware of them. Yet, we all have heard of situations in which subordinates do not know of the existence of policies. Management can, through the printed media, conferences or direct person-to-person contacts, transmit policies to those who are affected by them.

People also must know why policies are established and the reasons behind their adoption. Cooperation, loyalty and positive willingness to follow policies can be expected only of those who understand and accept them.

Formulation

Policy formulation must first initiate with a complete understanding of objectives. Functional as well as organizational objectives must be considered before making policies the guides to action.

Because policies also reflect the philosophy of the company and its management, policy formulation must include the consideration of a broad scope of factors such as trends in economic technology, social responsibility, politics, and international situations.[3]

Participation between and among various levels of management aids in the formulation of policy. Often those who participate in the formulation process will accept and support the ensuing formal policies.

Policy is often considered a part of strategy to both practitioners and students of management. Certain types of policies and strategies may appear to be virtually the same. For example, policies for the firms' growth through acquisition of smaller companies or through development of new products compatible with the present product line are also elements of strategy. But, if these statements are used as guides to decision making, they are considered policy statements. If the statements are coupled with resource commitments, they are considered strategic statements.

NATURE OF STRATEGY

The term strategy defines how an organization's objectives are to be achieved. It connotes the plan of action within policy guidelines coupled with the commitment of resources.

TYPES OF STRATEGIES

There are as many classifications of strategy as there are management textbooks. However, the following types are mentioned in figure 10-6 to illustrate the wide range of the strategy formulation process.

Master Strategies
- Refer to the total nature of the firm's basic objectives and policies as well as general and specific resource implementation
- Also referred to as grand strategies and strategic programs

Substrategies
- Strategies classified per organizational level. For example, a department within a division may develop a detailed department strategy to support the overall divisional strategy

Resource Strategies
- Most strategies deal with resources such as the use of management, personnel, equipment, money, energy or combinations of resources

Functional Strategies
- Various specific strategies must be developed for the commitment of resources to marketing, production, personnel, and finance

---

Fig. 10-6. Classification of strategies

STRATEGY FORMULATION

In the planning chapter it was emphasized that the first phase of strategy formulation was to forecast and analyze the firm's external environment. The discussion included such factors as economics, politics, society, technology, competition, and the structure of distribution. Necessarily, a firm must forecast those variables which it *cannot* control.[4]

The dimensions of strategy, however, encompass all the variables which a firm *can* control. These are plant, product, price, personal selling, advertising, promotion, plant location, research and development, and quality control, as well as other controllable variables.

Dimensions of strategy may also be considered along the time horizon. Strategies are often considered either long-range, over several years; intermediate range, a year or so; or short-range, from the present to a few months. Obviously, developing strategies requires the application of both art and science by the manager.

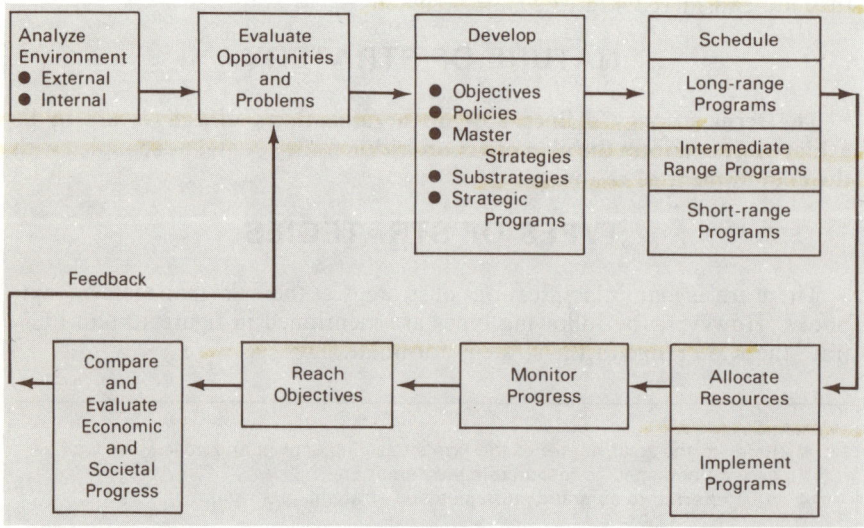

Fig. 10-7. Interdependence of objectives, policies, and strategies

INTERDEPENDENCE OF OBJECTIVES, POLICIES, AND STRATEGIES

To summarize, the management process begins with setting objectives. It begins at the top with clear and consistent objectives being developed throughout the entire organization. Long-range objectives must be developed, before short-range and immediate objectives can be considered, in order to establish continuity of action throughout the organization.

Policies are the guidelines to achieving these company objectives. They ensure uniformity of organizational actions that carry out goal attainment. Management must thoroughly analyze the external and internal constraints to the organization, such as economic trends, competition, or changes in technology, before policies may be developed.

Strategies, then, are the mix and implementation of objectives and policies specifically in that strategies require resources to be committed and action to be taken as we depict in figure 10-7. Success is achieved when the various kinds of strategies pay off in the desired goal attainment.

THE ROLE OF CENTRAL MANAGEMENT

Top management must necessarily be concerned with the total perspective of the organization. Managers should have an integrated understanding of the missions, priorities, and plans of running the organization.[5] This task of synthesizing all of the parts into the total thrust of the organization should be the distinctive responsibility of the firm's leadership.

Futuristic Approach

To maintain a forward thrust, top management must continuously analyze and develop strategies regarding all the controllable factors within the business organization. The executive group must then develop policies to clarify and guide managerial actions throughout the organization. This must be a formalized procedure that also indicates who is responsible for specific goals and objectives. Management must, moreover, set up an organization to carry out the various functional policies and strategies. And finally, top management is responsible for initiating and implementing these strategies throughout the total organization.

Therefore, top management initiates and designs the varoius policies and strategies with regard to the future of the organization. Management must develop the organization and direct the total organizational efforts with respect to carrying on the business. This is a continuous and dynamic process of integration.

QUESTIONS FOR DISCUSSION

1. Define and discuss the nature of policies and their relationship to objectives.
2. Differentiate among the terms *principle, objective, policy,* and *strategy*.
3. Explain some possible major functional policies of the business firm.
4. Discuss the characteristics of an effective policy.
5. There are many classifications of strategies. What types were mentioned in this chapter?
6. Summarize the interdependence of objectives, policies, and strategies.
7. Discuss top management's role with respect to policies and strategies.

REFERENCES

1. E. Raymond Corey and Steven H. Star, *Organization Strategy: A Marketing Approach* (Cambridge: Harvard University Press, 1971), chapter 1.
2. David C.D. Rogers, *Business Policy and Planning* (Englewood Cliffs, NJ: Prentice-Hall, Inc., 1977), pp. 211-13.
3. C. Roland Christensen, Kenneth R. Andrews, and Joseph L. Bower, *Business Policy*, 3rd ed. (Homewood, IL: Richard D. Irwin, Inc., 1973), pp. 229-33.
4. H.W. Lanford, *Technological Forecasting Methodologies* (New York: American Management Association, 1972), pp. 145-52.
5. Erich Jantsch, *Technological Planning and Social Futures* (New York: John W. Wiley, 1972), pp. 46-47.

SELECTED BIBLIOGRAPHY

1. Ackoff, Russell L. *A Concept of Corporate Planning.* New York: John Wiley and Sons, Inc., 1970.
2. Ansoff, H. Igor. *Corporate Strategy: An Analytic Approach to Business Policy For Growth and Expansion.* New York: McGraw-Hill, Inc., 1965.
3. Bonge, John, and Coleman, Bruce R. *Concepts For Corporate Strategy.* New York: The Macmillan Company, 1972.
4. McNichols, Thomas J. *Executive Policy and Strategic Planning.* New York: McGraw-Hill, Inc., 1977.
5. Murdick, Robert G., Eckhouse, Richard H., Moor, R. Carl, and Zimmerer, Thomas W. *Business Policy: A Framework for Analysis.* Columbus, OH: Grid Publishing, Inc., 1972.
6. Newman, William H., and Logan, James P. *Strategy, Policy, and Central Management.* 7th ed. Cincinnati: South-Western Publishing Co., 1976.
7. Steiner, George A. *Business and Society.* 2d ed. New York: Random House, 1975.

CHAPTER 11

UNDERSTANDING INDIVIDUAL BEHAVIOR

Purpose of Chapter 11:

1. To define and discuss the concept and process of individual motivation
2. To evaluate current motivational theories and their relevance to understanding behavior
3. To apply a program of motivational theories to everyday organizational settings

Essential elements you should understand after studying this chapter:

1. A definition of individual motivation
2. Need theories of Maslow, Herzberg, and McClelland
3. Vroom's Expectancy Theory and its assumptions
4. Money as a motivator
5. Application of motivation theory through job enlargement, flextime, and job enrichment

INTRODUCTION

For students of management concerned with the task of managing the efforts of others, clearly it is most crucial to have an understanding of both individual and group behavior. It is important to know what causes people to behave as they do in the same organizational setting. Just as important, too, is the need for the manager to translate this knowledge of behavior into distinct motivational opportunities in order to achieve desired and necessary goals within the environment of the firm.

MOTIVATION PROCESS

For working purposes, motivation is defined as an inner state or condition that activates and directs behavior toward the achievement of certain goals. It is a process of selecting and directing certain actions among voluntary activities to achieve those goals.[1]

```
1. Identification of Need
       ↓
2. Search for Means of Satisfaction
       ↓
3. Goal-directed Behavior
       ↓
4. Fulfillment of Needs
       ↓
5. Evaluation of Goal-directed Behavior
       ↓
6. Reassessment of Needs
```

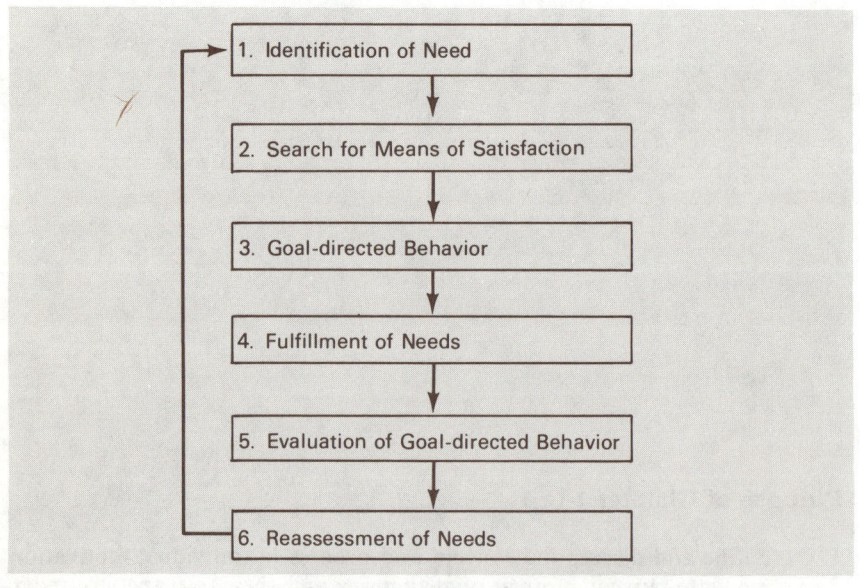

Fig. 11-1. Process model of motivation

As we illustrate in figure 11-1, the process of motivation begins with an initial urge, tension, or drive, followed by a search for the means of satisfying the need through the selection of certain goal-directed behavior, until the fulfillment of that need is achieved. At this stage performance is evaluated to determine its effectiveness in terms of whether it has satisfied the need. The process renews itself with the reassessment of need satisfaction and the subsequent identification of residual and/or new needs for satisfaction.

Certainly, the study of motivation is not an easy task. The task is, furthermore, complicated by the fact that the subject itself is not one totally founded on scientific principles—in other words, it is not yet a science in the truest sense of the word. As a subject it deals with many different variables that influence goal-directed behavior of the person. Individual characteristics such as needs, interests, attitudes, and goals all have a definite influence on motivated behavior. Moreover, within the organization itself characteristics such as the tasks being performed, managerial practices, the climate or setting in which activities take place also can profoundly influence the motivated behavior of people.[2]

Attaining both individual and organizational goals concurrently is, therefore, a function of motivated work behavior. Individuals within organizations are, and need to be, motivated to satisfy their personal goals as they simultaneously work to achieve certain desirable goals of the institution. In sum, then, highly motivated managers and workers are essential to the very survival of the institution.

What all this means to management is that there is an implicit responsibility to know and understand the motivational process and to incorporate its features into the organizational system so as to stimulate people to contribute their optimum effort.

MOTIVATIONAL THEORIES

While there are several theories of motivation for application within the organization, we will center our discussion on two major categories. These are the so-called need theories of motivation, and the expectancy theory of motivation.

Need Theories of Motivation

The foundation on which all need theories must be built is the satisfaction of human needs and wants. Patently, the actions of all normal human beings are for the purpose of satisfying, as far as possible, those needs, wants, or values that sustain and give meaning to life.

Basically, we live, act, and function, to maintain life through food, shelter, and clothing. We feel the need to protect ourselves from various risks of living, so certain security needs must be sought. We are emotional and gregarious beings, so sound emotional health and a satisfying social sense are obvious needs. We are continually growing and developing human beings, so creativity, personal challenges, and self-fulfillment are basic needs. Essentially, our individual need hierarchy is influenced by a combination of organizational, personal, and social determinations as shown in figure 11-2.

Consequently, in support of this, there are three important need theories to which we turn our attention: Maslow's Need Hierarchy, Herzberg's Two-factor Theory and McClelland's Achievement Need Theory.

Maslow's Need Hierarchy

Abraham Maslow's theory is based upon the assumption that basic human needs exist in a hierarchy that consists of five categories as charted in figure 11-3. Theoretically, at least, a person moves through the levels of this hierarchy stage by stage. After the lower level needs—physiological and security—are satisfied in that order, the individual procedes to the higher order of

ORGANIZATIONAL
- Status
- Role
- Responsibilities
- Level of Job Success
- Company Experiences

INDIVIDUAL NEED HIERARCHY

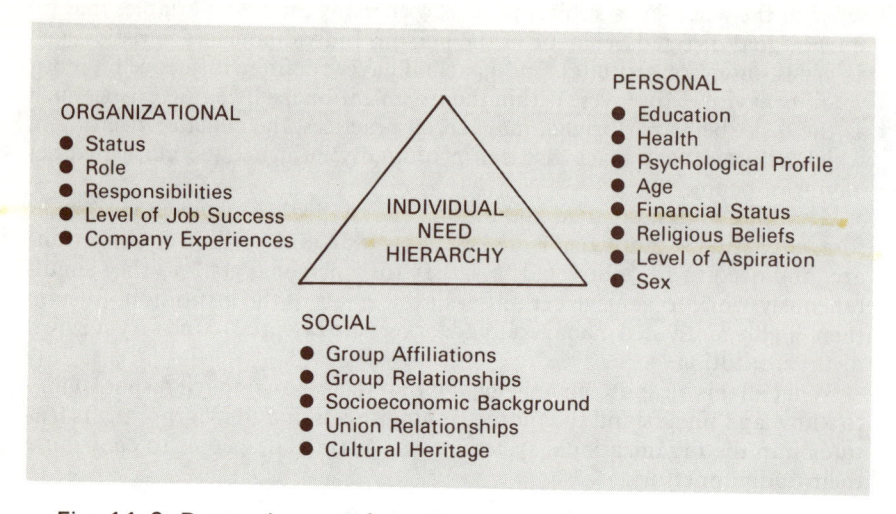

PERSONAL
- Education
- Health
- Psychological Profile
- Age
- Financial Status
- Religious Beliefs
- Level of Aspiration
- Sex

SOCIAL
- Group Affiliations
- Group Relationships
- Socioeconomic Background
- Union Relationships
- Cultural Heritage

Fig. 11-2. Determinants of the Need Hierarchy for an Individual

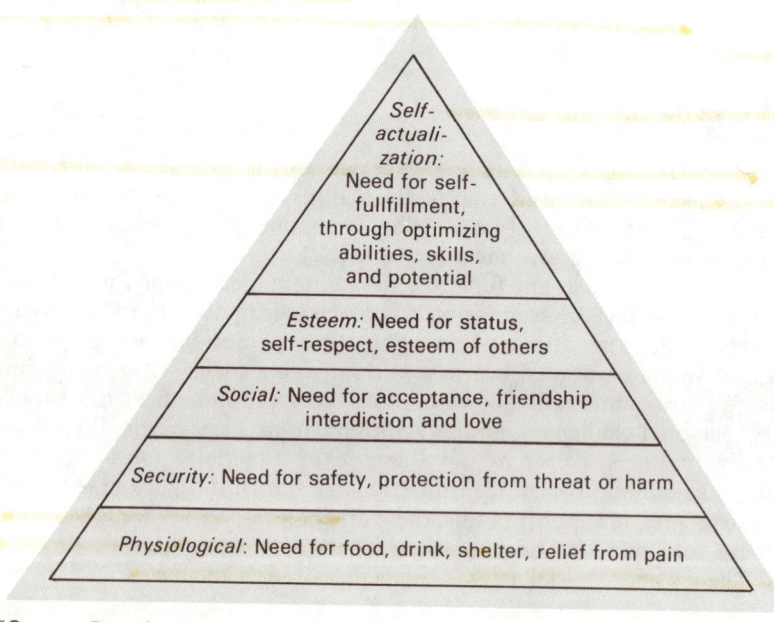

Self-actualization: Need for self-fullfillment, through optimizing abilities, skills, and potential

Esteem: Need for status, self-respect, esteem of others

Social: Need for acceptance, friendship interdiction and love

Security: Need for safety, protection from threat or harm

Physiological: Need for food, drink, shelter, relief from pain

*Source: Data (for diagram) based on Hierarchy of Needs in "A Theory of Human Motivation" in *Motivation and Personality*, 2d edition by Abraham H. Maslow, Copyright 1970 by Abraham H. Maslow, reprinted by permission of Harper & Row, Publishers, Inc.

Fig. 11-3. Maslow's hierarchy of needs

needs; social esteem and self-actulization. This implies that some needs such as physiological and security must be relatively satisfied before higher order needs such as creativity or self-fulfillment can be sought effectively. Critical, according to Maslow's theory, is that a need once satisfied ceases to motivate. For example, when an employee feels he is being adequately compensated for his efforts, then money itself may lose its power to motivate.

While such in general terms may be the case, it is still not easy to indicate the exact order of priority that individuals will establish for themselves. To illustrate, some people may well prefer to concentrate their activities on creative risk-taking at the expense of basic food needs. And since a manager often must deal with people on a one-to-one-basis, in contrast with employees in general, this difference should be recognized.

It would certainly be unrealistic to deny that people, generally speaking, have certain basic needs which motivate them to action. Fundamentally, all people have such basic needs and wants. But as yet we cannot specify with definite precision to what degree or in what order particular people are motivated by those needs.

Herzberg's Two-Factor Need Theory

Frederick Herzberg is the author of a two-factor theory of motivation. The original research underlying his theory is based on a study of 200 engineers and accountants. The two factors referred to are termed *satisfiers* and *dissatisfiers*. His study concluded that some job conditions operate to dissatisfy employees when the conditions are not present, but their presence, on the other hand, does not strongly motivate employees.

These strong dissatisfiers are also known as *maintenance* or *hygiene factors*, since they support satisfaction of a reasonable level. In other words, if these conditions are present, this does not necessarily motivate employees. But, if they are not present, then dissatisfaction results. Maintenance factors are concerned primarily with the job context or environment. Extrinsic in character, they, incidentally, lie mostly on the left half of the scale on figure 11-4, and include:

1. Company policy, procedures and administration
2. Quality of technical supervision
3. Salary
4. Quality of interpersonal relations among peers, with superiors, and with subordinates
5. Working conditions

Motivational factors or satisfiers are concerned more with the job content and the satisfaction gained from job performance. Intrinsic in nature, they lie mostly on the right half of the scale on figure 11-4. When present, these conditions can build strong levels of motivation which can result in good job conditions build strong levels of motivation which can result in good job performance. Employees are presumed to be motivated to obtain more of them.[3]

They are:

1. Achievement
2. Recognition
3. Work itself
4. Responsibility
5. Advancement

There are certain criticisms leveled at the Herzberg theory, such as it oversimplifies the nature of job satisfaction, and also that his theory is based on a limited, and not truly representative, sample of accountants and engineers. Yet his work clearly demonstrates those conditions necessary to effective motivation in the organizational environment. As such, his model is extremely popular, understandabale, and definitely applicable to work settings.

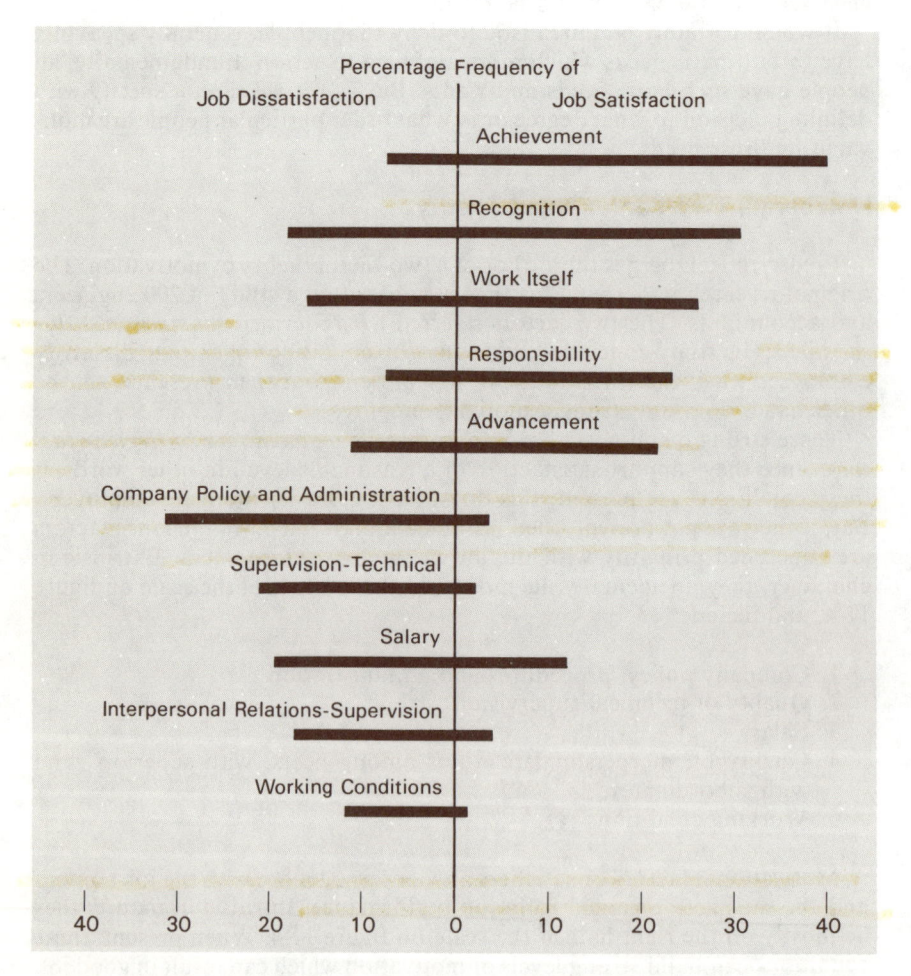

*Source: Frederick Herzberg, Bernard Mausner, and Barbara Block Snyderman, *The Motivation To Work,* (New York: John Wiley and Sons, Inc., 1959), p. 81. (Used with permission.)

Fig. 11-4. A comparison of satisfiers and dissatisfiers

McClelland's Achievement Need Theory

David McClelland of Harvard University has conducted motivational studies indicating that unlike Maslow's theory, many needs are neither physiological or universal in nature. Rather these needs are socially acquired and vary from culture to culture. McClelland, in his research, has identified three types of acquired needs: the need for achievement (n Ach), the need for affiliation (n Aff), and the need for power (n Pow).[4]

The need for achievement manifests itself in a high concern for success and an equal concern for failure. People with a high need for achievement prefer to set moderate task goals, to initiate decisions, to accept responsibility for their work, and to receive prompt feedback on their performance.

The need for affiliation demonstrates a desire to be accepted for social interaction with others. People with a high need for affiliation seem to evidence a concern for pleasant, interpersonal relationships.

The need for power reflects the desire for exercising influence and control over others. People with a high need for power generally seek power and authority and positions of leadership.

McClelland's theory holds significant meaning for managerial motivation. Different needs of people express themselves in different behavior patterns. Simultaneously, different managerial positions require different behavior patterns. Consequently, and although it is not an easy task, the organization can improve managerial performance by attempting to match the motivational characteristics of individuals with the requirements of the job.

Expectancy Theory of Motivation

The theories of Maslow, Herzberg, and McClelland are basically *content* in nature; that is, they focus on the needs and incentives that cause behavior. Expectancy Theory, on the other hand, is *process* in nature; it is concerned with the questions of how individual behavior is energized, directed, and maintained.

Expectancy Theory owes much to the efforts of Victor Vroom, who developed a model of motivation somewhat different from those of Maslow and Herzberg.[5] Whereas Maslow's concept is one structured along fixed need positions, and Herzberg's is dichotomized into a dual class of motivations, Vroom's model is based upon "path-goal" theory. Built into the "Path-goal" Theory is the assumption that individual motivation is a process of choosing between types of behavior to attain particular goals. More concretely, this means that if an individual's path-goal perception is positive, then productivity will be high. Conversely, if negative, that is, if the individual does not perceive his behavior will attain particular goals, then productivity will be low.

Expectancy Theory, according to its proponents, is predicated upon three main concepts: performance-outcome expectancy, valence, and effort-performance expectancy. *Performance-outcome expectancy* is defined simply as the individual's belief that certain behavior will result in certain outcomes or rewards. Each outcome, furthermore, has a valence (a value, worth, or attraction) to a specific individual. Outcomes have different valences for different individuals due to differing needs and perceptions. Effort-performance expectancy represents the individual's perception of the difficulty of achieving certain expected work performance and with it the probability of successful achievement.

When combined into one approach, these concepts construct a basic statement about motivation. In general, the motivation to attempt to behave in a certain way is greatest when:[6]

1. The individual believes that the behavior will lead to outcomes.
2. The individual believes these outcomes have positive value for him or her.
3. The individual believes that he or she is able to perform at the desired level.

A very useful interpretation of the Expectancy Theory model for understanding behavior in organizations is one based upon certain and specific assumptions.[7] These assumptions are:

1. Individuals have unique sets of needs and expectations about how organizations will treat them.
2. Individuals decide about their own behavior as a member of the organization in coming and staying at work and about the amount of effort they exert in performing their jobs.
3. Individuals differ in terms of needs, desires, goals, and rewards.
4. Individuals tend to do those things which they see as leading to outcomes (rewards) they desire and avoid doing those things they see as leading to outcomes that are not desired.

What implications does the foregoing Expectancy Theory hold for managers desiring to motivate improved performance of their people?[8] Managers who are ever conscious of their role in moving toward certain objectives should:

1. Determine outcomes each employee values. What turns on him or her?
2. Determine what kinds of behavior is desired. What are acceptable indicators of performance in terms of quantity and quality?
3. Make sure desired levels of performance are attainable.
4. Link desired outcomes to desired performance.
5. Analyze the total situation for conflicting expectancies.
6. Associate rewards with good performance.
7. Make sure changes in outcomes are large enough to motivate significant behavior. Trivial rewards result in trivial effort and thus trivial improvement.
8. Check the system for its equity. The system must be a fair one with good performers in the system receiving more desired rewards than poor performers.

Money As a Motivator

What is the importance of money as a motivational technique in the contemporary organization? During the scientific management period of Taylor, money was listed as a most significant incentive for the "economic man" during that period shortly after the turn of the century. Piece-rate incentive systems were much in vogue then to stimulate worker productivity. But as the concept of "economic man" changed over time to that of "social man," it was argued that worker behavior and productivity were more influenced by social factors such as group pressure and supervisory attitudes rather then economic factors.[9]

It is an obvious truism that money is important. But its importance varies with the need structure of the individual. It is most important, apparently, to individuals satisfying the lower level physiological and security needs. But as these needs are satisfied, it has less importance, unless it can satisfy other needs.[10]

When analyzed in the light of Herzberg's Two-factor Theory, money is not merely a hygiene factor. It can also be a motivator insofar as it represents factors that make up Herzberg's satisfiers. For example, increased pay may be given as a recognition of performance, or granted in connection with job advancement or even related to the individual's job achievement. As such, then, money is a motivating consideration. Money per see, though, is not a motivating factor; it is what money represents that is actually motivating.

David McClelland's research[11] of money motivation indicates that whether workers or managers are high or low in achievement motivation determines the effectiveness of financial incentives. People with relatively low achievement motivation will work harder for increased money rewards. Apparently, neither the task nor money itself interests the low achiever as a measure of accomplishment. Rather, and here again as with Herzberg, its importance lies in those things money can buy. High achievers, on the other hand, attach special significance to money and see it as a concrete measure of how well they have performed.

FROM CONCEPTS TO PRACTICE

With a better understanding of the concepts of the major motivational theories, it is possible for management to construct sound, workable programs for more effective employee motivation. Workable programs, in this context, constitute a course of action that allow the application of motivational theories to everyday organizational settings.

When constructing practical programs, management should certainly recognize that work motivation depends highly on the personal commitment of the worker since the institution, in and of itself, does not exert direct control over an individual's motivation. However, and beyond that, the organization can indirectly influence the behavior of its employees through the use of those extrinsic, social, intrinsic, and job-related incentives which incorporate the following strategical prerequisites.[12]

1. Organizational incentives should be matched to the needs of the people. This not only enhances the incentive's value, but also results in greater employee satisfaction.
2. Organizational rewards should be related to task performance. Identifying task performance with rewards, either individually or collectively, not only increases the value of the task, but also insures the mutual dependency of achieving individual as well as organizational goals.

3. Rewards should be challenging but attainable. If rewards are improbable to attain, they will quickly lose their incentive value.

Extrinsic Organizational Incentives

In generating organizational incentives, the institution can, as we cited, initiate those that are extrinsic, social, job related, or intrinsic in nature. By extrinsic we mean those substantive and positive elements relating to satisfactory pay, working conditions, and job security. These incentives have a special influence on worker motivation and productivity for those striving for basic physiological, lower-order need satisfaction and where incentive rewards are directly related to performance that is challenging but yet attainable.

Social Incentives

Social or interactive incentives are those related to established and accepted group norms, a higher degree of trust and openness in relationships with others, opportunity for risk-taking behavior in work, and effective supervision by management.

Job-related Incentives

Task or job-related incentives refer to those incentives developing out of such organizationally structures programs as job enrichment, job enlargement, and flexible working hours (Flextime).

1. **Job Enrichment.** The purpose of job enrichment is to incorporate higher levels of challenge and achievement in jobs by giving people more freedom in decisions about important job factors. It means allowing a participative voice in matters pertaining to equipment layout, work methods, and sequences. Job enrichment, moreover, includes involving people in decisions affecting work environment and conditions.[13]
2. **Job Enlargement.** This concept is often termed *horizontal job loading* because it expands tasks horizontally. The worker, instead of performing a segment or a fragment of the job, produces a whole unit of a major portion of a job. Job enlargement sometimes is considered synonymous with job enrichment. However, there is a big difference in that job enlargement requires changes in the technical aspects of the job, while job enrichment requires changes in the behavioral aspects of an organization.
3. **Flextime.** This is an increasingly popular system[14] that provides employee's incentives in the form of extended weekends or flexibility in scheduling their own work. Employees can work four ten-hour days each week or vary their starting or quitting times without reducing hours of work. While the program is practical for manufacturing personnel on continuous production schedules, the plan may not be suitable for jobs relating to shift work or to highly interdependent operations.

Intrinsic Incentives

Finally, intrinsic incentives have reference to the kind of motivation generated as a result of the task accomplishment. It means that satisfying and successful task performance produces feelings of success, achievement, and ego involvement. These intrinsic rewards, then, satisfy the high-order needs of self-respect and self-actualization. In addition, the task elements of the job such as its variety, autonomy, and built-in feedback mechanism directly control the probability that the effort will lead to task accomplishment.[15]

QUESTIONS FOR DISCUSSION

1. Define motivation. What is the relationship of effective motivation to effective management?
2. What are some of the important obstacles that must be overcome in motivating people?
3. Discuss the practicality of applying Herzberg's Two-factor Theory to an organization.
4. Compare and contrast the Maslow and Herzberg theories of motivation. What criticisms have been leveled at these two popular theories?
5. Describe McClelland's achievement need theory in terms of its acpplication by management.
6. The Expectancy Theory includes the concepts of performance outcome expectancy, valence, and effort-performance expectancy. What are the meanings of these concepts? Evaluate pay as a motivator.
7. Describe what you think might be major problems in applying Expectancy Theory concepts of motivation.
8. Differentiate between job enrichment and job enlargement.

REFERENCES

1. Kae H. Chung, *Motivational Theories and Practices* Columbus, OH: Grid, Inc. 1977), p. 7.
2. Ibid., p. 7.
3. Frederick Herzberg, Bernard Mausner, and Barbara Block, Snyderman, *Motivation to Work* (New York: John Wiley & Sons, Inc., 1959), p. 61.
4. David D. McClelland, *The Achieving Society* (Princeton, NJ: Van Nostrand, Inc., 1961).
5. Victor Vroom, *Work and Motivation* (New York: John Wiley & Sons, 1964).
6. David A. Nadler and Edward E. Lawler, III, "Motivation, a Diagnostic Approach," *Perspectives on Behavior In Organizations*, edited by J. Richard Hackman, Edward E. Lawler III, and Lyman W. Porter (New York: McGraw-Hill Book Co., 1977), pp. 26-34.
7. Largely taken from David A. Nadler and Edward E. Lawler III, op. cit.
8. Ibid., pp. 26-34.
9. Chung, op. cit., p. 138.
10. Chung, op. cit., p. 139.
11. David C. McClelland, "Money As A Motivator: Some Research Insights," *The McKinsey Quarterly* (New York: McKinsey and Co., Inc., Fall 1967).
12. Adapted largely from Chung, *Motivational Theories and Practices* (Columbus, OH: Grid, Inc.), pp. 10-11, 190-93.
13. This concept, popularized by Herzberg, is based upon the assumption that factors necessary for psychological growth such as responsibility, job challenge, and

achievement must be in addition to hygiene factors for satisfactory performance.
14. General Accounting Administration estimates about 1.5 million to 2.2 million federal employees on Flextime: *Cleveland Plain Dealer*, Cleveland, OH, 1 January 1978, sec. 6, p. 1.
15. Chung op. cit., p. 50-53.

SELECTED BIBLIOGRAPHY

1. Chung, Kae H. *Motivational Theories and Practices.* Columbus, OH: Grid, Inc. 1977.
2. Lawler, Edward E., III. *Motivation In Work Organizations.* Monterey, CA: Brooks/Cole, 1973.
3. Porter, Lyman W., and Lawler, Edward E., III. *Managerial Attitudes and Performance.* Homewood, IL: Richard D. Irwin, Inc., 1968.
4. Porter, Lyman W.; Lawler, Edward E., III; and Hackman, J. Richard. *Behavior In Organizations.* New York: McGraw-Hill Book Co., 1975.
5. Stogdill, Ralph M. *Individual Behavior and Group Achievement.* New York: Oxford University Press, 1959.
6. Vroom, Victor. *Work and Motivation.* (New York: John Wiley & Sons, Inc., 1964.

CHAPTER 12

UNDERSTANDING GROUP BEHAVIOR

Purpose of Chapter 12:

1. To define and discuss the concept and process of group behavior
2. To classify the different types of groups and their functions
3. To discuss certain characteristics common to group behavior
4. To clarify the effect of the larger organization upon the group

Essential elements you should understand after studying this chapter:

1. Reasons why people form groups
2. Different types of organizational groups
3. Task and maintenance group functions
4. Group norms, values, status and cohesion
5. Groups and their role in decision making
6. Effect of large organizations upon group members
7. How the group adjusts to the impact of larger organizations

WHY UNDERSTAND GROUP BEHAVIOR?

The contemporary manager recognizes more than ever the need to understand not only individual but, increasingly, the dynamics of group behavior. Historically, the emphasis has been on the study of individual and interpersonal behavior and its various components and factors. But since groups greatly influence our working lives and very much dominate the organizational setting and its activities, more and more attention is being directed to comprehending aspects of group behavior.

A group is much more than a collection of people who work, play, or live together. Groups have special characteristics and distinctive aspects, not readily apparent to the casual observer. But they are, nonetheless, aspects that exert a profound influence on group members themselves and group performance in the organization. Effective managers must have a good sense of these aspects of group behavior and their importance in achieving their personal objectives as well as those of the firm.

Managers must be aware that individual motivation and striving, personal satisfaction levels and feelings of right and wrong are very much affected by the groups in which people function. Moreover, there is the fact that these factors can and do change as people move from one group to another. Why? Simply because each group in the organization is different and since each group is different, people behave and think differently. For example, it is not unusual to find that basically competent employees can be rendered incompetent or ineffective as a result of the particular group in which they work. Similarly, an ineffective worker in one group can become highly effective in another. Clearly, management needs to know and understand much more than just the worker alone, if it is to predict future behavior.

WHAT ARE GROUPS?

A group may be defined as two or more people who are dependent upon one another to achieve some objective. Each person occupies a social position with respect to the others that heavily influences the work the individual performs alone and with others in the group setting. The interaction of its members is guided by informal rules of conduct, known as norms, and also by explicit formal rules or procedures of the firm. Finally, to be identified as a group, the members need to have some sense of "we-ness," of togetherness, a perception that they have a distinct entity with a specific mission in contributing to organizational goals, as depicted in figure 12-1, where two groups in an organization, each with its own position, norms, and goals, and affected by organizational rules, contribute to goal attainment of the larger organization.

REASONS PEOPLE FORM GROUPS

People in the organization seem to form groups for reasons that relate to the individual's needs for social interaction, identification, personal support and work situations, and goal achievement.[1]

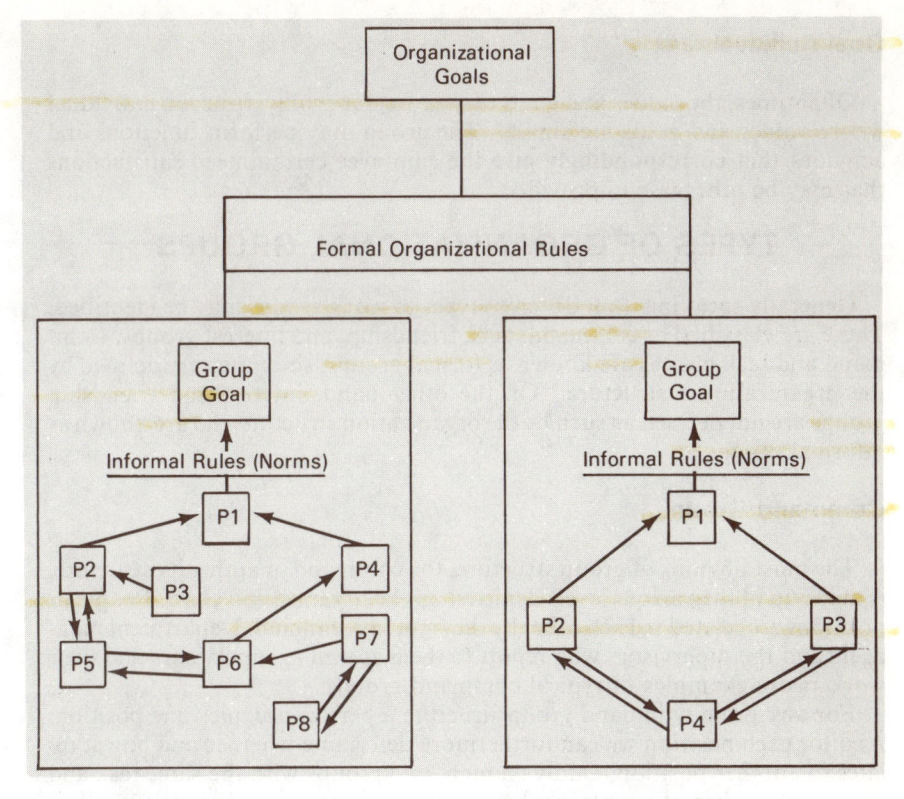

Fig. 12-1. Group formation in the organization

Social Interaction

Some individuals join groups to establish social contacts, to be able to share ideas, thoughts and attitudes about the work as well as outside activities. Working as a group often results in increased individual motivation and higher productivity.

Identification

People feel the need to belong, and while they may be part of a larger organization, they find job satisfaction in working with and sharing experiences with immediate co-workers in a smaller group.

Personal Support

As members of a group, individuals seek and receive support in work situations. The work group offers guides to correct behavior, skill development, and solutions to work problems that, however effective, may differ from established policy or procedure. The group, moreover, develops a certain loyalty to its members and leader as well.

Goal Achievement

Oftentimes, the values and goals of a particular group attract an individual whose values and goals are similar. The group may perform functions and activities that correspondingly give the employee certain need satisfactions that may be otherwise unprovided.

TYPES OF ORGANIZATIONAL GROUPS

Generally speaking, four different types of work groups may be identified. These are classified as command, task, friendship, and interest groups. Command and task groups are known as formal groups, since they are defined by the organizational structure.[2] On the other hand, interest and friendship groups are not defined as such by the organization structure and are known as informal groups.

Command Group

The most obvious of group structure, the command or authority structure, is made up of the various levels depicted on the organization chart. People or positions are related to each other by the right to command. Department managers and the supervisors who report to them as well as supervisors and their workers are examples of typical command groups.

For any given command group structure a person occupies one position. And for each position we can furthermore determine whether and how it relates to another position. Oddly enough, two groups with the same task and the same number of people can have a different structure. Figure 12-2 illustrates this idea for a five-person group structured according to command or authority.

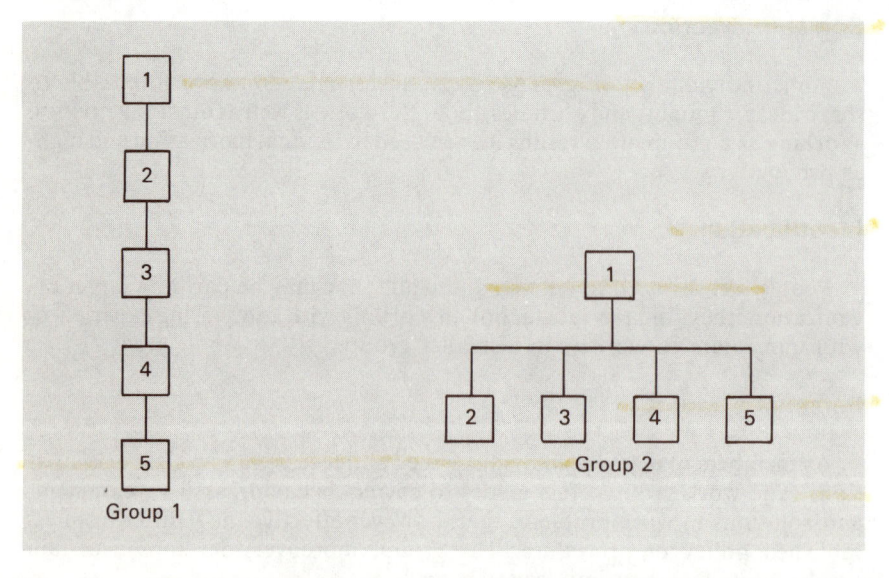

Fig. 12-2. Model of a command group structure

In group 1, you will note, there are five levels (positions) of authority. Position 1 has authority over position 2 and so on down to position 5 which has no authority. Group 2, however, has only two levels of authority. Position 1 has authority over the other four positions. Positions 2-5 have no authority over each other.

While it is important to remember that a work group can have different structural patterns, more important is the degree to which these different patterns affect group performance and member behavior.

How efficiently a group performs its tasks, the extent of completion, member anxiety, satisfaction, commitment, feelings about the task, and about other members are all affected by the way a group is structured.[3] Effective management, then, requires a sensitive awareness that structured group patterns, and not necessarily individual behavior, may be responsible for group success or failure in its work.

Task Group

A second type of formal structure in the organization is the task group. It is comprised of employees who must collaborate and work together to complete a particular project or task. A sales office work process requiring coordination and interdependency of activities is an illustration of a task group. A sales office group of three employees, for example, will receive an order from a customer. Procedure will dictate that one employee may be responsible for receiving the order, classifying it as to type of account, and for pricing the merchandise requested. Another is responsible for typing the order, while the third will procure the items from inventory stock, package them and specify the mode of delivery. All the tasks require communication through formal procedures that divide the work among the group and determine its flow. Figure 12-3 identifies the task group relationships.

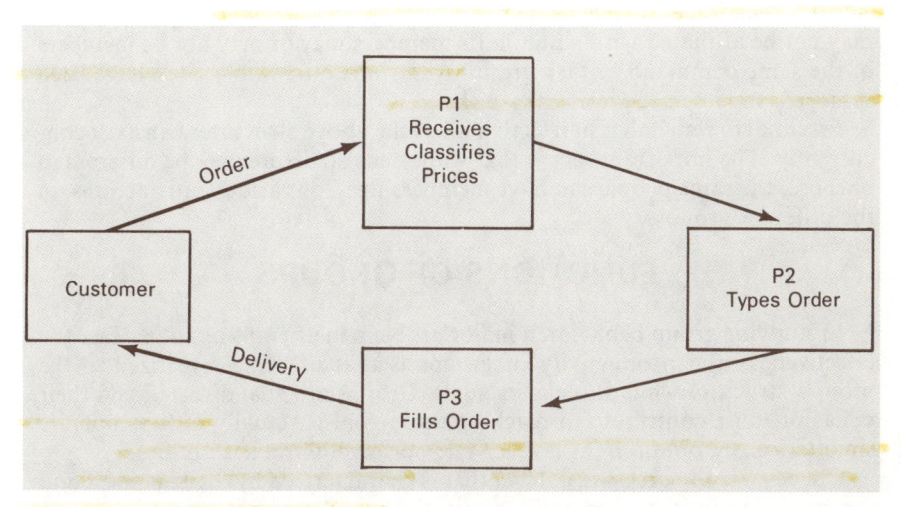

Fig. 12-3. Task Group structure: Sales office task group

Friendship Group

In the typical organization there are any number of friendship groups representing the diverse interests of its people. They are attracted together by certain common characteristics such as age, ethnic background, interest in hobbies or sports, and political or religious affiliation. Often, group interaction extends to relationships outside the organization. Communication channels generally are informal and usually by-pass the established ones of the formal organization. We have illustrated this in figure 12-4.

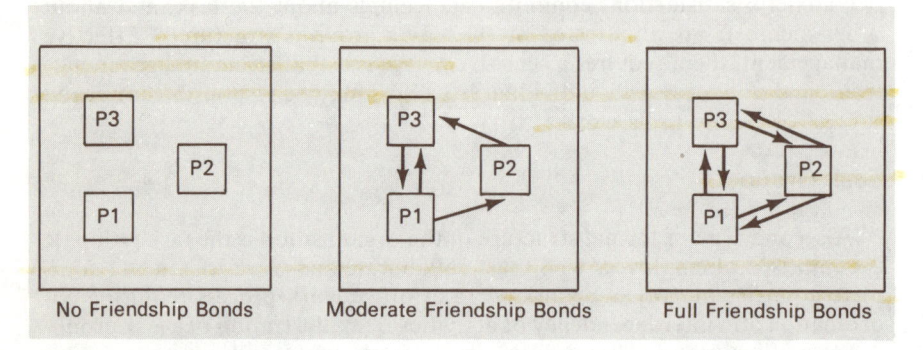

No Friendship Bonds   Moderate Friendship Bonds   Full Friendship Bonds

Fig. 12-4. Friendship group structure: Sales office friendship group

Interest Group

Whereas the friendship group is more stable and permanent, the interest group may exist for a shorter period of time. Normally, these are formed not only for protection of members but also to take advantage of opportunities. Their focus usually is on economic concerns such as wages, benefits, and working conditions, in their relationship with management. The group may or may not be affiliated with a union. Its members may or may not be members of the same command or task group. After the desired objectives have been achieved, the interest group may disband.

Essential to remember here is that all of the above structures can exist concurrently. The important fact is that while each structure may be different in purpose, the same people can have memberships, for various satisfactions, in the different groups.

FUNCTIONS OF GROUPS

In studying group behavior, a major problem in attempting to increase the effectiveness and productivity of groups is that of being sensitized to the group's structure while it seeks its goals. Groups are goal directed and their behavior must contribute to reaching those goals. Actually groups operate simultaneously on different levels while performing their activities.

One level is the group task level that is characterized by the task itself and the group's primary responsibility for it. The second is the group maintenance level. This has to do with people working together as a group on a task and the resulting and constantly changing interactions and relationships that can occur if the task is to be accomplished.

Group Task Functions

These are functions and activities that help facilitate and coordinate group effort in the selection and definition of a common problem and in the solution of that problem. They help the group accomplish the task.[4] They include:

1. Initiating: proposing tasks or goals, defining a group problem, suggesting new procedures or ideas for solving a problem
2. Information or opinion seeking: requesting facts or opinions; seeking relevant information about a group problem; asking for suggestions or ideas
3. Information or opinion giving: offering facts; providing relevant information about group concerns; stating a belief; giving suggestions or ideas
4. Clarifying: interpreting or reflecting ideas and suggestions; clearing up confusions; indicating alternatives and issues before the group
5. Summarizing: bringing together related ideas, restating suggestions after group has discussed them; offering decisions for the group to accept or reject
6. Consensus testing: checking to see if the group is nearing a conclusion; sending up a trial balloon to see how much agreement has been reached

Group Maintenance Functions

These are functions and activities that focus on and help strengthen group-member relationships and that help build and reinforce group feelings and attitudes. They help the group work together and develop loyalty to one another and to the group as a whole.[5]

1. Encouraging: being friendly, warm, and responsive to others and to their contributions; showing regard for others; agreeing with others
2. Expressing group feelings: summarizing what group feeling is sensed to be; describing reactions of the group to ideas or solutions
3. Harmonizing: reducing tension; reconciling disagreements; getting other people to explore differences
4. Compromising: compromising the group's position; admitting error; using self-discipline to maintain group cohesion
5. Gatekeeping: inviting others to participate; keeping communication channels open; suggesting procedures for sharing the discussion of group problems
6. Setting standards: expressing standards for the group to achieve; applying standards for evaluating group performance; stating values or ethics

Groups, it seems, are likely to operate at optimum efficiency when their members perform both task and maintenance functions and when the functions become the responsibility of all members. The functions are not necessarily mutually exclusive. While performing a task function such as suggesting a new approach to a problem, a member may also express the feelings of the entire group (a maintenance function).

CHARACTERISTICS OF GROUPS

True groups have certain definite and distinct qualities. Some of the more important features incidental to organizational group behavior should be identified.

Structure

A difficult aspect about understanding group behavior is the concept of structure. *Group structure simply means that the relationships among the members follow a pattern that can be determined, and those patterned relationships have consequences and effects for each member as well as the group as a whole.* People hold positions in the group and these positions are linked or related to one another by some definite criteria such as power, status, expertise, or skill.

In respect to the types of groups that we discussed earlier, each group has its own structure which may exist simultaneously with the other groups. Furthermore, within a specific organization individuals may belong to a number of different groups. And oftentimes membership in these groups may even overlap as in the case of members of a particular sales group (a task group) being on the same bowling team (an interest group).

Norms and Values

Norms are rules of behavior, or in other words, proper ways of acting that the members, in varying degrees, accept as legitimate for themselves. These norms specify the kinds of accepted social behavior that are expected of group members in their relationship with others, if they want to belong. For instance, all clothing buyers of a department store may lunch daily at a certain restaurant, while the clothing alterations workers, of the same store, may take their lunch daily at a certain table in the firm's cafeteria.

Values, on the other hand, are a much broader class. These are beliefs that group members share about legitimate or worthwhile goals to strive for. For example, a work group can highly value good interpersonal relations among its members. And norms usually are present to make these values attainable. To illustrate, there may be a norm that rejects borrowing or using tools and equipment of other group members. This norm and others like it would support the value of sound interpersonal relations.

Effective managers should remember that every true group has many norms and values that measurably affect not only group objectives, but also those of the manager and the larger organization's goals as well. Work groups establish norms that regulate, among other things, the speed of member work as well as the volume of production of the work group itself. On the other hand, there have been norms and values which truly support the larger organization. Finally, there are norms and values that have little effect on the institution.

A general rule of thumb, though, is that the longer a group has been in existence, the more norms and values will exist and the stronger they will be in controlling member behavior. Similarly, the longer a group has been in existence the more sanctions, in terms of rewards and punishments, it has developed to insure that members follow those norms and values. Of course, some norms and values do not have to be maintained by sanctions but instead are maintained voluntarily by the members who believe in and support those norms and values strongly.

Source of Norms and Values

The souce of norms and values is not always easily identified. Any given person can bring them into a group and then either impose them on the group members or convince the group of their usefulness. They can also arise as a reaction to the requirements or demands of the larger organization. Group leaders are frequently effective in imposing norms and values because they are either respected or have sanctioning power or both. For many professional work groups such as teachers, engineers, physicians, and nurses for instance, norms and values could, moreover, have their source in a professional code to which all have been exposed in their training.

Status

Status is defined as the amount of prestige that a person has within a group. It is directly related to the person's location within the various structures. Status identifies the individual's importance and is also an index as to how well that person helps the group fulfill its values besides maintaining its important norms.

The higher or more central a person's structural position, the more status and prestige there is in the group. Status, incidentally, may be either assigned or ascribed to a particular position.[6] Assigned status is a result of certain characteristics that differentiate one position from the other depending on the organization. In one firm high status may be assigned the research and development division, while sales in another firm may hold higher status. Ascribed status, on the other hand, derives from such factors as job seniority, age, work assignment, skills, or political influence or the particular group members.

Formal Rules versus Norms and Values

Formal rules are those that are imposed on the group members by the larger organization and its executives. These rules, unlike norms and values, are usually written and communicated. They can generally be found in job descriptions or in lists of organizational procedures. These rules are developed to help the organization maintain itself and also reach its goals. Rules about how to deal with customers or how to fill out forms, whom to see when a problem results, and so on would fall into this category.

One major distinction between rules and norms is that rules are usually imposed on the group while norms emerge from the group as a means of everyday functioning. The compatibility between formal rules and group norms can have important consequences. If the group's norms support the rules and goals of the larger organization, there will likely be a very smooth operation with satisfied group members. If, however, they are contradictory, then problems can result. When such a situation emerges, group members may possibly become devious in attempting to hide their violation of the rule of the larger organization.

If the rule is not terribly important, the organization may ignore the violation (if it is discovered). On the other hand, though, if the rule violation is important, or if the superior becomes uptight over it, then open conflict may result. At the extreme, a conflict between many organizational rules and group norms will result in severe demoralization of group members. This can lead to significant member turnover, lower productivity, and subsequently, a generally unhappy situation for all.[7]

Similarly, the more ability a person exercises in helping a group fulfill its values and maintain its important norms, the more status that person will enjoy. In understanding group behavior, it is important to assess this characteristic, since normally the more status people have the greater is their ability to influence other members. High status group members are usually the group leaders.

Deviant Group Behavior

Deviance exists when a member is not following the norms or official procedures of the group. One point to remember here is that no act or behavior is inherently deviant. For an act to be deviant the particular group must define it as such. In the case of a work group there are actually two potential sources of deviance.

The first is where an individual violates the norms or official rules of the work group itself. In this case the act will be deviant to the members of the work group but not necessarily to workers in other groups or to the larger organization. For example, a work group may have a long established informal rule as to how and when work breaks will be taken. If a member violates this regularly, then that person will be deviating from the group's rules. However, the larger organization will not see this as being deviant as long as the worker does not exceed the allotted time.

The second source of deviance would be where a group member violates some official rule of the larger organization, such as not filling out the time card as required or not dressing in the manner the large organization defines as appropriate. In this case the member would be deviating from the larger organization's rules, but the work group members would not care.

In all these instances the member is deviant because some artificially created formal or informal rule was violated. Obviously, groups which have many norms and rules are increasing the probability of member deviance. This is why many organizations and groups try to develop norms and rules only for important and necessary functions.

The problem with having norms and rules is that to be effective there must be sanctions (rewards and punishments) to maintain them. If an unimportant rule or norm is violated and no negative sanction is imposed then the group or organization may be "opening the door" for more deviance. On the other hand, if an unimportant norm is violated and negative sanctions do result, then member dissatisfaction or resentment could emerge.

The most effective norms or rules are those that "make sense" for reaching some valued goals, have clear and readily apparent sanctions surrounding them, and are supported by both the work group and the larger organization. If the norms of the work group contradict the rules of the larger organization, then problems may arise because a worker will automatically be conforming and deviant at the same time. Obviously, this may set up a confusing and destructive "we-they" situation between the group and the organization.

Individual Adaption and Functioning

It must not be forgotten that groups are made up of individuals who have identities, values, beliefs, likes, dislikes, and needs. A potential problem in groups is that each individual is placed in some position in each structure and must necessarily follow the group's norms in order to survive in the group. Many group problems can result from this when there is a lack of compatibility between individual and group characteristics. Conversely, groups can function well when this compatibility exists.

Each person has two sets of identities. One set is more visible with such factors as sex, age, and race, which everyone can observe. The other set is less visible with such factors as abilities, talents, and self-concept, which are subjective and privately held. These identities interact with a person's structural positions and role requirements to create either a compatible or incompatible situation.

If the structural positions that a person occupies provide demands, opportunities, and reactions from others that are consistent with the personal identities, then the chances for satisfaction and commitment will be reduced, and the individual will set up *role distance*. This means that the person tries to divorce himself from the role by not identifying with it. Demeaning the position, being very aloof and objective about what you "have" to do, stating that the role requirements are "silly," "foolish," and "immoral," would be typical expressions of this type of behavior.

A similar problem of commitment and satisfaction emerges when personally held values or beliefs are inconsistent with the practices or goals of the group. For example, a person who highly values fairness and honesty may have great difficulty working in an organization that encourages deception with its customers in order to make a sale.

Individuals who are in groups that maintain their personal identities, values, and beliefs will respect the group and be more committed, "self-sacrificing," and responsive to that group's influence. Conversely, if people do not find such a convergence then they will attempt to leave the group or, if that is impossible, will perform only the minimum to sustain membership and instead commit themselves to other groups more supportive of these personal characteristics. Three alternative groups could be family, religious or recreational groups as an example. In any event the effect is the same. The people are trying to maintain or enhance self-esteem. If this cannot be done in the work group, then they will commit themselves more to other groups.

GROUP COHESION

Cohesion, or group morale as it is sometimes called, is an important consequence of the group's norms, values, and structures. Cohesion is defined as the "sum of all factors influencing members to stay in the group." In essence, it is the attractiveness that group membership has for each member. Cohesion is important, because it affects such things as member retention, absenteeism, member participation, willingness to accept assignments and responsibilities, and the energy and persistence devoted to tasks and so on. All of these things are vital to a group's doing its job.

In groups of high cohesion you will find norms that prescribe positive interpersonal relations; norms that are seen as legitimate and important in helping the group reach its goals; norms that encourage and reward cooperation rather than competition; and norms and values that are compatible with the personal needs and values of the members.

Similarly, highly cohesive groups are characterized by structural patterns that "make sense" for goal attainment. By this we mean that the members see the structural patterns as being meaningful, useful, and necessary to reaching the stated group goals. You will also find that in cohesive groups the "liking" structure (interactions among people who like each other) and communication structure are such that all members are linked in some degree to one another. There are few if any isolated members.

Those normative and structural characteristics, which are part of producing a cohesive group, also aid in creating member satisfaction and commitment. No manager expects his or her employees to be satisfied with their jobs all the time. However, most effective managers see this as an ideal goal. Satisfied employees are not only better, more committed workers as a rule, but they are also more pleasant to have around as individuals. When group members are satisfied with their group situation, when they see it as a positive rewarding experience, they will want the group to maintain itself and subsequently will strive to see that it does. The result is better internal relations among members as well as measurable effort toward goals.

DECISION MAKING AND GOAL ATTAINMENT

In groups where decisions must be made about how to attain group goals, the issue of norms, values and structural patterns is important. The values of the leader and other group members are important determinants of whether and how hard the group will work towards goal attainment. This can be especially troublesome in groups where the goals are imposed upon the group by the larger organization. If the group leader and other members have values that are in conflict with the goals or have no valuation of the goals at all, then it follows that the amount of effort and commitment is reduced. By the same token, group goals that are supported by member values will have a greater likelihood of being achieved.

Norms that specify what kind of work is required of members, how members should relate to other members, who can participate in decision making, when one can participate, and so on, obviously will affect the quality of decision making and the speed, efficiency and quality of goal attainment. To illustrate, some groups have norms that prevent new members or junior members from participation in decision making. Not only are the potentially useful ideas and talents of these people lost to the decision-making process, but they are less likely to commit themselves to the decisions arrived at by the senior members.[8]

Structural patterns can similarly affect the decision-making process and goal attainment. The assumption is that for any given goal there is an optimum structural pattern for its attainment. Structural patterns can facilitate and also inhibit goal attainment. For instance, considerable research on the communication structure shows that a centralized structure (all communicate to one or only a few people) is faster and produces fewer effort when the job is a simple one requiring only the accumulation of information. On the other hand, a decentralized structure (members communicate to everyone else) is superior in speed and number of errors when the job is a complex one requiring reasonable and analytical processes.[9]

Another example of structure influencing decisions making and goal attainment is where the job at hand requires a high degree of close, positive, relationships among the members. In such a situation, structures that set up inequality in authority, or communication, or power may be counterproductive and result in just the opposite of what is needed for goal attainment. Scientific research teams working on the frontiers of knowledge could be an example of this.

EFFECT OF LARGER ORGANIZATION UPON GROUPS

The norms and structures of a group will form and stabilize over time. This stability provides an important foundation for member behavior in the group by allowing the members to realize fully what is expected of them and of the other group members in the firm.

All groups, however, are subject to change that is forced upon them by other groups. In the case of a work group, the larger organization frequently produces normative and structural changes by implementing decisions designed to help the larger organization reach its goals more efficiently or effectively. These changes usually fall into one of three categories: group size, task specialization, and formalization (rule forming). Each change produces certain expected effects upon group behavior.

Effect of Group Size

An increase or decrease in work group size automatically creates instability in the group. Whenever members are added or deleted, the structures will have to change. New positions will force a realignment among the remaining positions. The result is temporary instability, as the members learn and adjust to their new responsibilities and rights and learn the responsibilities and rights of the other positions.

This adjustment to the difference in group size also includes a certain amount of individual adaptation. The group members must now coordinate personal identities, values, and so on with the new position. If the group increases in size, there is an additional problem of teaching the new members the operating norms of the group. This is not an automatic process and sometimes can indeed result in the norms themselves changing.

Effect of Task Specialization

Frequently, organizations will produce normative or structural change in groups by increasing task specialization. This can be done by redistributing the work load in the organization so that a group that once had many jobs to perform will now perform only a few. But now it must do these jobs more thoroughly or intensely.

Another type of specialization change is that of redistributing the work load within a group such that members who once performed many tasks now perform only one or a few. Normative and structural change will of necessity occur because of the redefined positions and their new expectations.

Effect of Formalization

Finally, formalization, or an increase in rules and operating procedures, can affect the work group by conflicting with those norms presently in existence to which the members have already adjusted. Consequently, the group may reject or resist conformance.

GROUP ADJUSTMENT TO THE LARGER ORGANIZATION

It is not unusual for a work group to become insulated from the larger organization. This phenomenon though, occurs more often in mind than in actuality. In actuality, the group is part of a larger system which is arranged to achieve certain organizational goals. In day-to-day operations, however, many groups either fail to see or ignore this linkage and oeprate as an isolated system developing and legitimating their own normative and structural patterns.

As a result, when the larger organization requires changes in these patterns it is often seen as interference, which, even though legitimate, is nevertheless resented. Often this results in the development of protective norms such as "don't tell others what happens here," and may also cause the group to become not only more cohesive, but also defensive.[10] These types of reactions, while certainly strengthening the group, may, contrarily, make it less responsive to organizational demands.

Typically, if individual loyalty and commitment are to occur, they will be pledged to the group and not to the larger organization. This is understandable, since the work group is where individual relationships develop, where sanctions accrue, and where people are identified by others. Such isolation and the resulting problems can be minimized if the leaders or members of the group are involved, in some way, in the decision-making processes of the larger organization.

The involvement of the group in decision making keeps the group members aware of the group's linkage with the larger organization and reduces the probability of potentially destructive norms from developing within the group. Figure 12-5 illustrates the group's linkage to the objectives and goals

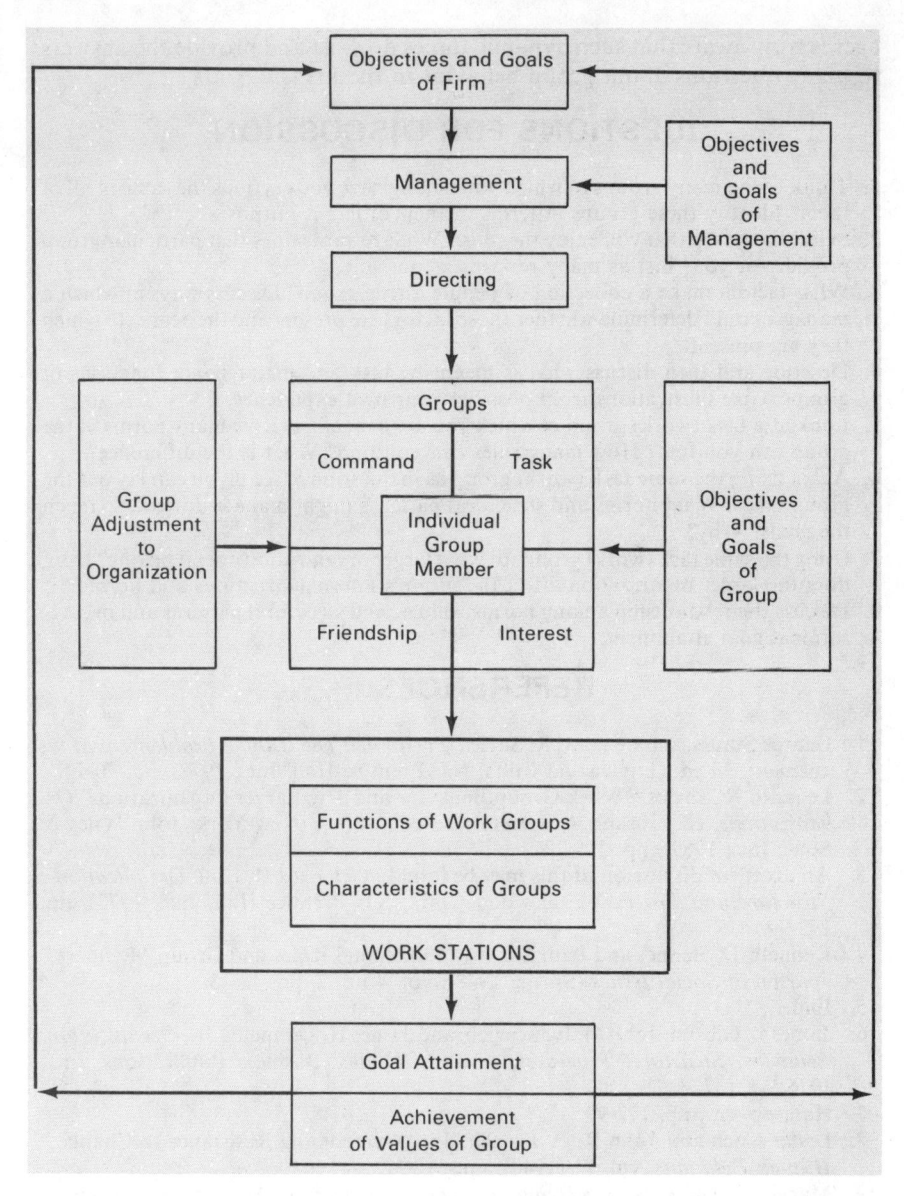

Fig. 12-5. Linkage of the group to organizational objectives and goals

of the organization in terms of the attainment of the group goals and values.

In summary, an understanding of group behavior requires an awareness of the dynamic forces that result when people come together. Structural arrangements and normative patterns have powerful effects on the quality and quantity of the relationships among group members.

Finally, structural and normative patterns affect the important issue of how efficiently and effectively the group reaches its goals. The effective manager is truly aware that such dynamic forces do exist and provide the answers to many questions about group behavior in the firm.

QUESTIONS FOR DISCUSSION

1. Think of the many groups to which you belong. Are your actions the same in all of them? Identify these groups in terms of their different purposes.
2. Select the group that you enjoy the most. What rewards does that particular group provide for you? List as many rewards as possible.
3. What factors make a collection of people a true group? Discuss ways in which a manager could determine whether those factors are present and the degree to which they are present.
4. Describe and then discuss what is meant by task and maintenance functions of groups. Give illustrations from possibly your own experience.
5. Look at a task (work) group of which you are a member. How many norms of the group can you find? How many rules can you find? What is the difference?
6. Again using the same task (work) group as in question 5, see if you can lay out the group goals. What norms and structural patterns might make it difficult to reach the goals? Why?
7. Using the same task (work) group, to what larger organization does it belong? How does the larger organization affect the group's internal structures and norms?
8. Discuss the relationship among norms, values, and structural patterns and organizational goal attainment.

REFERENCES

1. George Stauss, and Leonard R. Sayles, *Personnel: The Human Problems of Management*, 3d ed. (Englewood Cliffs, NJ: Prentice-Hall, Inc., 1972), pp. 70-74.
2. Leonard R. Sayles, "Work Group Behavior and The Larger Organization," *Organizations*, ed., Joseph A. Litterer, 2d ed., vol. 1. (New York: John Wiley & Sons, Inc., 1969), pp. 215-22.
3. An excellent discussion of this may be found in Richard H. Hall, *Organizations: Structure and Process* (Englewood Cliffs, NJ: Prentice-Hall, Inc., 1972), pp. 172-99.
4. Kenneth D. Benne, and Paul Sheats, "Functional Roles and Group Members," *Journal of Social Issues* (Spring 1948): vol. 4 no. 2, pp. 42-45.
5. Ibid.
6. James L. Gibson, John M. Ivancevich, and James H. Donnelly, Jr., *Organization: Behavior, Structure, Processes*, rev. ed. (Dallas: Business Publications, Inc., 1976), p. 157.
7. Hall, op. cit., pp. 172-99.
8. Lester Coch and John R. P. French, Jr., "Overcoming Resistance to Change," *Human Relations*, vol. 11 (1948): pp. 512-32.
9. Marvin E. Shaw, *Group Dynamics: The Psychology of Small Group Behavior* (New York: McGraw-Hill Book Co., 1976), pp. 142-44.
10. Morton Deutsch, *The Resolution of Conflict* (New Haven: Yale University Press, 1973), pp. 72-77.

SELECTED BIBLIOGRAPHY

1. Bales, Robert Freed. *Personality and Interpersonal Behavior.* New York: Holt, Rinehart, and Winston, 1970.
2. McFeat, Tom. *Small Group Cultures.* New York: Pergamon Press, Inc., 1974.
3. Phillips, Gerald M. *Communication and the Small Group* 2d ed. Indianapolis: Bobbs-Merrill Co., Inc., 1973.

4. Reitz, H. Joseph. *Behavior in Organizations.* (Homewood, IL: Richard D. Irwin, Inc., 1977.
5. Zander, Alvin. *Motives and Goals In Groups.* New York: Academic Press, 1971.

CHAPTER 13

COMMUNICATION: AN ORGANIZATIONAL VIEWPOINT

Purpose of Chapter 13:

1. To emphasize the critical importance of communication in organizational settings
2. To spotlight the structure and purpose of formal and informal channels of communication
3. To illustrate organizational and personal barriers to effectiveness
4. To offer basic ground rules for improving communications in the firm

Essential elements you should understand after studying this chapter:

1. Process of communication defined
2. Formal communication channels
3. Informal networks and their purpose
4. Organizational objectives in communicating
5. Structural barriers to effective communications
6. Socio-psychological barriers
7. Semantic barriers
8. Recommendations for improving organizational communications

NATURE OF COMMUNICATION

Communication is vital to any form of social activity requiring human interaction. Accordingly, it is a process that pervades all management activities. It accomplishes the functions of management and makes possible the work of an organization. The nature of information and ideas, the media and channels of transmission, the intentions and perception of both sender and receiver are all part of the communication process with which management is involved.

The important question about communication, then, is not whether managers communicate, since no organized activity can occur without it, but rather how effectively does management communicate? It is interesting to note that irrespective of startling advances in communication technology, communication between people and organizations still leaves much to be desired. Essentially, communication is not dependent on technology or instrumentation, but rather on forces in the people and their surroundings.[1]

Communication can be defined as the process of exchanging understanding through the use of commonly understood symbols both verbal and non verbal. The process is represented in figure 13-1. It is, moveover, a complex function involving the senses, experiences, feelings, attitudes, and interests, among other factors, which cause us to perceive the phenomena of actions, activities, and words in specific ways.

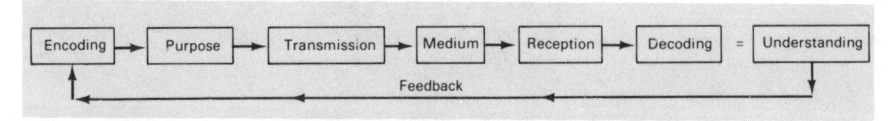

| Encoding | → | Purpose | → | Transmission | → | Medium | → | Reception | → | Decoding | = | Understanding |

Feedback

Fig. 13-1. The process of communication

Communication, furthermore, may be interpersonal, involving the exchange of understanding between two people or a small group. Or it may be organizational, involving a necessary system to exchange understanding by giving information and transmitting meaning to various organizational elements and groups of people both inside and outside the institution. A model of these factors is presented in figure 13-2.

FORMAL COMMUNICATION IN THE ORGANIZATION

Downward Channels

Formal communication in the typical hierarchical organization flows downward from the chief executive. Objectives, policies, directives, and decisions are issued to immediate subordinates who, in turn, retransmit the communication downward until it reaches the lowest level subordinate. The formal channels of a typical organization are depicted in figure 13-3. Theoretically, then, with an established chain of command, people know from whom they are to receive communications, and conversely to whom they are accountable. This vertical line from any superior to subordinate, moreover, needs to be standardized, personal, direct, and certainly explicit.

Communication: An Organizational Viewpoint 183

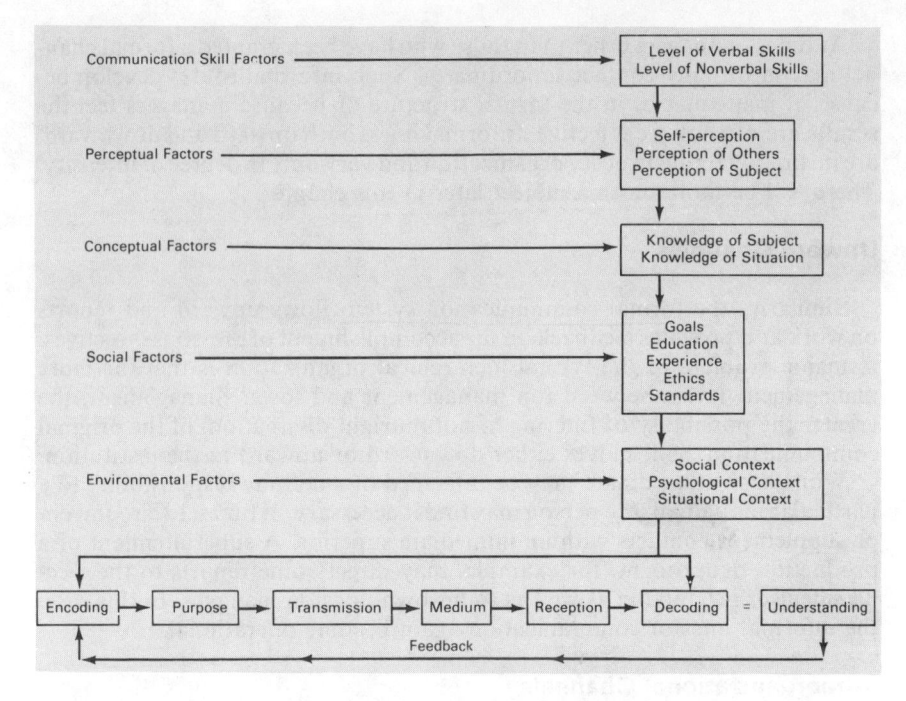

Fig. 13-2. Model of factors influencing fidelity of communication

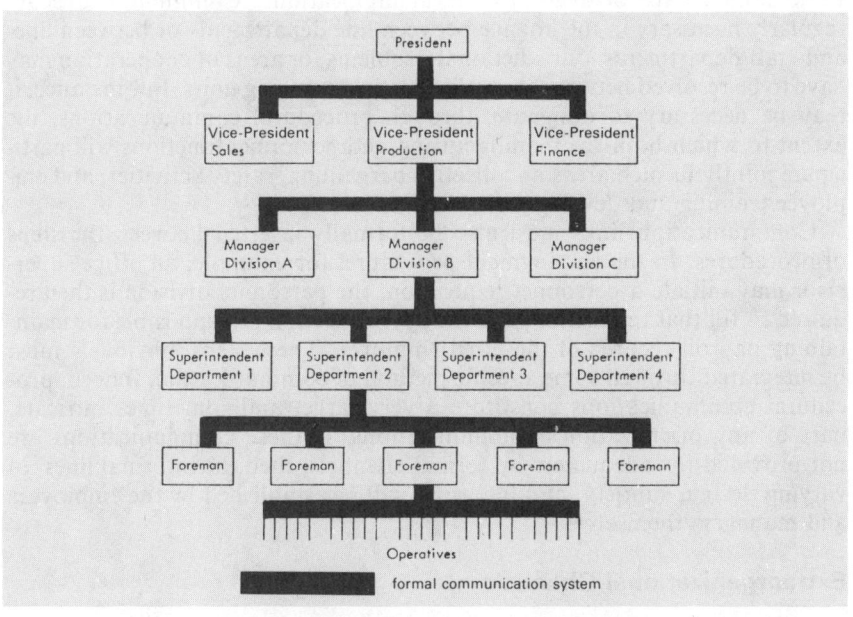

Fig. 13-3. Formal communication channels within the formal organization

At times, managers other than those who have been granted a formal channel may informally contact subordinates. Such informal routes develop because of inadequacies in the formal structure or because managers feel the results are often more effective. Informal lines, both upward and downward, are invariably found in every organization and vary only in degree of intensity. There will be more on this subject later in this chapter.

Upward Channels

Similarly, the formal communication system flows upward and reports on work and provides feedback on the accomplishment of previous directives. A major problem of the typical hierarchical organization is that the more management levels between top management and lower management, the greater the possibility of filtering, if not outright dissipation, of the original communication, as it moves either downward or upward in the institution.

While each subordinate may be informed of a definite responsibility to a particular individual, the person may find it necessary, at times, to circumvent or supplement contacts with an immediate superior. A superintendent of a production department, for example, may direct some reports to the vice-president of production as well as to his own division manager. In this case, the informal lines of communication again become operational.

Intraorganizational Channels

Formal communication lines may also be established horizontally across vertical organizational lines. Some of these are for organizational purposes, while others have distinct procedural implications. Communications are regularly necessary in the linkage between line departments or between line-and-staff departments. Jurisdictional problems, or areas of cooperation may have to be resolved between the various manufacturing units. For instance, it may be necessary to designate, through procedural communications, the extent to which both the manufacturing and personnel functions will participate jointly in such areas as collective bargaining, safety activities, and employee training and development.

Communication links must also be formally inserted between the steps of procedures. In the employment procedure, for example, an office supervisor may initiate a personnel requisition; the personnel division is then required to fill that requisition; and the payroll section is responsible for maintaining payroll records of the hired employee. These steps, obviously must be integrated through some specific method of communication. Indeed, procedural communications constitute a very large, and sometimes intricate, part of any organization's communications. If these communications are not provided for adequately by formal channels, then the informal lines, of varying design, subtlety, and intensity, will be established by the employees and managers themselves.

Extraorganizational Channels

Lines of communication are also extended to various external groups.

Among such groups are government offices, local and national, customers and suppliers, unions, community agencies, the educational community, homes of the employees, and the general public. Some of these contacts may be highly formalized as they are in certain governmental or union relationships. Most, though, are of an informal nature, whose purpose may be either informational, instructional, or persuasive in character.

INFORMAL COMMUNICATION IN THE ORGANIZATION

Informal System

A truly interesting phenomenon of organizational activity is the informal system of communication. This informal system which underlies the formal system has its own personnel subsystems. Figure 13-4 illustrates typical informal communication networks within an organization. Here the vice-president of production is a poker-playing friend of the superintendent of department 4, while all the foremen are on the firm's bowling team.

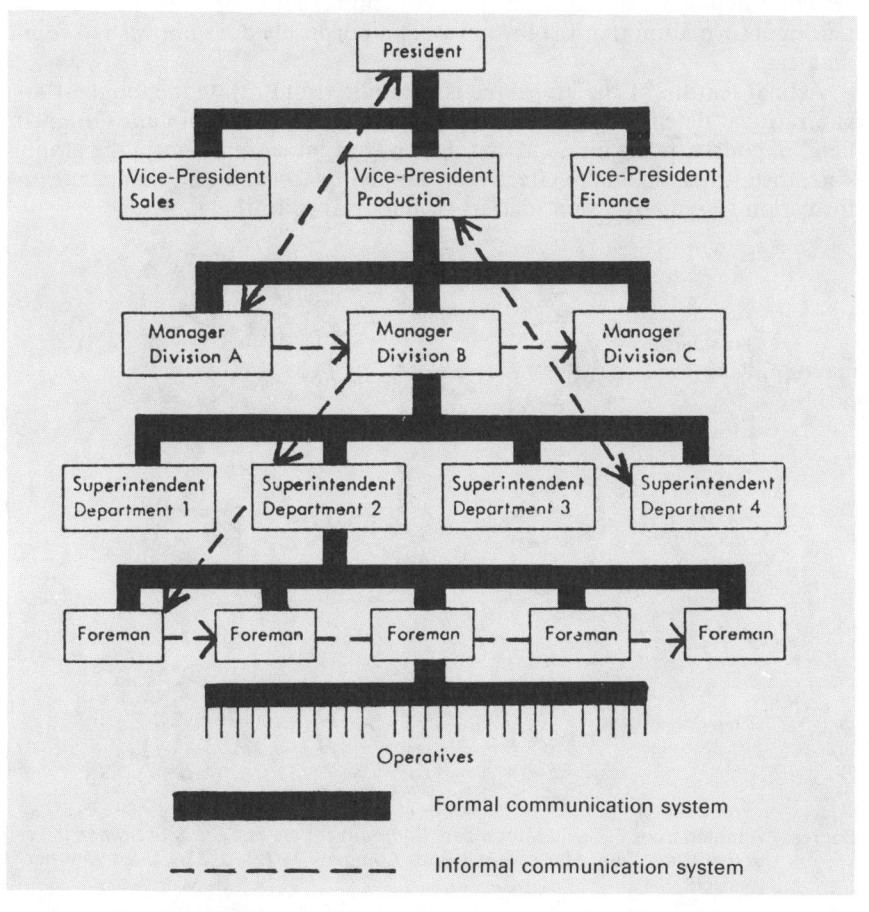

Fig. 13-4. Typical informal communication channels

The Grapevine

The prime medium of communication within the formal system is the well-known grapevine. It has a variety of purposes and features. It originates as a consequence or outgrowth of human interactions in the organization. As a by-passing mechanism, it satisfies the employees' needs for communication and socialization. When used effectively, it can help develop group integration and a feeling of identity among the individual employees. It can assist management in many ways: in orienting new personnel to work routines and in supplementing the downward flow of information from upper levels of management.

There are several interesting features of the grapevine. It has a tremendous capacity to carry information throughout the entire organization. As a positive medium, moreover, it can provide such needed feedback to management about employee feelings and attitude. Conversely, however, it can spread inaccurate information and unauthenticated rumors. Its rapidity of transmission is such that at times it will function more quickly than the formal system it bypasses. Management will often find the grapevine useful in transmitting information that the formal system purposely does not wish to communicate.

A final feature of the grapevine is its ability to infiltrate the toughest organizational defenses for both reception and transmission of data.[2] Implicit here, of course, is the message that if management is to minimize the grapevine, then it must be more effective in supplying accurate and immediate information to employees on matters of importance to them.

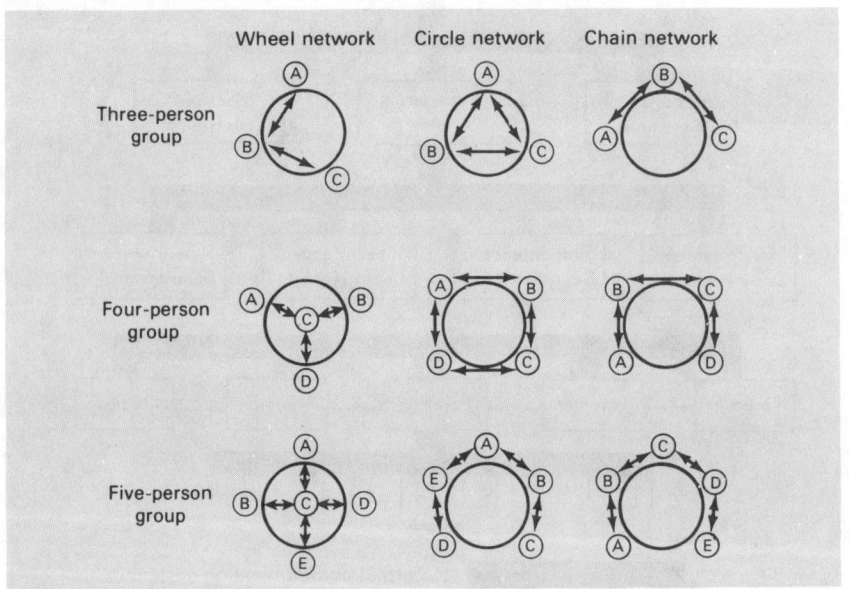

Source: Adapted from C. David Mortensen, *Communication: The Study of Human Interaction* (New York: McGraw-Hill Book Company 1972), p. 334. Used with permission.

Fig. 13-5. Interpersonal communication networks

COMMUNICATION NETWORKS AND INTERPERSONAL RELATIONS

While implementing communication in the organization, management needs to understand the network or pattern of relationships through which group members can communicate. Interesting to note is the differences among networks identified as "wheel", "circle", and "chain" in figure 13-5. In the wheel network only one person communicates with all others regardless of group size. The circle network, however, permits each person to communicate with two other group members. And the chain network allows two-way exchange between all but members on the outside. The essential difference in these three commonly used networks in the organization is their respective degrees of centrality or the amount of direct contact each person has with the others. The wheel network is the most highly centralized, the chain relatively centralized and the circle least decentralized. A centralized network depends on a central person to link communication among all other members.

OBJECTIVES OF ORGANIZATIONAL COMMUNICATIONS

After an organization has identified and established the various channels of communications it will plan to use them for different purposes.

Purpose of Downward Channels

The major purpose of downward channels may be translated into the following specific intentions of communication programs:

1. To gain understanding and support of company objectives, plans and policies so employees will support management actions essential for success of the operation
2. To inform about the organization, its history, progress, and prospects for new business and growth
3. To convey information about the day-to-day activities and operations of the institution and its personnel
4. To explain the rationale behind management decisions and particularly behind changes which may affect the personnel
5. To discuss regularly personnel and labor relations, objectives, policies, practices, and decisions
6. To present the firm's views on economic, political, and social affairs[3]

Purpose of Upward Channels

As a primary purpose, upward communications serve to inform management of results achieved by the organization, its groups and its personnel. Upward communications also describe progress in reaching objectives or in accounting for the efficient use of assigned resources: human, financial, and material.

But there are other important purposes to be served by the upward flow from employees. Some of these are:

1. As an aid to decision making, they serve to keep management informed of attitudes, trends, and reactions among employees
2. To allow for the expression of personal opinions, grievances, or complaints
3. To permit individual contribution of suggestions and ideas as they may affect employees in their work
4. To allow for worker participation and involvement in the decision-making process in areas of mutual interest and concern
5. To confirm employee acceptance of individual and group goals and obligations

The upward flow is a direct response to management's downward flow in a communications system. This free-flowing, two-way system of interchange is absolutely necessary if true understanding between management and the employees is to be achieved.

Horizontal Intraorganizational Channels

The purpose of cross organizational flows is to integrate the efforts of otherwise separated units. If the work of the production department, for example, is to be coordinated with that of the marketing department, cross contacts are certainly necessary. The plans of each, though, must be known and synchronized in terms of such elements as quantity, quality, production scheduling and distribution, and cost and pricing factors, as well as any promotion and advertising programs. Coordination is the purpose that must be served here by intraorganizational systems.

Horizontal flows also have other purposes, similar to those of vertical flows. Information, clarification, instructions, and persuasions may be transmitted and exchanged to either reduce misunderstanding or to support positions taken on various subjects. Indeed, a most significant function of horizontal channels is to reconcile differences and conflicts that may arise out of normal relationships between functional departments and line-and-staff units. Sometimes and unfortunately, the resolution of differences preempts the major work to be accomplished. Even so, it can be argued that this alone would justify the existence of horizontal communications.

Extraorganizational Channels

Formerly, these flows were limited since a firm's contacts were principally with supplier and customer. With the exception of incorporation procedures and a few simple reports to governmental agencies, formal contacts with government were few. Business contacts with unions were minimal because of the then relative insignificance of unionism.

Increasingly, though, organizations have enlarged their extraorganizational flows of communication. The reasons for this lie in the growing regulation of business by government; the intensified competition of rival business; pressure from community and social groups; the accelerated trend of consumerism and the growing impact of unionism. More specifically, companies may interest themselves in extraorganizational flows for a variety of reasons:

1. To promote favorable legislation on such subjects as taxes, labor, and corporate practices
2. To win understanding, approval, and support of the organization's position on vital economic, political, and social issues
3. To establish and enhance a positive image of the industry, the company, and its products or services
4. To explain and clarify its position in labor disputes

ORGANIZATIONAL BARRIERS TO EFFECTIVE COMMUNICATION

From what we have discussed so far, it would appear that good communications are easy to achieve. Effective attention to lines, purposes, content, and media of communications seemingly should guarantee success. Were this true, it would be difficult to see why communications in an organization fail so often.

But, on the contrary, there are a number of obstacles, some difficult and complex, which impair the communication process. Let us examine some of these prevalent barriers which may be classified as structural, socio-psychological, or semantic in origin.

STRUCTURAL BARRIERS

This type arises from the fact that the structural elements of an organization may block communication flows. The individual manager, by virtue of a select position in the structure, can potentially close down all communication between the manager and those with whom there is interaction. Important to remember here is that the attitude of management, beginning at the highest level, strongly determines the kind of organizational climate in which effective communication takes place.

At the immediate level of operation the supervisor may act as a filter of vertical communications. The supervisor may purposely block communications with subordinates by avoiding interpersonal dialogue or by a failure to listen. This can be disastrous, since the supervisor represents the organization to the group being sueprvised. Moreover, negative communication practices carry over and directly influence any personal effectiveness in such supervisory responsibilities as motivating, counseling, training, and performance appraisal.

Unity of Command

A major barrier may be the organization structure itself. The structure ordinarily has built-in principles that should facilitate communication. For example, the principle of unity of command states that an employee should report to only one manager. Naturally any orders and instructions from several different managers would obviate this principle.

Span of Control

Another principle, the span of control indicates there is a limit as to the number of subordinates a manager can effectively supervise. Too many subordinates obviously will prevent, or seriously dilute, the efforts of the manager in reaching all persons.

Excessive Layering

Excessive layering of authority levels is another barrier that is structural in origin. This refers to the number of hierarchical organizational levels that can cause eventual filtering of communication both downward and upward. The more levels and the more superiors, the greater the possibility of dilution or distortion or even disappearance of communication. A natural result of such blockage, incidentally, is the subsequent reinforcement of the grapevine which then conveniently bypasses the obstructed formal channels during the course of its operation.

SOCIO-PSYCHOLOGICAL BARRIERS

Sociopsychological barriers stem from certain potential and inherent factors that can manifest themselves in organized group activities. Problems arising from different frames of reference and stereotyping are two typical examples that fall into this category.

Frame of Reference

A person's perception is a complex of beliefs, judgments, experiences, truths and principles, and biases and prejudices that help determine or assess that individual's personal estimation of situations and circumstances. If management's communications are consonant with the perceptions of employees, then there is communication. Another way of saying this is that people will listen to and accept those statements that are in accord with their frame of reference, with what they already believe and will give less consideration to those things with which they do not agree.

Stereotyping

This barrier arises out of a person's preconceived ideas about what individual people and groups of people mean. It is a form of discrimination. Once an image or impression is determined, it is then universally applied to any individual irrespective of any differences or distinctions which may differentiate that person from the stereotyped group.[4]

Consequently, we hear what we expect to hear about a person or a particular group. This fault spills over into group versus group, or class versus class stereotyping. Some workers feel that as a class opposite to that of management, they must arbitrarily refrain from accepting any views expressed by management.

But stereotyping or typing of classes can occur in management levels as well. Staff people may categorize line executives as production-oriented, parochial, and mostly noncooperative. Line may return the compliment by classifying staff people as impractical visionaries who constantly scheme to control that which is line's responsibility. Upper levels of management may be suspicious of lower-level supervisors, feeling the latter are not company-minded enough. Front-line supervision, on the other hand, may view management as a group, mostly profit and cost-directed, with little regard for the daily problems experienced in the production areas.[5]

SEMANTIC BARRIERS

The purpose of language is to convey meaning. Actually, words do not mean anything but are simply vessels or containers of meaning. Meaning is in the people using the words, not in the words themselves. Moreover, the same words may have different "meanings" to different people or groups of people.

Words, it appears, have what is known as denotative and connotative meanings. The denotative meaning of words is the dictionary definition of the word. The connotative meaning, on the other hand, is the result of the emotional aura or atmosphere surrounding the word in its usage. *Collective bargaining* and *unions*, for example, are words that may infuriate some executives but have a pleasant influence on workers. Conversely, the words *Taft-Hartley* may generate hostility in the minds of many employees, while assuaging the feelings of management. Somewhat similar, but perhaps not so violent, reactions would result from such words as *productivity, cost reduction, profits, right to work*, and *management prerogatives*.

In-group Language

Normally, most occupational, professional and social groups will develop their own language consisting of words and phrases that have meaning only to those special group members. The language simplifies in-group communication, besides providing a feeling of identity and status to those using it. While in-group language facilitates effective communications within the group, its use with external groups will present a barrier to intergroup understanding.[6]

IMPROVING ORGANIZATIONAL COMMUNICATIONS

By this time, you should be well aware that effective communication is a vital function in organizational activity. In fact, effective management may be equated with effective communication. And if this function is to be carried out successfully, its practices must conform to sound principles and rules. Some recommendations in support of this are offered here in this section:

Consistency of Words and Action

Management's actions should agree with its words, thereby creating a climate of confidence. In the final analysis it is what the communicator *does* that really matters. Insincerity or superficial concern about employee opinion becomes apparent and will subsequently obstruct further communication. Actions that are contradictory to announced purposes or intentions result in future distrust and disaffection by the receiver.

Isolation of Purpose

The purpose of each communication should be specifically isolated. The target, either person or group, should be identified and the communication correspondingly adjusted to the intellectual and interest levels of the target.

Bilateral Exchange

Bilateral or two-way communications should be encouraged and cultivated through a spirit of openness and trust. The organization should incorporate media, such as regular meetings and conferences even at the operative level, along with established grievance procedures to provide available channels for continuing exchange of communication.

Encouragement of Feedback

Management should attempt to cultivate feedback on a voluntary and regular basis to insure a proper goodness of fit between the communicator and the recipient. Feedback is crucial to effective two-way communication, since it provides a channel for response that helps the communicator determine whether the message has been received and whether it has produced the intended response.

Effective Listening

Management should listen to all groups, middle management, supervisors, employees, and the public as well. It should listen as a technique for feedback on reactions, attitudes, feelings, and moods. This also means that management should listen to the results of employee morale surveys, consumer opinion surveys, community polls, and so on, in addition to the more immediate expressions of its subordinate management and employees.

Summing up, then, effective communication between management and its many groups, particularly the employee group, is possible if the organization truly strives to achieve it. Research indicates that employees evidence a desire for upward communications (one that would probably grow with proper encouragement and removal of frustration and obstacles).[7] In this there is both economic and social return in terms of profitable ideas, better ways of doing things, support for management actions and increased employee participation and involvement, as well as personal satisfaction within the environment of the enterprise.

QUESTIONS FOR DISCUSSION

1. Explain the differences among the channels of communication and lines of authority and responsibility.
2. Discuss the purposes of communication channels from subordinate to superior. Give several illustrations.
3. What are identifiable characteristics of the informal communication system? From

your own experiences, illustrate the effectiveness of the grapevine. Give an example of the grapevine operation.
4. In what manner can the organizational structure inherently present barriers to effective understanding?
5. From your own experience, cite a situation in which effective exchange of understanding was not possible because of certain barriers. What action might have been taken to avoid this problem?
6. Define what is meant by *feedback*. How can management be certain it is getting proper feedback from the groups to which it has communicated?
7. How can semantics affect communication? Give an example of this barrier from your own experience.
8. Of the recommendations offered for improving communications, which do you feel are more important? Support your response with logical reasoning.

REFERENCES

1. James L. Gibson, John M. Ivancevich, and James H. Donnelly, Jr., *Organizations: Behavior, Structure, Processes* (Dallas: Business Publications, Inc., 1976), P. 318.
2. Keith Davis, *Human Behavior at Work* (New York: McGraw-Hill Book Co., 1972), p. 267.
3. Adapted from "Employee Communication: Policy and Tools, Studies in Personnel No. 200" (New York: National Industrial Conference Board, Inc., 1966), pp. 15-19.
4. William V. Haney, *Communications and Organizational Behavior, Text and Cases,* 3rd ed. (Homewood, IL: Richard D. Irwin, Inc., 1973), pp. 55-56, 334-36.
5. George Strauss and Leonard R. Sayles, *Personnel: The Human Problems of Management,* 3rd ed. (Englewood Cliffs, NJ: Prentice-Hall, Inc., 1972), pp. 209-10.
6. Ibid., p. 212
7. See Alfred Vogel, "Why Employees Don't Speak Up," *Personnel Administration* (May-June): 1967.

SELECTED BIBLIOGRAPHY

1. Berlo, David K. *Process of Communication: An Introduction to Theory and Practice,* New York: Holt, Rinehart and Winston, Inc. 1960.
2. Burack, Elmer. *Organizational Analysis: Theory and Application.* Hinsdale, IL: The Dryden Press, 1975.
   Leavitt, Harold J. *Managerial Psychology.* 3d. Chicago: The University of Chicago Press, 1972.
4. Mortensen, C. David. *Communication: The Study of Human Interaction.* New York: McGraw-Hill Book Co., 1972.
5. Sigband, Norman B. *Communication for Management.* Glenview, IL: Scott, Foresman & Co., 1969.

CHAPTER 14

LEADERSHIP BEHAVIOR: STYLES AND DETERMINANTS

Purpose of Chapter 14:

1. To explore leadership as a management process and activity
2. To discuss and evaluate the importance of certain leadership theories
3. To analyze the different roles exercised in leadership

Essential elements you should understand after studying this chapter:

1. Definition of leadership
2. Bases for leadership power
3. Trait approach to leadership style
4. Personal behavior approach
5. Ohio State Leadership Studies
6. The Managerial Grid
7. Situational approach to leadership
8. Contingency approach
9. Different roles of leadership

NATURE OF LEADERSHIP

Probably few areas of management receive as much attention, investigation, and study as does leadership. Truly, there are decisive reasons for this, since it is leadership that gives dynamism, vitality, and substance to an organization's structure. Leadership is that force that galvanizes a firm and its people into achieving required and expected results. It is leadership that provides and reflects the character, soul, and in fact, the very life itself of the institution.

By definition, leadership is a process within a specific situation in which a central figure guides and influences the activities of others in the pursuit of individual and group goals. Essential to this definition of leadership is the behavior of a central figure around whom a group gravitates and performs certain tasks.

Where does leadership, one might ask, fit in the overall conceptual process of management? Theoretically, leadership is a subset of the managerial function of directing. As such, it serves alongside motivating and communicating as necessary subfunctions of direction. In other words, while directing the work group in the achievement of desired objectives, the manager alternately or synchronously motivates, communicates, and leads.

Are the terms manager and leader synonomous? Or is there, in fact, a difference both in definition and practice? The definition of a manager insists that there is a formal position on the organization structure from which the manager plans, organizes, staffs, directs, and controls the resources and activities of a work group. Moreover, the manager has the formal power of a designated and particular office to support that position in the institution.

Leadership, on the other hand, while essential in achieving desired goals is not entirely restricted to fomal management. Ideally, management should be equated with leadership. Optimally, of course, the manager should be an effective leader. But often this is not the case. Many times, leadership is found and provided through the informal rather than the formal organization. Informal leaders by virtue of their relationship, may often satisfy the goals of individuals and of the group.

Managers, conversely, must not only work toward satisfying these same goals, but must also satisfy the goals of the formal organization. The basic distinction between these two types of leaders is not predicated on their specific jobs, but on their sources of influence and authority.[1] Simply stated then, all managers have formal authority while leadership is based on earned authority.

Leadership, moreover, has additional connotative meanings in terms of its definition. It implies a conscious and deliberate followship. It stresses personal influence and interaction between leaders and their followers. Leadership also implies a genuine acceptance of that person by followers. It means the exercise of influence, of direction without the strict use of authority or power that is associated with a particular position. Effective leadership is, furthermore, structured on an awareness of group norms and values and on an awareness of the individual's goals and aspirations as well. It is the product of the deliberate structuring of a climate that can be conducive to highly motivated individual and group performance.

BASES OF POWER

What is the basis of power upon which a leader influences members of the group? In terms of influence upon the group and its members, there appear to be five bases that support a given type of power:[2]

1. **Reward power.** This is power whose basis is the ability to reward. Compliance with the wishes and actions of one's supervisor will lead to positive rewards. Rewards may be either monetary or psychological in nature.
2. **Coercive power.** This power is based on fear. A subordinate perceives that punishment is meted out for disagreement with the wishes and expectations of one's supervisor.
3. **Legitimate power.** This is power derived from the supervisor's position in the organization. It is authoritarian power in a formal organization and is a relationship between offices rather than between persons. It is the *right* of an office to lead.
4. **Referent power.** Has its source in the identification of a follower with a leader. The leader's personal traits and characteristics influence followers in their admiration and respect.
5. **Expert power.** Refers to the influence exerted by the leader's superior knowledge or ability in specific areas. The leader's possession of expertise results in respect and compliance of peers or subordinates.

This fivefold framework, incidently, provides a conceptual distinction among the bases of power. Reclassified into two major categories, it consists of power based primarily on organization factors and power based on individual factors.

Reward, coercive, and legitimate power are specified and controlled primarily by the individual's position in the organization. On the other hand, the degree and scope of a manager's referent and expert power bases are dictated primarily by the individual's personal characteristics. Therefore, it should be observed that within this framework the individual controls the referent and expert power bases, while the reward, coercive, and legitimate power bases are controlled by the organization.[3]

What is important here in this discussion of influence theory is that the organizational and individual characteristics of managers are interdependent. Leading or influencing others depends, among other things, on the organizational system and on the perceptions that subordinates have of their leaders.

SOME THEORIES OF LEADERSHIP

There are numerous theories of leadership, and many of them are worthy of analysis. Here, however, we will limit our discussion to four distinct approaches that have evolved out of research and study. These are: (1) trait approach, (2) personal behavior approach, (3) situational approach, and (4) contingency approach.

Trait Approach

Proponents of trait theory suggest that various physical, pesonality, or intelligence criteria may be valid in describing or predicting leadership success. But is there truly a specific grouping or cluster of traits that identify effective leadership? There have been many attempts to answer that question. Much research and study have been devoted in an effort to discover those characteristics that differentiate the leader from the follower. So far though, the evidence is inconclusive about any particular traits that are exclusive to leadership.

The physical trait approach centers on the fact that the physical stature of a person affects his or her ability to influence followers. Tall and physically powerful and dynamic individuals are viewed as being leaders or potential leaders more than their shorter and less powerful contemporaries. While certain studies do support the physical trait theory, they do so with reservations.[4] Evidence seems to show that physical characteristics are important to leadershiip only when they are demanded by the job.

The personality trait approach was particularly prominent during the 1940s when some theorists and practitioners felt that composite lists of traits could be developed and synthesized into desirable leadership profiles for use in managerial selection. These leadership profiles contained a wide range of qualitative attributes, many of which were difficult to define. Some typical traits were initiative, judgment, loyalty, aggressiveness, decisiveness, courage, persistence, and so on.

Intelligence as a prerequisite for leadership, conversely, finds support in certain studies that concluded that an individual's intelligence is an accurate predictor of managerial success within a certain range. Above this range, however, individuals with higher and higher scores are less likely to be successful managers. It appears, though, that individuals at very extreme high levels of intelligence deal with abstract ideas and concepts and do not find desired intellectual challenge in managerial activities.[5]

As we suggested earlier in this section, solid evidence supporting the trait approach is assuredly lacking. Leadership, it seems, appears on the organizational scene in all sizes, colors, and shapes. One needs only to be acquainted with an institution for a brief period of time before realizing the varied differences in the sex, racial, physical, and personality traits of its many capable leaders.

One major weakness of the trait approach is its failure to recognize the influence of situational factors of leadership. Trait theory focuses primarily on the individual factors of leadership. Leadership, on the other hand, must be discussed in relationship to the group as well as to the individual. A final shortcoming thoroughly highlights the weakness of the trait approach. While recognized leaders exhibited many of the described traits, it has been difficult to filter out those universal traits common to all leaders. And even more, the degree to which managers possess given traits has been hard to measure and predict.[6]

Personal Behavior Approach

This approach to the study of the institution's leadership asserts that leaders may be characterized by certain behavioral qualities or patterns. Within this framework we will limit our discussion to the Ohio State two-dimensional theory and to the Blake and Mouton Managerial Grid approach.

The Ohio State Studies

Since directly after World War II, researchers at The Ohio State University have engaged in extensive studies of leadership. Chief among those researchers has been Ralph M. Stogdill, whose work in the field of leadership has contributed measurably to an increased understanding of the subject.[7]

Probably the most significant contribution of Stogdill has been the isolation of certain discrete variables, or dimensions of leadership behavior. Of these, "consideration" and "initiation of structure" emerge as fundamental characteristics of leadership behavior in organizational settings.

These two behavioral characteristics evolved from research activities, involving literally hundreds of management personnel. Employed were measuring instruments known as the LOQ (Leadership Opinion Questionnaire), which measures how leaders think they ought to behave in their leadership roles, and the LBDQ (Leadership Behavior Description Questionnaire), which measures how subordinates perceive leaders in their leadership roles.

"Consideration" as a dimension of leader behavior reflects a basic concern for human relations, for the comfort and well-being of subordinates, for mutual confidence and trust, for respect for subordinate's ideas, contributions, and feelings. Managers scoring high on this variable are considered to be supportive, among other factors, allow for group participation in the unit's decisionmaking process.

"Initiation of structure" is a dimension that indicates the degree to which leaders define and structure their own roles and those of subordinates in achieving objectives. Leaders scoring high in this variable clearly delineate relationships with subordinates; develop well-defined patterns of organization; establish policies and procedures; and actively plan and schedule subordinate activities.[8]

A major contribution of the Ohio State studies is that the behavior of a leader can be depicted as some combination of both consideration and initiation of structure. Earlier approaches tended to classify leadership according to either/or models, e.g., people-centered versus job-centered or autocratic versus democratic. But the Ohio State studies supported the notion that a leader may be high or low in both dimensions simultaneously, depending on the situation, while still achieving organizational effectiveness.[9]

Blake and Mouton Managerial Grid®

The Managerial Grid concept was developed by the research team of Robert R. Blake and Jane S. Mouton and introduced in the early sixties.[10] A two-dimensional concept, this analysis recognizes two major variables of leadership: (1) concern for people and (2) concern for production. According to Blake and Mouton, a concern for people and a concern for production can be integrative rather than exclusive. That is to say, leadership is a combination of these two concerns in achieving operational results.

A contribution of this approach is that it, like the Ohio State studies, shows how a leader can simultaneously maximize both the methods that are production-oriented and those that are people-oriented. As such, it also permits leaders to avoid adopting either/or styles of leadership, such as an autocratic or democratic style or a production-centered versus a people-centered style. The Managerial Grid avoids these traps since many leaders feel they could not accept the either/or alternative.

The Grid approach is a highly popular concept and one used regularly in organizational development activities in industry. It allows leaders through use of questionnaires to assess their own particular style before their involvement in a laboratory training program, the purpose of which is to improve styles toward an ideal 9,9 point on the managerial Grid.

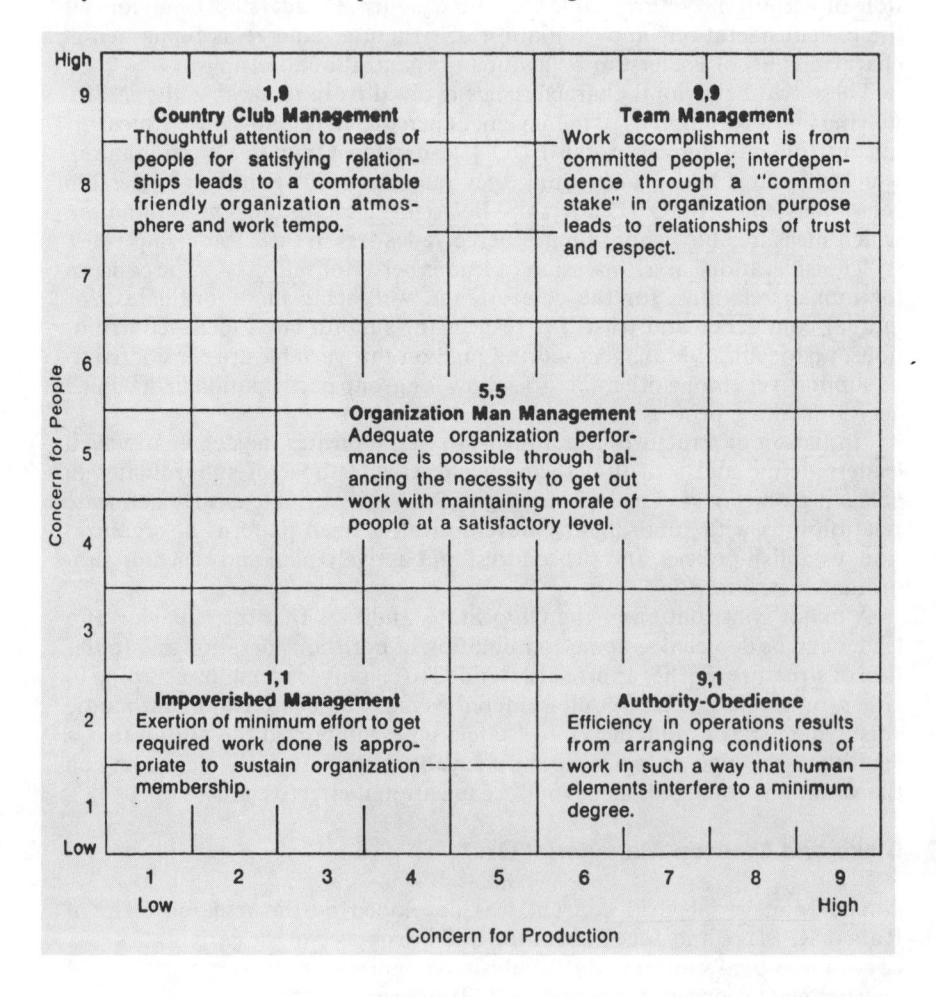

Concern for People (vertical axis, Low 1 to High 9) vs **Concern for Production** (horizontal axis, Low 1 to High 9)

1,9 Country Club Management
Thoughtful attention to needs of people for satisfying relationships leads to a comfortable friendly organization atmosphere and work tempo.

9,9 Team Management
Work accomplishment is from committed people; interdependence through a "common stake" in organization purpose leads to relationships of trust and respect.

5,5 Organization Man Management
Adequate organization performance is possible through balancing the necessity to get out work with maintaining morale of people at a satisfactory level.

1,1 Impoverished Management
Exertion of minimum effort to get required work done is appropriate to sustain organization membership.

9,1 Authority-Obedience
Efficiency in operations results from arranging conditions of work in such a way that human elements interfere to a minimum degree.

Source: The Managerial Grid figure from *The New Managerial Grid*, by Robert R. Blake and Jane S. Mouton. Houston: Gulf Publishing Company, Copyright© 1978, page 11. Reproduced by permission.

Fig. 14-1. The managerial grid

Figure 14-1 identifies five different basic leadership styles among altogether 81 possible positions on the Grid. These are:

1,1 Impoverished Management. Exertion of minimum effort to get required work done is appropriate to sustain organization membership.

9,1 Authority-Obedience. Efficiency in operations results from arranging conditions of work in such a way that human elements interfere to a minimum degree.

1,9 Country Club Management. Thoughtful attention to needs of people for satisfying relationships leads to a comfortable friendly organization atmosphere and work tempo.

5,5 Organization Man Management. Adequate organization performance is possible through balancing the necessity to get out work with maintaining morale of people at a satisfactory level.

9,9 Team Management. Work accomplishment is from committed people; interdependence through a "common stake" in organization purpose leads to relationships of trust and respect.

Situational Approach

Perhaps one of the better approaches to the situational theory has been that offered by Robert Tannenbaum and Warren Schmidt.[11] **Whereas trait theory emphasizes what a leader is, and personal behavior theory what a leader does, situational theory focuses on certain forces beyond these two dimensions. These dynamic forces which influence leadership style are present in the leader, the leader's subordinates, and also the situation itself.**

Situational theory proposed that leadership is or should be flexible and adaptable. The essence of this theory is that a leader should adjust an individual style according to the specific group being led at a given point in time in a particular environment or circumstance.

Forces in the Manager

According to Tannenbaum and Schmidt,[12] there are certain identifiable forces that function within the manager's own personality. The first is the leader's own value system and perception of people in general. Does the leader believe in delegating authority, in participative decision making, or is there the feeling that the leader is getting paid to make all the decisions?

The second is the leader's level of confidence in the subordinate's ability to make decisions. If the leader is unsure, or mistrusting of people, then the leader will, justifiably or not, have more confidence in the leader's own capabilities than in those of subordinates.

The leader's own leadership tendencies constitute a third force operating on the manager. Some managers function comfortably in a highly directive role. Issuing orders comes easy to them. Others may be more comfortable when sharing responsibilities with their subordinates.

A final force is the manager's own feelings of security. Some managers, more than others, require more predictability and stability in their environment. Decentralizing one's authority obviously requires relaxation of control over events and their outcomes.

Forces in the Subordinate

There are also forces affecting the behavior of subordinates, which influence the leader's style. The leader may allow subordinates greater freedom of action if they evidence strong needs for independence in their work and if they are willing to assume responsibility for decision making. Another determinant is the subordinates' degree of identification with the response to the goals of the firm. A final force is their present level of knowledge and experience in dealing effectively with problems facing the group.

Forces in the Situation

A third set of forces in addition to those existing in the manager and in subordinates are those present in the situation, in the organizational environment. The type of organization, its values and traditions are definite influential factors here. How does top management feel about subordinate participation in decision making? What is its expected behavior of the manager? What is the degree of cohesiveness within the group? Does the unit operate effectively as a team willing to work together in the delegated exercises of management?

Another important factor is the nature and kind of decision-making opportunities. Is the group equipped to handle certain complex problems or should these problems be left in the province of the manager? Finally, there is the all too important variable of time which permits little latitude and less opportunity for involving subordinates in the decision-making process.

Figure 14-2 presents a continuum of various leadership styles. You should observe that each style, or behavior point, simultaneously relates to the degree of authority used by the manager and the amount of autonomy or freedom for the nonmanager in reaching decisions. Most important for the manager is the assessment of the critical forces present in the situation and then a determination of a particular style that is best adaptable to those forces.

Contingency Approach

A contingency theory of leadership effectiveness is one that combines elements of both the trait and situational theories, and hypothesizes that the performance of a group is dependent on the interaction of both leadership style and the situation. Fred E. Fiedler, a leading proponent of this theory, offers the support of extensive research that suggests leadership is a relationship based on power, control, and influence. Leadership arises not only because of personality traits but also because of situational factors and the interaction between the leader and the situation.[13]

The contingency theory of Fiedler attempts to measure leadership effectiveness by employing three critical components that determine the favorableness of the situation for the leader. These are leader-member relations, task structure, and position power.

Leader-member relations refers to the degree of confidence the subordinates have in the leader. Good or bad relations with the group is considered the key factor in determining just how favorable a situation is for the leader. The leader's authority essentially depends on acceptance by the members.

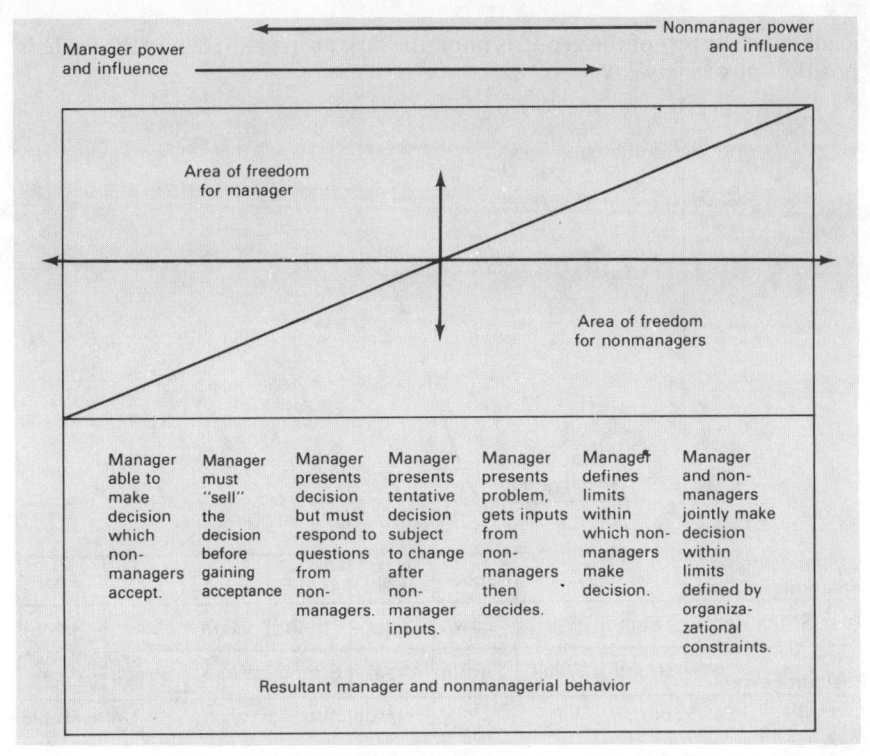

Leadership Behavior: Styles and Determinents 203

```
                                                    Nonmanager power
        Manager power                               and influence
        and influence
```

Area of freedom for manager						Area of freedom for nonmanagers	
Manager able to make decision which nonmanagers accept.	Manager must "sell" the decision before gaining acceptance	Manager presents decision but must respond to questions from nonmanagers.	Manager presents tentative decision subject to change after nonmanager inputs.	Manager presents problem, gets inputs from nonmanagers then decides.	Manager defines limits within which nonmanagers make decision.	Manager and nonmanagers jointly make decision within limits defined by organizational constraints.

Resultant manager and nonmanagerial behavior

*Source: Robert Tannenbaum and William H. Schmidt, "How to Choose A Leadership Pattern," *Harvard Business Review*, vol. 51, no. 3, May-June, 1973, p. 168. Copyright 1973 by the President and Fellows of Harvard College; all rights reserved. (Adapted with permission.)

Fig. 14-2.

Fiedler contends the leader-member relations variable is the most important, since it has to do with the degree to which followers are willing to follow their leader.

Task structure refers to the degree in which job requirements are spelled out, structured and defined in contrast to being unstructured and vague. Clear task assignments to subordinates seem to result in better performance. This factor determines greatly the leader's authority to give instructions and to evaluate performance.

Position power refers to the formal vested power in the leader's position. It includes the right to direct, evaluate, reward, and punish those being supervised. A leader with position power can more easily obtain a following than one without such power.

The combination of these three elements determines the favorableness of the situation for the leader. Eight different combinations of these elements ranging from favorable to unfavorable can be developed as in figure 14-3. A highly favorable situation is one where relationships between the leader and group are good, the task is structured, and the leader's position power is high. A highly unfavorable situation is one where the relationships between the leader and the rest of the group is poor, the task unstructured, and the leader's position power is weak.

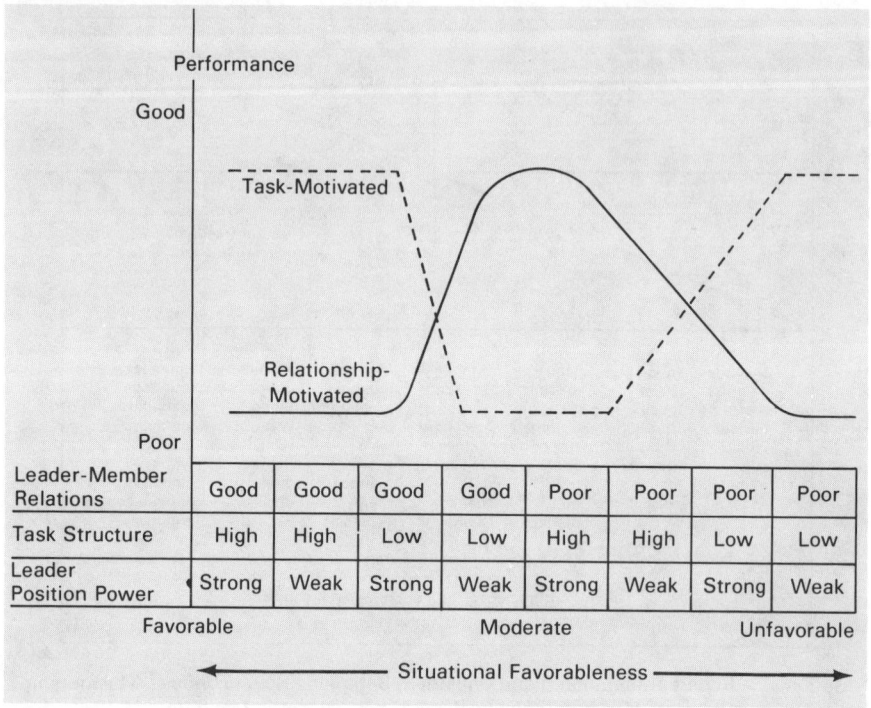

Leader-Member Relations	Good	Good	Good	Good	Poor	Poor	Poor	Poor
Task Structure	High	High	Low	Low	High	High	Low	Low
Leader Position Power	Strong	Weak	Strong	Weak	Strong	Weak	Strong	Weak
	Favorable				Moderate			Unfavorable

← Situational Favorableness →

Source: Adapted from Fred E. Fiedler, "The Contingency Model — New Directions for Leadership Utilization," *Journal of Contemporary Business* (Autumn 1974), p. 71. Reprinted with permission of the *Journal of Contemporary Business*, Copyright 1974.

Fig. 14-3. How the style of effective leadership varies with the situation

In essence, the research of Fiedler suggests that leaders who are directive and leaders who are permissive can operate best in certain situations. Leadership is a product of the leader's personality, the task to be completed, and the characteristics of the group which must be influenced. Ultimately, it is up to the leader to examine the situation and then to decide the required style of leadership.

ROLES OF LEADERSHIP

As you probably already perceived, the role of a leader is a highly complex one influenced by many subtle and, at times, elusive factors as suggested in figure 14-4. Irrespective, though, of the recognized limitations in describing leadership and its elements, certain roles of leadership may be identified:

1. **Representative.** Leaders assume, speak, and act as the representatives of

the group. They act as the office spokesperson through whom the flows of communication are channeled. Furthermore, they reinforce their representative roles by maintaining cordial contacts with their superiors and other superiors in the organization.

2. **Climate Creator.** Leaders create and nurture the kind of working environment that encourages the best efforts of people; that unleases talents, enthusiasm, and cooperation. It is the kind of climate that fosters personal growth, where people are encouraged not only to commit themselves but also to be a willing participant in the determination of the outcome of events and activities.

3. **Change Agent.** Leaders, while planning and directing, must become involved with change. They are sensitive to the changing needs of the organization and its people. They plan change, innovate it, apply it, and purposefully reduce any resistance by those affected. They also reflect a high sense of adaptability to the impact of change upon their own functions and roles.

4. **Goal Emphasizer.** Leaders exhibit a concern for goal realization. There is an emphasis on achieving goals, an emphasis not inconsistent with

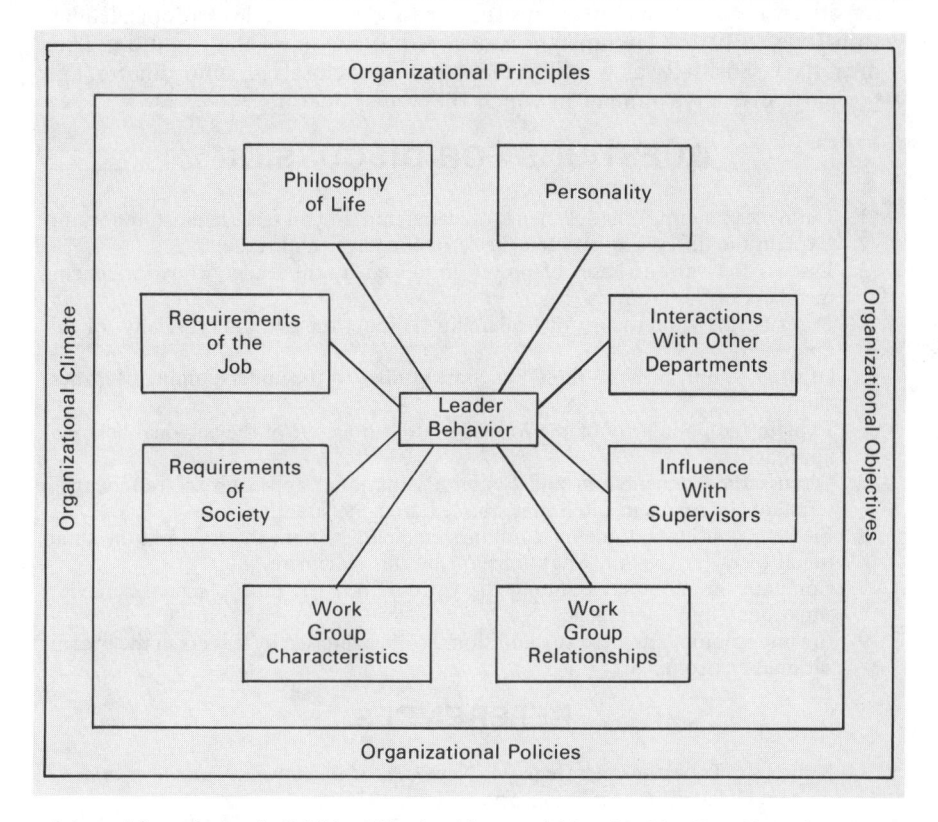

Adapted from James L. Cribbin, *Effective Managerial Leadership*, (New York: American Management Association Inc., 1972), p. 120.

Fig. 14-4. Factors influencing leadership behavior patterns

other desirable attributes of leadership, such as their feelings for people. By the same token, they apply, wherever required, necessary pressure to induce the desired contributions of their followers.
5. **Activist.** Leaders are activists who make things happen. Their energy is the catalyst that generates the drive to perform required work. Opportunities and dreams conjured up from behind a desk are nothing until they are physically activated. Intellect and knowledge are meaningless until put to use with applications of energy.
6. **Empathizer.** Leaders recognize that their success is effected through others. Consequently, they develop a strong sense of social awareness; and a sensitivity to others. They are positive and supportive in their interpersonal relationships. They exhibit enthusiasm and encouragement in the daily pursuit of objectives.

As a final wrap-up in our discussion of leadership, several points need to be reemphasized. First, there is no conclusive evidence of physical traits or personality attributes that are universally common in all leadership situations. Leaders, it seems, originate because of a combination of elements that include certain factors within the followers. Effective leaders must have the necessary sensitivity to assess and interpret situations and then be able to adopt a leadership style to fit the circumstances and requirements of the situation. They must have sensitivity as well in understanding themselves, subordinates, and the particular environment in which they must operate.

QUESTIONS FOR DISCUSSION

1. Define leadership. What elements of leadership do you feel are most important?
2. Explain the difference between the terms manager and leader.
3. Discuss the various bases of power employed by the leader while influencing members of the group.
4. Describe the trait theory of leadership. Discuss the credibility, if any, of this approach.
5. Of what significance are the Ohio State studies to the understanding of leadership?
6. Explain the popularity of the Managerial Grid as one of the personal behavior approaches.
7. Discuss the Tannenbaum and Schmidt situational approach to leadership in terms of the forces in the leader, the led, and the situation.
8. Fiedler's contingency theory combines elements of both the trait and the situational theories. Explain what is meant by this statement.
9. Compare the differences among the various theories: trait, personal behavior, situational, and contingency.
10. In your opinion, are there any additional roles exercised by leaders in the organizational environment?

REFERENCES

1. Robert L. Trewatha and Gene M. Newport, *Management: Functions and Behavior* (Dallas: Business Publications, Inc., 1976), p. 437.
2. John R. P. French and Bertram Raven, "The Bases of Social Power," *Group Dynamics* (New York: Harper & Row, 1960), pp. 612-21.
3. James H. Donnelly, Jr., James L. Gibson, and John M. Ivancevich, *Fundamentals of Management* (Dallas: Business Publications, Inc., 1971), p. 187.

4. Ralph M. Stogdill, "Personal Factors Associated With Leadership," *Journal of Applied Psychology* (January 1948): 35-71.
5. Research is by Edwin E. Ghiselli, as described in Alan C. Filley, Robert J. House, and Steven Kerr, *Managerial Process and Organizational Behavior*, 2d ed. (Glenview, IL: Scott, Foresman & Company, 1976), p. 213.
6. Dalton E. McFarland, *Management: Principles and Practices,* 4th ed. (New York: Macmillan Publishing Company, Inc., 1974), p. 486.
7. For a detailed review of these efforts the student should see Ralph M. Stogdill, *Handbook of Leadership* (New York: The Free Press, 1974).
8. Ralph M. Stogdill and Alvin E. Coons, eds., *Leader Behavior: Its Description and Measurement*, Research Monograph, no. 88 (Columbus, OH: Bureau of Business Research, The Ohio State University, 1967).
9. Steven Kerr, and Chester Schriesheim, "Consideration, Initiating Structure, and Organizational Criteria—An Update of Korman's 1966 Review," *Personnel Psychology,* (Winter 1974): 555-68, for a clarifying response to a critique of these studies.
10. Robert R. Blake and Jane S. Mouton, *The New Managerial Grid* (Houston: Gulf Publishing Company, 1978).
11. Robert Tannenbaum, and Warren H. Schmidt, "How to Choose a Leadership Pattern," *Harvard Business Review*, vol. 51, no. 3, (May-June 1973); 162-80.
12. Ibid. Treatment of the situational theory is mostly adapted from "How to Choose a Leadership Pattern."
13. For a detailed description and analysis, see Fred E. Fiedler and Martin M. Chemers, *Leadership and Effective Management* (Glenview, IL: Scott, Foresman & Co., 1974), pp. 63-69.

SELECTED BIBLIOGRAPHY

1. Campbell, John P.; Dunnette, Marvin D.; Lawler, Edward E., III; and Weick, Karl E., Jr.. *Management Behavior Performance and Effectiveness*. New York: McGraw-Hill Book Co., 1970.
2. Fiedler, Fred E., and Chemers, Martin M. *Leadership and Effective Management* Glenview, IL: Scott, Foresman & Co., 1974.
3. Reddin, William J. *Managerial Effectiveness*. New York: McGraw-Hill Book Co., 1970.
4. Stogdill, Ralph M. *Handbook of Leadership: A Survey of Theory and Research*. New York: Free Press, 1974.
5. Vroom, Victor, and Yetton, Philip W. *Leadership and Decision Making*. Pittsburgh: University of Pittsburgh Press, 1973.

CHAPTER 15

DEVELOPING THE MANAGERIAL TEAM

Purpose of Chapter 15:

1. To rationalize managerial development as an organizational necessity
2. To introduce relevant guidelines for developing the firm's leaders
3. To identify the content, methods and techniques emphasized in the developmental process
4. To outline a program for evaluating the results of developmental activities

Essential elements you should understand after studying this chapter:

1. Definition of management development
2. Purpose of developing managerial talent
3. Forces behind the need for managerial development
4. Basic concepts for developing managers
5. Important on-the-job methods
6. Off-the-job developmental methods
7. Developmental techniques employed
8. System for evaluating effectiveness

INTRODUCTION

Managing in today's progressive organization, one surrounded by ever-changing environments, requires a continual effort by management to keep pace with the effects of change upon both the institution and its members. Organizational growth, increasing product complexity, and advancing technological progress, among other factors, emphasize that the organization develop and maintain a system for on-going training and development of its management personnel.

Moreover, such emphasis applies not only to management in business firms but also, and more frequently, to such diverse industries as health care, government, and education. There are reasons, of course, for the increased acceptance of training as an organizational responsibility. They rest on the fact that firms must first insure the continuity of qualified leadership and second, maximize the contribution of sound management to the success of the organization.

Implicit in structuring a formalized plan of management development is the understanding that the institution cannot allow development to be a matter of either chance or random experiences. This means that careful consideration must be given to the many dimensions of development. That is what we attempt to do in this chapter.

PURPOSES OF MANAGER DEVELOPMENT

What should be the purposes of a formal system of management training and development? Generally they are these:

1. To raise the present level of managerial performance to its highest achievable level
2. To develop the latent potential of individual managers for ultimate broader assumptions of responsibility
3. To insure a reservoir of qualified manpower to satisfy the organization's present and future needs
4. To satisfy the manager's personal need for professional growth and career progress
5. To provide a favorable climate that encourages and sustains individual development and professional achievement

Management development includes both training and education. *Training* as used here refers to the acquisition or increase of skills and knowledge required to perform the specific tasks in a management job. *Education*, on the other hand, has a broader connotation. Its purpose is to enhance the decision-making aspects of management. It also refers to developing individuals, so they may acquire a greater understanding of the adaptability to their total environment.

When the managers' understanding of the factors that affect them are increased, a better adjustment to their role in the organization is expected to result. Similarly, understanding the relationship of the firm to the total business environment and even to the broad economic, political, and social environment should help develop in them the value judgments, attitudes, and the perspective of a leader. Ultimately, the result of sound training and education should be the acquisition of effective knowledge, skills, and attitudes in the manager who aspires to the role of leadership.

FORCES BEHIND DEVELOPMENT OF MANAGERS

More than ever before, institutions are facing up to certain dynamic environmental changes occurring in our society. A brief review of these economic, technological, social, and demographic changes is enough to present the need for better and more formal plans for management development.

Increasing Complexity

Today's organization is much more complex and complicated to manage. The manager must not only be concerned with the management of production but also with other disciplines and concerns, such as the behavioral sciences, marketing, finance, taxation, government, and law. Complexity in the modern organization also requires more advance knowledge and skills in new and emerging fields such as computerization, automation, logistics, and international management.

Technological Change

The applications of new technologies demand more sophisticated training and development. Technological advances while primarily replacing lower-level workers will require more qualified managers. This alone will compound the need for more effective management.

Executive Obsolescence

Changing technologies and a changing environment outdate the knowledge and skills of management, particularly those in the scientific and professional fields. This requires constant updating not only to keep abreast of the current developments in one's areas of expertise but also to prepare for future ones as well.

Occupational Shifts

Over the years, there has been a persistent increase in the aggregate employment of managers and administrators. In fact, manager employment is projected to reach 10.9 million in 1985, which is up from 8.9 million in 1974. This represents a slightly faster rate of growth (22 percent increase) than anticipated for total employment (20 percent increase).

Moreover, in terms of the share of total employment, manager employment is expected to rise slightly upward from 10.4 percent in 1974 to 10.5 percent in 1985. Important, too, is the fact that while manager employment is expected to increase 10 percent in the manufacturing sector from 1974 to 1985, in the service industries, the projection for the same period is 40 percent.[1]

Increased management development activities must be consistent with this shift and growth of occupations. This is particularly true as more women and minority members have access to management responsibilities.

Increased Professionalism

Management is recognized as a distinct and professional kind of work with professional status, an established body of knowledge, principles, functions, and techniques that can be learned and taught. Professionalism requires continued dedication toward individual improvement and progress.

Broader Social Consciousness

Within recent years, business has evidenced a deepening social responsibility for the development of its employees. There is an increasing reliance upon the organization to assist the employee's development.

This social responsibility is not only the result of societal influences and external pressure, such as civil rights legislation, but also arises out of the organization's recognition to assist people in dealing with the problems and changes that are associated with an advancing technology.

SOME CONCEPTS OF MANAGER DEVELOPMENT

Earlier attempts at developmental programs in business were often a heterogeneous collection of phases, fads, gimmicks, and unrelated methods and techniques. Many so-called programs were sheer experiments. However, out of much confusion, there has gradually evolved, through the combined experience and research of business and the university, certain fundamental principles of development.

Whereas 20 years ago only the larger, well-financed and-staffed firm could afford training and development professionals in their ranks, today even smaller organizations have these specialists. Indeed, training which formerly was a subfunction of minor importance in the personnel field now is capstoned with its own professional association known as The American Society for Training and Development (ASTD). Formed in 1945, it presently has over 9,500 members. The society estimates there are over 50,000 professionals in the training area including those in private and public education systems.[2]

The following concepts or guidelines are generally accepted as being relevant to manager development in the enterprise:[3]

1. All development is self-development. This accepted truism is pivotal to all other principles. It means that development is not something done to a person. The results of training and development should be change—change in knowledge, attitudes, and skills. This change cannot be imposed by some other person but, in contrast, must be self-induced and voluntarily accepted and assimilated by the individual. The motivation, the effort, the obligation, and the responsibility for development lies within the person.
2. Manager development must be for *all* managers in the organization. Its objective should be to challenge all to increased personal growth and progress. This means that programming opportunities should be geared to all levels, not necessarily a selected few "crown princes" arbitrarily

predestined for top management positions. Otherwise, the effect would be to discourage those not selected.
3. Responsibility belongs to the line. It is impossible for the manager to delegate the development process. While the manager can delegate certain activities, this responsibility remains with management. In fact, the manager must be evaluated on the degree to which subordinate development is facilitated.
4. Development requires action. By this is meant that if a person is to develop, there must be some kind of change. Yet, nothing changes by itself. Change is produced by some influencing agent or stimulus. Development occurs because of some action or reaction on the part of the learner. New knowledges, new behavior patterns, and skills require involvement by the learner. Increasingly, company developmental programs provide actual practice in applying management knowledge and actual use of skills required on the job.
5. Emphasis is on the present job. Current thinking stresses a manager's development on the present assignment rather than on possible future ones. While promotion is an important motivator, undue emphasis diverts the manager's attention to excessive looking ahead. The developmental process should be interfaced with the present job and its improvement. Simultaneously, the manager is helped and encouraged to prepare for future and sometimes unknown responsibilities.

CONTENT OF DEVELOPMENTAL PROGRAMMING

Essentially, all management developmental activities should have as fundamental objectives an increase in the person's knowledge, an acquisition or improvement in managerial skills, or a fundamental change in attitude or belief. More directly, the actual agenda and instrumentation to achieve such objectives vary widely with the different and particular needs of organizations and individuals. For illustrative purposes, however, the following are typical areas and topics of concern in developmental programming:

1. Ongoing growth and development in the manager's technical field. Improvement of functional expertise and skill in the fields of production, personnel, marketing and finance.
2. Improvement of skills and techniques, both qualitative and quantitative, for more effective decision making.
3. Understanding the application of the computer sciences. Using the computer as another language.
4. Better conceptual and pragmatic understanding of the process of management and its functions and elements. Development in planning, directing and controlling.
5. Development in the behavioral sciences. An understanding of the variables in individual and group behavior, of motivation and morale.
6. Development of interpersonal skills. The ability to communicate more effectively, to interview, and to lead conferences. Learning the techniques of coaching and counseling. Figure 15-1 illustrates a conceptual approach to management development.

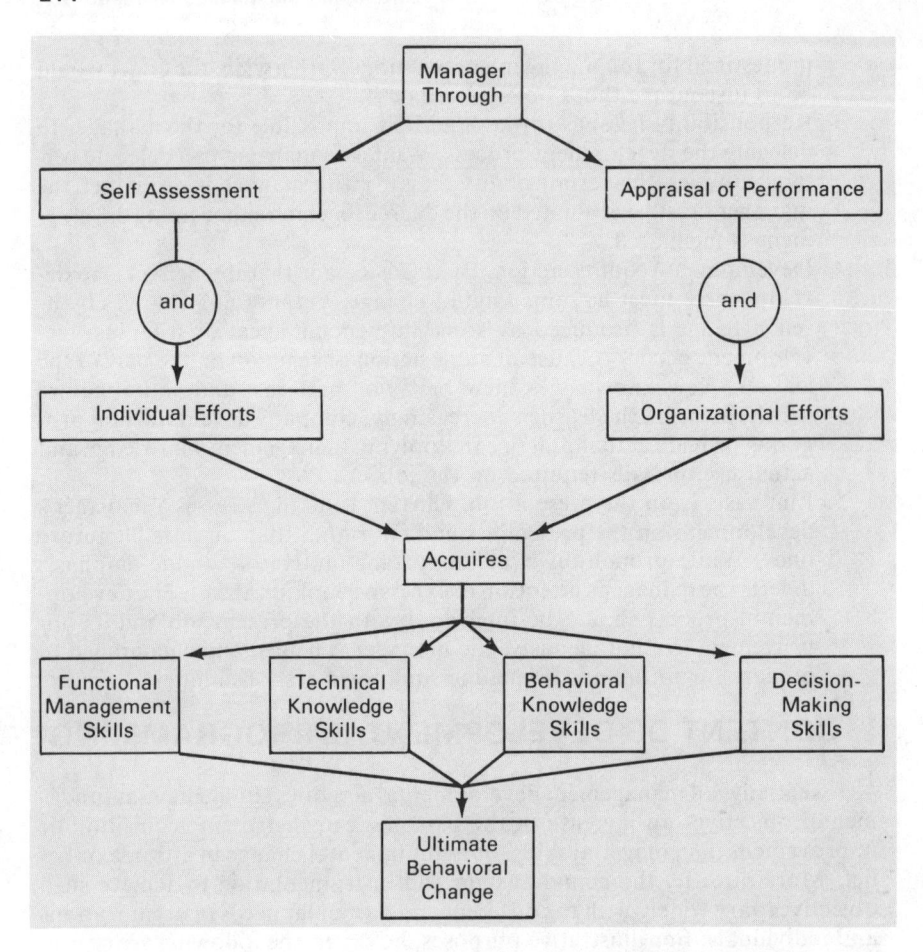

Fig. 15-1. Model of an approach to manager development

ON-THE-JOB DEVELOPMENTAL METHODS

On-the-job methods are considered important because of their relationship to the principles of development we mentioned earlier. While on the job, it is easier to diagnose the person's individual strengths and weaknesses. Through recognizing and assuming responsibility for job performance and results, the manager is motivated to continual self-development.

Guided on-the-job training, moreover, permits direct application of the person's new knowledge and skills. There is a concurrent responsibility for work performance and, also, direct and continuous feedback of results for evaluation purposes by the person's superior. The superior can then coach, counsel, and advise the subordinate on actual peformance in order to adjust it to required performance standards.

The success of on-the-job methods is based, however, on two important organizational principles. First, responsibility and accountability must be clearly and distinctly identified, preferably through written position descriptions.

Secondly, there must be a program for systematically evaluating the individual's performance and progress. Management appraisal, by the way, is the subject of chapter. 16.

There are a number of on-the-job methods. Some of the more common ones are discussed here.

Job Rotation

This method consists of transferring managers from job to job, department, or branch to branch in a deliberately planned program to broaden their knowledge and acquire diversified skills. Assignments may be either short or long range in time—anywhere from several months to several years depending on the assignment. The benefits of job rotation, as a method, are that it permits managers to develop a generalized rather than a specialized base necessary for top executive positions. It permits cross pollination of personnel concepts and ideas. It assists in breaking down barriers that arise out of misunderstanding between line and staff or between functional departments.

On the other hand, job rotation does entail certain limitations. The value received from short-term rotation assignments is oftentimes questionable. Frequent relocation can also affect the manager's morale and that of the family. There is, also, less pressure to perform if the trainee is rotated on short-term assignments in an "observer" capacity. The trainee should be in a position long enough to assume and perform functional responsibility. Otherwise, an understanding of the assignment is a topical rather than an integrative experience.

Planned Progression

Whereas one of the objectives of job rotation is generalized knowledge of the organization, the objective of planned progression is to program the manager for the acquisition of specific knowledge and skills within a specific functional area. It is directed toward a developmental need area as revealed by an audit of the manager's capabilites. It consists of assignments that fill in or complete certain needed aspects of development.

Managerial Trainee Programs

In many organizations, there are special training programs for recent college graduates. This type of program has a variety of names, but its purpose is to give the college graduate a general orientation to the firm and its operations prior to a definite assignment. Many times, the specific assignment is unknown, until after the organization has had the opportunity to assess the individual. Generally, placement is a function of mutual agreement between trainee and the firm. The program's length may vary from a few weeks to two years, and usually the trainees are directly controlled by the personnel or management development division.

Special Projects

This is a widely acclaimed method utilized by firms to provide challenge to the manager. The promising manager may need broader experiences or exposure in a particular area; or, conversely, the organization may have a specialized problem to solve or undertake. It may be a production problem, or research on a new product, or a distribution method. While the nature of assignments may vary, generally it is a temporary or part-time responsibility in addition to the person's regular duties. While doing so, the person is observed and guided by the superior.

If special projects are just additional work in the field of the manager's competency, then they are just added work. Conversely, challenging assignments outside the person's scope can help "stretch" a manager. If the person is required to develop new perspectives, learn a new knowledge, use new skills or methods, and become familiar with the unfamiliar, then true development will transpire.

Understudy Assignments

The understudy plan provides the conditions under which the manager learns the job of a superior so that the understudy is able either to substitute for or replace the superior if the position is vacated. The superior is responsible for coaching and instructing the understudy who is sometimes designated as "assistant to" or "staff assistant."

Advantages of this method are several. It allows the "trainee" to become familiar with the job's requirements before assuming its responsibilities. Relatively little time is needed by the successor to make the transition, thus assuring continuity of effective management. The superior is free for extended periods of time without fear of significant loss of departmental effectiveness. And when the superior is ready for promotion, it need not be delayed because lack of a replacement.

There are certain disadvantages, however. Effectiveness of the method depends solely on the understudy's relationships with the superior. Faults, as well as positive strengths, may be perpetuated. The understudy may become a replication of the boss. Furthermore, this method requires a conscious process of delegation by the superior who, for several reasons, may hesitate to delegate. There may be a lack of confidence in the understudy; or the superior may perceive the understudy as a threat to job security; or simply, the superior may not know how to delegate.

Group on-the-job Developmental Methods

A common practice of development is to assign special jobs or problems to a group of managers known as a task force. Its assignments span the organization, and its members come from different functions or locations within the firm. An assignment to a task force allows the manager the broadening experience of cooperating with managers of different backgrounds. This may be conducive not only to a broader-based understanding of the organization but also to better interdepartmental communications that result from the knowledge and awareness of the other managers and their units.

Multiple management is a practice similar to the task force. Sometimes known as the junior executive board, its members are generally drawn from middle management ranks. These boards, however, are purely advisory. Their purpose is to investigate, analyze, and offer recommendations to the board of directors or to the top officer of the function they serve, such as production or marketing.

Miscellaneous Methods

Some varied, and sometimes overlooked, methods of on-the-job development are also recommended, such as:

1. Substitute assignments. Assigning a potential manager to fill the temporary vacancy created when the present manager is away for extended periods, such as vacations.
2. Participation in company training programs. Allowing a manager to conduct training sessions in a field of competency can be extremely developmental to the growing executive.
3. Staff meetings. Permitting junior managers to attend or to sit in for the boss at relevant staff meetings can provide an added dimension of development.

OFF-THE-JOB DEVELOPMENTAL METHODS

There are a wide variety of off-the-job methods employable by an organization. *Off the job*, by the way, does not necessarily mean "outside the company," since many activities of this type are conducted by company personnel, either somewhere on the premises or away at some designated site, such as a hotel or conference center. Most commonly accepted, by definition, "off-the-job" development means those training activities that are not considered part of the manager's day-to-day work. Instead, more formal in character, these activities are additive or supplemental to the experiences gained on the job. A further advantage is the participant can devote full attention to the program in an atmosphere free of the pressure of job responsibility.

Company Training Programs

In this category are an endless variety of activities administered by the unit responsible for corporate development and training. Sessions are generally held in company conference rooms or training centers. The faculty for this type of program is usually company personnel with occasional use of the outside consultant.

Seminars, Conferences, Institutes

These are generally of a specialized character, sponsored off the premises by professional training associations or management groups. Their purpose is to augment development through participation in seminars conducted by professional learners in a field of expertise.

University Courses and Programs

Participation by universities in corporate executive development has been along two different lines. The first is illustrated by enrollment of managers in courses that are part of the regular curriculum offering. The second is represented by what is known as university development programs. These are generally designed for management at the middle and/or senior levels. There are approximately 45 major university development programs in existence.[4]

Most of the growth in university-sponsored programs has occurred since 1950. Such programs range in length from two to three weeks and may require on-campus residency by the participant. These programs should not be confused with the infinite number of shorter programs offered on the campus and often sponsored in conjunction with professional and trade associations.

An advantage claimed for university programs is that they encourage cross-fertilization of ideas among executives who represent different company experiences and viewpoints. Furthermore, executives feel more free to discuss their own weaknesses or to voice their opinions without fear of criticism or review by company colleagues or superiors. Then, too, executives can enjoy a learning environment without the pressures of their daily tasks.

TRAINING AND DEVELOPMENTAL TECHNIQUES

There are many useful techniques employable in developmental programs. The proper techniques depend upon the objective of the program or conference, its content, and for whom and by whom the program is conducted. In certain cases, a combination of techniques might be appropriate. The choice of technique is at the discretion of the company trainer or program leader. It must be remembered that the specific technique is really an instrument for helping effect change in the individual within a learning environment. Consequently, it must be chosen carefully for effects commensurate to its cost.

Lecture Technique

The lecture technique or the traditional classroom approach is by no means obsolete in management development programs. It consists of a verbal presentation with the learners engaging in a listening role. There is little interaction or feedback between the trainer and participant. While there are obvious limitations to this technique, it generally is applicable for large groups while conveying new information in a sequential, logical pattern of development. To enhance learner motivation, this technique should be employed in conjunction with other types of participative techniques, such as small group discussions, workshops, or panel discussions.

Role Playing

As the name implies, this is a technique of simulating situations, generally of a conflict nature between individuals and then having participants enact the part or role of the personalities. In management training programs, the emphasis is placed upon developing empathy with the attitudes and feelings of others and awareness of their reactions to one's own behavior. In addition, there is often an opportunity to practice the acquired human relations skills in specific problem situations. Sometimes, though, in sales training programs, for example, the emphasis is upon practice and delivery of sales presentations for eventual critique by the trainer.

Conferences

As a training technique, the conference is widely used in management development circles. It may be employed in several ways—as a training vehicle in solving specific management problems, or it may be used to acquire knowledge and understanding of concepts.

As a problem-solving technique, the conference enlists the participation of group members. A decision-making situation is offered for consideration, and the conference leader actuates and coordinates the group discussion so that individuals may contribute their thinking to the logical solution. Simultaneously, they learn the information and skills contributed by the leader and the others. When necessary information is not available from anyone in the group, individuals may be assigned responsibility for obtaining it.

As an informational or instructional medium, the conference combines the desired features of the lecture while allowing for ample discussion and feedback. Thus the conference technique has a number of advantages. It provides a learning atmosphere in which individual members benefit by sharing of experiences and ideas. Understanding is measurable through immediate feedback, and creative thinking is often stimulated through interpersonal exchange. It allows for suggestions and opinions and is conducive to improved motivation and morale. Since a sense of participation is generated, group members tend to assume greater responsibility for the decision and normally cooperate more willingly in effecting the solution.

To be successful, the conference technique requires a qualified leader skilled in discussion-leading techniques, along with a planned agenda with clearly stated objectives that identify the conference as either problem solving, instructional, or informative in character. It requires a properly equipped conference room and able conferees. Generally, a group should be limited to 15 or 20 members. Members should be selected on the basis of some interest or knowledge they already possess. This permits not only useful contribution to the solution of the problem but also provides knowledge, skill, and an additudinal framework for benefiting from the discussion experience. There is one word of caution, though, for management. The interchange so essential to efficient conferences should not be hampered by unreasonable differences in the rank, status, or experience levels among the participants.

Finally, this technique of development requires time for progress and cannot be precisely scheduled. By the same token, if the program is not carefully planned, the conference can readily degenerate into an unproductive "bull session."

Case Study

The case is a written description of a realistic situation in the business enterprise. It can be general or specific in its nature and approach. With considerable descriptive detail, it is presented for analysis and discussion. Usually, advance preparation by participants is required for the discussion. Practice is obtained in analyzing factual data, applying basic principles, separating symptoms from causes of behavior, evaluating alternative approaches, and then deciding upon a definite course of action. For managers with experience, cases furnish a manner of weighing personal judgment and analysis against that of other participants.

Management Simulation

A management game is a form of business simulation that actively involves the participants in decision-making roles. At the onset, a descriptive model of a firm is constructed. Participants are divided into management teams and then given various kinds of information about company operations, including data on investments, production capacity, sales, inventory, pricing, advertising, and other pertinent information. Decisions are generated in these functional areas with the management teams competing with each other to see which one can most effectively improve its market position or its profitability in relationship to the other teams. Participants have the opportunity to observe how a decision in one area, such as sales for example, will affect the other areas of the company in a competitive industry.

The model is often programmed on a computer; and, consequently, results of decisions are processed and made available almost immediately. Some business games are quite simple in design with a few variables as inputs for decisions. Increasingly though, a higher degree of sophistication involving many variables is being achieved so that the game more nearly approximates actual business situations.

T-Group Training

The T stands for training. It is also known as laboratory training and is sometimes equated with sensitivity training. However, there is a real distinction here, since sensitivity training is more related to group psychotherapy.

The T-group technique focuses on the development of a laboratory environment in which participants have the opportunity to learn about themselves, about interpersonal relationships, about groups and group behavior, and about larger social problems.[5] Its origin dates back to the National Training Laboratory (NTL) of the National Education Association, which held its first laboratory session at Bethel, ME, in 1947.[6] Presently, many kinds of institutions—business, education, services, as well as government—employ this technique, oftentimes using qualified consultants as group trainers.

The objectives of laboratory training are to assist the learner in achieving self-awareness and social effectiveness in interpersonal relationships. As managers develop new insight into individual effectiveness, they are expected to develop desirable changes in attitudes and behavior.

One suggested criticism of T-group training however is this. The target for change is essentially the individual and not the organization. When the participants return to their old structures, they normally step back in the same definition of their roles. The returning participants may have changed, but their superiors, colleagues, and subordinates more than likely have not. Nor has the organization changed. Critics say this aggravates any existing frustration and tension.[7]

Within recent years, though, there has been an expansion of laboratory programs, and innovations have been introduced and evaluated. One of these is the closer linking of the T-group to the realities of specific organizations. This is accomplished in part by dealing specifically with problems of change in the organizational setting involving members of that same organization who are ultimately responsible for implementing change.[8]

The results of T-group training, like all training, are difficult to measure. But, research seems to indicate that T-group training improves job performance for some people, but not all. The degree of benefit appears to be related to the extent people are willing to engage in "unfrozen" participation and their willingness to accept feedback.

Tangible results from applied research, the newer forms of application, and a growing corps of qualified trainers along with an evident interest by corporations seems to make T-group training an increasingly popular and acceptable form of development.

EVALUATION OF DEVELOPMENTAL PROGRAMS

Certainly, control activities must be exercised in the interest of effective management development. Obviously effectiveness should be measured or appraised. Yet, this is most difficult since the identifiable results of managerial development programs cannot always be readily traced to definite causal factors in the program. Other causal and nonrelated factors may influence favorable changes on the manager. Moreover, the work of a manger is such that changes in performance may transpire only over a protracted time period. Nevertheless, some assessment of developmental efforts is desirable, not only because of corporate cost and time factors involved but also because of the critical essentiality of the commitment to development.

Although no single method achieves complete satisfaction, several evaluative methods may be used to measure conclusively the impact of developmental efforts. Among these are: (1) measurement of changes in operational results, (2) measurement of change in behavior, (3) evaluation by participants, and (4) evaluation of the participants in the program.

Changes in Results of Operations

Since one chief objective of management development is improvement of current performance, changes in results of operations might be one index of effectiveness. Such information might be found in production or sales figures, budget, and other financial data, profit figures, turnover data, morale indices, and similar quantitative information.

Changes in Personal Behavior

Actually, there should be less concern with measuring the accumulation of knowledge and more with measuring the character and quality of attitude and action as they relate to improved job performance. Periodic appraisals will assist the superior in comparing personality and behavior traits, including attitudes, with ratings given the manager before training.

Evaluation by Participants

The participants themselves are frequently asked to evaluate a program. While it is difficult to achieve the participant's objectivity in assessing the effects of training on job performance, nonetheless, there is merit to this method. The participant's attitudes and any subjective opinion are important since these indicate the degree of influence exerted by the program. This method can offer constructive criticism with respect to program content, its application, method and quality of instruction, physical facilities, and similar topics.

Evaluation of Participants

This is best accomplished by attempting first to identify the desired objectives, benefits, or behavior of a specific management training program over a given time interval. Ideally, the desired objectives would be compared with a similar group of managers who did not experience the training program. Any differences then in the benefits, as measured by improved job performance of the group who were exposed to the training program, could be attributed to the training effort.

Such a procedure would take the following steps, as diagrammed in figure 15-2:

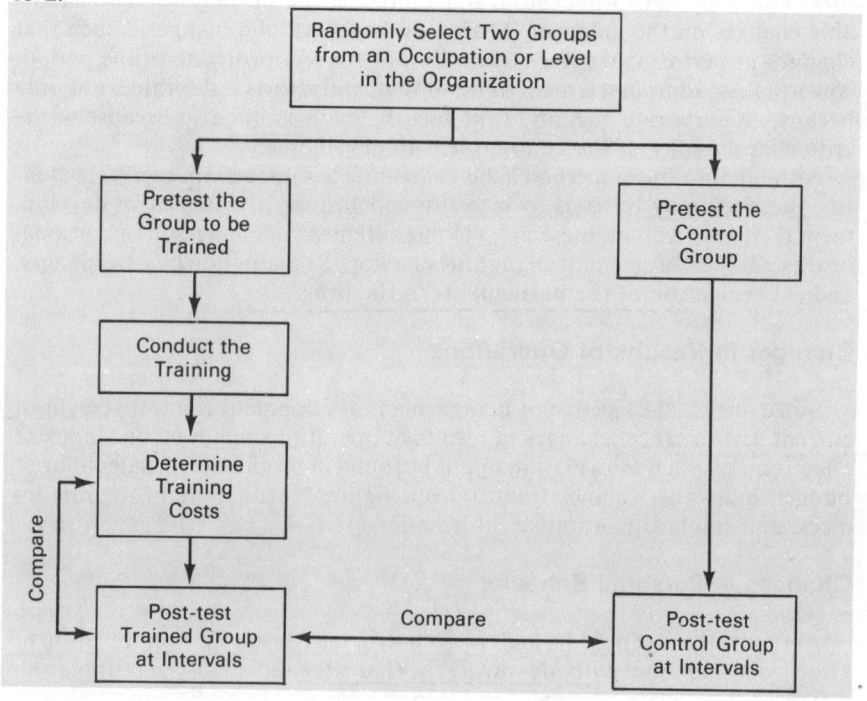

*Source: *Management of Human Resources,* William P. Anthony and Edward A. Nicholson, Columbus, Ohio, Grid, Inc., 1977, p. 173. (Used with permission.)

Fig. 15-2. Training and career development systems

1. Randomly establish two groups of managers from similar jobs or organizational level. One group will be exposed to the training program (experimental group), the other will not (control group).
2. Pretest both groups in terms of behavior and/or knowledge to determine present levels or stages.
3. Administer the training program for one group.
4. Determine all costs of the training effort, including instructor costs, manager expenses, media costs, facilities, and manager time away from the job.
5. Conduct a post-test measure of behavior or knowledge of both groups at periodic intervals after completion of training.
6. Compare the benefits of the program as measured by improved behavior or job knowledge with the costs of the program for the trained group.
7. Compare the post-test behavior behavior and job knowledge of the trained group with the control group.[9]

Need for Better Evaluation Methods

Unquestionably, much can yet be done to improve evaluation methods. More precise methods need to be developed through research and continual experimentation. Often, measurement is difficult because of ill-defined objectives and standards for developmental activities. Unless specific objectives are established, then measurement techniques are useless.

Finally, while it is recognized that certain programs do not lend themselves to evaluation, top management should nevertheless continue to support research using those techniques and instruments for the quantitative as well as qualitative measurement of programs. The purpose of development should be recognizable change in the behavior of the participants. This is the most significant function of training; and if organizations are to spend their money wisely, then continuous evaluation attempts are necessary.

QUESTIONS FOR DISCUSSION

1. What should be specific objectives of management development programs?
2. Why do training and development programs not always achieve desired effectiveness?
3. Describe the process and content of a training program with which you are familiar. How does it measure up to the standard methods and techniques of this chapter?
4. Evaluate the statement that manager development processes are for the larger firm only.
5. Discuss the arguments for and against the use of sensitivity training as a developmental technique.
6. How can exectuive development programs be evaluated? Identify certain problems associated with the present methods of evaluation.

REFERENCES

1. U.S. Department of Labor, *Monthly Labor Review*, Bureau of Labor Statistics, vol. 99, no. 11 (nov. 1976): 12-14.
2. J.S. Jenness, "Change for the Future," *Training and Development Journal* (Jan-

uary 1972): 2-4.
3. Largely adapted from Walter S. Wikstrom, "Developing Managers: Underlying Principles," *Management Record* (November 1962): 15-18.
4. "Executive Development Programs in Universities," *Studies in Personnel Policy*, no. 215, National Industrial Conference Board, Inc., New York, 1969, p. 1.
5. Leland P. Bradford, Jack R. Gibb, and Kenneth D. Benne, *T-Group Theory and Laboratory Method: Innovation and Re-education* (New York: John Wiley & Sons, Inc., 1964), p. vii.
6. Ibid, p. 8.
7. Daniel Katz and Robert Kahn, *Social Psychology of Organizations* (New York: John Wiley & Sons, Inc., 1966), pp. 390-91.
8. Ibid., p. 558.
9. William P. Anthony and Edward A. Nicholson, *Management of Human Resources* (Columbus, OH: Grid, Inc., 1977), p. 172).

SELECTED BIBLIOGRAPHY

1. Anthony, William P., and Nicholson, Edward A. *Management of Human Resources.* Columbus, OH: Grid, Inc., 1977.
2. Campbell, John P.; Dunnette, Marvin D.; Lawler, Edward E., III; and Weick, Karl E., Jr. *Managerial Behavior, Performance, and Effectiveness.* New York: McGraw-Hill Book Co., 1970.
3. French, Wendell L., and Bell, Cecil H., Jr. *Organization Development.* Englewood Cliffs, NJ: Prentice-Hall, Inc., 1973.
4. Goldstein, Irwin I. *Training: Program Development and Evaluation.* Monterey CA: Brooks/Cole Publishing Co., 1974.
5. Patten, Thomas H., Jr. *Manpower Planning and the Development of Human Resources.* New York: Wiley Interscience Division, John Wiley & Sons, Inc., 1971.

CHAPTER 16

APPRAISING THE PERFORMANCE OF MANAGEMENT

Purpose of Chapter 16:

1. To introduce the concept and purposes of systematically appraising the performance of the organization's management
2. To identify the specific variables employed in evaluation
3. To review the methodologies of measurement
4. To recommend an integrated program for organizational adoption

Essential elements you should understand after studying this chapter:

1. Purposes of management appraisal
2. Dimensions employed in measuring performance
3. Limitation of personality traits in appraisal
4. System of management by objectives as an appraisal approach
5. Different methods of appraisal
6. Procedure for an appraisal program

INTRODUCTION

By this time you should be thoroughly aware that the success of an organization is largely dependent upon the effectiveness of its management personnel. Critical, then, to serving the fundamental concepts of management is the need to measure and evaluate the performance of the institution's management people. More than this, such evaluation besides being fundamental to effective management itself, must also be based upon the distinct contributions of management personnel to the attainment of organizational goals. Accordingly, operational programs for regularly appraising performance should be established by management throughout the entire organization. **Performance appraisal is the process of measuring and evaluating the performance of management against certain and verifiable criteria. Performance appraisal is usually listed under the staffing function as a responsibility.** But even so, it also is firmly linked to the functions of planning and controlling. For is is through planning that the goals are established against which management performance is measured. And it is through controlling that managerial performance is evaluated, and then redirected, if corrections are necessary. Furthermore, the appraisal process is pertinent to all levels of management.

PURPOSES OF MANAGER APPRAISAL

The contemporary organization finds it important to employ a system of management appraisal for several reasons. First of all, it is used to assess the performance of each manager when framed against previously established goals and objectives. And assuming a consistent and well-planned effort to reach verifiable goals, then the best criteria of appraisal are the goals themselves, the planning programs used to accomplish them, and the manager's success in achieving them.

Appraisals can also be used by the institution to identify managerial strengths and weaknesses. More specifically, they can assist in identifying individual as well as group developmental needs. These need areas subsequently become targets or objectives for developmental activities. Another value of management appraisal is that a formal and periodic system encourages supervisors to observe regularly the behavior of their subordinates. When viewed in this respect, properly conducted appraisals, when implemented with effective counseling and coaching, can surely enhance mutual understanding between the supervising managers and their subordinates.

One further purpose of appraisal is the benefit that can result from a person's receiving an objective assessment of individual worth and contribution. Organizations discover the process of appraisal can serve as an influential force on the person's future performance. Moreover, many firms use the appraisal program as a basis for both salary adjustments and promotion purposes. Finally, when appraisals are conducted on a regular basis over a period of time, they are useful in job transfers and possible terminations.

DIMENSIONS OF MEASUREMENT

What, one may ask, should be measured if the purposes of appraisal are to be satisfied? Management appraisal should primarily focus on measuring *performance as a manager* as well as *performance as a manager in meeting objectives.*[1] Ideally, a top-rated manager operates effectively in both areas. Oftentimes, though, an executive may excel as a manager in contrast to a detrimental performance of assigned responsibilities in, say, personnel, finance, marketing, or production.

To satisfy desired performance as a manager certain standards or measurements can be established such as the person's level of managerial skills and to a lesser degree, the person's character or personality traits. To satisfy performance of a manager, when measured against objectives, the organization can establish certain standards based on identifiable and acceptable goals that are both quantitative and qualitative in nature.

But certainly an initial comment on these standards in in order. They must be considered with relevance to the organization and the job in which, and for which, they will be used. Therefore, standards should be selected by knowledgeable executives and technical staff. Moreover, selected standards or factors should represent significant and key aspects of job performance and should be clearly defined so there is no misunderstanding of meaning by either management or the subordinate being appraised.

Managerial Skills

A logical basis for appraising performance is to isolate the basic functions involved and required in satisfactory management and then to identify those factors that evolve when the functions are effectively performed.

Planning. Appraising the manager as to: forecasting; establishing objectives (both short- and long-range) policies and programs to accomplish those objectives, budgeting, scheduling, and overall decision making.

Organizing. Appraising the manager as to: assigning responsibilities, delegating authority, coordinating activities, and developing work relationships.

Staffing. Appraising the manager as to: recruiting, selecting, training and appraisal of subordinates, utilizing their skills and abilities, and structuring plans and programs for continual subordinate progress and development.

Directing. Appraising the manager as to: leadership style, initiating action, communications skills, resolving conflict situations, initiating and instrumenting change, developing positive attitudes and morale of the group, managing by objectives, and motivating improved performance.

Controlling. Appraising the manager as to: developing standards of performance, implementing means to measure results, monitoring plans and programs, appraising subordinate performance, and executing corrective action.

Character Trait Factors

The use of character or personality traits as factors in evaluation was widely employed in the past. More recently this approach has been minimized because of the difficulty of accurately measuring the impact of traits upon the individual's performance.

Basic to this approach is a strong dependency upon the evaluator's subjective opinion of predetermined personal characteristics that were assumed to be associated with successful performance of the job. The focus here is on personality traits rather than on identifiable and measurable factors of achievement. As a result, such subjective and almost indefinable and immeasurable characteristics as "initiative," "aggressiveness," "dependability," and "loyalty," to name a few, constitute some of the criteria used for evaluation.

A major criticism of the trait method of rating, however, is that not only are standards unclear but also the trait method is predicated on the assumption that there is a psychological constellation of traits that make up the best executive. On the other hand, it should be recognized that individual performance or behavior is the cumulative result of personality traits, however difficult those traits are to measure.

Perhaps social scientists of the future will be able to measure traits more definitely, but presently trait evaluation entails certain distinct disadvantages. The ambiguity of such descriptive terms leads to judgments that are biased by the rater's subjectivity and may, therefore, be unreliable and invalid. Also, any judgments generated by this approach are often difficult to communicate to the subordinate who assumes possession of such traits to a high degree. Finally, a rating of traits does little to provide a subordinate with adequate guidance for improving the person's performance.[2]

Performance Measured Against Objectives

Consistent with the need to appraise the performance of management is the need to assess performance against verifiable goals. Such is the basis for management by objectives (MBO), or appraisal by results programs. This approach represents a departure from certain traditional methods of appraisal in that the emphasis is on the evaluation of results—both quantitative and qualitative—of objective achievement—of what the manager *does* more so than what the manager *is*.

Explicit in the use of this approach are two basic concepts. first, the clearer the idea the manager has about what is to be accomplished, the greater the chances of accomplishing it. Secondly, progress can only be measured in terms of what one is trying to make progress toward.[3]

While management by objectives programs may differ in their methodology, there are certain essential stages to the program as depicted in figure 16-1.

1. Superior and subordinate at all organizational levels jointly agree upon the specific and precise results to be accomplished by the subordinate.
2. Both superior and subordinate agree upon the criteria for measuring and evaluating performance.
3. Periodically, the superior and subordinate review the degree of progress toward the predetermined and agreed-upon goals. Objectives and plans are subsequently revised or updated as required.
4. The superior operates as a coach and counselor in assisting the subordinate to achieve objectives. Emphasis is at all times on mutual planning and problem solving. The role of the superior is primarily supportive rather than coercive.

Appraising the Performance of Management   229

Key Result Areas Defined →	Superior and Subordinate Agree upon Objectives and Expected Results.
Agreed-upon Standards of Performance →	Superior and Subordinate Agree upon Measurement Criteria.
Job Improvement Plans Developed →	Subordinate Progress is Periodically Reviewed in Light of Objectives and Plans.
Results Delineated →	Subordinate Prepares Report on Achievements as Well as Variances from Expected Results.
Performance Appraised →	Superior and Subordinate Discuss Performance and Progress in Goal Achievement.
Prescription for Future Goal Achievement →	Superior and Subordinate Develop Program of Activities for Goal Accomplishment in the Future.

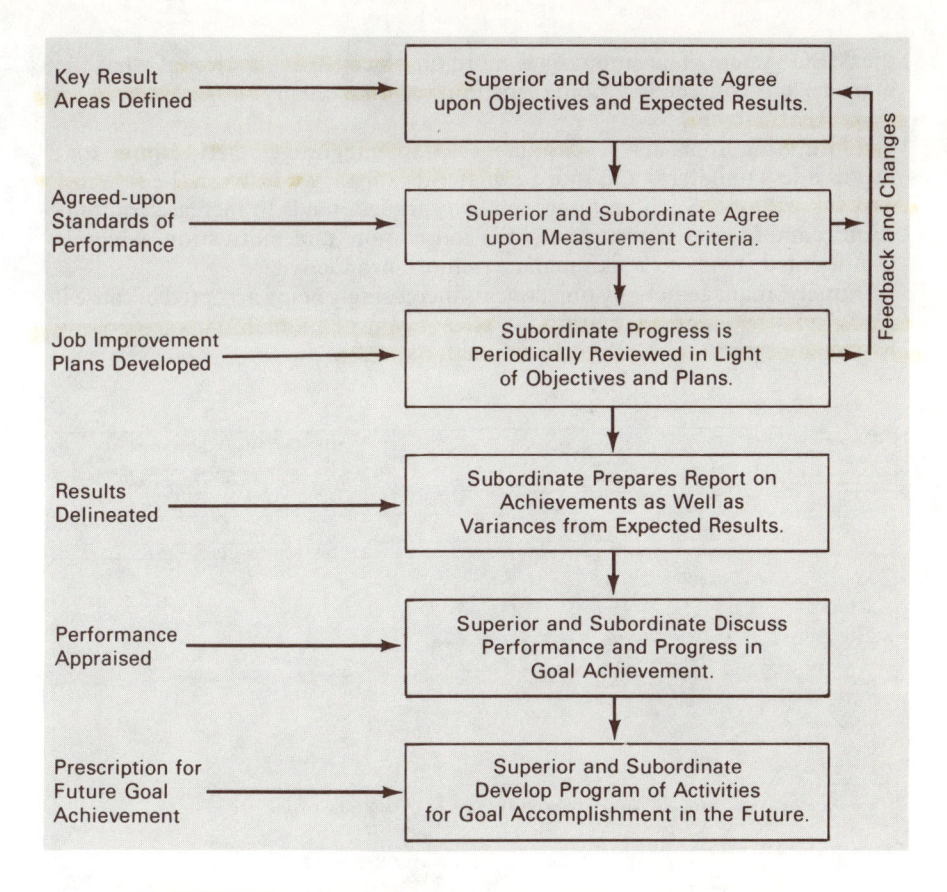

(Feedback and Changes)

Fig. 16-1. The process of management by objectives

5. At the conclusion of the reporting period, the subordinate prepares an achievement report that lists all major accomplishments and indicates variances between the expected and actual results.
6. In an interview setting, superior and subordinate discuss the variance in goal achievement and then develop subsequent objectives and methods of accomplishment for the ensuing time period.

Advantages of Management by Objectives

The proponents of the MBO approach stress that goal setting and not criticism should be used to improve a manager's performance. Superior results are observed when the supervisor and subordinate together set specific goals to be achieved, rather than merely discussing needed improvement. Moreover, it is felt that frequent reviews revolving around presently occurring needs are more productive and less threatening to the subordinate than the usual annual appraisal discussion.

Secondly, personality does not exert a strong influence in evaluation under the MBO system. The emphasis is more on objective evaluation of what the manager has concretely accomplished rather than on any subjective opinion about that person.

Third, this approach is conducive to an integrative relationship—that means a less unilateral and more a bilateral exchange—between the superior and subordinate. Such an approach, it is argued, tends to increase commitment; commitment tends to heighten motivation; and motivation, which is job oriented, tends to make managers more productive.

Finally, management by objectives is increasingly being accepted because it lends itself better to evaluating the efforts of professional managers whose work may be creative rather than functional.

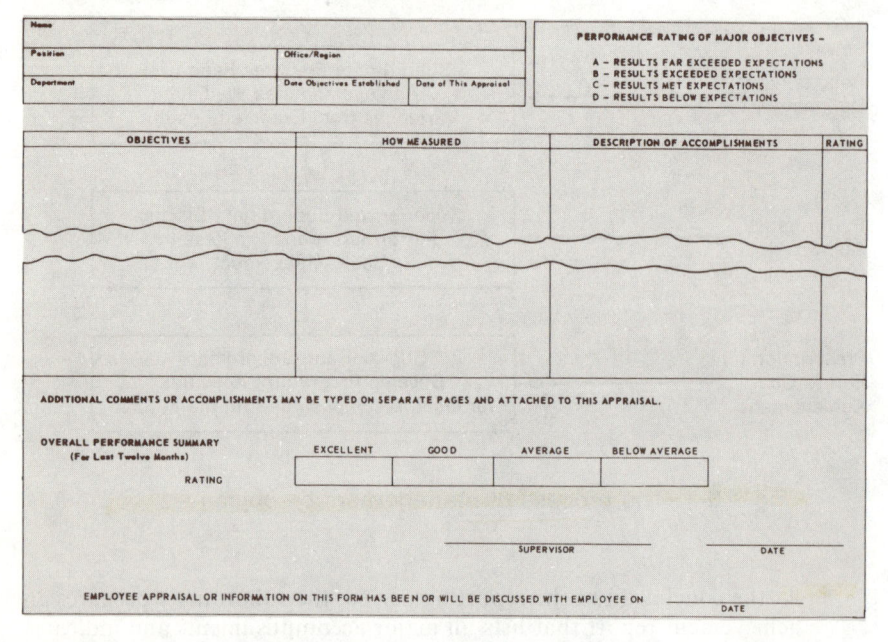

Fig. 16-2. Management for results performance appraisal

Figure 16-2 represents a typical instrument used where a management-by-objectives program is employed with middle and upper management levels. The superior (1) lists the preestablished objectives mutually agreed upon for the appraisal period; (2) indicates the basis on which performance is measured (this will involve scheduling both for completion and quality of performance); (3) indicates the rating for each objective or accomplishment, using the scale shown on the form; (4) supplements the evaluation with any additional comments or accomplishments; and (5) summarizes the overall performance for the 12-month period.

METHODS OF APPRAISAL

In view of the authority relationship, the immediate superior executive should always be the chief appraiser. However, other individuals, such as the superior's supervisor or peers of the executive may, at times, also be involved. The organization, furthermore, depending on its needs and preferences, may elect to use one or various methods by which the appraisal factors can be considered. Some of these methods are:

1. Ranking method
2. Graphic rating methods
3. Forced-choice method
4. Group appraisal method
5. Assessment center method
6. The clinical interview
7. Critical incident method

Ranking Method

This approach requires the superior to evaluate the subordinate on both performance and value to the organization when compared to others in the firm. There are several varieties of this method. The simple ranking technique permits the evaluator to array all subordinates from the most valuable to the least. It is an overall rating, and usually without consideration of specific factors. As such, it has little value in deciding the developmental needs of an executive. Furthermore, it has little value since almost every management position is different from every other one.

Graphic Rating Methods

This method provides for evaluating the executive on the basis of individual factors. For each factor, a range of measurement is provided by breaking down the factor into degrees such as superior, above average, average, below average, and poor. To assure accuracy and uniformity of measurement, it is important that each factor and the degrees of each factor be clearly defined for the rater. Many rating forms also require written statements that further describe the ratee in the light of the factor, or give specific examples from job behavior that substantiate the rating. A rating scale that uses defined and semantically different degrees would look like this:

Factor: Ability to Motivate

- ☐ Inspires subordinates to excellent, consistent, and willing effort.
- ☐ Usually gets employees to give very willing and above-average effort.
- ☐ Gets employees to respond in an average manner to his supervision.
- ☐ Frequently fails to get cooperation and adequate effort from subordinates.
- ☐ Consistently fails to get subordinates to produce in a satisfactory manner.

Forced-choice Method

This is considered an improvement in accuracy over other systems in that it reduces the effects of rater bias. The rater is provided with sets of statements, each set consisting of both favorable and unfavorable descriptions. The rater must check what is considered to be the most applicable favorable statement and the most applicable unfavorable one. The manager, however, does not know which statements actually are counted and which are meaningless for purposes of the evaluation. Thus, the superior cannot knowingly evidence either positive or negative bias. Here is an example:

      _____ Anticipates problems
      _____ Lacks drive and initiative
      _____ Posesses social maturity
      _____ Tends to be tactless with subordinates

Obviously, the construction of a set of statements, properly discriminating, is a complex and difficult task. Also, since the rater does not know how the subordinate is being rated, the rating offers little value for an appraisal interview. There is also the question of indifference in such a program where the feeling may prevail that a randomly selected judgment is as good as a carefully selected one.

Group Appraisal Method

As generally administered, this method combines the ratings of several supervisors in the firm. The appraisal group usually is composed of the subordinate's supervisor as well as other supervisors who have knowledge, through work contact, of the person's performance.

Group ratings may be conducted in the form of a conference among the raters, or such ratings may be made independently by each appraiser, then combined for discussion purposes. The former appears to have an advantage because lack of information by one rater about some aspect may be supplied by another who happens to have such information. There is danger, however, of constructing a compromise appraisal rather than one incorporating the true judgment of each appraiser. It is preferable, therefore, to have each appraiser first work independently and then later join the group for a collective rating.

The theory underlying group rating is that a better coverage of the individual's strong and weak points will result. Also possible bias on the part of the superior may be modified by other, more impartial, ratings. This rating method has merit, but it must be remembered that no one is in a more advantageous position than the immediate superior for evaluating the performance of a subordinate.

Assessment Center Method

A recent innovative adaption of the group approach used by some large corporations is the use of assessement centers to assess corporate talent formally. An assessment center is simply an off-job site where managerial assessments take place.

Military assessment techniques were originally employed by the Office of Strategic Services for officer selection during World War II. Since then, The

American Telephone and Telegraph Company has been a pioneer in using the assessment center approach for management selection.

Assessments of managers at the centers are a combination of data-gathering techniques such as personal questionnaires and projective tests, along with an intensive personal interview. Additionally, there are usually the collective evaluations of several trained specialists who observe the manager's actual performance in such areas as planning and organizing, leadership and communications skills, and decision making.

Among various techniques employed during these simulated exercises are the in-basket technique, role playing, and the management simulation game. At the conclusion of all tests and situational exercises, which last several days, each member of the evaluation staff independently prepares an individual assessment. This is further synthesized into a summary report that includes an overall assessment of the individual's strengths and weaknesses as well as recognized potential to the organization.[4]

The Clinical Interview

This type of interview is conducted by clinical psychologists, usually consultants, who are trained and skilled in interviewing and in administering and interpreting certain standard tests, including the so-called "projective techniques."[5] These are tests in which a person responds verbally to relatively unstructured or ambiguous material such as ink blots, pictures, or partial sentences. Generally, the psychologist is familiar with the position for which a person is being assessed and has established the criteria of personality characteristics important to success or failure in this particular job.

The clinical psychologist evaluates the test responses, the interview responses, and conduct of the person being assessed and then balances these against the personality patterns and characteristics known to the psychologist by virtue of previous training and experience. Finally, a report is prepared, based on the personality and potential of the person being assessed, in relation to the particular position or responsibility in the firm.

Some companies use this kind of assessment technique for several announced purposes. First, to supplement the regular appraisal program; secondly, to interview candidates for management positions; and finally, as a counseling method in the hands of a trained expert. Advantages of this approach, according to its proponents, are that it permits the clinical psychologist to apply professional expertise to a particular situation. It is also suited for bringing out personality characteristics that may be closely related to success and failure in jobs.

On the other hand, certain disadvantages of this technique are that its accuracy depends largely on the degree of expertise of the clinical psychologist. It also takes more time and is somewhat more costly than conventional techniques.

Critical Incident Method

This method focuses on the predetermined critical requirements of a job. Critical requirements are those critical behaviors that determine whether a job is being done effectively or ineffectively. Critical incidents of both effective and ineffective behavior are obtained from managers, the incumbent person being evaluated, and others close to the job under analysis.

The incidents are then analyzed and refined into a composite picture of the required essentials in a particular job. From this a checklist is developed, which forms the framework against which the manager is eventually evaluated.

PROCEDURE FOR APPRAISAL

At this point our discussion, it should be recognized that when the appraisal process is divided into a logical sequence of steps, the result can be a more accurate measurement of the individual's value to the organization. Moreover, the results of appraisal constitute a sound basis for judging the individual's future possibilities with the firm. The steps in the appraisal process may be summarized as follows:

1. Determining job needs
2. Appraising performance—present and potential
3. Conducting the appraisal interview and determining individual needs
4. Suggesting a developmental program
5. Putting the program into action
6. Follow-up

Determining Job Needs

The job duties, responsibilities, authority relationships, and other information included in the job description, form the basis for developing criteria to be used in the measurement. The criteria selection and their development was discussed, as you will recall, in the preceding section.

Appraising Performance—Present and Potential

The actual appraisal consists of measuring the individual's performance and the characteristics that influence that performance in terms of the appraisal factors which have been developed for the particular position or organization.

A distinction should be made between appraisal of the executive's *current performance* and of the *potential* that may be shown through performance. Figure 16-3 illustrates a typical instrument employed for appraising the potential of managment personnel. Current performance should be the first concern in evaluation—that is, how well does the person discharge the actual job responsibilities for which there is present accountability? Following this there should be a considered judgment as to the person's aptitude for future development and promotability.

For obvious reasons, the appraisal of current performance should be discussed with the individual being rated. Beyond this, the appraisal of potential should be of great interest to higher management, especially for such purposes as long-range organizational personnel planning.

1	SOC. SEC. NO.	NAME (LAST) (INITIALS)	COST CENTER	DEPARTMENT
	POSITION TITLE	SECTION	JOB CLASS	AGE / SENIORITY

2 CANNOT BE EVALUATED FOR PERFORMANCE OR PROMOTABILITY
(Enter corresponding code in the box to the left and do not complete remainder of form. Proceed to Block 7)

☐ (A) On assignment less than 6 months; will be evaluated on 6 month anniversary.
(B) Other *(Explain)* ______

3 PRESENT PERFORMANCE *(Check corresponding box to the left)*

☐ Exceptional — Performance and behavior are outstanding in all aspects. Employee **substantially exceeds goals** and responsibilities.
☐ Very Good — Performance and behavior are consistently high. Employee meets all and **exceeds some goals** and responsibilities.
☐ Good — Performance and behavior are usually at a high level. Employee **meets goals** and responsibilities.
☐ Satisfactory — Performance and behavior are satisfactory. Employee **meets most goals** and responsibilities.
☐ Marginal — Employee **meets some goals** and responsibilities.
☐ Unsatisfactory — Performance and behavior do not meet minimum standards on present job.

4 ACCOMPLISHMENTS *(List significant accomplishments during past year. BE SPECIFIC)*

______

5 EVALUATION OF PROMOTABILITY
List below the position(s) to which the person is promotable. Enter in the box(es) to the left of each position, "0" if employee is currently promotable, or an estimate of the number of years until he is promotable. Mark "X" in the appropriate box if the person is not promotable.
Note: If the position to which the person is promotable is a top level decision making position, i.e., no lower than two management levels below Group Vice President, check Block 6.

☐ ______
☐ ______
☐ ______
☐ Not Promotable

IF THE INDIVIDUAL IS NOT PROMOTABLE, INDICATE REASON(S) BELOW: *(Enter corresponding code in the box to the left)*

CODE
☐ (A) More Experience (C) Unique Skills (Explain) (E) Other
(B) Additional Training (D) Fully Utilized

Briefly explain ______

6 This box is to be completed only if the person is an outstanding individual considered eventually promotable to a top level decision making position. If this block is used, this form is to be forwarded to the Division/Group Staff Department Head for concurrence and initials.

☐ MARK "D" in the block if the employee is eventually promotable to a DIVISION staff position (e.g., reports to a Division Head).
MARK "G" in the block if the employee is eventually promotable to a GROUP staff position (e.g., Division Head).

7 Estimate of Potential By: ______ (Immediate Supervisor) ______ (Title) ______ (Date)

Reviewed By: ______ (Next Higher Supervisor) ______ (Title) ______ (Date)

Fig. 16-3. Estimate of potential

Appraisal Interview and Determination of Individual Needs

The manager who has been evaluated will normally, and justifiably so, want to know the results of appraisal. An appraisal interview, well-planned and conducted, besides divulging results can assist the individual in developing potential attributes and in taking corrective action regarding those areas of deficiency. Thus, the superior should determine in advance the points to be discussed with the person in terms of strengths, problem areas, and weaknesses.

When these points are constructively covered in an interview setting, it is much more likely that the subordinate will welcome any evaluation of personal performance, will make additional suggestions for self-improvement, and will cooperate in taking subsequent action. Usually it is more effective to discuss the positive points of the evaluation at the onset of the interview in order to convince the subordinate of the constructive purpose of the process. Constructive suggestions and a program for improvment that involves and elicits the participation of the subordinate can then be developed.

The appraisal of the individual's potential may include judgment as to the subordinate's qualifications for further responsibility, the approximate length of time to achieve those qualifications, and also the type of development to be prescribed. The determination of individual needs can often be made in conjunction with the appraisal interview.

Sufficient time, of course, should be allowed for the appraisal interview, and a friendly atmosphere should prevail. Privacy should be assured even if it means getting away from the work scene. Whenever possible, too, subordinates should be encouraged to talk about their own performance. With encouragement they are more likely to bring out specific job weaknesses and suggest ways of overcoming them.

Suggesting a Developmental Program

When a clear understanding has been reached with the subordinate manager as to individual needs, then a program of development can be evolved. Some firms follow a policy of having individuals develop their own program of self-development and then submit it to their superior (and perhaps, the staff director of management development) for approval. The help of a staff person is usually sought at this point so that means of improvement can be matched as closely as possible with needs. Certain courses may consequently be prescribed to increase technical knowledge in an area.

Additionally, it may be that a variety of work experience is indicated in order to give the executive a company-wide point of view and a better knowledge of relationships existing among organizational units. Or plans may be made to develop needed human relations skills. It is possible, too, that present methods of acquiring behavioral skills need to be augmented with more teaching in order to accelerate the process of development, and a further system of coaching may need to be initiated.

Putting the Program in Action

Plans for development as a result of the appraisal should include the time, place, content, and type of development. When programs of the understudy, coaching, or on-the-job type are prescribed, sufficient time should be set aside for instruction, discussion, and counseling. Otherwise, this important phase may be neglected. Definite procedures should be established so that training or education is carried out in a systematic manner and adequate control can be exercised.

Follow-up

No program of appraisal is complete without a follow-up to assure that development is actually taking place. The methods of follow-up differ little from regular methods of appraisal—the results of development should, after all, show in performance. Some specific review of the proposed development program itself and of the manager's participation in it may be in order. Superiors and others may analyze the executive's progress. Counseling interviews with the manager can be scheduled at appropriate intervals to discuss personal progress and perhaps to modify the development program so as to coordinate it more closely with individual needs and concerns.

BENEFITS OF APPRAISALS

While methods of appraising managers are still far from being perfect, there are few functions that can have a more impressive impact upon managerial climate and organizational effectiveness. When the superior recognizes the importance of evaluation and is willing to take the time and effort to do a conscientious job, when there is mutual understanding between the manager and the subordinate of what is expected and what is important in the job, and when evaluation is not viewed by the subordinate as a disciplinary measure, then the benefits can indeed be great.

Resultingly, subordinates are given an opportunity to learn how they stand with their superiors and with the company. They are given the chance to state both their own feelings about their performance and their own reaction to the appraisal of their work. Invariably the principle of participation is invoked.

The appraising executive ultimately stands to benefit from the process too. A beneficial result is encouragement to analyze continually the responsibilities of subordinates, which, after all, is part of the appraising executive's own broader function. This may lead the executive to greater self-analysis, which in turn should produce a sounder basis for the executive's own progress and promotion opportunities. Better executive control generally results too, and in short, better executive performance.

QUESTIONS FOR DISCUSSION

1. Discuss the overall value of executive appraisal to both the organization and its management.
2. To what extent do quantitative performance standards meet the need for effective evaluation criteria?
3. What activities should be covered in a comprehensive appraisal process?
4. Identify and discuss the chief reasons for the popularity of the management-by-objectives type of appraisal programs.
5. Discuss the chief principles of conducting the postappraisal interview.
6. Why is it important to distinguish between current performance and potential performance in making the appraisal?
7. How can management utilize the results that derive from management appraisals?

REFERENCES

1. Harold Koontz, *Appraising Managers As Managers* (New York: McGraw-Hill Book Co., 1971), p. 11.
2. Stanley Sloan and Alton C. Johnson, "New Context of Personnel Appraisal," *Harvard Business Review* (November-December 1968): 14.
3. For a study of corporate practices in MBO see "Managing By and With Objectives," *Studies in Personnel Policy*, no. 212, 2d ed., (National Industrial Conference Board, Inc., (1970); 2.

4. For a more detailed analysis of this concept see Walter S. Wikstrom, "Assessing Managerial Talent," *The Conference Board Record,* National Industrial Conference Board, Inc. (1967).
5. For a more thoroughly delineated description and evaluation of the clinical interview, see Robert B. Finkle and William S. Jones, *Assessing Corporate Talent* (New York: Wiley-Interscience, Division of John Wiley & Sons, Inc., 1970), pp. 28-30.

SELECTED BIBLIOGRAPHY

1. Cummings, L.L., and Schwab, Donald P. *Performance in Organizations: Determinants and Appraisal.* Glenview, IL: Scott, Foresman & Company, 1973.
2. Finkle, Robert B., and Jones, William S. *Assessing Corporate Talent.* New York: Wiley-Interscience, Division of John Wiley & Sons, Inc., 1970.
3. Kellogg, Marion S. *What To Do About Performance Appraisal* Rev. ed. New York: Amacom Division, American Management Association, 1975.
4. Koontz, Harold. *Appraising Managers As Managers.* New York: McGraw-Hill Book Co., Inc., 1971.
5. Reddin, W.J. *Effective Management By Objectives.* New York: McGraw-Hill Book Co., 1971.

CHAPTER 17

CONTROLLING DESIRED PERFORMANCE

Purpose of Chapter 17:

1. To investigate the management function of control; its definition and requirements
2. To illustrate the nature and characteristics of a basic control system
3. To delineate the relationship of control to other managerial functions

Essential elements you should understand after studying this chapter:

1. Definition of control
2. Requirements of control systems
3. Organizational factors requiring control
4. Interrelationship of functions and factors with the control process
5. Organizational responsibility for control
6. Basics for information control systems

NATURE OF CONTROL

As we discussed earlier, the contemporary manager is a specialist who seeks to coordinate the efforts and activities of other specialists, while pursuing group and organizational objectives.

In the process, we have learned, management must necessarily plan, organize, staff, direct, and control both human and physical resources. So far, we have treated the first four of these basic functions. Here, in this chapter, we concern ourselves with the important and final managerial function of control.

Simply defined, control is the responsibility to see that activities are completed as planned, organized and directed. Thus, control is particularly concerned with overall coordination. Consequently, some authorities use the term as a synonym for coordination. In fact, some are so impressed with the significance of control that they equate control with management itself.

As a result, one often encounters such terms as financial control, material control, marketing control, quality control and personnel control. In these instances control is really given the meaning of management. Thus, financial control is essentially financial management, material control is material management, and so on. It is felt here, though, that control defines a portion—however, a major portion—of the work of management.

DEFINITION OF CONTROL

Controlling is that management function that determines, evaluates, and makes corrective adjustments on operations, activities, and processes according to predetermined standards.

As a management function, control must be employed in all organizational systems. Under idealistic systems, management's objectives and goals would be achieved after the planning, organizing, staffing, and directing functions have been completed. In the real world, however, this is rarely the case. Performance, oftentimes, is just not equal to the predetermined objective, because of imperfections that occur in reality.

For example, planning focuses on the future, with most decisions being made under conditions of uncertainty. Later on, and in an ever-changing environment, when more is known about the future, it may be that the objectives were inappropriate, or too difficult to meet, or in some cases, not practical at all. Obviously, there is a definite and continuing need to measure and compare deviations from preestablished goals and standards.

Since businesses sometimes do not exist under conditions of certainty, it is important, as a manager, to have continuous, dynamic control systems throughout the many levels of the organization. This must be done to monitor desired performance within the firm, and to correct deviations to planned and desired results. The foundation for control then is comparative information in the hands of management, so that corrective action may be taken on deviations from standards.

THE BASIC CONTROL SYSTEMS

One of the most generally accepted approaches to managerial control utilizes the closed-loop model shown in figure 17-1. This model graphically shows the basic requirements for managerial control systems.

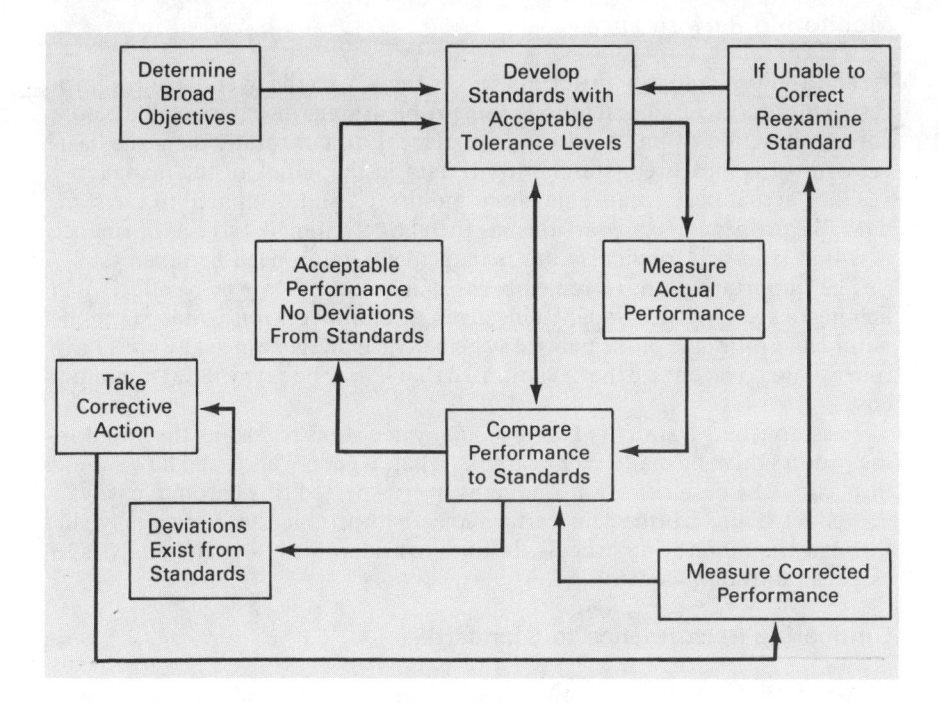

Fig. 17-1. The basic control system

REQUIREMENTS OF CONTROL SYSTEMS

There are several important requirements for installing and maintaining control. These are: (1) establishing reasonable standards; (2) monitoring performance; (3) comparing performance to standards and; (4) corrective actions to bring necessary deviations in line with standards.

Establishing Standards

A standard is a measurable specific goal used for comparing performance and satisfying the overall objectives of the company or department. Since much of the manager's work deals with quantity, quality, budgets, and personal performance, there should be control standards determined for all of these topical areas. Ideally, standards should be definable, measurable, communicated, and sometimes flexible.

Some common types of standards deal with production output per man hour, shift, or work week. Production schedules normally developed by the manufacturing engineers also constitute a standard. Moreover, quality control, as demanded by the quality control engineer, design engineers, and ultimately the customers, also serves as standards. The techniques of setting and measuring control standards are discussed in greater depth in the next chapter.

Monitoring Performance

The ability to identify problem areas is the key to the overall control process. This is critical, since it follows that problem areas msut be isolated before corrective action of any kind can take place. Fundamentally then, the basis for control is measured (standardized) data in the hands of the manager.

Once actual performance has been monitored and compared to the standard, the proper corrective action may then be determined. If the performance is within standard, obviously, no management action need be taken.

The important point to remember is that if controls are to be effective in helping to accomplish company objectives, all employees must understand the nature and rationale of the control system. The manager especially must have timely data to recognize the deviation, so that it may be corrected at minimum cost.

In establishing a system of control, many decisions regarding the monitoring process must be made. For example, what, where, where, and how should inspections be designed? If a product is overinspected this becomes costly; if a product is underinspected, performance and production defects may slip through the monitoring process. It takes considerable effort and analysis to establish optimum controls.[1]

Comparing Performance to Standards

In practice there are a number of different kinds of standards that require comparison to performance. Some of these are profit standards, cost standards, work measurement standards, and capital standards, to mention only a few. Management must be able to select critical points of control and be able to determine how best to measure and analyze any differences.

Taking Corrective Actions

In order for managers to initiate corrective actions, they must know when unsatisfactory performance exists. Too often, managers set up controls and monitor results but do not follow up with corrective action. If standards are being met, no corrective action is necessary. However, when standards are not being met, it is the manager's job to initiate corrective action and follow up to insure it has been accomplished according to standards. Sometimes managers must also redefine those standards as designs, products, or materials change over time. This is symptomatic of the process of change as it affects the control function.

GENERAL CHARACTERISTICS OF THE CONTROL PROCESS

In initiating and activating the control process, management should make sure the following guidelines are incorporated throughout the entire cycle.

Understandable Controls

Any communications relating to control, both written and oral, must be clear, so that everyone affected by controls can interpret them. Standards should be easily applied and understood and stated in nontechnical terms. Any methods of implementation should be both accepted and clear to those applying them.

Flexible Controls

Controls must be developed that fit the situation. Frequently, management's objectives may be too difficult to meet because of the changing environment. This could lead to unattainable standards, which must be changed to fit the new and ever-changing business situations. For example, flexible production schedules provide a sliding standard depending on orders and other manufacturing priorities.

Timely

Timing cannot be overstressed. The sooner deviations from standards are reported to management, the quicker corrective action can be taken and the problem brought under control. Rapid and almost instantaneous feedback is essential to the process.

Economical Controls

Controls must be worth their cost. Each control must fit the particular situation. Economy is relative, since the control must vary with the size, complexity, and importance of the situation. General Motors, for example, can afford extensive control systems. This is true especially on manufacturing lines affecting steering, braking, and other vital parts of automotive production. On the other hand, a small company cannot afford extensive controls.

FACTORS TO BE CONTROLLED

If desired objectives are to be accomplished, then the manager must exercise control in relation to everything that contributes to, or affects, attainment of those objectives.[2]

Accomplishing objectives, therefore, serves as the ultimate test of control. If, for example, an objective of a businessman has been to earn $10 million in a given year, this becomes the yardstick against which results are finally measured. But, this yardstick is somewhat limited for use on any given day to any given person. Other control elements are also needed.

Working backwards from the objective, it is reasonable to ask what action is necessary to help earn $10 million? The answer is a variety of projects or activities. These, then, also must be controlled. Within these projects will be found activities related to marketing, manufacturing, finance, engineering, accounting, logistics, and research, just to mention the obvious ones. In most companies, control goes beyond the mere listing of projects or factors such as quantity, quality, cost, and time that are to be controlled.

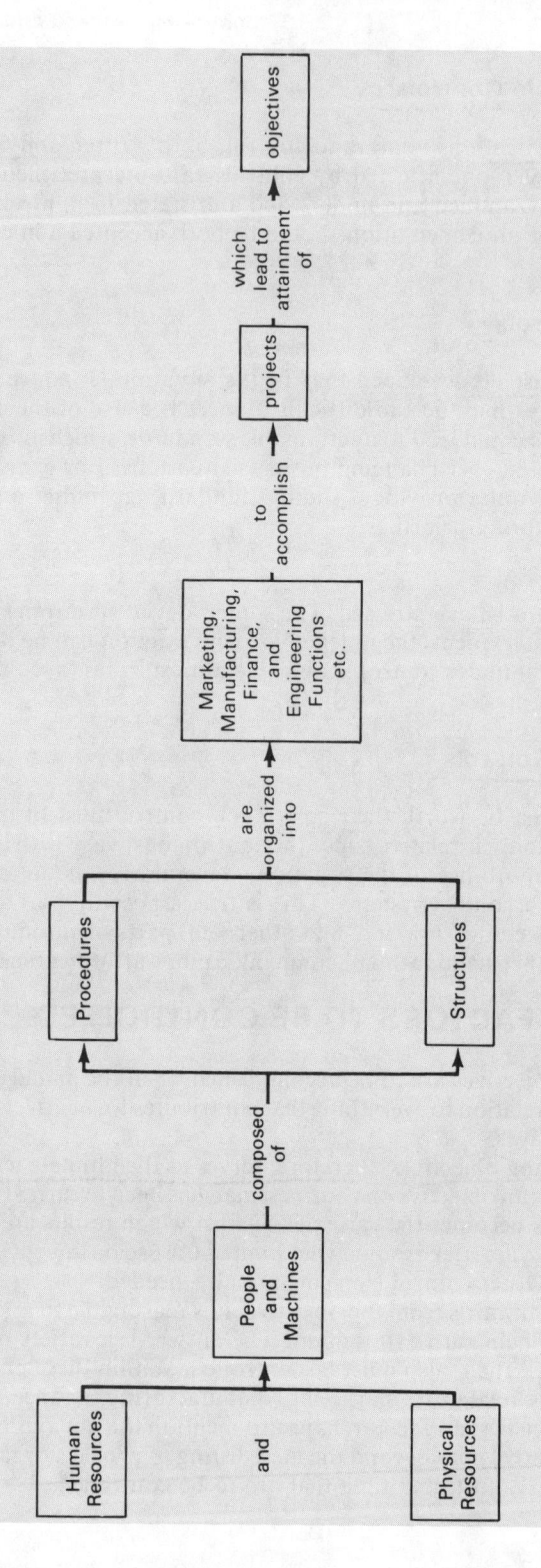

Fig. 17-2. Relationship of factors to be controlled in the business enterprise

As we illustrate in the following diagram, figure 17-2, control must be performed in relation to functions, procedures, structures, people, and resources.

The following is a description of each of the important factors making up the model.

1. Functions. for example, control the work done by a representative performing the function of selling a particular commodity.
2. Procedures. A sequence of selling operations from the initial planning of sales, to selecting and training salesmen, to the actual selling, and evaluation of results could be controlled.
3. Structures. The work done in each organization unit such as the engineering department or sales department, and subdivisions thereof, could be subject to control.
4. Personnel. Each person on the job makes an excellent unit of control, particularly at the supervisory level. Each has specific work that must be controlled.
5. Resources. Control may revolve about:
    (a) Machines: each drill press, cash register, workbench, or truck, for example, may be controlled.
    (b) Materials: each class of materials or supplies in each storeroom or department could well be considered for purposes of control.

The extent and amount of detail involved in control will largely depend upon how important it is to regulate and restrain the details of operations. If any possible losses or gains are great, obviously it will pay to spend more on control. If losses or gains are small, then it would be foolish to spend more on control than the controls themselves can save.

How much control is exercised depends upon how much planning is originally performed. The less planning, the more management will have to control and vice versa. Whether emphasis is placed on planning or controlling depends upon the situation, the skills and attitudes of management, as well as the types of problems faced.

Functions	Factors			
	Quantity	Quality	Time	Cost
Manufacturing	Output Scheduling Inventory	Tolerances Clinical tests	Daily output Shift absences	Production Budgets
Marketing	Units sold Market share Salespersons	Corporate Image Advertising	Yearly sales Inventory Turnover	Marketing Budgets
Finance	Cost of Goods Sold working Capital Direct labor Costs	Cost per unit Versus Competition Value for dollar Return goods	Short-term or Long-term Borrowing and	Wages Interest Insurance

Table 17-1. Relationship of control factors to organizational functions

INTERRELATIONSHIP OF FACTORS AND FUNCTIONS

The function of planning is most important when anticipating the need for controlling activities. Obviously, any activity can be controlled with respect to any or all of the previously discussed factors, such as quantity, quality, time, and cost. In every organization, assuredly, there should be an integrated plan to show the interrelationships between controlling factors and organization functions. We have developed such a typical plan in table 17-1.

Using a matrix of this type, one can easily target critical control areas throughout the organization. From this base, significant variations in these areas can subsequently be followed by management. After all, the basis for control is information in the hands of the manager. Fundamentally, the degree to which the factors and functions are interrelated, and control systems designed to support them are the essence of good management.

RESPONSIBILITY FOR CONTROL

A basic problem in management is to identify specific responsibility for control. Of course, it has been argued that controlling is a function of every executive. However, it can even be further argued that every person—whether a manager or not—performs a certain amount of control. From an organizational point of view, there are a number of ways through which managerial control may be performed. Our discussion of these may be conveniently taken up under the following headings: (1) internal control of each organization unit, (2) staff control relationships, (3) information systems for control, and (4) external control forces.

Internal Control of Each Organization Unit

Managers, no matter what ramifications of control may be developed in an organization, must, to a greater or lesser extent, be responsible for controlling their own units. The simplest plan, of course, is for managers to perform in relation to their subordinates all necessary control functions. Prior to, during, and after the performance of work, the managers concern themselves with control functions outlined earlier in this chapter. By performing control functions, superiors can keep closer contact with subordinates, evaluate more intimately their own planning, and minimize the amount of record keeping both by themselves and by their subordinates.

The internal control of each unit may also be accomplished by the appointment of a staff assistant or through control procedures. The assistant may keep records of work progress, check quantity of output against program quantities, check quality of work against standards, compile reports, and analyze deviations of actual from planned action. Or, the managers may themselves design procedures that serve to control their subordinates.[3] Report forms, statistical and graphical displays, and routines regarding how and when to report are certainly useful control devices.

Staff Control Relationships

As an enterprise grows, it is usually found desirable to establish separate organizational units to perform control functions. A rather common example of an interdepartmental control unit is the production control department. Very simply, it has responsibility for taking care of details necessary to get customer orders through the many departments of a production system.

For example, if Customer Smith ordered 100 No. 18 wheels to be shipped on June 30, the production control department would arrange to have the hub, spoke, rim, and assembly departments work on their respective parts of this order at the right time. A production control unit, by keeping appropriate records of other customer orders in the factory, and of available capacity of the various manufacturing departments, can fit Customer Smith's order into the maze with efficiency and with due consideration for all variables involved. Other examples of staff units concerned with operative projects are sales control units, engineering control units, and transportation dispatching units.

The top levels of an organization may also have administrative control staffs. Such units are responsible for coordinating the efforts of the major divisions of an enterprise. To illustrate the work of such staffs, take the case of a company that has decided to introduce a new model of its product every year during the first week of October.

Working backwards from that date, it is necessary to calculate how much time each department—engineering, advertising, sales, production, finance, personnel—will need to carry out its share of this annual project. Starting and finishing times for each department must be calculated. And checks must be made to see that each department keeps on the scheduled times. All of this would be the responsibility of an administrative control unit, reporting to the president or executive vice-president. This staff unit relieves the top executive of all the details of coordination, thus freeing up time to concentrate on creative planning and high-level policy making.

Staff control units may also be established to assist in the control of particular factors or resources in the company. For example, the cost department is responsible for, among other things, gathering cost data, comparing them with cost estimates, and making recommendations for cost reductions. The inspection department is another staff unit that assists in quality control, through its work of comparing quality of output with standards of quality. A standards department may be established to check on the maintenence of all types of mechanical, chemical, engineering, and specification standards. And one more example: the auditing department is responsible for checking financial expenditures and accounting records to see that honesty and accuracy are maintained in all parts of the business.

Such staff control units just mentioned are desirably established on a independent basis, because their work cuts across the activities of many departments, and because their integrity can best be safeguarded by separating them from the units they are intended to control.

Information Systems for Control

Usually information systems are designed by staff groups to provide managers with specific inputs from internal and external sources. The data that flows through these systems are the bases for management decisions in many of the functional areas.[4]

Basically, there are four major kinds of information systems: quantity, quality, financial, and personnel. with the increasing implementation of computers, applications for the four kinds of information systems are growing rapidly.

Information systems can be successful only when managers integrate the physical with the financial measures as the basis for control. The following example is a materials-requirements planning information system (for quantity) that utilizes a central computer.

This information system, programmed for a central corporate computer, connects the advance planning group, sales, production planning, inventory control, a manufacturing division for component A, and four different plant locations within the corporation. All use component A in their daily manufacturing. (See figure 17-3.)

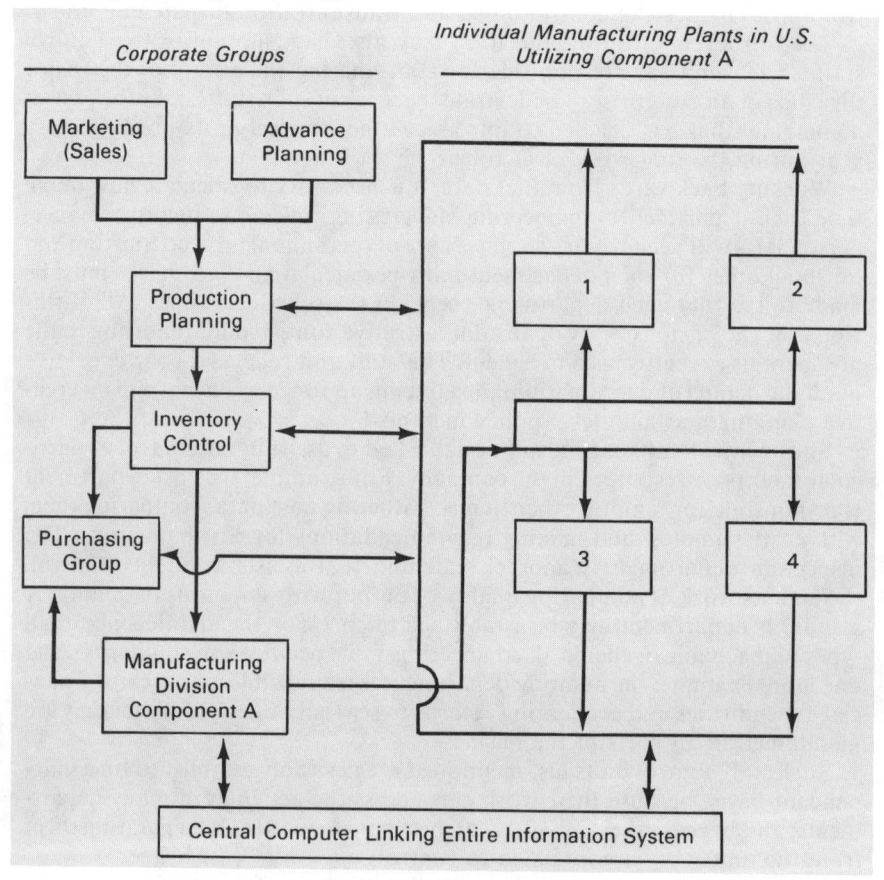

Fig. 17-3. Production planning information system

Two main groups initiate the beginning step in this system, which is the forecast for the numbers of component A that will be required throughout the four manufacturing plants. Both short-range and long-range estimates are made by the advance planning and marketing departments. These estimates are stored in the computer. When these two groups meet and agree on the numbers of component A that the company needs to manufacture for the coming year, they then coordinate with the production planning department.

The production planning department's responsibility then is to schedule during the current year each individual manufacturing plant's production that utilizes component A. These production schedules are also an input into the computer. Moreover, they are incorporated into a master production plan for the entire corporation. This plan or master computer program lists all of the current production specifications, sizes, grades, and so on of all products manufactured within the company as well as those utilizing component A. Computers are often programmed to determine the capacities, product mixes, and daily schedules for each plant for at least six months to a year in advance.

At this point, the master computer has final schedules for each plant location. The program is then released to inventory control, which previously has stored into the computer records of all inventory materials in stock, on order or partially made up. These are corrected daily. The inventory control group then determines the amounts of materials necessary to produce to the current production schedules. If the necessary materials needed to manufacture component A are on hand, the order is sent to the manufacturing division. If the materials are short, the inventory control group orders the necessary materials through the purchasing group.

Component A is then manufactured and sent to the four outside plants to be made into their respective products. As discrepancies in manufacturing occur daily, they are reported to production planning, which initiates the proper corrective action.

All of the information is stored in the central computer. It is updated each day so that management may, at any time, view the quantity aspects of manufacturing's master schedules for any, or all, of the four outside plants. This kind of information system is utilized throughout industry to keep data in the hands of management for control purposes.

External Control Forces

And, finally, forces and controls of a variety of kinds outside an organization itself may affect managerial controlling. Common to all enterprises are, of course, governmental legislation, judicial decisions, and rulings and procedures of administrative bodies that surround practically every managerial action.

There are, too, various community agencies, welfare groups, trade associations, educational institutions, unions, and churches that have an impact upon the controls management can and does exercise. Along somewhat similar lines, the social mores and customs of the community (local and national) in which a business operates have a tremendous effect upon the kinds of, and the degree of, controls that can be exercised by management. It should be noted, too, that favorable or unfavorable public relations have an important impact upon management controls.

These external factors and forces are often overlooked in studies of managerial controls. This oversight may be due to the fact that the work of managers seems to be concerned solely with what happens within the organization. The manager is controlling the flow of work through the procedures of the company. But it is apparent that much of what is done is influenced by the external controls listed in the preceding paragraph, and the same influence is felt by every other executive in the company. Hence, in exercising managerial controls, the import and significance of these external forces should be carefully weighed and taken into account.

QUESTIONS FOR DISCUSSION

1. Discuss the relationships among planning, control, coordination, and management.
2. What functions are performed in control? What is meant by each?
3. Describe the factors used in the exercise of control.
4. Specifically, what is controlled when control is being exercised?
5. Show the relation of control to objectives, procedures, and resources.
6. Who may control, and over what would his, her, or their jurisdiction extend?
7. Discuss staff control units and how they evolve.
8. Give some examples of external controls that may affect a business enterprise.

REFERENCES

1. J. Timothy McMahon and G.W. Perritt, "The Control Structure of Organizations: an Empirical Examination," *Academy of Management Journal* (September 1971): pp. 327-39.
2. Thomas E. Vollmann, *Operations Management* (Reading, MA: Addison-Wesley Publishing Co., Inc., 1973), pp. 34-38.
3. Richard I. Levin and Charles A. Kirkpatrick, *Quantitative Approaches to Management*, 3d ed. (New York: McGraw-Hill, 1975) pp. 216-221.
4. Franklin G. Moore, *Manufacturing Management*, 5th ed. (Homewood, IL: Richard D. Irwin, Inc., 1969), pp. 568-71.

SELECTED BIBLIOGRAPHY

1. Anthony, Robert W. *Planning and Control Systems: A Framework for Analysis.* Cambridge: Harvard University Press, 1965.
2. Bonini, Charles P.; Jaedicke, R.K.; and Wagner, Harvey M. *Management Controls.* New York: McGraw-Hill Book Co., 1964.
3. Duncan, Acheson J. *Quality Control and Industrial Statistics.* Homewood, IL: Richard D. Irwin, Inc., 1965.
4. Mockler, Robert J. *The Management Control Process.* New York: Appleton-Century-Crofts, 1972.
5. Tannenbaum, Arnold S. *Control in Organizations.* New York: McGraw-Hill Book Co., 1968.

CHAPTER 18

CONTROLLING TECHNIQUES AND THEIR APPLICATION

Purpose of Chapter 18:

1. To introduce the application of quantitative control techniques within the firm
2. To present specific quantitative techniques for decision making in financial and manufacturing control situations

Essential elements you should understand after studying this chapter:

1. Definition of financial control
2. Financial control techniques
3. Quality control defined
4. Relationship of quality to product design
5. Manufacturing process control

INTRODUCTION

Quantitative control techniques are applied in many special situations as managers attempt to monitor certain aspects of the total performance of the firm. Increasingly, special tools have been used to improve the manager's ability to control. These tools, which are closely related to the other quantitative decision-making tools, are a significant aid to management's decision-making capability.

Consequently, this chapter reviews several quantitative types of control that have particular significance to the manufacturing organization such as financial control, quality control, and manufacturing process control.

FINANCIAL CONTROL

Managing and controlling any business requires an understanding of the basic accounting statements that represent the operations and financial position of the firm. Accounting, therefore, is the basis for quantitative control, and the chief accounting officer is generally titled the controller of the firm. Financial control is accordingly accomplished through profit analysis. Profits obviously are essential for the survival of the firm and its ability to expand or diversify. In the final analysis, all management decisions must be weighed in terms of their effect upon profitability and ultimate survival.

The major function of an accounting system is to report necessary financial information to managers. To implement this responsibility there are two basic financial statements, the balance sheet and the income statement, which serve as instruments for analysis of the firm's profits.

The Balance Sheet

The balance sheet reports the company's financial position at a specified time. It shows the assets, liabilities, and owner's net worth as of a given date as depicted in table 18-1. Assets owned by the firm include such things as buildings, materials, machinery, land, and claims on others. Liabilities are amounts, goods, or services that are owed to others. Net worth is the owner's claim to the assets after the liabilities are subtracted. Accountings' basic equation therefore is:

$$\text{Assets} - \text{Liabilities} = \text{Net Worth}$$

If liabilities are greater than assets, net worth is a minus quantity. Profits add to net worth as they are carried from the income statement to the balance sheet.

The Income Statement

In contrast to the balance sheet, the income statement summarizes financial results for some period of time as in table 18-2. It summarizes the revenues received and the expenses incurred by a unit or group of units over a certain period. Usually statements are issued for a one-year period, with interim statements, for the month or quarter, and generally are issued at the convenience

Table 18-1
COSMOS COMPANY
BALANCE SHEET
December 31, 1979

ASSETS

Current Assets		
Cash	$2,000	
Accounts Receivable	3,000	
Inventory	5,000	
Total Current Assets		$10,000
Fixed Assets		
Equipment	$20,000	
Less Depreciation	5,000	
Total Fixed Assets		$15,000
TOTAL ASSETS		$25,000

LIABILITIES

Current Liabilities		
Accounts Payable	$2,000	
Notes Payable	1,000	
Total Current Liabilities		$3,000
Fixed Liabilities		
Contracts Payable	$6,000	
Long-Term Notes	1,000	
Total Fixed Liabilities		$7,000
TOTAL LIABILITIES		$10,000
NET WORTH		$15,000
Total Liabilities plus Net Worth		$25,000

Table 18-2
COSMOS COMPANY
INCOME STATEMENT
January 1 - December 31, 1979

Sales		$95,000
Cost of goods sold:		
Beginning Inventory Jan. 1	$25,000	
Purchases during year	30,000	
Goods available for sale	$55,000	
Less ending inventory Dec. 31	20,000	
Cost of goods sold		$35,000
Gross Margin	$60,000	
Selling and Administrative Expenses:		
Rent	$10,000	
Salaries	27,000	
Advertising - Promotion	1,000	
Insurance	2,000	
Transportation	3,500	
Utilities	5,000	
Miscellaneous	1,500	
Total Operating Expenses		$50,000
NET PROFIT FROM OPERATIONS		$10,000

of management.

Sales usually account for most of the income received by a manufacturing firm. Costs are the expenses incurred during the same period of time. The difference between income received and costs is profit.

The income statement has three basic parts: (1) income received, (2) cost of goods sold, and (3) operating expenses. The difference between sales income and costs of goods sold is termed gross margin. Net profit is obtained when operating expenses are subtracted from gross margin.

All the accounts that record income and expenses are summarized at the end of each period. The profit, resulting from these calculations is then transferred to the balance sheet's net worth account. Unless an asset is disposed of, or liability is paid off, or a change is made in the ownership of the firm, the balance sheet accounts remain open. Usually, corporate income tax is deducted from net profit from operations to determine net income accruing to the owners.

Analysis of Statements

There are various relationships within the balance sheet used for control. First, note that every asset, liability, and net worth account is presented on the balance sheet. (from table 18-1)

Assets – Liabilities = Net Worth
$25,000 – $10,000 = $15,000

The other relationships that are often used from the balance sheet are:

$$\text{Current Ratio} = \frac{\text{Current Assets}}{\text{Current Liabilities}}$$

$$= \frac{\$10,000}{\$\ 3,000} = 3.33$$

This ratio for the Cosmos Company of 3.33 to 1 is good, since a rule of thumb of 2 to 1 is usually acceptable within the industry.

$$\text{Quick Ratio} = \frac{\text{Cash} + \text{Receivables}}{\text{Current Liabilities}}$$

$$= \frac{\$5,000}{\$3,000} = 1.66$$

A conservative rule is that this ratio should be at least 1 to 1. Therefore, Cosmos' quick ratio also looks good.

$$\begin{aligned}\text{Working Capital} &= \text{Current Assets} - \text{Current Liabilities} \\ &= \$10,000 - \$3,000 \\ &= \$7,000\end{aligned}$$

This measurement of adequate cash on hand is necessary to insure that Cosmos can meet payroll and pay daily expenses, purchases, and so forth.

$$\text{Proprietorship Ratio} = \frac{\text{Owner's Investment}}{\text{Total Assets}}$$

$$= \frac{\$15,000}{25,000}$$

$$= 60\%$$

Usually a conservative minimum of 50 percent is desired; however, in this case 60 percent is safely above the minimum. When this ratio becomes too small, it indicates that owners have too little of their own funds in the business and possibly may have problems obtaining capital. When this happens, it is often called trading too thin on the equity.

The income statement indicated that the company had $95,000 net sales. The gross margin was $60,000 with a cost of goods sold of $35,000. These relationships are often compared to other companies in the industry to determine if gross margins are too low, or possibly inventory too high. The company also paid out $50,000 in sales and administrative expenses. These too, must be studied since they have a direct effect on profits. Most companies have continual cost reduction programs in effect at all times.

Internal Control Systems

Internal control refers to the systems, methods, and procedures that companies use to protect assets and to insure honest and accurate accounting statements. In general, internal control ascertains that these statements are prepared in meaningful form for management decision making and control.

The prevention of errors and fraud and the development of bases for taxes by the federal government make internal control procedures mandatory. There must always be continuous cross checking and auditing to find even unintentional errors that may occur in the accounting system.

Internal control attempts to insure that measurements of business performance are accurate and honest. These accounting tools may help management make decisions on factual knowledge and are designed to supplement, not supplant, management judgment. To insure overall efficiency of use of funds, measurements and controls must be effectively designed for each operating level of the organizational structure.

Importance of Budgeting

A budget is a plan of action, expressed in financial terms, for a given period of time. It is a device used for controlling operations. During its existence, management uses the budget to check and control performance on the various levels of the organization. Most companies use their fiscal year as the time period for budgeting.

The key problem for any business is that of planning and controlling the future financial resources of the company[1]. To facilitate this process there are a number of budgets employed such as: (1) the operating budget, comprised of sales, prices, revenue, costs and profits; (2) the cash budget, concerned with the firm's liquidity position; and (3) the planning-programming budget, related to all strategic plans of the company such as new products, processes, advertising, and training and development, to mention a few.

The very process of budgeting demands planning and control at all levels of the organization, since budgets become the standards of performance by which comparisons are made and corrective actions are developed.

QUALITY CONTROL

Quality control is the use of quantitative techniques developed to identify and remove causes of defects and variations from set standards during the manufacturing process. to explain further, each product has numerous properties that define its nature. For instance, a piece of synthetic rubber has dimensional, elongation, tensile, and impact properties, as well as a myriad of other technical characteristics.

Each of these characteristics in turn is measurable and has specifications usually set and evaluated by rubber compounders. For technical quality control to be uniform throughout the industry, there exist standards that are used to interpret and set forth methods of measurement. Some available standards are set by the U.S. government, the American Society for Quality Control, International Standards, and American, British, or Canadian Standards. Quality, then, is a problem of conformance to specifications interpreted by various available standards.

Phases of Quality Control

There are four phases of quality control:[3] (1) the desired level of customer quality characteristics, (2) the engineering design phase to determine proper specifications for customer characteristics, (3) the production stage to implement the design specifications, and (4) the use stage often referred to as reliability, or quality over a period of time, as illustrated in figure 18-1.

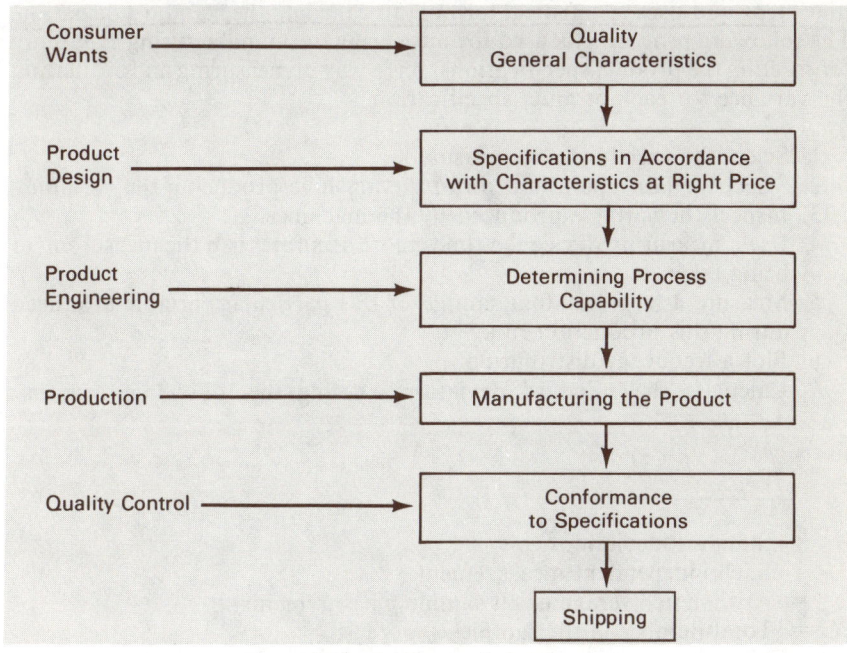

Fig. 18-1. Control of quality

QUALITY AND PRODUCT DESIGN

The design engineer sets forth the detailed specifications of quality to be produced in accordance with the quality characteristics desired by the customer. The engineer determines the complex design for quality—which materials should be used and their technical dimensions, tolerances, and requirements. There is a close working relationship with marketing, which often represents the customer, and also with product engineers, who know the manufacturing and process capabilities of the plant. The specifications and standards designed into the product subsequently become the basis for quality control throughout the manufacturing process.

Once the product has been designed, the manufacturing or production quality phase is comprised of raw materials acquisition, the production process and its control, and finally inspection and testing for quality conformance.

Throughout the process of quality control there are a number of probable causes of variance from designed quality. These consist of differences among materials, workers, and machines. And, there are differences within each over time, and each in relationship with the other variable.

Calculating Process Capability

One of the most important quantitative management techniques for control is the procedure for calculating process capability. This procedure has nine steps and uses a statistical formula to calculate the standard deviation. The following procedure is used for measuring the manufacturing capability for meeting the product specifications. It is a way of measuring and evaluating the variance for each product specification.

1. Select the variable to be measured.
2. Select the best operation to run the machine producing the variable.
3. Inspect the variable produced by the machine.
4. Use a measuring device ten times more accurate than the measurement being taken.
5. Measure a large random sample of this particular variable produced during this production run.
6. Plot a frequency distribution.
7. Calculate the standard deviation σ using the following formulas:

$$\sigma = \sqrt{\frac{\sum_{i=1}^{N}(x_i - \bar{x})^2}{N}}$$

σ = Standard deviation
x_i = Each independent measurement
$\bar{x}$ = Arithmetic average of all sample measurements
N = Total number in the sample

8. Calculate the process capability 6σ or $\bar{x} = 3\sigma$
9. Plot $\bar{x}$ and $\pm 3\sigma$ on the frequency distribution

The value 6σ represents the best effort of the process. Each study should be made under controlled conditions obtainable in the production environment. This should help minimize assignable causes of variation such as defective materials, unskilled workers, dull tools, and the like. Figure 18-2 shows the process capability diagram.

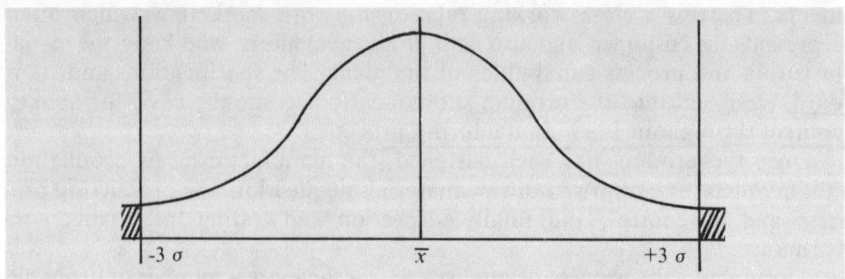

Fig. 18-2. Process capability for a normally distributed quality measurement

Controlling Techniques and Their Application   259

The area under the curve between the ±3 limits would contain 99.74% of the measurements of the quality variable being studied. For example, in the following table 18-3, 60 measurements of tensile strength in pounds per square inch (psi) were taken for 60 tires sampled at random.

Table 18-3
Tensile Tests for 60 Random Tires

20	22	15	26	24	21
20	17	19	14	13	25
16	19	22	17	16	29
19	21	16	18	20	10
21	15	20	23	21	12
17	20	22	25	26	15
18	23	12	13	12	19
23	16	17	15	14	21
16	18	18	20	16	24
18	22	23	23	19	27

Thus, with the data gathered, the next step (figure 18-3) is to plot a frequency distribution to determine if the data belongs to a normal (bell-shaped) curve.

Since the data appears to be normal, the $\bar{x}$, mean, and standard deviation can be calculated.

$$\bar{x} = \frac{\sum_{i=1}^{N} x_i}{}$$

$$\bar{x} = \frac{1142}{6}$$

$$\bar{x} = 19 \text{ and,}$$

$$\sigma = \sqrt{\frac{\sum_{i=1}^{N}(x_i - \bar{x})^2}{N}}$$

$$\sigma = \sqrt{\frac{1030}{60}}$$

$$\sigma = \sqrt{17.2}$$

$$\sigma = 4.2$$

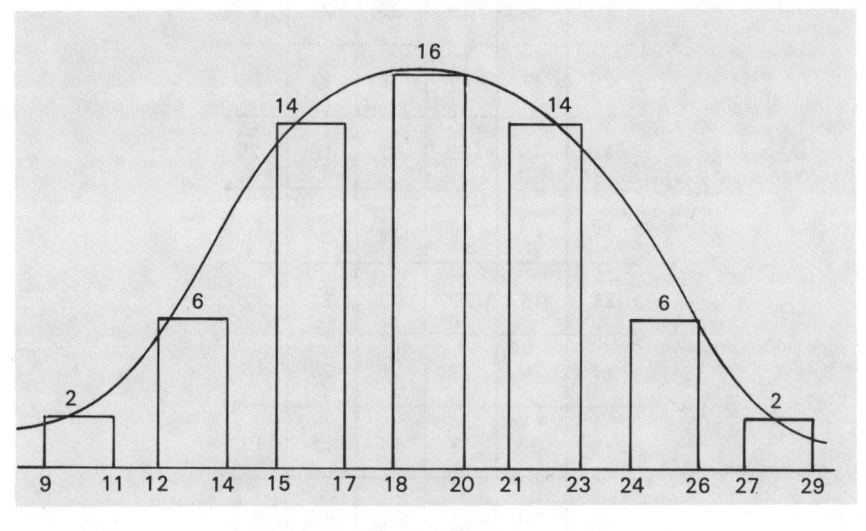

Fig. 18-3.

Therefore, 6σ or the process capability would be approximately 7 to 31 pounds per square inch for these tires.

CONTROL CHARTS

A control chart such as figure 18-4 could now be constructed and maintained near the tire production area. This chart would have three horizontal lines: the average line 19 psi; the upper and lower control limits previously calculated $\bar{x} + 3\sigma$, or 31; and $\bar{x} - 3\sigma$ or y. Each individual tire could then be plotted to see if the tensile tests meets the established specifications of process capability.

MANUFACTURING PROCESS CONTROL

Manufacturing process control utilizing a computer is a sophisticated kind of information system that functions over a short decision time frame, from minutes to even a week or two. The function of control implies frequent manufacturing decisions. This particular function of control encompasses the planned cycle of activities by which a series of manufacturing events is made to conform to a standard level of performance.

Both the control and information about a manufacturing system imply feedback and comparison to a given standard of conformance. This means

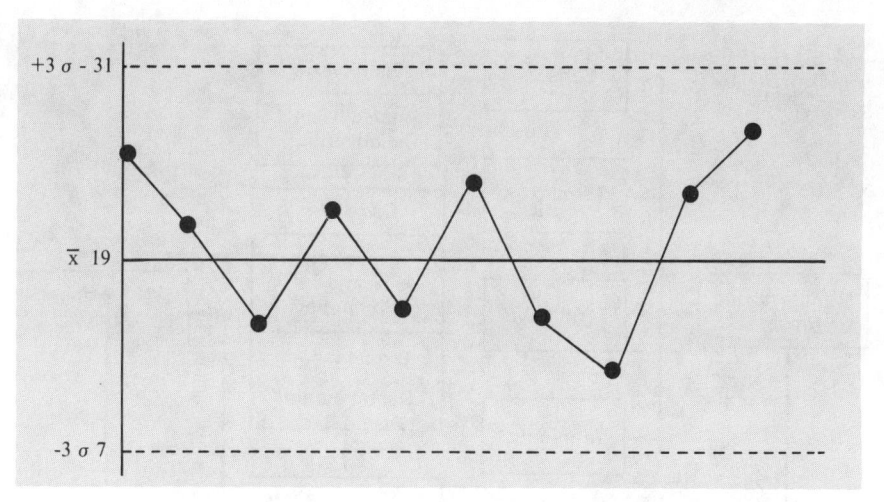

Fig. 18-4. A variable control chart for tire tensile results

then that the process information must be delivered to the reporting system in time for corrective decisions and action about the process, products, or materials.

An effective process control system, especially one linked to a computer, must perform four basic operations with minimum delay. These basic operations depicted in figure 18-5 are discussed in the following sections.

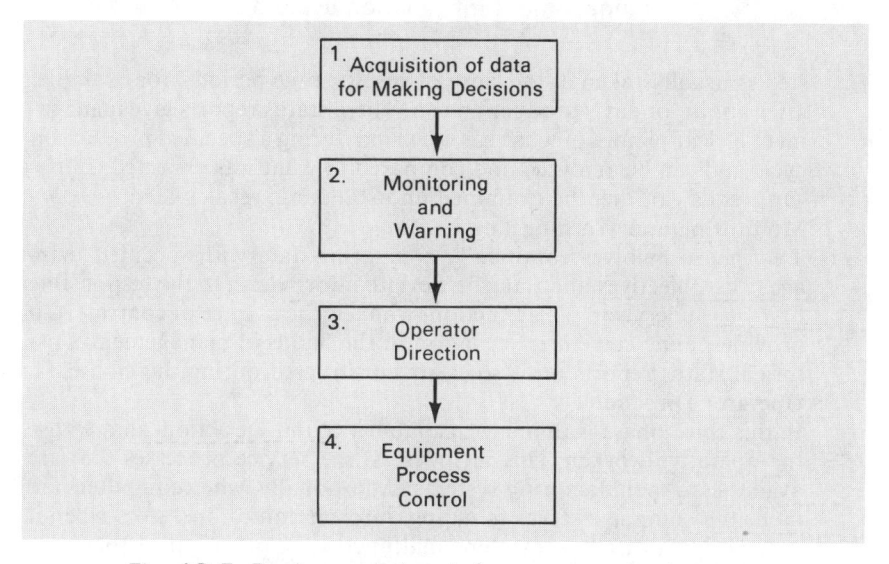

Fig. 18-5. Basic operations of process control system

1. Initial Data Aquisition Phase

The basic fundamental transaction data is collected from the plant floor and recorded for later consolidation and reporting to management. This

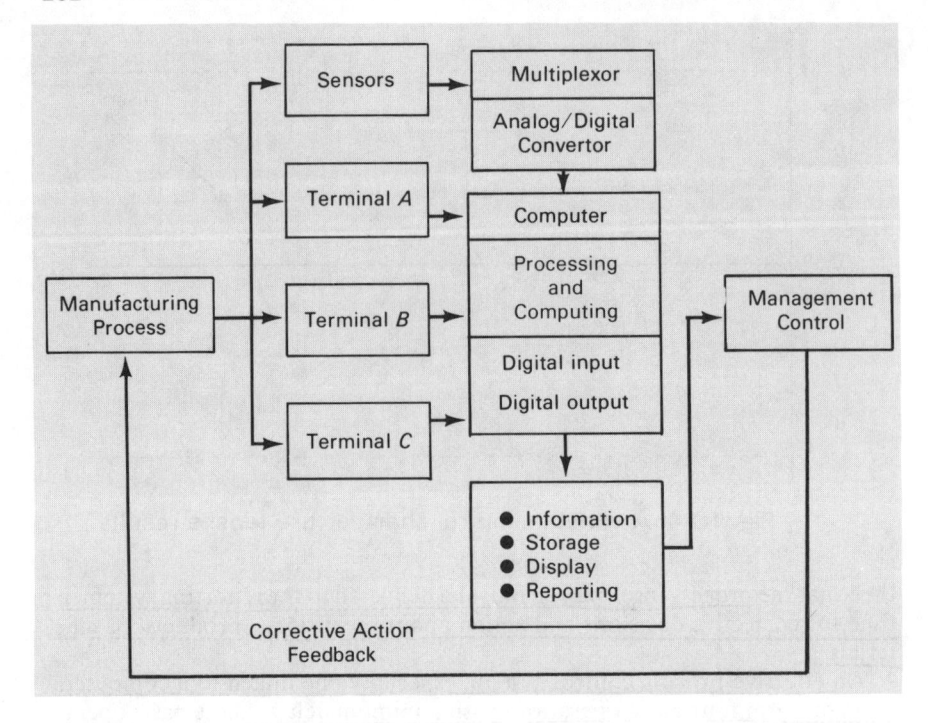

Fig. 18-6. Computerized manufacturing control and management information system

step is usually taken at the close of specific time periods, for example, after a shift, or day's production run. These status reports give management a clear picture of what has occurred during a specified production cycle and can be analyzed and compared to what was expected. Long-run trends can then be examined and standards recalculated.

2. **Monitoring and Warning Level**
This phase involves continually comparing data with specified management objectives and flagging deviate information to the responsible first-line supervisor. This function, which is the essence of control, is to provide online current information in the hands of management. Historical status reports are also easily constructed during this phase.

3. **Operator Direction**
In this third phase is found the capability to initiate actions that advise the operative worker. This includes all the service processes that are available to manufacturing systems. Additionally, when computers are used, the computer serves to supply information to operators when it detects operator error, machine malfunction or other out-of-tolerance operating conditions.

4. **Equipment Process Control**
The last phase integrates all services performed in the factory into a real time process of direct control of the operating machinery. Typically, real time control systems consist of a central computer, auxiliary processing equipment, and a number of remote terminals. These terminals

are located throughout the manufacturing cycle to communicate with and receive data from the computer, as we have illustrated in figure 18-6.

The information being processed by the system would provide several important monitoring functions. First, it would provide trend or historical information for alerting management to possible problems before they are out of control. Second, the deviate data gathered by the system could be utilized to diagnose and isolate particular operator and/or machine malfunctions, which require management's attention. Third, it facilitates a more efficient utilization of plant equipment.

OTHER QUANTITATIVE METHODS

Some other quantitative methods should be mentioned, even though they may be beyond the scope of this text.

Probability Theory

Many of the descriptive and classical statistical techniques are used by managers from time to time. The usefulness of statistics is well known and accepted throughout management literature on planning and controlling. For example, one of the most interesting contributions to decision making is in the area of probabilistic decision making. Here the theory of probability is used to expand the alternatives to managers. Take the case of a prospective store location. If a company that operates a chain of stores plans to build a new store in either of two cities the company might analyze the following data:

If the store is located in Town A and has a probability of ¾ of being successful, the store might make an annual profit of $8,000,000 a year. If it is not successful it might lose $2,000,000 a year.

If the store is located in Town B and has a probability of ½ of being successful, the store might make $12,000,000 annually. If it is not successful it might lose $2,400,000 a year. Where should the company locate the new store?

First, the manager must look at the alternatives.

Table 18-4

Town	Success $	Probability	Not a Success $	Probability
A	$ 8,000,000	¾	($2,000,000)	¼
B	$12,000,000	½	($2,400,000)	½

If the manager is an optimist, location B would be chosen in order to maximize profits ($12,000,000). On the other hand if the manager is a pessimist, location A would surely be chosen to minimize losses (−$2,000,000).

However, if the manager utilized all the data and multiplied the probabilities times the conditional values, logically location A would be chosen as follows:

A $8,000,000 × ¾ - $2,000,000 × ¼ = $5,500,000
B $12,000,000 × ½ - $2,400,000 × ½ = $4,800,000
∴ A would be selected

The rationale is that in the long run, given these probabilities, possibly from past experience, the manager would tend to maximize profits.

Operations Research

To many management scholars, operations research has become a common term for the use of more complicated quantitative techniques. Operations research consists of bringing into focus in mathematical terms, every important variable and the reasonable outcome involved in a set of decisions. These alternatives are usually developed and tested mathematically, often using the computer before the actions or decisions are adopted.

Some of the more popular quantitative techniques used in operations research are linear programming, simulation, monte carlo, queuing, and gaming. These, however, are beyond the scope of this text.

Finally, you should be aware that decision making in its most sophisticated sense is a complex, dynamic process combining many of the above tools, both quantitative and nonquantitative, and often utilizing the computer.[4] These complex approaches frequently go by the names systems analysis, formal corporate planning and control, as well as management science.

QUESTIONS FOR DISCUSSION

1. Discuss the major function of an accounting system for control.
2. Define accounting's basic formula.
3. What are the various accounts on a balance sheet?
4. The income statement has three basic parts. Discuss each.
5. Show how ratio analysis can be meaningful for control.
6. Why is budgeting such an important control procedure?
7. Explain how to measure process capability.
8. Show how to calculate a standard deviation.
9. There are five probable causes of variation in quality. Explain.

REFERENCES

1. Andrew C. Stedry, *Budget Control and Cost Behavior,* (Englewood Cliffs, NJ: Prentice-Hall, 1969).
2. Elwood G. Kirkpatrick, *Quality Control for Managers and Engineers,* (New York: John Wiley and Sons, Inc.), pp. 3-12.
3. A.V. Feigenbaum, *Total Quality Control,* (New York: McGraw-Hill, 1961).
4. Karl A. Shilliff, and Bernard A. Deitzer, "Computer Control of Human Resource Development," *Manufacturing Engineering,* (December 1978): pp. 65-67.

SELECTED BIBLIOGRAPHY

1. Elwood S. Buffa, *Operations Management* (New York: John Wiley & Sons, Inc., 1968).
2. Peter P. Schoderbek, *Management Systems* (New York: John Wiley & Sons, Inc., 1967).
3. Acheson J. Duncan, *Quality Control and Industrial Statistics,* 3d ed. (Homewood, IL: Richard D. Irwin, Inc., 1965).
4. Gilbert Gordon and Israel Pressman, *Quantitative Decision-Making for Business* (Englewood Cliffs, NJ: Prentice-Hall, Inc., 1978).
5. Robert J. Thierauf, *An Introductory Approach to Operating Research* (Santa Barbara, CA: Wiley/Hamilton Publication, 1978).

CHAPTER 19

MANAGEMENT AND ETHICAL BEHAVIOR

Purpose of Chapter 19:

1. To discuss the significance of ethics in managerial behavior
2. To identify the sources of a managerial code of conduct
3. To outline the basis for professional conduct in the firm

Essential elements you should understand after studying this chapter:

1. Ethical behavior defined
2. Standards of managerial behavior
3. Role of individual value systems in behavior
4. Basis for professional conduct
5. Guidelines for personal ethical behavior
6. Program for corporate ethical behavior

INTRODUCTION

So far in our discussions we have concentrated on the manager's role in exercising responsibilities of planning, organizing, staffing, directing, and controlling of group leadership and decision making within the organization.

Our discussion of management, though, would certainly be remiss if we did not include those functions and responsibilities of management that are related to the firm's character and to its public existence. Essentially, management responsibility is public responsibility. There inevitably exists a fundamental responsibility of management to the public interest.

The basis for this, of course, lies in the fact that the enterprise is an organ of our society and its activities decisively influence the social fabric of that society in which it operates.[1] All institutions, then, are actually tools of society. They are established by society and, in the long run, continue to exist with the granted consent of society. It is public policy and public good that determine and limit the range of actions and activities of the enterprise. Each institution in the final analysis is considered a social asset for performing some useful, constructive purpose for the public good.

It follows then that those managers entrusted with the responsibility for running the enterprise not only have power over its physical and human resources, but more broadly still, their managerial decisions have great impact upon society, its economy and its people. Clearly then, management in pursuit of its own self-interest cannot consider its decisions to be divorced from society and the public good. On the contrary, it must assume responsibility for the public good and accordingly subordinate self-interest to an ethical standard of conduct that supports the interest of both society and its people. This public responsibility of management must, therefore, underlie all corporate behavior and form the basis for the ethical behavior of management.[2]

CHANGES IN THE ENVIRONMENTAL CLIMATE

Within recent years four important developments have contributed to a change in business climate. These four changes have not only produced a positive result but also have created strong implications for increasing ethical sensitivity in the business community. They are: (1) the advancement of the social ethic and with it the human relations approach to society and people; (2) an increasing professionalism of management; (3) the rise of consumer-oriented marketing concepts; and (4) the generally adopted new concepts of corporate commitment to the public.

As a result, organizations have made major changes in organizational policy. The fact that many changed policies were promoted by business because they were good for the enterprise in no way alters their significance. Management increasingly realizes that good ethics is good business.

Throughout the 20th century, the moral and ethical behavior of businessmen has been improving and increased awareness of ethical problems will bring out even more explicit and professional ethical standards.

Over the years, institutions, and particularly business, have attempted to demonstrate their responsibility for ethical conduct in our free enterprise society. They have attempted to meet the challenge of ever higher ethical goals through objectives, policy, and action. Accordingly, ethical standards which guide business conduct have gravitated to a point where they now exert a profound influence on the performance of the business community.³

So as the ethical conduct of U.S. business has improved, so the public demand for responsible conduct has increased correspondingly. To realize fully future opportunities and to maintain simultaneously public confidence requires then a continuing pursuit of high standards of conduct.

For business to attain this objective is not without some difficulty. The business institution has many faceted relationships—with the owners, stockholders, employees, customers, suppliers, government, and the public in general.

Concurrently, the traditional emphasis on freedom, competition, and progress in our economic system often brings the varying interests of these groups into conflict. This gives rise to many difficult and complex problems. And while relationships of an enterprise to these groups are in some degree regulated by law, compliance with the law provides only a minimum basis of behavior. But beyond the law, the policies and actions of business itself must be counted on to recognize the proper claims of all affected groups.⁴

Central, then, to a discussion of ethical behavior in the organization is indeed the fact that the interests of the public, management, and employees—their purposes, goals, needs and values—are often and seemingly opposed.

Stockholders, for example, usually expect the highest return on their investments. Labor desires higher wages, increased security, and other benefits. Customers want highest quality at lowest possible prices. Suppliers desire the best prices for their goods and services; and the public, generally speaking, wants business operations to be without harmful and polluting effects. Assuredly each interested party attempts to justify its own demands. Each and all exert various influences and pressures on the institution and its management as in figure 19-1.

Reconciling or balancing these opposing interests and pressures often requires an individual exercise in managerial ethics—an exercise in considering the "right" and "wrong" in decision-making situations. While the manager certainly may be helped in decision making by the quantitative forces in the competitive markets—whether of goods, finances or labor—the manager, in large part, must arrive at conclusions by the qualitative standards of ethics.

NATURE AND SIGNIFICANCE OF ETHICS

In an open and pluralistic society such as ours, unethical behavior sometimes associated with organizations makes interesting copy for the information media. In fact, it is commonplace to find examples in the daily press of some kind of unethical practice in either the public or private sector—in government or in the business community.

Within recent years, for instance, a major scandal occurred in which a "Watergate" forced the resignation of our president. A foreign government was charged with purchasing influence among our congressmen. Corporations have been found guilty of breaking the laws governing political campaign contributions. A U.S. firm is cited by the Securities Exchange Commission for giving brides to the president of a foreign country to gain a lower tax advantage. Another company has been accused of using a multimillion dollar fund for payoffs to local officials of other nations to gain an unfair and

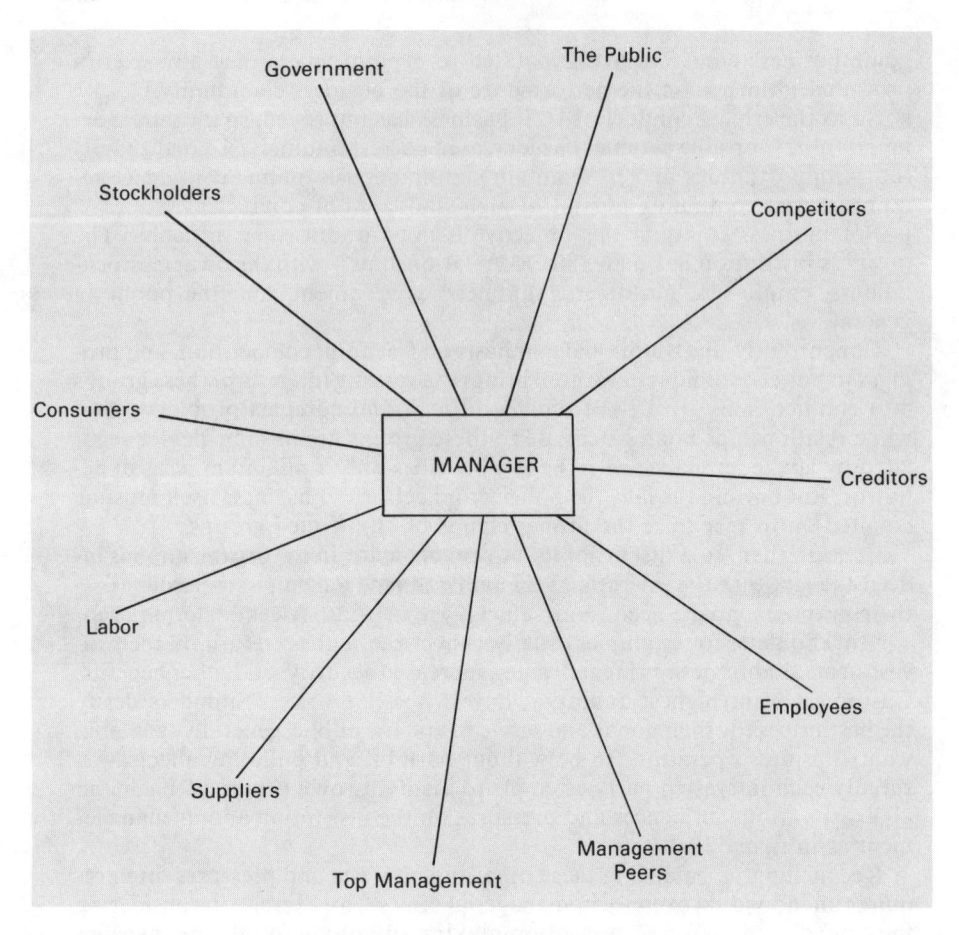

Fig. 19-1. Managerial pressure points

perhaps illegal advantage over competitors. A major equity fund is guilty of issuing "phantom" life insurance to improve its market position.

Similar reports of tax dodgers, mishandling of pension funds, shoddiness of product quality, improper financial practices, discrimination in employment, and lack of concern for worker health and safety have appeared in the media and, of course, all tend to raise questions about the ethical standards of organizational conduct.

The unethical practices just described are indeed immoral and unconscionable. And while unethical practices are not representative of organizational behavior, nevertheless they are symptoms of inappropriate behavior. In our open society any excesses of managerial conduct are readily visible to the public, irrespective of the many transactions conducted every day in an atmosphere of honesty and integrity.

To be sure, the U.S. business community, for example, has come a long way since the era of the antisocial, unbridled, profit-seeking capitalists described in *The Robber Barons*.[5] Today, through a combination of self-regulation and federal legislation, the average firm evidences increasing interest and concern for its ethical behavior. It recognizes a responsibility to the society that permits it to exist and function. It recognizes too, that the unrestrained use of social and economic power to the detriment of public and societal good can only result in increased government intervention and control through restrictive legislation.

DEFINITION OF ETHICS

A basic problem in any discussion of ethics is common agreement as to the meaning of a term that indeed lends itself to broad and subjective interpretation. In our culture, ethics has been defined variously by different sources as: "due regard for other people," "conforming to moral standards," "determining what is right and wrong in situations," "what the law requires," and "what my conscience allows."

But this very lack of uniform agreement on a common definition compounds the problem for management in the perception and treatment of ethics. **For purposes of discussion, ethics, then, is the study of the morality of human conduct and the standards for that conduct. Ethics strives to delineate what conduct is good or bad or what conduct is to be acceptable or unacceptable.** A code of ethics, thus, would exist of a recognized standard of ideal and acceptable behavior in organizations and society.

SOURCES OF A CODE OF ETHICS

Just how does a manager go about developing a personal code of ethics? How does ethics, as practiced in the organization, originate? And from what sources does it spring?

A manager's personal and ethical behavior is largely shaped by certain standards against which individual conduct is framed. There are four generally recognized standards which are the subjective, the normative, the objective, and associational standards.[6]

The Subjective Standard

The manager's morality is viewed intuitively—subjectively, if you will. If the behavior of others is similar to that of the manager, it is considered moral. If the behavior of others is sufficiently different, in terms of patterns of action and beliefs, then such behavior is likely to be considered ethically unsound.

The Normative Standard

Morality is that standard approved by the greatest number of people. This is the expression of society, the culture, and the group as established through its norms of behavior. Thus, a norm is a standard, developed by the group against which behavior can be measured. Norms identify that behavior that is important to a group. Reward and punishment systems are rigidly established to support conforming behavior while rejecting disapproved behavior.[7]

Legal standards, incidentally, are the legal criteria of morality and are but the norms of past society, so to speak. The question is to what degree does the normative behavior of others influence the behavior of the manager?

The Objective Standard

This standard of behavior is that reflected against the religious criteria of morality. It is that behavior encouraged by the precepts and teachings of the Judeo-Christian faiths and typified by the Ten Commandments and the Torah. The objective standard is a more permanent basis for establishing one's behavior. While managers will employ the Judeo-Christian ethic in varying degrees of application, it nonetheless constitutes a widely known, recognized and accepted basis for individual behavior.

The Associational Standard

A fourth standard or criterion for the manager's ethical performance is the persuasive influence of certain people who, through close personal contact, exert a significant effect upon the manager's actions. In this class and according to rank order of importance are: father, mother, teachers, clergy, wife, and business associates.[8] Again, arises the question as to the significant impact of these sources in influencing managerial behavior. Certain associational sources, it appears, such as one's superior, exert a more pronounced influence on managers in their work environment than does one's associates or peers. (Figure 19-2 represents a model of influential factors in the determination of ethical behavior.)

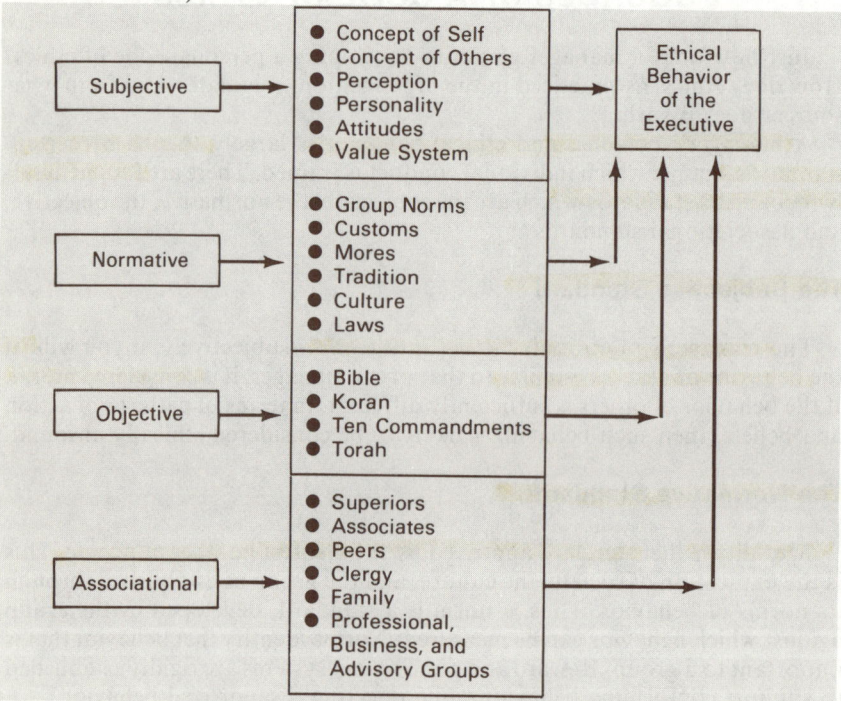

Fig. 19-2. Influential determinants of ethical behavior

Summarily then, the behavior of a manager is a composite of beliefs and attitudes and reflects influences from a variety of sources. Obviously, some sources will exert stronger influence than others. Each manger exhibits a peculiar, ethical profile and while individual behavior in the decision-making process may be comparable to that of other managers, the basis for decision or action may be distinctly different.

ROLE OF VALUE SYSTEMS

Any discussion about business ethics, about "what is" in contrast to "what ought to be" in terms of the manager's ethical behavior, must also concern itself with the manager's value system. Whereas norms constitute rather specific codes of conduct desired by a group in particular situations, values describe what individuals consider important. Values represent preferences for particular things, conditions, or circumstances compared with others.

Understandably, within an organization are reflected many of the characteristics of society as a whole. The institution, public or private, production or service, profit or nonprofit, is a subculture of the larger society. The values and attitudes that prevail outside are generally exhibited by organizational members inside the firm.

The organization itself, as we described in chapter 12, is instrumental in the creation of a climate of behavior. It also creates and establishes feelings, attitudes, beliefs, and a value system of its own. The value system of the firm strengthens people in their relationships with the economic and competitive environment. It, furthermore, reinforces cohesion by offering to its members readily applicable guidelines which suggest appropriate and acceptable behavior.

An individual's value system, therefore, is intrinsic, highly perceptual, and reasonably permanent. It provides a framework that influences individual behavior and social expectations. It provides the basis for making value judgments. Values that are internalized and exert the greatest influence on behavior might be defined as *operational*. Those that are outwardly professed, but not fully accepted internally, might be termed *adoptive*.[9]

What this means, simply, is that many people function in organizational life with a dual value system that is apparently inconsistent. A typical example of this would be a personnel director, primarily a service-oriented individual, who works for a firm that is devoid of humanistic feelings in its approach to employees and views the personnel function as "the office to hire and fire the rank and file." Another instance would be a sales representative, highly moralistic, who works for a business that knowingly ships defective products.

Eventually, however, one's value system determines one's actions. The personnel director and the salesman must either change their value systems— or leave the firm. Obviously, the value system of the manager is important because it influences:

1. A manager's perception of situations and problems being faced
2. A manager's decisions and solutions to problems
3. The way in which a manager looks at other individuals and groups of individuals—thus influencing interpersonal relationships
4. The perception of individual and organizational success as well as its

achievement
5. The limits for the determination of what is and what is not ethical behavior by a manager
6. The extent to which a manager will accept or resist organizational pressures and goals[10]

SELF-PERCEPTION OR ETHICAL BEHAVIOR

Any discussion of the manager's ethical behavior must begin from the viewpoint of the manager. How, then, do average modern managers view or perceive their own behavior in terms of relationships with the firm, client, and society?

Average executives, various studies show, feel they are ethical in their practices and that extensions of themselves (their department, company, industry, and country) are also concerned about the ethical implications of their decisions. They also feel that good ethics is good business in the long run, especially in employee and customer relations.

The golden rule, most executives believe, while useful as a starting point, is inadequate as a norm for solving most ethical problems in business. Furthermore, studies bear out that the executive who does not attend church or synagogue appears to have attitudes just as ethical as those of the church-affiliated manager.[11]

Again, and to reemphasize, more than any other singular influence on the job is the influence of one's superior. The executive's behavior is profoundly influenced by the behavior of superiors in the making of decisions both ethical and unethical. This points out, of course, that improvement of standards of conduct in the organization rests with management itself. Therefore, any expected change in ethical behavior must stem from the conscious actions of the organization's leadership.

A BASIS FOR PROFESSIONAL CONDUCT

A major frustration encountered by the executive is the relative inability to place the ethical issues in clear-cut categories. There are many gray areas where issues are borderline, and applicable rules are difficult to find. It is hollow logic to assume that all executives instinctively know what guidelines to follow:

Consequently, if executives base their ethical behavior *on the law alone*, then this supports the idea that anything *not in the law* is permissible behavior. This, of course, is questionable thinking. "While our system of laws provides a substantial basis for ethical conduct, ethics is much more comprehensive. Law deals with man as he is, setting a minimum standard of conduct. Ethics seeks to lead man to what he *ought to be and do*; it establishes a maximum standard."[12] Business ethics concerns itself with the *is* of business behavior versus the *ought to be*. The *ought to be*, according to many managers, apparently needs to be defined more clearly.

And many organizations are doing just that—indicating required behavior in the firm. Increasingly, business is spelling out in policy terms both its definition and interpretation of business conduct. In addition to self-initiated statements by the firm on required ethical behavior, there are strong in-

> **Independence, Integrity and Objectivity.** A certified public accountant should maintain his integrity and objectivity and, when engaged in the practice of public accounting, be independent of those he serves.
>
> **Competence and Technical Standards.** A certified public accountant should observe the profession's technical standards and strive continually to improve his competence and the quality of his services.
>
> **Responsibilities to Clients.** A certified public accountant should be fair and candid with his clients and serve them to the best of his ability, with professional concern for their best interests, consistent with his responsibilities to the public.
>
> **Responsibilities to Colleagues.** A certified public accountant should conduct himself in a manner which will promote cooperation and good relations among members of the profession.
>
> **Other Responsibilities and Practices.** A certified public accountant should conduct himself in a manner which will enhance the stature of the profession and its ability to serve the public.
>
> Source: American Institute of Certified Public Accountants, *Code of Professional Ethics*, (New York: American Institute of Certified Public Accountants, 1972). Copyright 1972 by the American Institute of Certified Public Accountants, Inc. (Adapted with Permission.)

Fig. 19-3. Ethical principles of The American Institute of Certified Public Accountants

fluences by other external groups and organizations that interact with the firm. These organizations may be classified as professional associations, public advisory groups, and business associations.[13]

Professional Associations

This group offers codes of conduct that support, among other things, fairness, full disclosure, and decisions free of influence. These codes govern the ethical conduct of members in business, for instance, as with the Certified Public Accountants (figure 19-3).

Advisory Groups

Codes of behavior are also offered by foundations, religious action groups, and minority groups. However, there is a difference with professional groups. The professional groups are self-generating a code for their own self-control, both in business and out of it. Advisory groups, on the other hand, offer to raise the standards of others.[14]

Business Associations

In this category are the many business associations representing specific groups such as florists, retail druggists, and grocers. The National Retail Druggists Association, the National Merchants Assocation, and the National Grocers Association are some examples. While these groups primarily serve their own interests, they also set ethical standards for dealing with consumers and others. In this manner they control unscrupulous members, maintain a public image, and expel offenders who consequently are denied the values of membership.

GUIDELINES FOR PERSONAL ETHICS

Suggesting guidelines of ethical practices for the modern manager goes well beyond both the law and the universal golden rule. What is offered the manager, during any deliberations involving ethics, are the following guidelines designed to cover the widest range of possible managerial behavior.

1. Does the contemplated activity violate the tenets of the Judeo-Christian beliefs (the Ten Commandments or the Torah)?
2. Even though the manager's anticipated action will *not* be audited by the firm's superiors would it be the same if it were?
3. How would the contemplated action appear to the public if all the facts, motives, interests, and profits were divulged?[15]
4. If the proposed act is questionable, regardless of the fact that it is a familiar practice in which almost everyone indulges, the act should be tested by assuming that it is the sole instance of commission. How does it appear in this light?
5. If the environment is political, how would the contemplated act appear to an ordinary member of the community whose authority (and vote) made it possible?
6. How would the act be characterized if it had been performed by the firm's most detested business adversary?

DEVELOPMENT OF PROFESSIONALISM

Obviously, at this stage, it can be concluded that ethics, as that behavior permitted by the law, is not enough. Nor is a code of ethics built solely upon the Golden Rule enough to form a basis for ethical decisions. Nor is it enough for business behavior to be predicated exclusively on religious principles. All these assist, of course, in establishing a code of behavior. What is additionally needed, though, is more constructive support, another standard, which along with the law and religion serves as a basis of conduct for the manager.

Accordingly, the following operational ground rules of professional ethical behavior are offered for the manager's consideration.

1. Professional business managers affirm that they will place the interest of the business for which they work before their own private interests.
2. Professional business managers affirm that they will place their duty to society above their duty to their company and above their private interests.
3. Professional business managers affirm that they have a duty to reveal the facts in any situation where (a) their private interests are involved with those of their company, or (b) where the interests of their company are involved with those of the society in which it operates.
4. Professional business managers affirm that when business managers follow this code of conduct, the profit motive is the best incentive for the

development of a sound, expanding, and dynamic economy.[16]

AN ORGANIZATIONAL PROGRAM FOR BUSINESS ETHICS

Finally, what advice can be offered management, advice that both supports individual professionalism and is conducive to maintaining an atmosphere of ethical corporate behavior?

Promotion of Corporate Organizational Understanding

The organization should promote well-considered policy statements of ethical principles to guide both management and employees in specific situations arising in the course of business activities both domestic and foreign. Obviously, this policy should be clearly delineated, communicated, and enforced by regular audits of performance.

Management can further support this through personal example for others to emulate; example that helps establish a positive organizational climate of ethical conduct.

Compliance With the Law

Recognizing complexities and the ever-changing patterns of modern law and governmental regulation, the firm should insure that its officers and employees are both informed about and comply with legal requirements affecting their activities. Beyond this, management needs to encourage and support codes of conduct espoused by professional groups for industry in general and especially for functional groups such as marketing, personnel, finance, production, and so on.

Conflicts of Interest

The firm needs to issue and promote statements of policy regarding potential conflict of interest problems of its directors, officers, and employees. Policy statements should cover conflicts that may develop in relation to transactions with or involving the firm; acquiring interest in or performing services for customers; distributors, suppliers, and competitors and the buying and selling of company securities, to cite a few examples.

Entertainment and Gifts

Company policy needs to define and communicate required managerial behavior with regard to accepting gifts and favors from institutions having an interest in the firm. It should also cite policy on expenditures for gifts and entertainment. Criteria as to both situation and amount should be clearly established. Moreover, company policy needs to be communicated to both the organization and to its many publics.

Customers and Suppliers

In its business relationships, the firm insures that marketing activities, including advertising and merchandising representations, are honest and truthful. Both its product and service should measure up to basic obligations and responsibilities. Favoritism and discrimination are avoided in relationships with all clients.

In summary, one final comment must be made here. That is this. While we have already discussed the continually increasing expectations of the firm by society, it goes without saying that unrestrained business behavior leads only to more regulation by government through law and its many enforcing agencies. If the organization in a free enterprise system wants to avoid more constraints, it would do well to be highly sensitive to its ethics.

QUESTIONS FOR DISCUSSION

1. Discuss what you feel are the reasons for the increased concern for more positive ethical conduct in business.
2. Just how do aspects of ethics arise in the decisions of management? Give several examples.
3. Describe how an individual, possibly yourself, develops a code of ethics for use in relationships with people and groups.
4. In what ways does one's value system influence behavior?
5. To what degree have associations and social groups modified questionable business practices? Cite examples.
6. In what manner is the concept of managerial professionalism related to a positive code of business behavior?
7. Compare the exercise of ethical responsibility between large and small companies; between the federal and local governments.

REFERENCES

1. Peter F. Drucker, *The Practice of Management* (New York: Harper & Bros. Publishers, 1954), p. 381.
2. Keith Davis and Robert L. Blomstrom, Business and Society: Environment and *Responsibility*, 3d ed. (New York: McGraw-Hill Book Co., 1975), p. 383.
3. George A. Steiner, ed., "Standards For Business Conduct," *Issues in Business and Society* (New York: Random House), p. 256.
4. Ibid., p. 257.
5. This book by Matthew Josephson (New York: Harcourt Brace and World, Inc., 1962) is an expose' of unethical conduct of certain businessmen during the 19th century.
6. Adapted from V. Clayton Sherman, "Business Ethics: Analysis and Philosophy," *Personnel Journal* (April, 1968).
7. Ralph M. Stogdill, *Individual Behavior and Group Achievement* (New York: Oxford University Press, Inc., 1959), pp. 71-83.
8. Raymond Baumhart, *Ethics In Business* (New York: Holt, Rinehart, and Winston, Inc., 1968), p. 68.
9. Clarence C. Walton, *Ethos and the Executive* (Englewood Cliffs, NJ: Prentice-Hall, Inc., 1969), p. 33.
10. George W. England, as quoted in Walton, *Ethos and the Executive*, p. 34.
11. Baumhart, op. cit., pp. 4-5.

12. Stephen C. O'Connell, "Ethics in Business," *The Appraisal Journal,* American Institute of Real Estate Appraisers, Chicago (July 1966): 359.
13. Adapted from Keith Davis and Robert L. Blomstrom, *Business Society and Environment* (New York: McGraw-Hill Book Co., 1971), pp. 143-145.
14. Ibid., p. 344.
15. Edmund Cahn, as quoted in Walton, *Ethos and the Executive,* p. 91.
16. Robert Austin, "Code of Conduct for Executives," *Harvard Business Review,* vol. 39 (September-October, 1961), 53-61. As quoted in Walton, *Ethos and the Executive,* p. 90.

SELECTED BIBLIOGRAPHY

1. Davis, Keith, and Blomstrom, Robert L. *Business and Society: Environment and Responsibility.* 3d ed. New York: McGraw-Hill Book Co., 1975.
2. Garrett, Thomas M. *Business Ethics.* New York: Appleton-Century-Crofts, 1966.
3. Steiner, George A., ed. *Issues in Business and Society.* New York: Random House, 1972.
4. Walton, Clarence C. *Ethos and the Executive.* Englewood Cliffs, NJ: Prentice-Hall, Inc., 1969.
5. Walton, Clarence, ed. *The Ethics of Corporate Conduct.* Englewood Cliffs, NJ: Prentice-Hall, Inc., 1977.

CHAPTER 20

EMERGING DIMENSIONS IN MANAGEMENT

Purpose of Chapter 20:

1. To summarize significant developments and their implications to management
2. To identify changing dimensions of the work force and to project certain occupational and demographic trends
3. To outline the effects of computer technology and management science techniques upon the organization
4. To discuss the question of corporate social responsibility and its impact upon management decisions

Essential elements you should understand after studying this chapter:

1. Projected differences in the demographic composition of the work force
2. Growth of computerization in business
3. Effects of the computer upon management
4. Increased role of social responsibility
5. Technology and social responsibility
6. Human resources and social responsibility

INTRODUCTION

The business organization is a dynamic, changing entity operating in a complicated, changing environment. It simultaneously contributes to and receives from the societal environment within which it functions. It must seek, therefore, to adapt itself to ongoing changes, to support research for improved management techniques, and to incorporate new knowledge from other disciplines. The firm can neither stand still nor stand alone. It must be sensitive to the pervasive and compelling influences that emerge around it.

While it is difficult, to be sure, to predict the future, it is possible to discern certain emerging trends or developments that will assume even larger significance for the firm and its management. Needless to say, if there is one organizational requisite more germane than others, it is the need for creative innovation and adaption as the organization plans for the future.

THE CHANGING WORK FORCE

An organization perpetuates itself by regularly drawing its leadership and productive human resources from the many groups it serves. Projections through 1985 seem to indicate that certain distinctive differences will appear in both the occupational and demographic makeup of our population.

In terms of the basic scenario, total employment is expected to increase by about 20 percent between 1974 and 1985, from almost 86 million to a little over 103 million. The number of white-collar workers, the largest major occupational category is projected to rise by almost 28 percent during this period from 41.7 million to 53.2 million as depicted in figure 20-1. Blue-collar workers, the second largest major occupational category are expected to increase by only 13 percent from 29.8 million in 1974 to 33.7 million in 1985. A decline of about 39 percent is anticipated in the number of farmworkers from 3 million in 1974 to 1.8 million in 1985.[1]

By 1985 white-collar workers are expected to account for slightly more than half (51.5 percent) of the economy's total employment. This is up from 48.6 percent in 1974 as described in figure 20.2. The share of the total attributed to service workers also is expected to increase during this period from 13.2 percent to 14.1 percent. The blue-collar share of total employment, however, is expected to decline from 34.6 percent in 1974 to 32.6 in 1985. Farmworkers are expected to account for only 1.8 percent of total employment, and this is down from 3.5 percent in 1974.

In terms of specific occupations, the group of professional and technical workers, which include physicians, lawyers, scientists, and engineers, is expected to grow from 14.4 percent to 15.5 percent during 1974-85. Expansion in this category reflects the needs for more goods and services for a rising population concurrent with simultaneous and increased national efforts in the areas of energy exploration and production, mass transportation, urban renewal, and environmental protection.

Concurrently, the employment of managers and administrators is projected to reach 10.9 million in 1985. This is up from 8.9 million in 1974. Total employment, moreover, attributed to management is expected to increase about 10 percent through 1985 in the manufacturing sector and more than 40 percent in the service industries. The demand for salaried managers it seems

Emerging Dimensions in Management 283

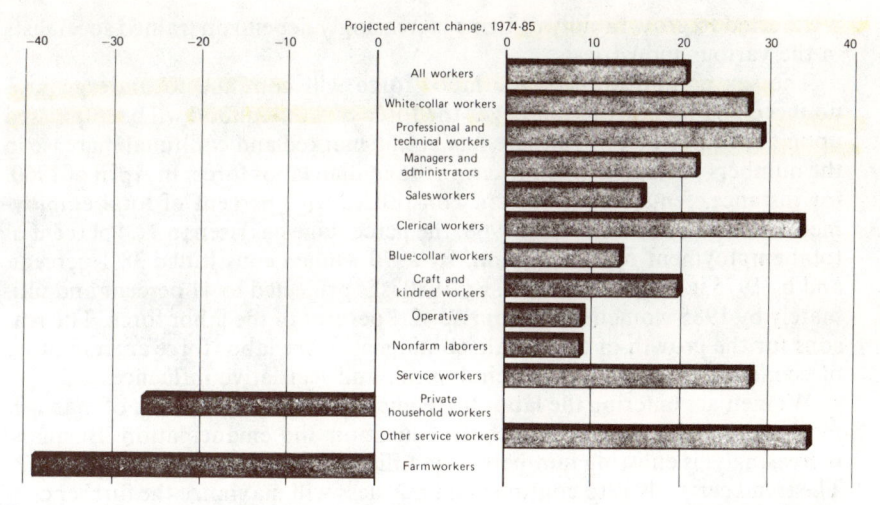

Source: *Monthly Labor Review,* U.S. Department of Labor. Bureau of Labor Statistics, November 1976, p. 11.

Fig. 20-1. Through the mid-1980's, employment growth will vary widely among occupations.

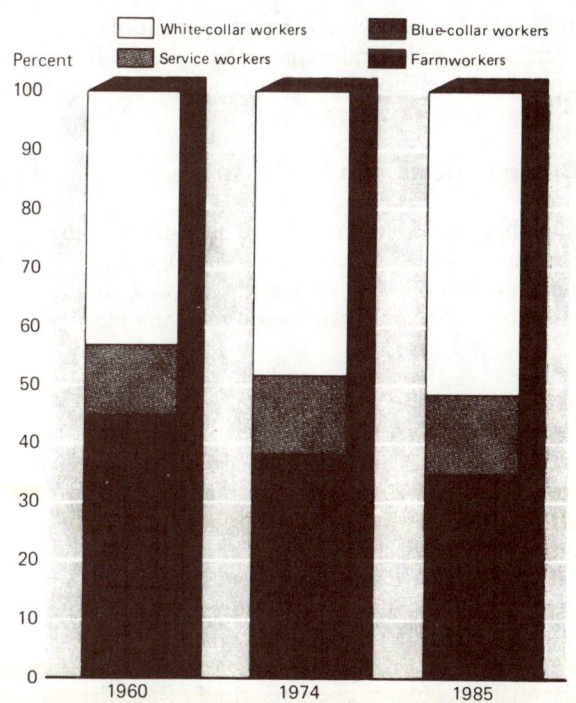

Source: *Monthly Labor Review,* U.S. Department of Labor. Bureau of Labor Statistics, November 1976, p. 12.

Fig. 20-2. Employment is expected to continue to shift toward while collar and service occupations.

is expected to grow rapidly as firms increasingly depend on trained specialists in the various industries.

The sex composition of the labor force will continue to undergo pronounced changes. More than ever the force of womanhood wil be impressed upon the firm. Since 1920 there has been a marked and continual increase in the numbers of adult women entering the civilian labor force. In April of 1960, for instance, female employment constituted 31.9 percent of total employment of 66.1 million. In April 1968, the percentage has risen to 37.4 percent of total employment of 75.6 million. By 1970 women constituted 38.1 percent, and by 1975 it was 39.9 percent. By 1980 is is projected to 41 percent and ultimately by 1985 women will comprise 42.1 percent of the labor force. The reasons for the growth of the female contingent of the labor force are a mixture of economic, sociological, psychological, and legislative influences.

Women are entering the labor force and, accordingly, the field of management, with a higher degree of both education and emancipation. Business, increasingly, is enlisting numbers of qualified women in managerial positions. The trend certainly is to continue and business will maximize the further contribution of women through providing increased developmental and promotional opportunities at all mangerial levels of the organization.

IMPACT OF THE COMPUTER

The computer makes possible better management of the modern corporation and its social, economic, and managerial systems. It facilitates through the use of management science techniques the planning, measurement, and control of the organization's systems.

Growth of Computerization in Business

The computer has made the knowledge industry possible. In 1960 there were 90,000 computers; in 1977 there were 155,000; and by 1985 it is estimated there may be as many as 500,000 in use at sites twice that number. In other words there probably wil be one installation for every business with over fifty employees.[2]

Effects upon Management Levels

The effect of the computer appears to vary with each level of management. The application of data processing has normally automated, for lower level management, decisions of a routine and menial nature. Furthermore, decisions on inventory control and manpower scheduling, formerly made by control supervisory staffs, are now being made by the computer. In turn, this is providing middle management with more accurate data for effectively evaluating the operating results of its supervision.

At the top management level, the computer is being utilized to analyze better data essential to a better understanding of the firm and relationship between it and its environment. It is being used to evaluate the effects of various corporate strategies over the long run. Furthermore, the computer is regularly being enlisted to forecast, among other contingencies, the success potential of new products and services as well as the probable effectiveness of changes in sales, sales promotion, distribution techniques, and human resource development programs.

Effects upon the Manager

The computer is a dual-edged tool. Just as it will provide needed assistance to managers of the future, it will also hasten their obsolescence, if they are not in tune with its expansive uses. If present and future managers desire to maintain their productive vitality, they will certainly prepare for personal compatibility with computerized information systems. The middle manager who incorporates and applies computer technology should not become extinct but will find increasing personal worth and satisfaction in the responsibilities of management.

Future Management and the Computer

While the information revolution will continue at an accelerated pace, the manager will have more control of the computer and information processing. Management experts predict a highly decentralized information system that will respond more to inquiries rather than issuing periodic reports.

Management, furthermore, will receive most of its data through electronic displays on portable minicomputers or conveniently located terminals which access a central computer. Managers of the future will have at their disposal immediate data on their machines, people, money, unit performance, corporate performance and national trends. Managers will be able to test alternative actions before making major decisions. They will be able to anticipate the impact of decisions on other operations of the firm. The computer, more than ever, will give management more useful information in a more timely fashion.[3]

CORPORATE SOCIAL RESPONSIBILITY

At the center of much management decisions is the question of corporate social responsibility. We discuss the subject here in terms of, first, developing concepts; second, management and technology; and third, management and human resources.

Developing Concepts

The question of whether or not business should exercise a sense of social responsibility is almost an academic one. The question itself is less and less debated, and more recently the focus is on the *degree* of social involvement by business. By social responsibility is meant the obligation of the firm to consider the impact of both its decisions and actions on the larger social system. Moreover, if the public interest is affected by management decisions and actions, then there is no question about the need to exercise social responsibility.

It is felt here that there is a decided interdependence, a distinct relationship between business and the social system within which it functions. Just as the business institution reflects the values and mores of a consuming society it also creates social values for that society. Why, the student may inquire, is there a growing concern about the exercise of social responsibility? There appear to be several main reasons.

First, there is an increased sensitivity by business itself to its role and responsibility in the exercise of social consciousness. A progressive and professional management is aware more and more of the interdependencies of business and society. Business, through the application of advancing technology, is instrumental in causing social change. Increasingly, business feels responsible for ameliorating the effects of social change upon society.

Second, there is pressure from society itself—composed of the many groups that business serves. More and more the parameters of corporate responsibility are felt to extend beyond the performance of economic functions alone. The social concerns—of unemployment, environmental pollution, resource conservation, and ecological stabilities—are felt to be considered along with the problems of market and profit performance. Since business possesses the resources and talent to assist in solving social problems the expectancy level of business behavior rises accordingly.

Finally, the regulatory pressure of government against business will be as intense as today except there will be a more cooperative relationship between industry, government, and society. Society's increased expectations of industry, which is expressed through the force of law, and while requiring more accountable behavior will also result in a more collaborative rather than antagonistic relationship. Future demands on the firm in terms of a variety of expectations by society such as equal employment, improved working conditions, a better environment, growth and profits, will force a rededication to quality production and distribution.[4]

Spinning off from a discussion of social consciousness are two important problem derivatives. There is first the impact and influence of technology upon the organization, and secondly, the responsibility of the firm in utilizing human resources.

Management and Technology

Our advanced civilization owes much of its economic progress to the innovation and application of technology. But a fundamental question is where will technological progress lead us? Will it be servant or master of management in its relationship to the concerns of society? In answer to these questions, management will need to evaluate continually the applications of technology, for consumer benefits, in terms of the longer range benefits to mankind itself.

Historically, in our affluent and consuming society, the overriding concern of the enterprise has been the acceptable ratio of goods and services to factor inputs. However, with the newer wisdom—the quality of life—our economic operations will have to be conducted in the future, not only with an eye to the successive lessening of labor inputs relative to output but also, and increasingly, with a more deliberate approach to environmental and ecological concerns. Management will need to address itself to the use of technology for, among a growing list, the reduction of land, sea, and air pollution; the conservation of natural resources; and the renovation and redevelopment of our depressed urban and industrial areas.

Management and Human Resources

The firm of the future will assume even greater responsibility for the development of all its human resources. Its own survival is the primary objective of the organization. Markets, products, technology, and financial resources will no longer be the predominant assurances for economic and social achievement. The survival of the corporation in the future will depend increasingly on its capacity for adapting innovation. This will require well-educated and highly motivated people. Corporate survival, essentially then, will derive from the quality of intellect and activation that its people possess.

As advancing technology accelerates the erosion of human physical skills, the organization will more concernedly plan for the development of its human assets through ongoing and continuing activities at all levels, and with all peoples, of the organization. The financial allocations for the development of human resources will not be considered optional allocations after all other monetary claims on the firm have been satisfied, but will be fixed charges or necessary costs incurred in the conduct of the corporation's social performance in conjunction with its profit performance.

QUESTIONS FOR DISCUSSION

1. Of what real significance to the organization is the changing composition of the work force?
2. Describe and discuss the impact of computerization upon the firm and upon management itself.
3. Explain the rationale for the social responsibility doctrine of the U.S. enterprise. How does this doctrine differ from that exercised, say, about 100 years ago in the average firm?
4. What do you foresee in the way of future developments in the exercise of social responsibility by the business community?
5. Do you believe that management is now or will become a profession? What are your reasons for believing as you do?
6. Do you believe that concern with the social responsibility of management will change the basic nature of management, as some observers predict? Why or why not?

REFERENCES

1. "Revised Occupational Projections to 1985," *Monthly Review*, Bureau of Labor Statistics, U.S. Department of Labor, vol. 99, no. 11 (November 1976): 10-22.
2. "Management and the Computer," *Industry Week*, (Cleveland, OH: Penton Publishing Co. [July 1977]); 65.
3. Ibid, p. 76.
4. "Future Focus Management," *Industry Week*, (Cleveland, OH: Penton Publishing Co. [January 1978]), 75-94.

SELECTED BIBLIOGRAPHY

1. Carroll, Archie B. *Managing Corporate Social Responsibility*. Boston: Little, Brown and Co., Inc., 1977.
2. Davis, Keith, and Blomstrom, Robert L., *Business Society and Environment*. New York: McGraw-Hill Book Co., 1971.

3. Luthans, Fred, and Hodgetts, Richard M. *Social Issues in Business.* 2d ed. New York: Macmillan Publishing Co., Inc., 1976.
4. Lynch, Robert E., and Rice, John R. *Computers: Their Impact and Use.* New York: Holt, Rinehart & Winston, 1977.

INDEX

Ackoff, Russell L., 24
Appraisal, executive, 225
Argyris, Chris, 24
Arnoff, E. Leonard, 24
Assistant to, staff position of, 69
Authority 80
   acceptance theory, 80
   bilateral dimensions of, 83
   competence theory, 81
   defined, 80
   delegating, 82
   formal theory, 80
   informal, 81
   in organizational structure, 89
   limits of, specifying, 87
   management behavior and, 89
   nature of, 87
   organizational, 87
   procedural, 87
   responsibility and, 81
   sources, 80
   staff assumption and, 73

Barnard, Chester I., 23
Bertalanffy, Ludwig von, 25
Blake, Robert R. 199-201
Break-even analysis, 117

Case study, technique, 219
Central staff, relation to regional, 77
Channels, management, 182
Churchman, C. West, 24, 25
Closed-end feed-back, 33
Communication
   barriers, 189
      structural, 189
      socio-psychological, 190
      semantic, 191
   channels downward, 182, 187
   channels upward, 184, 187
   defined, 182
   extraorganizational, 184, 188
   formal, 182
   grapevine, 186
   group stereotypes, 190
   improving, 191
   intraorganizational, 184, 188
   informal, 185
   horizontal, 188
   layering and, 190
   nature of, 182
   purposes of, 187
   downward, 187
   upward, 187, 188
Completed staff work, 71
Computer Technology, trends in, 284
Conference technique, 219
Control
   characteristics, 242
   defined, 240
   external, 249
   factors, 243
   internal control, 246
   information systems for, 247
   nature of, 240
   requirements, 241
   responsibility, 246
   span, 53-55
   staff relationships, 246
   systems, 240-241
Controlling techniques
   charts, 260
   financial
      analysis, 254
      balance sheet, 252
      budgets, 256
      control defined, 252
      income statement, 252
   manufacturing process, 260
   quality control, 256
   process capability, 258
CPM, 114
   internal control systems, 255
   quantitative methods of, 263

Davis, Ralph C., 22
Decision making, 30
    closed-end model, 34
    components, 31
    computer use of, 247-249
    experience and, 31-33
    general survey method, 37
    implications, 31
    interdisciplinary nature, 35
    managerial, 30
    methods, 37
    open-end model, 33
    scientific method, 38
    scope of, 29
    subject matter, 34
Delegation
    authority and, 81
    delegator and, 82
    recipient and, 82
    specific, 88
Directing
    defined, 7
    staff function in, 71
Drucker, Peter F., 23

E.O.Q. Model, 121
Economic service objectives
Emerson, Harrington, 19-20
Ethics
    associational, 272
    basis for, 274
    business organization and, 271
    defined, 271
    environmental climate of, 268
    guidelines, 276
    influence agents and, 272
    nature of, 269
    normative, 271
    objective, 272
    organizational program of, 277
    perception and, 274
    plan for, 277
    professionalism and, 274, 276
    sources of, 271
    subjective, 271
    unethical practices, 269-270
    value systems and, 273

Factors
    control, 243
    decision making, 31
    management, 7
    organization structure design, 45
    philosophy,
        planning, 102
Fayol, Henri, 22
Feed-back
    closed-end, 33
    open-end, 33
Fiedler, Fred E., 202
Follett, Mary Parker, 23
Formal organization structure, 45

Forrester, Jay W., 24
Functional organization structure, 47
Functions
    controlling, 7
    defined, 8
    directing, 7
    managerial, 101
    nature of, 8
    organizing, 5
    organizational, 5
    planning and, 5
    staffing, 5

Gantt Chart, 111
Gantt, Henry L., 111
Gilbreth, Frank B., 20
Gilbreth, Lillian, 20
Grapevine, 186
Groups
    adjustment to larger organizations, 176
    effect of larger organizations, 175
    characteristics, 170
        norms, 170
        status, 171
        structure, 170
        values, 170
    cohesion, 174
    decision making, 174
    defined, 164
    deviant behavior, 172
    formal rules, 171
    functions, 169
        tasks, 169
        maintenance, 169
    individual adaptation to, 173
    reasons of formation, 164
        identification, 164
        goal achievement, 166
        personal support, 165
        social interaction, 165
    types
        command, 166-167
        friendship, 168
        interest, 168
        task, 167
Group training methods, 216

Herzberg, Frederick, 24

Informal communications, 185
Informal organization structure, 57-58
Information systems, and decision making, 247

Koontz, Harold, 23

Layering, organizational, 53
Layering, communications, 190

Leadership
  bases of power, 197
  contingency approach, 202
  defined, 196
  forces in, 201-202
  managerial guide, 199-200
  Ohio State studies, 199
  personal behavior approach, 198
  roles of, 204
  situational approach, 201
  trait approach, 198
Likert, Rensis, 24
Line-and-staff, 66
  authority aspects of, 73
  human relations and,
  kinds of, 68
  organizational growth, 66
  reasons for,
  relationships, 77
  staff specialists, 70
Line organization structure, 45
Linear programming and control, 264
Logic
  decision making and, 37

Management
  behavioral science approach, 24
  careers, 12
  characteristics, 10
  computer and, 285
  constraints, 9
  control function, 7
  defined, 3
  directing function, 7
  dynamic model, 9
  early contributions, 16
  factors of, 7
  functions, 5
  human relations approach, 23
  human resources and, 287
  objectives defined, 9
  organizing function, 5
  organizational factors, 7
  organization structure, 9
  philosophy, 8
  planning function, 5
  policies, 9
  procedures, 9
  process management approach, 20
  quantitative approach, 24
  scientific management approach, 19
  scope of, 2
  staffing, 5
  static model, 4
  systems approach, 24
  technology and, 286

Management philosophy
  communicating the, 8
  defined, 8
Management trends
  computerization, 284-285
  human resources, 287
  social responsibility, 285
  technology and, 286
  workforce composition, 282-284
Managerial appraisal
  appraisal interview, 235
  benefits of, 237
  current performance, 234
  defined, 225
  development programs and, 236
  dimensions of measurement, 226
    achievement of objectives, 228
    character traits, 227
    managerial skills, 227
  follow up and, 236
  management by objectives and, 228-229
  methods of
    assessment center, 232
    clinical interview, 233
    critical incident, 233-234
    forced choice, 231-232
    graphic rating, 231
    group appraisal, 232
    ranking method, 231
  procedure for, 234
  program for improvement, 236
  purposes, 226
Managerial development,
  concepts of, 212
  content of programs, 213
  defined, 210
  evaluation of, 221
  forces behind, 211
  off-the-job methods, 217
    company training, 217
    seminars, 217
    university programs, 217
  on-the-job methods, 214
    group training, 216
    job rotation, 215
    miscellaneous, 217
    planned progression, 215
    special projects, 215
    trainee programs, 215
    understudy plan, 216
  purposes of, 210
  techniques, 218
    management simulation, 220
    case study, 219
    conferences, 219
    lecture, 218
    role playing, 218
    t-groups, 220
Managerial specialists, 2
Maslow, Abraham H., 24
Mayo, Elton, 23

McClelland, David C., 24
Mencius, 16
Mooney, James D., 22
Moses, 16-17
Mouton, Jane S., 199, 201
Motivation
  achievement theory, 157
  concepts, 153
  defined, 152
  dissatisfiers, 155-156
  expectancy theory, 157
  extrinsic incentives, 160
  flextime, 160
  Herzberg, Frederick, 24, 155
  intrinsic incentives, 160
  job enlargement, 160
  job enrichment, 160
  job-related incentives, 160
  Maslow, Abraham H., 24, 153-156
  McClelland, David D., 24, 157
  money, 158
  need theory, 153
  satisfiers, 155-156
  social incentives, 160
  two-factor theory, 155
Munsterberg, Hugo, 23

Network analysis, 113

Objectives, 126
  control and, 133
  criteria of, 136
  defined, 126
  environmental factors influencing, 135
  immediate, 130
  influences in formulating, 135
  intermediate, 130
  kinds of, 126
  long term, 130
  maintaining, 137
  management development and, 132
  nature of, 126
  organizing and, 132
  personal, 128
  planning and, 132
  primary, 132
  profit, 128
  responsibility for, 132
  secondary operational, 129
  short-term, 130
  social, 129
O'Donnell, Cyril, 23
On-the-job executive training, 214
Open-end feed-back, 33
Operations research and control, 264
Organization
  defined, 45
  departmentation, 49
  formal types, 45
  functional, 47

functional analysis, 49
functional differentiation, 50
informal, 57-58
kinds of, 44
layering, 53
line, 45
line-and-staff, 49
management philosophy and, 8
matrix management, 61
nature of, 44
office of the president, 61
project management, 59
purpose, 45
systems management, 59
tests of effective, 57
types of, 45
Organizational resources, 8
Organizational functions, 8
Organizing
  defined, 5

Personal staff, 68
PERT,
  defined, 114
  example of, 114
Planning
  breakeven analysis, 117
  business factors, 101
  critical path method, 114
  defined, 96
  development of, 96
  factors affecting, 102
  guides, 104
  inventory analysis, 120
  models, 106, 111
  nature, 111
  network analysis, 113
  preliminary phase, 96
  process, 105
  qualitative methods defined, 110
  quantitative methods, 110
  responsibilities, 99
  specialist phase, 98
  strategic projects, 102
  subject matter, 100
  time aspects, 97
Plato, 16
Policies
  characteristics of, 139, 144
  coverage of, 142
  defined, 139
  examples of, 142
  functional, 145
  objectives and relationship to, 145
  organizational, 143
  nature of, 140
  purposes, 142
  responsibility for, 149
Position rotation plan, 215
Project management, organization for, 59-60

Quantitative models,
  planning, 110-120
  controlling, 257-263

Reiley, Alan C., 22
Responsibilities, specifying, 90
Responsibility, 83
  authority and, 85
  bilateral dimensions, 83
  defined, 83
  formal, 83
  informal, 84
  nature of, 91
  organization structure and, 86
Roethlisberger, Fritz J., 23
Roleplaying, 218
Roman Catholic Church, 18

Secondary operational objectives, 129
Schmidt, Warren, 201
Scientific management, period of, 19-20
Semantic, communication and, 191
Sensitivity training, 220
Simon, Herbert H., 24
Social objectives, 129
Social responsibilities, 285
Span of control, 53
Specialized Staff, 69
Staff
  authority, 73
  central and regional, relation of, 77
  characteristics of, 70
  development of, 66
  domination of line, 76
  influence without line authority, 75
  limitations of use, 77
  procedural authority of, 74
  specialists, functions of, 70
  surveillance of regional units, 77
Staff work, completed, principle of, 65, 71
Stogdill, Ralph M., 24
Strategy, 147
  defined, 147
  types of, 147
  steps in formulation, 148
Structure, organization, 45-49
Structure, tests of, 56
Systems management, organization for, 59

Tannenbaum, Robert, 201
Taylor, Frederick W., 19
  management process, 20
  scientific management, 19
  management philosophy, 19
  management principles, 20-22
Tead, Ordway, 23
Therbligs, 20
Trends in management
  labor force composition, 282-284
  management and technology, 286
  social responsibility, 285

computer impact, 284
human resources, 287

Understudy plan, 216
University courses and programs, 217

Values, objectives as, 126

Wiener, Norbert, 25
Work force, changing composition of, 282-284

Xenophon, 16